D1468239

CIRCLES
OF
POWER

THE
MOST INFLUENTIAL
PEOPLE IN CANADA

JAMES FLEMING

DOUBLEDAY CANADA

Canadian Cataloguing in Publication Data

Fleming, James MacLean, 1951-
    Circles of power: the most influential people in Canada

Includes bibliographical references and index.
ISBN 0-385-25312-5

1. Elite (Social sciences) — Canada.   2. Power (Social sciences).   I. Title.

HN110.Z9E44 1991   305.5′2′0971   C91-094136-X

Jacket design by David Wyman
Jacket illustration by Valerie Sinclair
Printed and bound in the USA

Published in Canada by
Doubleday Canada Limited
105 Bond Street
Toronto, Ontario
M5B 1Y3

Contents

For Christine

Acknowledgements

There are many ways to study, probe and ponder Canada. For many thinkers, Canada is an abstract concept, a political creation that is more an act of faith than a spontaneous expression of community. For others, it is, above all, a huge grid of transportation and telecommunications links; a collection of far-flung population centres that find escape from loneliness through road, rail and phone connections with each other. These approaches have their merit. Yet there is only one way to truly *understand* Canada, and that is in terms of human relationships, not political or communications theories. Human relationships are the animus of Canada. How we relate to each other, view each other, and treat each other is the way by which Canada is ultimately defined. A collectivity of human beings can turn so acrimonious, bigoted and close-minded in nature that it has few commendable traits. As Thoreau once commented: "What men call social virtue, good fellowship, is commonly but the virtue of pigs in a litter, which lie close together to keep each other warm." Alternatively, human beings can forge a more noble-minded society where the ideals of compassion and justice are pursued. Canadians have always prided themselves on having created a society that doesn't fit Thoreau's barn-yard metaphor — although they've been slipping toward it lately.

I was motivated to write this book by my fascination with human relationships and the principles that govern them in Canada's power structure. Power is an inescapable part of those relationships, but power in human hands is never anodyne; it is sometimes benign and often malign. Canada, like all societies, is divided into the rulers and the ruled. Who gets power, how they use it and who is shut out from power, ultimately determines the justness and ethical tenor of our society.

I could not have undertaken so ambitious a study of who runs Canada without the help and inspiration of numerous people.

When it was conceived almost four years ago, this book benefitted greatly from the enthusiasm and insights of my agent at the time David Colbert, who later left the agency business to join Harper-Collins. Thereafter, agents Carol Bonnett and Linda McKnight of MGA Inc. provided me with the sort of support, shrewdness and judicious counsel that many authors only dream about.

I was aided immensely by several researchers. Alexander Bruce served as my research associate on the East Coast. A journalist based in Nova Scotia, he advised me and provided information on the members of the social establishment of the Atlantic provinces. Several other people aided me in conducting surveys of the ruling elites. They were Peter Scott, Shelley Cathers and Christine Fleming, my wife, who co-ordinated and cross-checked all five surveys. Diane Gee was of great help in researching the religious elite; and librarians Celia Donnelly and Roberta Grant both provided generous and patient assistance. Fran McNeely provided prompt and expert service transcribing interview notes.

The book might not have been written were it not for Anna Porter, the former chairman of Doubleday Canada and John Pearce, the editor-in-chief of Doubleday Canada, who seized on its potential and signed me up. John Pearce then played an irreplaceable role in overseeing the book from the idea to manuscript stage. His insights and deft editing skills improved the manuscript immensely through each of four successive drafts. I owe a debt of gratitude to Shaun Oakey for his fine line-editing skills and his ability to catch inconsistencies, spelling mistakes and other flaws in the text; and also to several members of Doubleday's staff: Maggie Reeves, the company's production and design manager who turned a messy manuscript into a readable book; Dara Rowland, the dynamic head of marketing and promotion; and to Christine Harrison, Jill Lambert and Susan Folkins who all played valuable roles in getting the book into print.

Several individuals were kind enough to read over sections of the manuscript and offer criticisms. They were Mark Starowicz, executive producer of CBC's *The Journal*, Patrick White, professor of history emeritus at the University of Toronto, and David Olive, editor of *Report on Business Magazine*. All remaining flaws or errors remain solely my responsibility.

Many others provided inspiration or invaluable counsel, including Chuck Macli, Ernest Hillen, and Peggy Wente, as well as my former Queen's University professors Ned Franks, George Perlin, Alastair Taylor, Charles Pentland, Nils Orvik and Jock Gunn who nourished and guided my intellectual curiousity. Thanks also to the late John Porter, whose book *The Vertical Mosaic* inspired me to write *Circles of Power* and to Peter Newman who was the first to show that such a topic could be entertaining as well as informative.

I owe my greatest debt to my wife, Christine and two children, Sarah, 13, and Iain, 8, who lived with this book while it was in gestation just as if it were a fifth member of the family.

James Fleming
July 1991

Introduction

First impressions — whether of people or parties — count a lot, and this black-tie affair was designed for maximum effect, from the first sip of white wine to the last nibble of pastry. I mounted the stairs to the Vanity Fair ballroom at the King Edward Hotel with the usual sense of reserve required for surviving at high-society parties where the egos come in sizes roughly equivalent to the party-goers' credit lines. Judging from the roar of voices, rising like the cacophony of a throng of alarmed jungle birds, the pre-dinner reception was already in full swing. Just another party, I thought. Then I came within sight of the crush of people who had gathered, at the invitation of publishing mogul Conrad Black, to celebrate the 100th anniversary of *Saturday Night* magazine in January 1988. It was, to say the least, a unique tableau. Crammed shoulder-to-shoulder in a cramped foyer outside the ballroom were about 200 of Canada's best-known and most accomplished citizens from almost every field of endeavour. The room was so packed that manoeuvring to see and be seen was not required. Turn on your heel and you might be standing nose-to-nose with billionaire Peter Bronfman chatting with novelist Margaret Atwood. Pivot the other way and you might elbow John Turner, then federal Liberal leader, chatting with Black (Brian and Mila Mulroney were invited but couldn't make it); back away two inches and you might bump into Emmett Cardinal Carter chatting with Fred Eaton, the department store scion. Making it to the bar was a 15-minute journey of excuse me's and shoulder lunges. There were dozens of business blue bloods

(Dixon Chant, Argus Corp.; Grant Reuber, Bank of Montreal). Media giants seemed to be everywhere (John Fischer, Southam; David Jolley, the Toronto *Star*; Allan Slaight, Standard Broadcasting; Pierre Des Marais, Unimedia). Justice Charles Dubin and James Spence from Tory, Tory added a certain gravity to the affair. A smattering of media personalities added wit or celebrity (Martin Knelman, *Toronto Life*; Andy Barrie, CFRB; David Olive, then with *Toronto Life*; Sandi Rinaldo, CTV; Kevin Doyle, *Maclean's*). Rounding out the ranks of the intelligentsia, there were academics like Jack Granatstein and such celebrity writers as Christina McCall, Graeme Gibson and Robertson Davies.

The charge of power that pervaded the congested room was the psychological equivalent of atoms being crushed together to produce nuclear fusion.

Later, inside the Vanity Fair ballroom, John Turner proposed a toast to the country, glass of white wine in hand, and dinner got under way. After Calabaza pumpkin soup, roast loin of veal stuffed with spinach, and petits fours, the guests listened to progressively witty remarks by Black, *Saturday Night* editor John Fraser, and in a toast to the magazine that was the highlight of the evening — celebrated novelist Robertson Davies. With his flowing, pure white beard, longish hair and quicksilver tongue, Davies came across like an Old Testament prophet with a merry sense of humour. He enchanted the guests with his lifelong memories of the magazine, including a recounting of his own stint as literary editor.

The party did more than confirm Black's skills as the consummate social tactician (right names plus big crowd plus small room equals success). It provided a glimpse in microcosm of Canada's haute monde. Call it the ruling class, the Establishment or the power elite, every society has an upper stratum of people who run the show. They are the flesh and blood answer to the question: Who's in charge here? They are not just the super-rich whose forebears made a fortune in the trades or business and now sit atop the social pecking order dictating social standards like Lady Astor in late-nineteenth century New York. They are also the bishops, the bureaucrats, the cultural czars, the politicians and others who make up the separate yet linked elite groups that run Canada. Elites, in the words of sociologist C. Wright Mills, author of *The Power Elite*, "occupy the strategic command posts of the social structure."[1]

In his celebrated study of American society, Mills used the term *power elite* to describe a powerful coalition of economic, political and military leaders in the 1950s. But institutional leaders rarely merge into a unified group that could be called a true power elite in Mills's sense. Usually, relations among elites range from harmony to conflict, as they do in Canada.

In fact, leading members of the major elites that run Canada are rarely even gathered together in one room. Those in the Vanity Fair ballroom came from the political, bureaucratic, business, media, religious and cultural fields. Normally these elites operate in circles of power that at times overlap and at others remain separate; that sometimes compete and often cooperate to keep society working as a going concern.

The word *elite* has many meanings in popular usage; people generally use it to describe any socially superior group, from athletes to soldiers. Often it suggests snobbery, as when someone complains about a person's "elitist attitudes". In this book the word *elite* is not used in a pejorative way. Elites per se are not bad or good; they are a necessary part of any working society. Whether there should be elites is not at issue; how they use their power and who is denied entry to their ranks is.

Webster's Dictionary defines *power* as the "possession of control, authority, or influence over others." In those terms, the power of Canada's elites is indisputable: they have the recognized right to make decisions for the rest of Canadians. They are the top politicians who pass laws; they are the business leaders who oversee the lives of thousands of employees and who are practised at the art of political lobbying; they are the senior bureaucrats who oversee almost every aspect of our lives, from what we pay in taxes, to what we can legally read, to what we can bring across the country's borders; they are the cultural powerbrokers who decide what we will see on TV or at the movies; they are the religious leaders who decide on the moral standards we ought to obey.

These leaders determine the nature of Canada's social contract; how we interact with one another; what behaviour is socially permissible or will land us in jail; and even, in the case of the religious elite, how we ought to behave in bed.

Of course, power is not always used in naked, straightforward ways. Indeed it is more fascinating, and potentially insidious, in its more subtle manifestation called influence.

Influence is intangible and often untraceable. *Webster's* notes that in one of its earliest uses (in the fourteenth century) the word referred to "an ethereal fluid held to flow from the stars and to affect the actions of humans." Influence is the ability to affect the course of events with a timely phone call to a friend, through an informal chat at a dinner party. It's the ability to direct the actions of lesser mortals with only a look or a quick comment. Very often, it is getting one's way through implicit rather than explicit expressions of will.

This book takes the reader inside the major elites that run Canada and analyses how power works within each one. Not all of Canada's elites are covered in this book. Owing to space considerations, I do not undertake an in-depth look at the legal, academic and labour establishments, although many members of these groups figure in this book. The elites I do study arguably rank as the most powerful in our society at present. They overlap when there is a marriage of goals and attitudes between one group and another, as when the business elite and the federal political elite work together to achieve common economic ends. At a more subtle level, they are also linked by the network of friendships and family ties that often bind them together, and by the movement of powerbrokers from one elite to another. Often, the influence of the powerful is not confined to one elite; rather, their clout extends beyond their own community into others, say from culture into politics, or from business to politics.

But these elites sometimes operate separately when their collective wills collide, as when the Canadian Conference of Catholic Bishops denounces the moral underpinnings of federal social or economic policies. Leftist scholars often paint a picture of ideological collaboration between these ruling elites. This book assumes that the elites share a general belief in the value of liberal democratic traditions but doesn't read anything conspiratorial into that fact. It is not a

Marxist class analysis. The idea of class is used in the following pages only in more generally accepted ways; that is, to divide Canadians into lower-, middle- and upper-class categories on the basis of their occupations and incomes.

In the case of each elite, I will identify who is powerful, how they wield their power and to what ends. Power tends to ripple in concentric waves from key powerbrokers. I will identify the people at the centre of these spheres of influence and the networks of friends and enemies that surround them.

Canadians expect a lot of the elites that rule them, expectations that are rooted in secular and religious values. Our democratic traditions lead us to assume that our leaders will wield power in a way that promotes the common good or serves the collective interests of society rather than the narrower interests of any one person or group. Likewise, our Judaeo-Christian religious traditions, a major force until the last few decades, remain potent to the extent that we still assume that society's rulers ought to be uncommon men and women who are deserving of obedience and respect in so far as they seek justice, rewarding good citizens and punishing the unjust and corrupt. The Protestant work ethic is commonly thought to have played a major role in the building of Canada as we know it. It is my view that a Protestant power ethic has been just as influential. The disciple Peter expressed it best: "Submit yourselves for the Lord's sake to every human institution," he tells his followers, "whether to a king as the one in authority, or to governors as sent by him for the punishment of evildoers and the praise of those who do right." This Protestant power ethic helps explain why Canadians have traditionally been deferential to authority figures, a national trait that is usually attributed solely to our monarchist political roots and peaceful evolution from colony to country.

The assumption that our rulers are generally deserving of uncritical deference has never been more challenged than in the past decade. Canadians seem profoundly disillusioned with the idea that our rulers, especially in the political realm, serve the collective interest of society or, on the whole, deserve respect for the integrity and justice of their actions. In researching this book, I was motivated, in part, by curiosity about whether this disillusionment is justified.

I will also consider the power of the elites in relation to one another. How much has the influence of the business elite risen in society? How much has the influence of the religious elite fallen? Has the media become the dominant force shaping the ideology and moral values of the population? Does the power of the federal cabinet rest solely on its constitutional right to move the levers of power and not on a wider legitimacy based on the support of the population? If so, why? As Frederic Cople Jaher noted in *The Rich, The Wellborn, and the Powerful*, "Like other social organizations, elites and upper classes rise, peak, and fall; they experience periods of triumph, challenge, and defeat."

But the book is not simply a study of power plays within and between elites. By determining who has power, it is possible to say who does *not* have it. This book is a modest effort to determine how the makeup of the ruling elites has changed since 1965, when John Porter published his more exhaustive, academic book, *The Vertical Mosaic*, which was 10 years in the making. Canadians of British descent, white complexion and Protestant belief have been a minority in Canadian society since the 1940s. Do they still dominate its elites? (WASP is a derogatory, imprecise term that I choose not to use.) Has the Old Boys' network, based on birth, family ties and graduation from the right schools, broken down? To what degree are outsiders allowed in to the elites? What kinds of inroads have women made?

The Dream of Mobility

By measuring the openness of the elites to newcomers based on merit, not birthright, race or sex, it is possible to draw conclusions about the truth of a central myth (one of the few remaining) that binds Canadian social society together: the dream of mobility. In this usage, a myth isn't an untruth, it is a great, often unspoken, belief that binds communities together. Myths can be untrue and destructive, like Hitler's Aryan race, or positive and at least partly true, like Pierre Trudeau's Just Society. The dream of mobility fosters a belief that individual effort is responsible for success, that every person can determine his or her own fortune, since equality of opportunity exists for everyone.

In reality, social climbing has never been easy. Since the beginning of recorded history, those at the top of the ladder have tended to close ranks against newcomers. In ancient Greece, leading philosophers like Pericles and Aristotle railed against the entrenched power of the noble and the rich in their society as being contrary to the democratic principles that supposedly governed it. But their protests were to little avail.

In Victorian England, getting ahead was tough for everyone but aristocrats and large landowners. The idea of granting a peerage to a mere industrialist or financier was still causing conniptions among the nobility into the late nineteenth century. When Disraeli recommended a barony for the relatively landless banker Lionel Rothschild in 1868, Queen Victoria noted that she "could not think that one who owed his wealth to contracts with foreign governments for loans, or to successful speculation on the stock exchange, could fairly claim a British peerage." Rothschild's son Nathaniel, a country gentleman of substance, had better luck in 1885, when he obtained the peerage that eluded his father.

North America was supposed to be a haven from such upper-class conceits. The dream of mobility has been engraved in the North American subconscious since the mid-1800s. It had its intellectual origins in Herbert Spencer's notion of social evolution, where the fittest survive, and in Adam Smith's "invisible hand" of the free market, in which the greater economic good is served by individuals pursuing their selfish ends. Immigrants seeking better opportunities in the New World fostered the dream in North America and it has served as a myth ever since. Yet the reality has never quite measured up to the myth. For example, ideas of equality didn't count much for anyone who wanted to make it into New York's high society in the late 1800s, where wealth, birth and style counted for everything. Probably the most famous social circle of the day was Lady Astor's Fashionable Four Hundred in New York. One leading member of the Four Hundred, Ward McAllister, who also coined the term, once explained to the New York Times why only 400 people made the inner circle. "If you go outside that number you strike people who are either not at ease in a ball room or make others not at ease." To this day, the upper class only admits newcomers who don't make them feel uncomfortable in social situations. Etiquette and attitude remain just as important as cash.

True or false, the mobility myth has motivated generations of would-be Horatio Alger–style heroes in North America. In Canada, it has blended with the myths of cultural pluralism and government-sanctioned multiculturalism. Made official in 1971, Ottawa's multicultural policies, as prime minister Pierre Trudeau told the House of Commons, were intended to "break down discriminatory attitudes and cultural jealousies . . . [and] form the base of a society which is based on fair play for all." In other words, new Canadians could keep their distinct ethnic identities without fear of suffering economic or social penalties. Partly because of multicultural policies, Canadians have bought into the mobility dream. In 1986, a *Maclean's/* Decima poll asked 1,575 Canadians what it takes to get ahead. A full 82 per cent replied hard work, 10 per cent said luck and 7 per cent said privilege. Are the 82 per cent just happy fools? What does it really take to get ahead in Canada?

The Big Picture

This book doesn't pretend to measure social mobility within the entire Canadian system. It focuses on a much more manageable group: those who occupy the pinnacles of institutional power. First, however, the larger social context should be provided. Academics have been busy studying social mobility in Canada, especially as manifested within ethnic groups. They agree that Canada's society is highly stratified, measured by job status and income.

This is likely to come as a rude shock to millions of middle-aged baby boomers who have spent the last decade spending and borrowing their way toward some ill-defined notion of prosperity. Powered by the cash flow of two-income households, a whole generation of Canadians has aspired to the sort of lifestyle that at one time only the upper classes enjoyed — private school for the kids; annual vacations in international hot spots that go in and out of style as fast as fashion colours; designer outfits with *de rigueur* accessories that cost a week's pay; fully loaded imported luxury sedans; sprawling homes with as many bidets as telephones. Such acquisitions feed the hubris of people who can't bear to think of themselves as limited by class. They refuse to recognize that there are limits to what they can buy, and likewise they refuse to place limits on their self-esteem by admitting to themselves that they are just middle-class parvenus on the make.

Knock a zero off the six-figure family income it takes to chase these dreams and you have a sub-level of social climbers with their own illusions of prosperity. They travel to Florida instead of France, drive an Accord instead of an Acura and send their kids off to take French immersion classes at public school rather than etiquette classes at private school. There's an undertone of quiet desperation to their acquisitive struggle (to paraphrase Thoreau), which is made more acute every time interest rates jerk upward, squeezing their two-income budgets even tighter. But they have the trappings of success to console them: a big-screen TV with stereo sound, a VCR, a bone-china dinner service and, perhaps, a family ski membership. Marx once remarked that religion was the opium of the people. Today, materialism has taken its place as the source of hope for the middle class. The "good life" has come to mean material comfort rather than wisdom.

In the 1990s many of these acquisitive baby boomers have had to confront social and economic realities for the first time. Many thousands of them have lost their jobs as companies have pared excess middle management; those who remain have had to scale back their career ambitions since there are far fewer jobs at the top than applicants for them. Loaded down with record levels of household debt and full of middle-age angst, the baby boom generation is headed for a collective case of acute depression.

All along, leading Canadian sociologists haven't bought the myth that material possessions are the great equalizer. They have used a more reliable measure of social status, namely the type of job a person holds, the education required to qualify for it and the income it generates. They measure social mobility by the openness of these jobs to newcomers of various ethnic backgrounds and both sexes.

In this country, the most commonly used job status rankings were developed by York University social scientist Bernard Blishen in the 1950s and have been updated several times since. Blishen ranked jobs using census data on educational requirements and income. Here's a sampling of the rankings he has come up with in the past decades. The first three categories correspond to the middle class. The second three correspond to the working or blue-collar class. There is no category for the upper class, which is generally defined as at least second-generation wealth with vast amounts of money vested in property.[2]

Class One:

Physicians and Surgeons
Lawyers
Dentists
Nuclear Engineers
Meterologists

Secondary School Teachers
Chemical Engineers
Optometrists
Chiropractors

Class Two:

Computer Programmers
Pilots
Social Workers
Writers and Editors
Sociologists
Dieticians
Economists

Mathematicians
Librarians
Elementary and Kindergarten
    Teachers
Financial Managers
Government Administrators
Producers and Directors

Class Three:

Funeral Directors
Insurance Salespeople
Members of Legislative Bodies
Ministers of Religion

Nurses
Actors
Railway Conductors

Class Four:

Photographers and
    Camera Operators
Musicians
Tellers and Cashiers
Dental Hygienists

Nuns and Brothers
Mail Carriers
Subway and Streetcar
    Operators

Class Five:

Messengers

Auto Workers

Taxi Drivers

Telephone Operators

Bookbinders

Bus Drivers

Hotel Clerks

Metal Working Machine
Operators

Class Six:

Bartenders

Fishermen

Farmers

Barbers

Babysitters

Janitors

Chefs

Chambermaids

Guards

Labourers (Manufacturing)

Using job status rankings such as these, sociologists have come to conclusions about the degree of social mobility in Canada.

First the good news.

- The vertical mosaic, as John Porter defined it, no longer exists. Ethnic groups can no longer be slotted into ascending occupation levels as they could be a few decades ago, with recent immigrants at the bottom and the charter groups (British and French) in the upper ranks. (Porter himself concluded this before he died in 1979.)
- Over the past 50 years, level of education has become more important in determining occupation status. This suggests that other factors such as skin colour have become less important and means that attaining status increasingly depends on individual achievement.
- Some major academics have optimistically concluded that ethnic stratification in Canada is breaking down; ethnicity, they say, is steadily becoming less important as a factor in the type of jobs Canadians seek or obtain. Most experts agree that there has been greater change in this regard in Canada than in the United States, which has a more settled industrial structure.

But it's not time to rejoice about equality of opportunity in Canada. Here's the bad news, at least for fair-minded Canadians.

- Those of British and Jewish origin still dominate the top occupational groups in English Canada, the professional, managerial and financial jobs.
- Ethnic group and family background remain important factors in determining a student's chances of acquiring a university education, which, in turn, affects his or her chances of getting a high-status job.
- The vertical mosaic may no longer exist, but there are obvious ethnic differences in the class structure, based largely on educational attainment. For example, largely because of their poorer education, Canadians of South European origin have low-status jobs. For the opposite reason, those of Jewish origin have high-status jobs.
- Ethnic groups also tend to be concentrated in certain industrial sectors. For example, South and East Europeans are overrepresented in manufacturing; Greeks and Chinese are overrepresented in the service sectors; Germans, Dutch, Italians and Scandinavians are strongly represented in the primary and construction industries. These economic concentrations reflect the historical pattern of immigration in Canada, in which certain ethnic groups tended to begin their new life in certain types of jobs.

Those of British origin tend to be well distributed throughout the workforce, probably reflecting the length of time this group has been in the country. Interestingly, a large percentage of nonwhites have professional jobs. Since an overwhelmingly large proportion of Chinese and blacks are foreign-born, this probably reflects selective immigration policy designed to meet the demands of the economy. But overall, the persistence of ethnic inequality in the workplace is well documented in the 1984 and 1988 Royal Commissions on Equality in Employment.

- Certain ethnic groups make, on average, a lot more money than other groups, with those of West European and Jewish origin at the top and those of South European and nonwhite origin at the bottom.

• Women face tremendous discrimination in the workplace. They tend to enter the workforce better educated and in higher-status jobs than men, but they find their upward mobility limited.[3]

On the whole, many academics see signs of improvement in equality of opportunity and the importance of individual achievement. But even the most optimistic feel that there's been too little improvement to conclude that Canada is becoming a more open society. Many would concede that family origins, ethnic background and sex are still strong determinants for attaining status in Canadian society.

This is the broad context for this book's attempt to measure the openness to newcomers of the major elites. It is fine to say, for instance, that more blacks or women hold professional or upper-managerial positions in the workforce. But that success palls if those blacks or women are shut out of the ranks of the elites where real power lies.

The Method

This is not the first book to study the manners, mores and methods of the people who run Canada in various spheres of power. There have been major journalistic books, such as Peter C. Newman's ground-breaking *The Canadian Establishment* in 1975, which provided Canadians with the first intimate glimpse of the people who form the country's social and business elites. Diane Francis continued the study of the wealthy upper class in her 1986 best-seller, *Controlling Interest: Who Owns Canada*. There have also been a few major academic studies of elites since Porter wrote *The Vertical Mosaic*. Two of the most notable have been left-wing analyses by Wallace Clement (*The Canadian Corporate Elite*, 1975) and Dennis Olsen (*The State Elite*, 1980).

This book is indebted to the contributions of these earlier works, but it is not quite like any of them. First, I am convinced that the popular study of power in Canada must extend beyond the privilege and prestige of the wealthy. They are in this book, but so too are the not-so-wealthy who wield very real power and influence over the lives of Canadians. Power is not measured simply by the size of a person's bank balance. It has a lot to do with the size of his or her Rolodex as well. Many of the powerbrokers in this book have influence that can make a typical well-paid corporate chief executive, whose power doesn't extend beyond producing widgets and hiring and firing people, seem like a eunuch.

This book is meant to be an entertaining, insightful look at the people who have power and how they use it. For that reason, it relies a great deal on first-hand portraits of the powerbrokers rather than treating them as faceless cogs within an institutional structure. The profiles are also intended to provide balance to more analytical sections and so make the book more enjoyable. Often, to include at least the names of those who are the most influential members of the elites, I have used lists that rank the most powerful at a glance. I felt that to merit inclusion in this book, the subjects had to have qualities and achievements that would make them leaders regardless of their job title. Hundreds of first-hand interviews have rendered insights into what drives these people and where they have come from. My extensive travels across the country and into the corridors of power have been instrumental in helping me determine who merits inclusion in the book. But the process is ultimately subjective, and others will no doubt dispute some of my choices.

To help draw conclusions about the openness and makeup of Canada's elites, I also conducted extensive biographical surveys to determine the family, ethnic and educational backgrounds of several key elite groups. This was done to show not only who has power but who is still shut out. These surveys were carried out in 1988, 1989 and 1990. They yielded in-depth information about the directors of the country's 20 largest corporations and the five largest banks, the federal deputy ministers who run the Ottawa bureaucracy, the members of the federal cabinet, the publishers and editors of the country's largest daily newspapers, and the religious leaders of the Anglican and Roman Catholic churches.

The response rate was high, and in many cases my findings were complemented by information from biographical sources, such as *Canadian Who's Who* and the *Financial Post Directory of Directors*. Since responses were not forthcoming from all the subjects, the surveys have limitations. There are no bold assertions that can be applied conclusively to the entire group. But they offer insights into the makeup of each elite and permit inferences to be made about who belongs to these elites and why. (The surveys are reproduced in detail in the appendices.)

This book studies five major elites. Part I provides an analysis of the federal and bureaucratic elites before moving on to study the current upsurge of regional resentments toward the way power is practised in Ottawa.

In Part II, the reader meets the most powerful business leaders in Canada, and learns how they wield influence both within the business community and in the political arena. The role of women in business and the multibillion-dollar world of wealthy business heirs is also examined.

Part III is a cross-country tour through the nation's social establishment.

Part IV provides an overview of the diminishing influence of organized religion in Canadian society.

Part V delves into the power and pervasiveness of the nation's media, with special emphasis on print journalism and the CBC, then examines two important cultural industries: film and book publishing.

The conclusion assesses how much Canada's dream of mobility applies to the elites and the extent to which they remain closed to newcomers.

This attempt to measure the openness of Canada's ruling elites is extremely relevant considering the vast changes in the makeup of Canada's population over the past few decades. According to leading sociologist Reginald Bibby, author of *Mosaic Madness: The Poverty and Potential of Life in Canada*, in 1986 only 34 per cent of Canadians claimed British origin (Irish, Scottish, English and Welsh) and 24 per cent claimed French origin. Another 4 per cent claimed both British and French ancestry, and 13 per cent claimed a mix of British, French and some other ethnic group in their ancestry. That left a full quarter of Canadians who hailed from neither of the two so-called founding cultures. They comprise other European (16 per cent), Asian (4 per cent), Native (3 per cent) and other (2 per cent). In recent years, continued intermarriage between Canadians of British, French and other ethnic descents has stopped the decline in those who claim British as one of several ethnic origins.

But any way you measure it, the numerical dominance of those with British roots is down from 57 per cent in 1901 and 55.4 per cent in 1921 as measured by census takers. In fact, the British have been a minority since the 1941 census, when 49.7 per cent of Canadians claimed British roots. (It should be noted that until the 1981 census respondents were asked to list only their father's ancestry.) Do they still lay claim to the bastions of power in society?

And what about women? They constitute a majority of the population, yet they haven't obtained a proportionate share of power. This book will explore the extent of the problem.

I hope to offer readers some insight into the nature of the society Canadians have created after a brief 124 years of existence as a country. This sort of assessment seems appropriate at a time when the nation's social contract has been strained to the limit by competing demands for justice and power. I conclude with some modest proposals on how we can promote a more just society for all Canadians and the sort of values that will be required.

Part I

POLITICS

Chapter 1

The Politics of Elitism

It had to happen. Sooner or later Canadians were bound to recognize and resent the overly exclusive character of Canadian politics. The despair and cynicism that voters feel about politicians and their art, as recorded by numerous opinion polls, is not a shortlived response to any given set of unpopular policies or to any one party. Rather, it is the result of a growing awareness that, in Canada, government is not of the people, by the people, for the people; it is of, by and for elites — and only sometimes for the people.

Canadians, from disgruntled truck drivers to white-collar office workers, are no longer satisfied with our brokerage form of government, in which extraordinary powers are given to the prime minister and cabinet that surpass the powers of their British counterparts. Even the American system, with its checks and balances, places more constraints on presidential power than our system places on the prime minister. The government leader gets and holds power by means of an intricate system of rewards for party faithful and by cajoling, accommodating and brokering between the interests of increasingly vocal elites, whether they be the well-organized professional interest groups lobbying in Ottawa or the grasping regional powerbrokers seeking this or that grant or construction project.

It's no mystery to the public which interest group has the most clout in Ottawa. As the 1978 Royal Commission on Corporate Concentration reported, "There is little doubt that the representatives of major corporations can and do have a greater access to both politicians and public servants than do other individuals through trade associations, their own professional representatives and perhaps most effectively, private conversations between corporate officers and those involved in the policymaking and legislative process."

For the voting public in Canada, the 1980s marked the end of innocence, or more accurately, of naiveté. Ottawa's time-honoured tradition, which began in Sir John A. Macdonald's day, of brokering between elites and ruling by doling out favours and patronage posts is simply no longer acceptable to voters.

Arguably, twin forces account for the mounting vexation of the public. One is the powerful example of U.S. congressional politics at work; the other is media coverage, which has laid bare the inner mechanisms of government as never before.

The intoxicating American example raises false expectations in Canadians. America's powerful Congressmen and -women make our MPs look like party lapdogs, mainly because U.S. politicians are free to vote in the best interests of their constituents, while our MPs are forced to vote along party lines. Heavily indoctrinated with the American example of direct representation, a theory honoured in rhetoric but not in practice in Canada's parliamentary system, Canadian voters feel frustrated when government MPs vote en masse for some contentious policy, such as the GST or free trade. Little wonder that fewer than half of federal MPs had less than five years' experience, according to a 1988 study — the voters take out their frustration on their MPs at election time. Constituents seem to realize that in vain do they phone the local MP to protest about a government policy, since the MP will be whipped into line by the party caucus anyway, or risk losing his or her chances for advancement or other rewards handed out by the prime minister.

In Canadian politics power is centred in the prime minister and the cabinet, not in the MPs who sit in the House of Commons. In the jargon of political scientists, Canada's government is executive-centred, not Parliament-centred. This notion that MPs are elected to speak for their constituents, and not primarily to uphold the government's agenda, is a widespread misconception among Canadian voters. It lays the ground for the cynicism, hostility and often apathy that voters feel when they are confronted by the reality of politics as conveyed by the news media.

The influential and exhaustive nature of today's media coverage has produced in the public a sophisticated awareness of how politics works in Canada. Through television newscasts and newspapers, the public is bombarded with information on who's cutting what deal with whom, what's wrong with the deal, and who peddled what influence to get it. Voters know who is getting what patronage post and for what (frequently) questionable reasons, and which region is getting what stupendously costly megaproject or government contract. There are almost always winners and losers, and hence there is reason for outrage from some interest group or region. This outrage, in turn, is given full play in the news. For politicians, the interplay of increasingly vocal interest groups and media coverage has made governing more difficult than ever. As Deputy Prime Minister Don Mazankowski puts it: "You have more special interest groups than you had before and they're more vocal and have more access to the media. Nothing happens without the whole country knowing it. So what you do in Alberta is reported immediately in Atlantic Canada or Quebec, and if there is a sense that there is some favouritism being shown, they say, 'Hey, what about me?'"

Canadians have been bathed in a continual stream of TV images of elitism at work. They've seen first ministers' conferences where white males in business suits wrangle over the country's constitutional future. They've seen almost monthly coverage of opposition outrage over the latest government patronage appointments when they know that the opposition will be just as hooked on the patronage game once in power. They've seen innumerable instances of scandal where MPs and cabinet ministers have been accused of illegally lining their pockets or abusing their powers.

Public resentment at back-room powerbrokering has deepened over the decades. In the 1957 election John Diefenbaker, then an outsider from Prince Albert, whipped up this brand of resentment by railing against the arrogance and back-room decision-making style of Louis St. Laurent and the all-powerful C.D. Howe — as exemplified by their controversial resort to closure in the famous pipeline debate — and won in an upset. Pierre Trudeau became a focus of anti-elitist resentment in the early 1980s, when he was increasingly perceived as arrogant, isolated from the public will and surrounded by tiresome advisers of overweening ambition. His successor as Liberal prime minister, John Turner, could never shake the widespread view that he was a creature of Bay Street, a representative of the corporate elite, even though he put enormous effort into bashing big business and portraying himself as a man of the people. After serving two months in office (the shortest tenure in history), Turner lost the 1984 election to Brian Mulroney, in part because Mulroney captured the middle ground of Canadian politics that prime ministers have traditionally straddled to win elections.

Resentment toward the politics of elitism is the main ingredient in the poisonous atmosphere in politics that had spread nationwide by the end of the 1980s. Amidst the malaise, *populism* became the new buzzword that somehow crystallized a whole range of grievances against the political system. Ominously, though, this nascent populism became a catalyst for the release of the unseemly side of Canadians: the bigotry, pettiness, racism and intolerance that spilled into the open when a disparate group of misfits burned a Quebec flag in Brockville in 1988. Worse, these same unsavoury elements in the Canadian population found deceptively articulate expression in some policies of Preston Manning's Reform Party. An excellent profile of the new western-based party shown in December 1990 on CBC's "The Journal" revealed that the party's more respectable objectives were a thin veneer for the anti-immigrant, anti-French views of some of its followers.

The same resentment lay behind the surly, inchoate bitterness against incumbent politicians of any stripe that in Ontario trounced the Liberal government of David Peterson in 1989 in favour of the untried New Democrats led by Bob Rae. Peterson was seen as just another manipulative politician when he called an unnecessarily early election, and the smug Bill Davis–style persona he had adopted on the advice of his handlers only compounded that view. By late 1990, the same brand of resentment was focused squarely on the federal Conservative Party, which had sunk to a record low of 14 per cent in the polls.

It is unfair to blame the Mulroney government entirely for the national distemper that afflicted the nation in the early 1990s, but in the years since 1984, when he won a majority, Mulroney and his policies had managed to fuel the mood of alienation to an unprecedented level. The fascinating question is how the Mulroney government managed this feat. How could such a savvy, vote-conscious group of politicians like Mulroney and his cabinet lead the party so far into the political wilderness that pundits were talking about the obliteration of the party at the next election, the surging fortunes of the New Democrats, and the potential of the Reform Party to become a major force in the House of Commons? Their conundrum is better understood when placed in the context of the past.

Canadian Political Traditions

It has taken Canadians about 120 years to become fed up with who has power and how they use it in federal politics. The pols in power in this era are arguably no more venal, crafty, manipulative or otherwise corrupt than they were at any time during our history. In fact, modern-day rules governing such areas as conflicts of interest, graft and election spending probably make our legislators some of the cleanest in history. For instance, Canadians would be appalled if Prime Minister Brian Mulroney and his cabinet served as the executives of major corporations at the same time as they governed. Imagine them hobnobbing with well-heeled merchants at a board meeting in the morning, then convening a cabinet session to talk about corporate tax laws or economic policy in the afternoon. Yet this is exactly what politicians did in Sir John A. Macdonald's time. Our first prime minister was simultaneously the first president of Manufacturers Life Insurance of Toronto and held the post until his death in 1891. Scholars of Canadian politics describe Macdonald's era as a time when the government spent most of its energy doling out patronage and presiding over the location of everything from post offices to wharves and railway stations. Sounds familiar.

From Macdonald's day to the present, Canadian politics has been dominated by a highly centralized, elitist approach to power whose origins can be traced to the pre-nineteenth-century Tory traditions of Great Britain. It was from these pre-liberal traditions, in which society was viewed as hierarchic, with the crown at the top and the lords, knights, burghers and commoners arranged in layers below, that our parliamentary division of powers sprang. In Canada, thanks in part to the monarchist leanings of the United Empire Loyalists, power has been highly concentrated at the top. Power still trickles down from the crown, now represented in theory by the governor general, and is wielded by the federal cabinet and the prime minister, who act on behalf of the crown.

Party discipline is so rigid that the members of the House of Commons have almost no independence. If they are members of the governing party, they are expected to pass legislation that originates in cabinet and the powerful civil service. If they are members of the opposition parties, they are expected to protest loudly but, of course, along lines determined by their party leadership. Ordinary MPs are little more than the yea-sayers of the party bosses.[1]

In modern Tory thinking, the old hierarchy based on rank and degree is no longer relevant, but the concept of social class — as in lower, middle or upper — has taken its place. Notes academic C.E.S. Franks, "society is still hierarchical, and the realm should be governed by an elite, a ruling class of the few who are able to acquire the art of governing. This elite is formed through heredity and the co-opting of those of merit from the lower classes to the higher. Mass suffrage is accepted but the electorate is passive, not active. Their participation is limited to voting and support of the party."[2] If you think this sounds like Canadian parliamentary experience, you're right. There's a further comparison to be made. Tory thinking, writes Franks, includes a belief in not only strong but big government. It professes that "elite leaders, the wealthy and the advantaged, have a responsibility for the welfare of others. Thus state education, universal health-care schemes and welfare programs are quite compatible with Toryism. So also is a strong role for government in planning the economy and restructuring industry."

Through the postwar period, Canada has been ruled by governments whose style has been dominated by the traditions of Toryism, not classic liberalism as it was practised in nineteenth-century England. In that liberal tradition, parliament, namely the House of Commons, was the focus of political power, not the cabinet, which was viewed as a powerful committee of parliament and was accountable to it. For example, Walter Bagehot, a leading nineteenth-century constitutional thinker and celebrated editor of *The Economist* magazine, described the cabinet as "a board of control chosen by the legislature, out of persons whom it trusts and knows, to rule the nation."

The early liberal theories developed by thinkers like Adam Smith in the 1700s and John Stuart Mill in the 1800s espoused a philosophy of *laissez faire*, of small government and a free market economy. In the liberal scheme, the primacy of the individual in theory led to the primacy of parliament in politics. During the heyday of liberalism in England, members of parliament were regarded as independent, rational human beings free of allegiance to interest groups and powerful patrons, and free from the bondage of party discipline.

By contrast, politics in Canada has been characterized by centralized power, elitism, patronage and a weak role for the people's representatives. In recent years the centralization of power at the top has increased. During Pierre Trudeau's administration, power was increasingly concentrated in the central agencies of administration, particularly the Privy Council Office (PCO) and the Prime Minister's Office (PMO). Joe Clark continued the trend by creating a powerful inner cabinet during his nine-month fling with power in 1979. Brian Mulroney, after a disastrous early flirtation with a looser style of government that saw his office become overwhelmed with decision-making, has resumed the trend. Not only are the PMO and the PCO as powerful as ever but Mulroney further centralized cabinet decision-making in two elite cabinet committees, the 19-member Priorities and Planning committee and the more powerful eight-member Operations committee.

The Balancing Act: Centralized Power and Collective Policies

Since the 1940s, federal governments have managed — until now — to avoid a widespread sense of alienation and anger among voters by one major means: implementing collectivist policies, often borrowed from the socialists of the CCF and the NDP, that address the needs and concerns of common folk. Like beneficent parents, the cabinet and civil service hatched policies that created the welfare state (universal health care, the Canada Pension Plan, unemployment insurance), stimulated industry (through generous tax provisions, loan guarantees and grants), promoted nationwide communications (through the CBC and postal subsidies for domestic magazines) as well as nationwide transportation. They also furthered regional development through transfers to the provinces and handouts to regional energy megaprojects.

This father-knows-best style of government fitted with the peculiar, long-standing tendency of Canadians to defer to authority — government authority in particular — a tendency that only lately seems to have broken down amid a national mood of distemper roughly comparable to the emotionalism of a beer-hall brawl. "People are sick to death of the established system. That disgust will not go away," comments Thomas Courchene, an economist and director of the School of Policy Studies at Queen's University.

The present Conservative Government is in trouble for one major reason. It has continued the tradition of highly centralized government, but its brand of free-market economics, coupled with the rigours of deficit-cutting, has meant that it is falling short on collectivist policies that keep the electorate content. To the majority of voters in mid-1991, the Conservative government seemed to be made up of politicians with the social conscience of Marie Antoinette, who pass policies that seem designed to inflict maximum pain on the middle class, and whose free-market views seem to be undoing everything Canadians once had in common, from the CBC to Via Rail, to Crown corporations like Petro-Canada and Air Canada. C.D. Howe must be railing in his grave.

Tories in the Wilderness

The highly centralized nature of power in Ottawa, and the alienation from the voters of those who hold it, aroused my curiosity about exactly who it is who governs us. What are their social and ethnic origins, their career and educational backgrounds? Do they fairly represent the demographic makeup of the country, or are they as homogeneous as the members of a wealthy yacht club? How open is the federal political elite to newcomers of varying backgrounds? To what degree does the federal political system enhance social mobility within Canada and, if so, for whom?

A survey I carried out in December 1989 and used with other biographical sources revealed that the 39 members of the Conservative cabinet were a well-heeled, well-educated group, drawn almost exclusively from the ranks of the upper middle class. The vast majority were men (there were in 1989 only six women) and middle-aged. Most were successful professionals or businessmen with solid educational credentials. About one-third had attended private school. Fully 33 ministers had attended university, and 11 had completed graduate studies. In addition, 22 had professional degrees or certifications. As might be expected, lawyers dominated the cabinet (12). But a good many ministers (11) also had a background in business, sometimes in combination with another professional degree such as law or engineering.

The ministers also tended to adhere to traditional, mainstream religious faiths. Of 25 ministers who claimed to adhere to a religion either in their survey response or biographical listings, most (18) were Protestant. Of the Protestants, seven were Anglican and seven were United Church. Six ministers were Roman Catholic and one was Jewish.

Most cabinet ministers were of British or French descent. There were notable exceptions, such as Deputy Prime Minister Don Mazankowski (Polish), Harvie Andre (Ukrainian), Otto Jelinek (Czech) and Frank Oberle (German), but hardly enough to reflect Canada's cultural mosaic. (In the House of Commons, only 49 of 295 members — 16.6 per cent — elected in the 1988 election were neither French nor British in origin. The number of visible-minority MPs increased to four from one in 1984. They were Howard McCurdy, NDP, a black; Filipino Canadian Rey Pagtakhan, Liberal; Lebanese Canadian Mac Harb, Liberal; and Ethel Blondin, Liberal, a native Indian.)

All but two cabinet ministers were born in Canada. Most (23) represented central Canada, nine represented the four western provinces, and five represented the four Atlantic provinces.

The cabinet ministers also had a taste for the trappings of prestige. A sizable number (11) belonged to one or more private clubs, ranging from the Ranchmen's in Calgary (Joe Clark) to the Toronto Club (Michael Wilson). The prime minister has memberships in five clubs, including the Mount Royal in Montreal and the Albany in Toronto.

(The Albany was the most popular club for ministers, with six as members.)

The picture emerges of a cabinet drawn from an exclusive section of society. Even so, for most of the group, politics offered another step up the social ladder to the ranks of power elite in Canada. Before they entered public life, very few held positions that would put them in the upper ranks of other elite groups. A notable exception is Brian Mulroney, who, as CEO of the Iron Ore Company of Canada, was a member of the business elite; former investment executives Barbara McDougall and Michael Wilson were also headed for the upper ranks of the business elite (defined here as holding memberships on powerful corporate boards or being CEO of a major company). Conversely, only two cabinet ministers, both of whom were farmers, left lower-class occupations to enter politics.

If the occupation of their fathers is considered the starting point for social mobility, the picture of cabinet ministers as social climbers emerges even more clearly. At least seven ministers grew up in lower-class, or blue-collar, homes. Among their fathers' occupations: farmer, auto mechanic, barber and cabinetmaker. Brian Mulroney's father was an electrician. Most ministers were born into the middle class; their fathers were white-collar managers, small businessmen or clergy. Only a handful had fathers who were members of an elite group, including Michael Wilson, whose father was president of the National Trust Co., and Kim Campbell, whose father was a chief magistrate in British Columbia.

In sum, the cabinet is dominated by upwardly mobile, upper-middle-class men who represent traditional power bases in Canadian society. Most have backgrounds in law or business, have French or English origins and represent central Canada. Before exploring what this means for the efficacy of the political system, I will take a closer look at the most powerful individuals in cabinet.

A Pragmatist in Power

"The prime minister of Canada is no place for a philosopher. If you're going to philosophize, then you should do that in the sanctity of one of our finer universities," asserts Prime Minister Brian Mulroney.

Mulroney is an arriviste. He was born in 1939, in Baie-Comeau, Quebec, a one-company town on the north shore of the St. Lawrence River. He is the third of six children born to Ben and Mary Mulroney, whose ancestors immigrated from Ireland to Canada in the 1840s to escape the great potato famine, settling first at Ste. Catherine-de-Portneuf, just outside Quebec City. During the 1930s, Ben and his family were among the settlers who built Baie-Comeau out of the bush while working at a new paper mill on the site. Mulroney grew up in a modest house on Champlain Street, and by Baie-Comeau standards enjoyed a comfortable life. His father worked his way up to foreman at the mill and moonlighted as an electrician. "There was always enough to eat and a proper place to live, a good education and summer jobs," Mulroney once told a *Maclean's* interviewer. "If we were poor, no one realized it."

Ben imbued Brian with a healthy respect for education. "There's only one way out of a paper mill town," he told his son, "and that's through a university door." Education would be the vehicle for Mulroney's rise from bush town to Parliament Hill; that and a self-confessed big mouth. "I was ambitious, and not always in the most pleasant way. I was a bit of a loud mouth," he once conceded. There was no high school in his hometown, so, at age 14, Mulroney left Baie-Comeau for Chatham, New Brunswick, where he attended St. Thomas High School, a school run by diocesan priests on the campus of St. Thomas Collage.

While at St. Francis Xavier University in Antigonish, Nova Scotia, Mulroney flowered into the proverbial Big Man on Campus. He was active in drama, playing in "The Caine Mutiny" and "Everyman," and was undefeated in intercollegiate debates. He was president of the Maritime Progressive Conservative Students' Federation and served as prime minister in Maritime university students' model parliament. After a disastrous year (1959) at Dalhousie law school, Mulroney completed his law degree at Laval University in the early 1960s. He was called to the Quebec bar in 1965, after having to rewrite one of his bar admission exams.

In law, there are essentially two routes to follow. One is small-time: working on your own or with a few colleagues and pulling down a middle-class income. The other is big-time: landing a job with a major Montreal or Toronto firm where the incomes are counted in six figures. Mulroney was among the lucky minority of lawyers who follow the second route. His ticket to upper-class wealth came when he was asked to join the prestigious Montreal firm that is now Ogilvy-Renault.

Mulroney began as a junior in litigation but soon found his feet in labour law. By all accounts he was first-rate, renowned for his legal skills and his now well known talents as a conciliator who would wring compromises out of the most intractable opponents. Mulroney's major clients were the employers involved in such disputes, not the workers. Those clients included The Maritime Employers Association, which represented major ports across the country, and the Iron Ore Company of Canada, which would later hire him as an executive.

During his days as Montreal labour lawyer, Mulroney was known variously as a workaholic, party boy and social climber nonpareil. He did copious amounts of work, drank copious amounts of booze (which he later forswore) and networked so intensely at fashionable social events that he became acquainted with just about everyone who counted in Montreal's business and political establishment. He made one of his best connections at the Mount Royal Tennis Club. It was there, beside the pool, that he met bikini-clad Mila Pivnicki, 18, the daughter of a prominent psychiatrist (whose patients included Margaret Trudeau). They married in 1973.

Mulroney had nurtured ties to the federal Conservative Party since his days in university. He was national vice-president of the Youth for Diefenbaker movement in 1956, later became a Quebec organizer for Diefenbaker and, in the summer of 1962, worked as a special assistant to federal agriculture minister Alvin Hamilton. At the 1967 leadership convention, he supported Davie Fulton, then followed Fulton to the Stanfield camp after Fulton placed third. But it was Mulroney's high-profile membership on the three-member Cliche Royal Commission, created in 1974 to investigate corruption in the Quebec construction industry, that made his name a household word in Quebec and set the stage for his first bid for the leadership of the PC Party in 1976. When Mulroney lost to Joe Clark, he took defeat hard, leaving politics to work at the Iron Ore Company in Schefferville, Quebec, first as a corporate affairs executive, then as president. As a sore loser, he spent his time plotting against Clark. As a corporate boss his major task was to shut down the operation — and by extension, the town — on behalf of Hanna Mining, its parent company in Cleveland. Mulroney accomplished the task — while garnering headlines about generous severance deals for laid-off workers — in November 1982, just in time for his successful bid for the leadership of the Conservative Party in the next year.

Mulroney personifies the triumph of pragmatism over principle in Canadian politics. Used wisely, pragmatism is a prerequisite of longevity for any politicians, but it is a poor replacement for a well-ordered political philosophy. If success in politics rests on the balancing of what we might call the three Ps — pragmatism, partisanship and principles — Mulroney scores high on the first two and poorly on the last. Instead of a personal political vision for Canada, Mulroney has offered a patchwork approach to governing, in which short-term compromises take the place of long-term goals based on a political philosophy. He is like an auto mechanic who has busied himself doing spot-welding jobs on a rusting car and failed to notice that the steering wheel doesn't work — until it's almost too late.

Mulroney doesn't even have a road map for where he wants to drive the car if it holds together. He's willing to take directions from everyone. "I like to listen to people. I get the best advice I can and then act in the interests of the Canadian people." The trouble is, acting in the interests of the people is far easier said than done. First, the people seldom agree on what their common interests are, and second, Mulroney's views on what is good for the people have rarely conformed with the people's views. No one can disagree that Mulroney's emphasis on achieving economic prosperity by keeping Canada united is a worthwhile endeavour. But economic prosperity is not a noble enough goal around which to forge a sense of national purpose. Economic prosperity is not an end in itself, it's a means to a higher goal, such as a society in which human rights, equality before the law or social justice are paramount.

Still, to characterize Mulroney as being totally without political principles is going too far, as is the tendency of some disgruntled voters to dismiss him as an insidious cad. Even Mulroney's harshest critics concede that one of his redeeming qualities is a genuine concern for the disadvantaged in society. One pundit, Ron Graham, author of *One-Eyed Kings*, went so far as to characterize Mulroney as a '60s-style liberal, but this makes too much of his humanitarian streak. Mulroney was elected partly because he promised to stop the Liberal Party's magnanimous ways that had left the government with an annual deficit of $35 billion by the end of 1984.

Despite the current neoconservative tack of his government, Mulroney has shown that he has acute instincts on how to occupy the political centre in Canadian politics. This has more to do with his desire to win elections than with any socialistic streak of well-thought-out collectivism. It is true that Mulroney spent his early months in office backtracking on and overturning Finance Minister Michael Wilson's early attempts to cut government spending. But his recalcitrance was mainly the result of the strenuous opposition the cuts engendered from the cabinet ministers and interest groups affected; it did not reflect a philosophical stand. For example, Mulroney initially agreed to Wilson's 1985 plan to partially de-index old age pensions. Mulroney overturned the plan a few months later in the face of mounting public opposition. He explained to reporters: "We are not here as emperors, we are in Parliament as commoners, servants of the people. We never contended we were perfect, but we have always said we would try and be fair. I think we violated that rule of fairness, as it turns out, and we had to correct it."

Flip-flops have marked Mulroney's career from the start. This is the man who opposed free trade during the 1983 leadership campaign, and who insisted that Joe Clark's "community of communities," the conceptual precursor of the Meech Lake accord was wrong for Canada and would be suicidal for the PC Party. By the end of the decade he had embraced both concepts (and was desperately trying to persuade Canadians to do the same). Such reversals are hardly the mark of a rigorous political philosophy. As journalist Jeffrey Simpson, a close observer of Mulroney, points out, the prime minister "does not have a well-ordered philosophy of government, he is driven by his instincts, and all of his political instincts are those of moderation. He believes the party can win only by being moderate. He has neither the emotional nor the intellectual equipment for trenchant analysis or radicalism."

Mulroney is a political sphinx who can be at turns thoughtful — he's legendary for his kind gestures to ailing colleagues and friends — and spiteful. Should a fellow politician or journalist cross Mulroney, he has been known to mutter a morbid "His time will come," as if exhorting voodoo spirits to strike down his opponent.

In social outlook, Mulroney is just as ambiguous. It's as though he can't figure out whether to be true to his roots as a working-class boy from Baie-Comeau or to his later incarnation as a prosperous labour lawyer with a Westmount mansion. At turns, Mulroney talks in the lugubrious phrases of a business brahman, then in the salty language of a stevedore. (In a phone interview with me in 1982, Mulroney immediately launched into barroom talk, apparently assuming that journalists always swear when they converse.) He has the emotional sensitivity of a true Celt and the belligerence of a schoolyard bully.

Mulroney's major political strength is his fierce partisanship. It divides the world into allies to be supported and adversaries to be bullied and it also seems to give him the strength to fight back after countless setbacks for his government. This same partisanship also marked his rise to power, as his propensity to hire old school chums as aides and advisors reveals. Partisanship keeps the world simple, but it is no alternative to a well-ordered philosophy of government. If anything, Mulroney's ascent to the prime minister's office is a remarkable example of how someone can gain power without much of an idea of what to do with it. How Mulroney managed this is not a great mystery.

He equipped himself with the right education, made an art form of nurturing the right contacts with the wealthy and politically well-connected, then refused to accept defeat until the leadership of the party was his. This is all to his credit. Yet without a well-ordered political philosophy, his use of power has fallen into disrepute. His gradual shift to the right of the political spectrum, as he matched his conservative rhetoric with action, seemed to be a belated attempt to stake out some philosophical ground.

Mulroney's first term as prime minister, from 1984 to 1988, was marked by his vacillation between moderation born of political necessity and the neoconservative economic attitudes that surfaced in his rhetoric. In 1983, while sitting as opposition leader in the House,

Mulroney consistently denounced the Liberals for running up a $31-billion annual deficit. On CTV's "Question Period," he said that the Liberals showed "no respect for the taxpayer's dollar." Elsewhere, he railed against Ottawa's bloated bureaucracy and promised "tough but fair" economic measures to get the deficit down and the economy on track. The election of his party, he promised, would unleash the economic energy of Canada and create "jobs, jobs, jobs."

The rhetoric continued in his campaign for re-election in 1988. The free trade debate dominated the campaign, but the deal was part of a wider notion of how Canada must adjust to compete in a fiercely competitive global economy. "We're talking about prosperity. We're talking about what Margaret Thatcher calls the wave of the future. You don't hide behind barriers any more," he told reporters on a November 1988 campaign stop.

During the campaign, Mulroney said that the objectives of his next four years would be to reduce the federal deficit, complete his government's tax program, continue to unleash the private sector from deregulation, attract international foreign investment and strengthen the country's research and development sector. Canadians got most of what Mulroney promised in his second term. But in the course of living up to much of his conservative rhetoric, Mulroney alienated his government from most voters. For example, a *Globe and Mail*-CBC poll in October 1990 showed that more Canadians (49 per cent) thought free trade had hurt Canada than thought it had helped or made no difference. During the Meech Lake crisis, in February 1990, another *Globe*-CBC poll showed that 47 per cent of Canadians opposed the deal, while only 24 per cent favoured it. And a Gallup survey conducted in November 1990 showed that 76 per cent of Canadians opposed the infamous Goods and Services Tax.

It is hard to blame any one policy for turning droves of voters away from the Conservatives. The Meech Lake process certainly was crucial. Andrew Cohen, author of *A Deal Undone: The Making and Breaking of the Meech Lake Accord*, has probably summed up the aftertaste best. "The accord itself," he wrote in the *Financial Post*, "based on a strategy of co-opting, rather than confronting Quebec nationalism, awakened emotions best left undisturbed. But the meth-

ods of its proponents — the brinkmanship, the cynicism, the man-
ipulation — suggested to every group with an agenda that anything
goes: that all means were legitimate, that everything was up for grabs.
When the highest law of the land seemed a matter of such casual
concern to the prime minister — a roll of the dice, after all — small
wonder some began to think otherwise."

As dismayed as the public was with the fractious state of the nation
in early 1990, there was another issue that evoked rage rather than
bewilderment: soaring taxes. The PCs had come to office promising
a fairer tax system, but the vast majority of Canadians believed that
the government had failed miserably. A Gallup survey released in
December 1990 revealed that only 12 per cent of Canadians thought
the government had made the system fairer for the average Canadian.
Almost three out of four thought it had failed. They were right.
Between 1984 and the end of 1989, the government increased its
income tax revenues by 70 per cent, with most of the increase coming
from middle-class earners. Canadians were beginning to feel taxed
to the hilt. Meanwhile, taxes eased for groups on both sides of the
middle class. Even before the imposition of the Goods and Services
Tax, Vancouver's Fraser Institute calculated that taxes from all sources — federal and provincial income taxes, consumption taxes and
municipal taxes — consumed about half of a taxpayer's income.
Little wonder that the Tories had nowhere to go but up in the polls.

By early 1991, the cabinet was a team under duress, united in
a hang-tough attitude that they were doing what was best for the
country. Joe Clark, the new constitutional affairs minister and faded
Red Tory, was touring the provinces in search of a compromise on
constitutional reform. Benoît Bouchard, the new health minister and
Mulroney's Quebec lieutenant, faced two daunting tasks: persuading
Canadians that the Tories cared about social programs, and rebuild-
ing the party's fragmenting power base in Quebec. Defence Minister
Marcel Masse, who made a name for himself as a cultural crusader
in his former job as communications minister, was getting used to
his new role as a hachetman charged with imposing severe cutbacks
at his new ministry. Perrin Beatty, the minister of communications
and self-styled future prime minister, was enjoying the limelight as
the latest defender of Canadian culture. Other ministers were licking

their wounds after receiving demotions in the spring cabinet shuffle. Among them: Robert de Cotret, who moved from minister of environment to minister of state, and John Crosbie, who was shifted from Trade to Fisheries and Oceans. Senator Lowell Murray, the former minister of federal-provincial relations and the man who was a major player in the Meech Lake mess, was left as Government Leader in the Senate.

Perhaps most amazing, Mulroney's cabinet was not splintered by grumbling defectors or open rebellion. This was partly a testament to the prime minister's remarkable ability to inspire loyalty in his lieutenants. But it was also a result of the fierce ideological convictions of Mulroney's mainstays in cabinet: Michael Wilson and Don Mazankowski, neoconservatives from opposite ends of the social spectrum. With them to prop up his resolve, Mulroney seemed as resolute as the Iron Lady of London.

The Patrician: Michael Wilson

Michael Wilson is in his element. It's a Saturday morning in February 1990, and Wilson, then the finance minister, is recovering from tabling a get-tough budget. He is back in his Etobicoke riding, eating a hearty breakfast of sausages and scrambled eggs along with 500 party faithful at the exclusive Old Mill Restaurant. It is a partisan crowd of well-off urban professionals, many of whom live in the multimillion-dollar mansions nestled in the nearby South Kingsway neighbourhood. The men wear business suits, the women wear variations on a wealthy theme, everything from kilts and pearls to evening gown glamour. (These women are the same crowd who can be seen regularly at the nearby Loblaws on a weekday morning, picking up a few groceries in their best sables and minks, their hair in classic buns and their necks adorned with a smattering of jewellery.)

After Wilson delivers his standard tough-guy message on the deficit, the questions begin. They are predictably mild: Why not just cut every government department by 10 per cent? Why not get rid of foreign aid? And so on. Wilson responds politely, soaking in the acceptance as if he's soaking in a good hot bath.

Michael Wilson displays a bland political persona that, rather remarkably, has won him election to the House of Commons four times since 1979. He's a one-man contradiction to the observation that "you cannot adopt politics as a profession and remain honest" — oft-quoted words of Louis McHenry Howe, secretary to President Franklin D. Roosevelt. Wilson's physical appearance reinforces the good-guy image. The high forehead, kind eyes and melon-sized chin would make him a perfect stand-in for Dudley Doright of the Mounties.

Wilson's views on economic policies haven't wavered since he entered the political game; he's only had to slow down the timetable whenever he's confronted with political realities. The Canadian public, most of whom disapprove of those policies, view Wilson as something akin to a dentist. Each one of his budgets was dreaded like an annual checkup, and each one produced pain like that associated with a few fillings on one extreme, to a root canal on the other. Even those who agree that social program cuts and tax hikes are necessary long for a relief from the discomfort.

After a frustrating first term in government, Wilson emerged in the second as an unsurpassed philosophical force in the Mulroney cabinet. In 1984, the fledgling finance minister laid out his neoconservative economic agenda in a tidy little document called the *Agenda for Economic Renewal*. It contained a list of Wilson's pet programs: free trade, privatization, deregulation, corporate and personal tax reform, deficit reduction and financial institution reform. By the time he left the finance portfolio in April 1991, he had taken action, with mixed success, on every one of those fronts.

Backed by a band of deficit-cutting disciples in the Finance Department and central bank, Wilson had cast over the government his austere vision of what's good for the country through budgets and his membership on key cabinet committees, including Operations, which decides what issues deserve attention, Priorities and Planning, which then deals with those issues, and a special expenditure-review committee set up in 1989 to hunt down spending cuts. Wilson's switch to minister of trade in the 1991 cabinet shuffle did not lessen his influence over economic policy; it simply broadened his sway to include trade and industrial policies.

There's a good chance that history will judge Wilson to be the man who set the finances of the country back on track, especially if the GST turns out to be the means for reducing the national debt. But the long-suffering public is in no mood to buy that line of reasoning. According to the findings of Decima research, Canadians claim that they want government to cut spending sharply, but they also want it to spend more in some areas, particularly health, education and social programs.

But the Tories had little room, thanks to the horrid state of the Canadian economy in 1991 and the recalcitrant deficit, to implement collectivist programs that could win back the public's heart. The prime minister admitted as much in the House in December 1990. After blaming the Liberals for the country's $380-billion debt, Mulroney said Ottawa couldn't help the country's 1.2 million jobless. Interest payments on the debt alone, he said, consume 35 cents of every dollar. "That limits severely the kinds of government programs that can be initiated."

Thus cornered, the government seemed, at least to the unemployed and poor in the country's burgeoning food lines, unaware of what aid was needed. Wilson didn't help the impression with his ill-timed comments about knowing what it's like to take a pay cut. A month before, reacting to another bout of bad economic news from Statistics Canada, he had told reporters that when he was an executive at Dominion Securities (now RBC Dominion) in 1973, he took a 25 per cent cut in pay during difficult economic times. The lunacy of comparing the temporary sacrifice he made as an upper-income investment executive with the hardship faced by the country's jobless was evident to everyone but the finance minister.

Wilson's definition of economic sacrifice, and his neoconservative agenda, are very much in tune with his upper-class origins and career on Bay Street. Born in Toronto in 1937, the son of Harry Wilson, president of National Trust Co., Wilson grew up in a comfortable Rosedale home. He attended Upper Canada College and the University of Toronto, graduating with a B-average in Commerce. His first job was with a blue-chip British merchant banking house, Baring Brothers, which he joined in 1959 with a helping hand from merchant banker Sir Edward Peacock, a friend of his father's. (A generation later, Wilson's son Cameron works at the same firm.) After apprenticing on the Euro-bond market for two years, Wilson returned to Toronto to sell commercial paper for Harris & Partners Ltd. When that firm merged with Dominion Securities in 1973, Wilson emerged as executive vice-president. By then a pillar of the Conservative Party, Wilson was first elected to Parliament in 1979 as part of Joe Clark's ill-fated government. He was re-elected in 1980, 1984 and 1988.

Throughout, there's little doubt that he has remained true to his roots and to the principles that sprang from them. Unfortunately, the road to political oblivion is paved with cost-cutting intentions. Perhaps, however, like good dentists, he and his successor, Don Mazankowski, will recognize before the next election that patients deserve a lollipop every once in a while.

The Prairie Puritan: Don Mazankowski

When fledgling Justice Minister Kim Campbell tried to get tough new gun controls passed, she discovered that nothing happens in the government without Don Mazankowski's approval. In June 1990 Campbell introduced a gun-control bill that banned combat-type weapons and ammunition clips containing 30 or more bullets and required a 28-day cooling-off period between the application for a gun permit and its issuance. Mazankowski, an Albertan, stepped forward to protect the interests of enraged gun owners in the west who feared their hobby was facing undue restrictions. There ensued a cabinet battle, and, to nobody's surprise, Campbell lost. The bill was referred to committee for watering-down.

Brian Mulroney may get the TV coverage, Michael Wilson may get profile after profile in leading newspapers and magazines, but Mazankowski makes the government work. As deputy prime minister and finance minister, he is Mulroney's most trusted confidant and right-hand man. Yet his power doesn't stop there. He is a major force on the most powerful cabinet committees: the Operations committee, the Priorities and Planning committee and the expenditure review committee, the cost-cutting powerhouse of cabinet that has whittled away relentlessly at the spending of government departments. As Jim Hawkes, the party whip and a fellow Alberta MP has put it, "Nothing moves in Ottawa without Maz. He is at the centre on a daily basis."

The MP for Vegreville, a farming town east of Edmonton, comes across as every inch the tough cost-cutter. He is physically imposing, but not in the muscular way one would expect of a man who grew up on a prairie farm. He has a tense, vaguely menacing air about him, created by his bone-dry demeanour and the jet-black eyebrows that arch like falcon wings. This man is all business. It's easy to see why the prime minister counts on him to make things run on the Hill.

There was nothing in the political environment to make a deputy prime minister smile on the rainy day in October 1990 when I interviewed him in his wood-pannelled East Block office. "We're going through some very difficult times," he says stonily, "but I don't feel any sense of defeat or sense of difficulty that cannot be overcome. That's not to disregard the current view of the voters," he adds. "We have embarked on a program which we believe is important, is critical, and we believe we're doing the right thing."

If Mulroney is the moderate who has mastered the neoconservative rhetoric and Wilson is the guru, Mazankowski is the practitioner who makes it happen. Under his watchful eye, program spending by government departments has been cut from a $16-billion annual shortfall to a $10-billion surplus — a $26-billion turnaround during the Tories' tenure. A veteran of seven election wins since 1968, Mazankowski has served the Mulroney government since 1984 as minister of transport, president of the Treasury Board, minister responsible for privatization and regulatory affairs, and agriculture minister. As transport minister, he deregulated the airline and trucking industries, revised the Railway Safety Act and the National Aeronautics Act and privatized Northern Transportation Co. As privatization minister, he announced the privatization of Air Canada. He's viewed in western Canada as the father of the Western Economic Diversification Plan, which has pumped more than $250 million into the region's economy. As agriculture minister, he launched an ambitious overview of the whole industry system of farming, marketing boards and food processing with a view to making it more competitive, more sensitive to consumer demands and more market-oriented. He's proud of his accomplishments. "In terms of revitalizing the private sector and the kind of job creation that we've had from the private sector, I think those policies have been correct," he says.

Mazankowski developed his own brand of rugged individualism while rising from humble origins. He was born on a farm outside Viking, Alberta, in July 1935. His parents, Frank and Dora, both of Polish descent, had immigrated from Nebraska in 1921. Mazankowski describes his father as a "very quiet, very kind and compassionate person." But his mother had most influence on him. "My mother was more aggressive and more business-oriented, and she gave us the element of drive and initiative and enterprise."

The youngest of five children, Mazankowski spent his boyhood tending dairy and beef cattle first thing in the morning and last thing at night. During the day he attended a one-room schoolhouse in nearby Coburg. School wasn't high on his agenda, though, and he dropped out at age 16. "I had good marks," he says. But, he adds, "I really wanted to get into business because as a kid my father used to take me to town. I yearned for the day that I could be standing on the other side of the counter running the cash register and writing up orders."

He left Viking to visit one of his older sisters, who was married and living in Chicago. "She asked me to come and spend a few days with her and I ended up staying a year and a half." Mazankowski worked at his sister's trucking company as a dispatcher and part-time driver.

When he was 21, he decided to go into business for himself. By then back in Alberta, he opened a North Star gas station and service centre in Vegreville, just a tractor ride north of Viking. Later, with his older brother, Ray, he opened a General Motors car dealership. Mazankowski was joint owner of the business until 1980, when he sold out to his brother. The business failed in 1985.

Mazankowski credits his mentor, John Diefenbaker, with attracting him into politics. "In the election of 1962, he came to Vegreville. He asked for some vehicles to move chairs, and I got included on the list of supporters." Mazankowski was thrilled by Diefenbaker's speech. "My attraction to him came as a result of our business. He was seen as being very helpful to western Canada, in particular the farmers."

After 1968, when Mazankowski was first elected to Parliament, he became fast friends with the Chief, who by then was an ordinary MP, having lost the party leadership to Robert Stanfield in the convention of 1967. "We campaigned together in elections and by-elections. He was an amazing fellow. He had a very keen mind and a memory that was very sharp. We never missed a speech of his in the House of Commons." When Diefenbaker died in 1979, Mazankowski was a pallbearer at his funeral.

Mazankowski also credits Robert Stanfield with helping his career enormously. "He gave me more opportunities than I ever could have imagined, opportunities to take an active role, and he gave me that sort of quiet confidence that I guess I needed."

Throughout his career, Mazankowski has been known for his clean living (he goes to mass regularly) and an ability to stay out of scandals that have felled other MPs by the dozen. He can sound as ingenuous as Jimmy Stewart in the movie *Mr. Smith Goes to Washington.* "The most satisfying moment of my life," he says, " was being elected for the first time and having the privilege of walking up the steps of the Parliament Buildings, under the Peace Tower, and knowing that I really belong there." He adds: "The last thing in the world I ever wanted to do was embarrass my constituents by my conduct. That has been the kind of discipline I have imposed on myself."

Mazankowski's economic views round out the picture of Prairie Puritanism. "I think I'm economically quite conservative," he says in understatement. "My brother Ray, who was with me in business, was perhaps more of a risk taker than I was. I was more cautious. I am fiscally conservative." He considers himself more liberal on social issues, although he makes a typical Red Tory look leftist. "Being a good conservative economically gives you the strength to be socially liberal," he says. As proof of his liberal streak, Mazankowski cites his legislative efforts to make airports more accessible to the disabled and to provide better housing for seniors. "It goes back to my western upbringing and small-town living. If your neighbour needs help or if your community needs help, you all pull together."

But if Mazankowski has a socially progressive impulse buried deep under his furrowed brow, it's not one that his fellow cabinet ministers or, indeed, Canadians have seem much of lately. He's been too busy counting the costs of the government's past beneficence.

Barbara McDougall and the New Wave Tory Women

They carry briefcases, wear elegant clothes with a corporate executive cut, drink scotch more than spritzers, make the members of REAL women look like throwbacks to the '50s and radical feminists look like left-over college sophomores from the '60s. There are a total of 21 of them in the federal Tory benches, and seven now have seats at the cabinet table. Of those, Kim Campbell, first female minister of justice, is viewed as a comer, but Barbara McDougall, minister of external affairs, has arrived. McDougall, who has served two terms to Campbell's one, has Mulroney's ear like few other ministers.

Of the seven, only McDougall and Campbell are full departmental ministers. The others are more junior ministers. They are Monique Vezina, minister of state (employment and immigration) and minister of state (seniors); Monique Landry, minister for external relations and minister of state (Indian and northern development); Shirley Martin, minister of state (transport); Mary Collins, associate minister of national defence and minister responsible for the status of women; and Pauline Browes, minister of state (environment).

In 1967, an editorialist in the Calgary *Herald* had this to say in a rant against the creation of the Royal Commission on the Status of Women: "Men and women are not equal. Nature has ascribed roles to women that make it impractical for them to be regarded on the same basis [as men] in many instances." If there's a woman politician who best dramatizes the lunacy of the *Herald*'s remarks, it's Barbara McDougall. Not since Flora MacDonald has a woman been touted so often to become Canada's first female prime minister. McDougall has been endorsed as prime ministerial material by a variety of publications, from *Chatelaine* to the *Globe and Mail*.

McDougall looks every inch the part as she paces the floor of her office in Toronto's financial district. Unlike her predecessors in federal cabinets, such as Judy LaMarsh, known for her sombrero-like hats, and Flora MacDonald, who perfected the Maritime matron look, McDougall has the art of power dressing down pat. She's clothed in Rosedale chic with a dash of extra colour thrown in. The vibrant mauve of her business suit highlights her chestnut-tinted hair. Her gaze is steady and assured. Her words ooze out in a throaty Rosedale drawl; all the better to intimidate the guys back at the cabinet table, who speak variously in spruced up Baie-Comeau slang (Mulroney), Newfie twang (Crosbie) and Alberta tough-guy talk (Mazankowski.) The expansive office, one of a suite maintained by the party for the use of Toronto cabinet ministers when they're in town, is done up according to CEO standards of power decorating. There's the requisite deep brown hardwood desk in one corner, collector's art on the walls and a neat little arrangement of armchairs, sofa and coffee table for entertaining the steady stream of supplicants seeking a hearing with the most powerful woman in cabinet.

McDougall epitomizes the new wave of Tory women in Ottawa. She's a party loyalist who can talk about deficit-cutting with the best of them; she's a fiercely independent woman with a knack for getting along in the boys' club without behaving "like a man in drag," as B.C. cabinet minister Carol Gran once observed about women in power. She's committed to the cause of winning more political power for women, but in a moderate way that leaves women's rights activists enraged.

Surviving in the political game is hard enough, without the added burden of being viewed as a torch-bearer for women's power inside the male bastion by just about every women's group in the country. McDougall has survived with a mix of moxy and moderation that may win her the leadership of the party someday, but it's left radical feminists shaking their heads in dismay.

This is an inescapable jam for McDougall, who has never tried to curry favour with the more radical women, like the leaders of the National Action Committee on the Status of Women (the NAC). The fact is that it's tough to be both a Tory and a women's rights booster in Ottawa these days. Economic realities are number one on the agenda, and that means that all variety of spending programs of special interest to women, such as money for women's shelters and long-promised daycare legislation, are far down the list. McDougall is a member of a cabinet that, after the 1988 election, scrapped national daycare legislation that would have provided $4 billion to create an additional 200,000 daycare spaces. She's part of a cabinet that in the February 1990 budget slashed $1.6 million in spending on 74 women's centres. (It partially restored the funding after a storm of protest.) She's part of a cabinet that cut funding to the NAC in half but gave a grant to its ultraconservative rival, REAL Women (Realistic Equal Active for Life).

The pressure on McDougall and the other women in cabinet is understandable in many respects. They are the indisputable standard bearers for the advancement of women in politics. The significance of their positions can be understood only within the wider context of the incredible degree to which women have historically been shut out of politics.

The problem is not confined to Canada. In *Women and Politics in Canada*, Janine Brodie writes that, statistically, "women are the most underrepresented social group in the elected assemblies of western democracies. Women constitute more than one half of the population, but rarely more than a handful of its elected representatives are women. Few aspects of social life are more completely and universally male dominated than politics."

The facts on women's political participation in Canada would be enough to turn a Pollyanna into a Cassandra. Men have voted in elections in Canada since 1791. Women couldn't vote federally until 1919, following a passage of the Women's Franchise Act in 1918. (Some women had voted in 1917, under the Wartime Elections Act, which enfranchised women serving in the forces and female relatives of men in the forces.) Most provinces were faster to grant women the vote. First came Manitoba, Saskatchewan, and Alberta in 1916. British Columbia and Ontario followed in 1917, Nova Scotia and New Brunswick in 1918, Prince Edward Island in 1922, Newfoundland in 1925. Quebec didn't grant women the vote until 1940.

The recognition of women as "persons" under the law came in 1929 after the British Privy Council overturned a Supreme Court of Canada ruling that "persons" did not include women when it came to Senate appointments. In the decades since, women's progress into the ranks of the country's male-dominated political elite can best be described as incremental. Just 13 per cent of federal MPs are women in Canada. In both Britain and the U.S. the percentage of women legislators is about 6 per cent. In large part, this poor showing is explained by the deep-rooted sexist attitudes women must overcome among their political peers in order to win nomination contests in the first place, then among the electorate at large on voting day.

The first woman elected to the House of Commons was Agnes Macphail, in 1921. Between then and 1984, a mere 65 women became members of the federal Parliament. Little wonder that Commons debates, dominated by strutting lawyers and preening businessmen and with women sometimes drawn into aping their behaviour, have become the glorified equivalent of a cock fight.

In the mid- to late 1980s, women made more progress in politics than they had for decades. The 1984 election saw 27 female MPs elected, and six of them were given seats at the cabinet table. In 1988, a record 39 women went to Ottawa and, once again, there were six female cabinet members. This sounds like good progress until you consider that while women make up 51 per cent of the population, in the 1988 election they counted for only 20 per cent of all candidates and won just 13 per cent of the total 295 seats in the House of Commons.[3]

This historical record explains why women's groups intensely scrutinize the performance of McDougall and her female cabinet colleagues. But a good deal of the criticism directed at McDougall is unavoidable because it is based on left-wing ideology. For example, the Conservatives passed a law promoting employment equity for women and minorities in federally regulated companies, but that falls short of more militant women's demands for hiring quotas to redress the workplace inequity. Quotas smack of the sort of government intervention in the marketplace that is rejected outright by the Conservative government.

Then, too, some left-wing women critics spread the banner of women's rights across so many issues that it becomes meaningless. Audrey McLaughlin, the leader of the federal New Democrats, is an example. In a speech to a women's conference organized by the Canadian Labour Congress, she argued that simply electing more women to Parliament will not change the political culture, and lumped McDougall, then minister of employment and immigration, in with former British prime minister Margaret Thatcher as examples to prove the point. In Canada, she said, "we have a minister of employment and immigration who is a fine person, but who believes in privatization, deregulation and free trade with the United States." These policies, she said, are hurting women, which is as useful as saying acid rain discriminates against women.

Other legislation, like the 1990 abortion law that was defeated in the Senate, reflects the limits pro-choice female MPs, including McDougall, face in getting the feminist point of view across to male legislators. The law almost universally outraged women's groups because it would have made abortion a criminal offence, punishable by up to two years in jail unless a women received a doctor's opinion that the pregnancy was a threat to her health.

McDougall is not happy with the lack of influence women have in federal decision-making, but she says her approach is to work within the system rather than try to effect change from outside. "The structures have to change, but if we all wait we won't get anywhere," she says. Far from being oblivious to the advancement of women, McDougall is a charter member of an unofficial coalition of female Conservative MPs and politicos who meet regularly to discuss the state of women's power in politics. The movement was started in 1981 by Ottawa veterans like Jean Pigott, then a defeated Tory MP, and Jocelyne Côté-O'Hara, senior policy adviser to Brian Mulroney between 1983 and 1986. As journalist Charlotte Gray observed in *Saturday Night* magazine, this group has expanded the notion of Tory women beyond the blue-rinse set, and it has been a major reason for the makeover of the female Tory elite into professional go-getters.

McDougall takes her sense of sisterhood seriously and says she makes a point to befriend women newcomers to Parliament. "I always try to reach out a hand," she says.

But politics isn't a game that you can win if you play favourites based on gender. McDougall prides herself on her ability to fit right in at the cabinet table. "I get along with just about everybody. It sounds trite to say but that's one of my skills." That skill comes in handy when it's time to move bills through cabinet. "Anything that comes to cabinet gets chewed over and argued about, and eventually one builds a consensus. One builds a consensus by building allies. That means first of all you have to know what you are doing. Secondly, you have to pay attention to cabinet colleagues when they have something they are trying to pull together, and you have to be able to get along with them or you don't get policies through cabinet."

Like many other successful women of her generation, McDougall has risen to the top thanks to character traits that can't be confined to either sex: resilience, independence and an ability to find new beginnings after misfortune. Born in Toronto in 1937, she is the oldest of three sisters. When she was just 11, her father, Jim Leaman, who was the head of the Physical Education Department at Lawrence Park Collegiate, died of polio.

McDougall and her sisters, Nancy and Janet, were raised by their mother, Jean, who worked as a clerk for the Ontario government and later as secretary to a provincial cabinet minister. McDougall remembers her childhood as "hyperactive and busy. It was wall-to-wall lessons. Piano, tap dancing and ballet." Her mother, now in her eighties, seemed to have had resolve to spare. "Mother always took three things for granted," McDougall has often said. "One, that we'd all take piano lessons. Two, that we'd attend Sunday school. And three, that we'd go to university. None of that ever changed, with or without my father." Growing up without a male influence around the house "had some obvious negatives," says McDougall. "But it gave us the confidence that we could do things that fathers and brothers do."

McDougall graduated from the University of Toronto with an honours B.A. in political science and economics in 1963. "I was fairly competitive by nature," she recalls. "I was vice-president of the students' council." In the fall of 1963, she married an architecture student, Peter McDougall. The marriage was the second major disaster in her life. She followed Peter out to Vancouver, where he enrolled in the University of British Columbia. She worked as a business reporter for the *Vancouver Sun* (with a young Pat Carney, later a cabinet colleague), then as an investment analyst with Odlum Brown. But her personal life became increasingly strained. Peter found his career disappointing, and he suffered from depression, compounded by his drinking. Barbara left the childless marriage in 1974. With her prospects in Vancouver seemingly limited, she set out for Edmonton. Four years later Peter was dead of a heart attack.

Although McDougall didn't know a soul in Edmonton, her poise and audaciousness soon landed her a job as an on-air business reporter for CITV. When the show was cancelled, McDougall landed on her feet again. Dr. Charles Allard, the station's owner, gave her a job as an investment manager at NorthWest Trust.

McDougall's career in the investment business began to take off in 1976, when she returned to Toronto and signed on with the prestigious A.E. Ames brokerage firm. During her investment career, McDougall says she faced subtle and not-so-subtle obstacles as a woman. "When I first looked for a job, they blatantly didn't hire women and were prepared to say so," she says. Once she had a job, she noticed the discrimination was more subtle. "Mostly it was being ignored or overlooked. Being ignored affects your confidence." She adds: "I had a fair amount of determination." In 1981 McDougall became the company's first female vice-president. Soon afterward, though, Ames merged with Dominion Securities, and in May 1982 McDougall lost her job.

Until that point in McDougall's life, politics had been a pastime (she had managed David Crombie's successful campaigns in the 1979 and 1980 elections). But after her setback in the investment business, it became a profession. McDougall ran all-out for the 1984 election in Toronto's St. Paul's riding and won handily. She remembers well the day in 1984 when the prime minister asked her to be in the cabinet. "I was absolutely on cloud nine — the day we were sworn in the first time. There is nothing, *nothing*, that will ever compare with that invitation to be in the cabinet."

Now late in her second term in Ottawa, McDougall has performed yeoman service for Mulroney without losing credibility under the strain. There's been plenty of controversy. As minister of privatization she sold Canadair to Bombardier in Montreal; as minister of state for finance, she handled the failure of two western banks — Canadian Commercial and Northland — and then withstood the opposition outrage at the government's abortive $255-million bailout bid. She remembers the end of each Question Period. "I used to collapse in

Erik Neilsen's office. I would get out through the government lobby, through the scrum into Erik's office, and just sit like this" — she sprawls in her seat.

As immigration minister, McDougall increased the annual quotas for immigrants despite public opposition, and as minister of employment, she toughened up the requirements for collecting benefits and moved toward handing responsibility for UIC over to employers and employees. Her promotion to external affairs minister in 1991 was a reward for work well done. Too bad her arrival was marred by the eruption of controversy over the Mashat affair. McDougall's damage-control skills were tested once again as she and other senior ministers attempted to explain how Mohammed Mashat, the former Iraqi ambassador to the U.S., gained fast-track entry into Canada without their knowledge. By blaming the bureaucrats involved, McDougall and her cabinet cohorts managed to avoid serious political damage. Shaking off the Tories' unpopularity will be harder.

McDougall is in full agreement with the neoconservative bent of the Tory cabinet. And her support for Mulroney seems unshakable: "I have enormous respect for the man as a leader," she says. "I feel I will always be proud to have been a part of his team." The question left hanging over McDougall's career is whether her place on that team will prove to be a ticket to nowhere after the next election, or whether, like so many times before in her life, she'll have the resilience to sidestep misfortune and re-emerge unscathed.

The Invisible Hands

Cabinet may be the ultimate arbiter of political power in Canada, but there are other, barely known practitioners of powerbroking in Ottawa who are neither elected representatives nor members of the professional civil service. The single most influential of these is the prime minister's chief of staff.

The Richelieu of Parliament Hill

The beauty of being a trusted adviser to the prime minister is that you can formulate political strategies, convince the prime minister to follow them and then dodge public disapproval if they don't work out. Political power without public responsibility: that's the name of the game. No one knows this better than Norman Spector, chief of staff to Prime Minister Brian Mulroney since the fall of 1990.

Forty-two year-old Spector is a virtual unknown to most Canadians. They might have seen him, bearded, bespectacled and balding, on TV, hovering at the prime minister's shoulder at constitutional conferences; a few Ottawa residents might recognize him scooting around town in his dark-blue Fiat Spyder. But to Parliament Hill denizens, he's known as the *éminence grise* behind Mulroney's thinking.

Canadians should know Spector a lot better. They're certainly aware of the end result of his influence. Before he was promoted to the PMO, Spector spent four years as secretary to the cabinet for federal-provincial relations. Along with Senator Lowell Murray, himself a student of the Stealth-bombing school of politics, Spector was an architect of the 1987 Meech Lake accord. He was also an author of the federal strategy to get the accord ratified by all 10 provinces by 1990. That process, carried on in a style of shuttle diplomacy so secretive that it would likely please even the machinating Henry Kissinger, came to represent for many Canadians all that was wrong with federal politics. As back-room politics goes, it was too secretive even for some of the key players.

In the months following the first ministers' agreement on the constitutional deal in 1987, the chances of ratification by each provincial legislature by June 1990 had slipped away, primarily because several premierships, in New Brunswick, Manitoba and Newfoundland, had changed hands. To achieve ratification, Spector and Murray engaged in countless backstage negotiations with premiers, but that process left some provinces feeling left out. In Manitoba officials tried, in 1988, to convey their concerns to the Federal-Provincial Secretariat that Quebec might invoke the notwithstanding clause in the 1982 constitution to outlaw English signs. They couldn't get through. In Newfoundland, it didn't go unnoticed that the two federal emissaries didn't even meet Newfoundland premier Clyde Wells until six months after his April 1989 election. In Ontario, "we got the sense," commented David Cameron, a University of Toronto professor then advising the Ontario government, "that [Spector and Murray] wanted our vote but not our voice."[5]

When the Meech Lake accord died in June 1990 because it lacked ratification by the Newfoundland and Manitoba legislatures, Mulroney refused to the end to acknowledge that the federal government had failed. (After all, he argued, the accord did have the signatures of all 10 premiers and it fell apart mainly because Wells had not honoured his commitment to put the deal to a vote in his legislature.) But even Mulroney agreed publicly that future constitutional negotiations should not be carried out in smoky back rooms. Despite his part in masterminding the process, however, Spector was not banished to political oblivion; shortly thereafter Mulroney hired him as his top adviser.

Spector has many credentials that help explain why he still enjoys Mulroney's esteem. Montreal-born, he's a veteran bureaucrat who gained respect for his intellectual abilities serving as a transportation policy analyst for the Ontario government and later as chief policy adviser to former British Columbia premier Bill Bennett.

Just as significant, Spector has impeccable neoconservative credentials. In the 1960s, while a student at McGill University, he was part of a right-wing backlash to student radicalism. Later, his doctoral thesis for Columbia University argued that government regulation had stifled Canada's cable-television industry. As Bill Bennett's right-hand man, Spector earned a reputation as a neoconservative ideologue and anti-union tough guy.

As Mulroney's chief of staff, Spector's influence reaches throughout Ottawa. He is in charge of the Prime Minister's Office (PMO), which, along with the Privy Council Office (the top echelon of the bureaucracy) oversees the operation of government. Spector's task is to impose order on the chaotic affairs of state, acting as an arbiter of what issues make it to the top of the political agenda and in what order.

Mulroney's choice of chief of staff has typically said much about which issues top the prime minister's agenda. Mulroney's first chief of staff, Bernard Roy, is an old friend and fellow Laval graduate in law who played a crucial role in the government's constitutional dealings with Quebec. Next, former bureaucrat Derek Burney brought much-needed organizational skills to the job. His successor, Stanley Hartt, is a tax lawyer whose penny-pinching skills came in handy when cutting the deficit topped the agenda.

As the current incumbent, Spector has as his main task helping the prime minister formulate a national unity strategy. For Canada's sake, one hopes one of Spector's as yet unrecognized attributes may be an ability to learn from his mistakes.

The Lobbyists

Their taste in cars runs to Jaguars and Mercedes; their taste in lunch spots runs to the prestigious Rideau Club or Le Cercle Universitaire. But when it comes to deal-making their preferred style is to avoid attention. They are the throngs of lobbyists who swiftly and silently chase just about everything with a title on the banks of the Rideau. Everyone from lowly backbench MPs to cabinet ministers and mandarins is fair game for these political paladins, who phone, lunch and brief Ottawa decision-makers on behalf of corporate clients.

Comprised of former government aides and civil servants, they sell their expertise in government policy and often their personal friendships with politicians and bureaucrats. They like to say they're not peddling influence on behalf of the corporations who hire them, they're simply "clarifying and providing orientation" to decision-makers, as lobbyist Fred Doucet once put it, which only goes to prove that semantic skills are a requisite of the lobbying profession.

There have always been professional interest groups with representatives in Ottawa to twist elbows, but they've generally been of a benign variety whose allegiances and interests are an open book. The Chamber of Commerce, the Canadian Manufacturers' Association, the Canadian Medical Association: their names alone have pretty well spelled out whose views they represent. The other acknowledged hotbed of lobbying has always been the Senate, which has traditionally housed corporate heavyweights, such as Senators Leo Kolber, Trevor Eyton and Claude Castonguay, who doubtless take their roles as providers of sober second thought seriously but also make no secret of their continued ties to their former corporate fiefdoms.

However, since 1984, American-style lobbying has become the premier form of influence-peddling in Ottawa. Most often, the secret of the success of these paid lobbyists has been their access to the people at the apex of power; access based on their longtime friendships with insiders, Tories, former government employees, or all three.

The first Tory insiders to set up a lobbying business in Ottawa were Bill Neville and Bill Lee, in 1968. Yet the new style of lobbying took off in 1984, with the creation of Government Consultants International (GCI) by three Mulroney cronies: Frank Moores, former premier of Newfoundland and a close Mulroney friend since the 1970s; Gerry Doucet, a university pal of Mulroney's from St. Francis Xavier University (and brother of Fred, another Mulroney friend and former aide); and Gary Ouellet, a key organizer in the 1984 election campaign who includes Mulroney and Deputy Prime Minister Don Mazankowski among his friends. These three pioneered "advocacy" lobbying in Ottawa. While other firms simply provided strategic advice or phone numbers for clients, GCI proudly promised to make the phone calls and do the hustling themselves.

Since then Ottawa has been pervaded by former political aides, MPs, bureaucrats and even generals selling their knowledge of the inner workings of government, as well as their friendships with former colleagues, to the highest corporate bidders. It is the most blatant example possible of the interplay of three elite groups: the political, the bureaucratic and the corporate, represented in this case by hired guns.

Corporations or interest groups (generally representing some type of business) hire the lobbyists most often for three reasons: they want a government contract (departments like Supply and Services, National Defence and Transport each year hand out contracts worth tens of billions of dollars); they want to influence the legislative process in their favour; or they want regulatory approval or a licence for some business venture, such as American Express's successful bid for a Schedule B Banking licence in 1988.

Perhaps the fiercest lobbying battle ever seen in Ottawa erupted in 1991 over which companies should have the right to offer long-distance phone service in Canada. The fight began when Unitel Communications Inc. of Toronto applied to the government regulator, the Canadian Radio-television and Telecommunications Commission, for the right to compete in the $6-billion long-distance market traditionally monopolized by Bell Canada and eight other regional phone companies.

The warring parties hired a who's who of lobbyists with the best connections. Unitel signed up Public Affairs International, the busiest lobbying firm in Ottawa. Among those working on the account for PAI were Pierre Fortier, PAI president and former national director of the Progressive Conservative Party, and David Crapper, a former senior aide to Deputy Prime Minister Don Mazankowski. One of Unitel's corporate parents, Rogers Communications of Toronto, added reinforcements in the form of three law partners from Johnston & Buchan, an Ottawa-based firm with a winning record in lobbying on telecommunications issues.

On the other side, Bell Canada signed on Government Consultants International. GCI put three key men on the Bell account: Ouellet; Francis Fox, a former Liberal communications minister; and Patrick MacAdam, who in the past has served in the Canadian High Commission in London and is past head of Mulroney's caucus liaison office.

Not to be outdone, several major regional phone companies also sent lobbyists into the fray. The three Prairie phone companies joined forces to hire Government Policy Consultants, headed by Jon Johnson, a former policy adviser to Mulroney. Newtel Enterprises of St. John's retained John Lundrigan, a close associate of Frank Moores of GCI.

Even before executives of the rival companies had a chance to make their pitches before the CRTC beginning in April 1991, these platoons of lobbyists were hard at work, advising their clients on strategy and using all the influence they could muster in the highest levels of the cabinet and Department of Communications, since everyone expected that whatever ruling the CRTC issued would be appealed before cabinet.

Regardless of the outcome of the phone fight, which was still under way as this book went to press, it illustrated the degree to which lobbyists have become a crucial part of the decision-making process

in Ottawa and insinuated themselves intractably into the machinery
of government. Earlier, American Express used at least three lobbying
firms to win cabinet approval to become a bank in Canada. Toronto
developer Huang & Danczkay signed on three lobbying firms for
its successful bid to build the third terminal at Toronto's Pearson
International Airport. French pharmaceutical giant Institut Merieux
SA relied on an Ottawa lobbying outfit, the Capital Hill Group,
to win Investment Canada approval for its takeover of Connaught
Biosciences. Scarcely any piece of legislation affecting corporate interests or any government contract is handed out before teams of
lobbyists have tried to cajole, harass or politely convince politicians
and mandarins to see things from the point of view of interested
corporations.

In 1989 the government attempted to bring the whole back-room
lobbying business into public view by requiring lobbyists to register
their clients with a new federal agency. But lobbyists have filled up
the registry with lists of so many clients that it's hard to tell who's
lobbying who at any one time. As Bill Neville, now head of the
Neville Group, commented to the *Financial Post*, "There's so much
registering going on that [the registry] is losing its meaning." The
problem, he says, is that because lobbyists can register clients at any
time — not just when they make contact with a government official
— it's tough to track lobbying activity accurately.

The registry does, however, give a good reading of which lobbying
firms have the largest client rosters. There are an estimated 5,000
so-called Tier One lobbyists in Ottawa, who work for specialized
lobbying companies. The Lobbyists Registration Act differentiates
them from Tier Two lobbyists, who represent their own companies,
such as Bell Canada or General Motors, or associations like the
Chamber of Commerce. Here's a list of the busiest Tier One lobbying
firms according to the March 1990 registry, and the best-connected
lobbyists in their employ.

Public Affairs International (PAI): 54 clients. Owned by Hill and
Knowlton, which in turn is owned by the British WPP Group. Run
until 1989 by Mark Daniels, a former deputy minister of consumer
and corporate affairs, PAI employs such well-connected Ottawa fig-

ures as David Crapper, former aide to Don Mazankowski; Douglas Frith, once a Liberal MP; Alec MacPherson, a career civil servant and formerly special adviser on trade and finance in the Finance Department; and Paul Curley, a former Tory party president. PAI also shares common ownership with Decima Research, of Toronto, the public opinion polling firm run by the hippie Tory pollster Allan Gregg, and Public Affairs Resource Group (PARG), run by senior Liberal David McNaughton. PAI's clients have included IBM Canada, Imperial Oil and the Japanese Manufacturers Association of Canada.

Government Consultants International (GCI): 50 clients. Founded by Frank Moores and fellow Tories Gary Ouellet and Gerry Doucet. GCI made personal access to the prime minister and key cabinet committees a crucial part of the lobbying game. Major clients have included Bell Canada, General Electric Canada and the Pharmaceutical Manufacturers Association of Canada.

Fred Doucet Consulting International: 35 clients. Run by Fred Doucet, a former adviser to Prime Minister Mulroney and brother of Gerry, of GCI. Brascan and Noranda rank as its most notable clients.

Osler Hoskin and Harcourt: 33 clients. This Toronto law firm handles work for three national poultry marketing agencies and the Dairy Farmers of Canada.

S.A. Murray: 33 clients. Headed by Toronto Tory Susan Murray, the firm's influence in Ottawa is growing rapidly, especially after it handled a winning bid by Hughes Aircraft of Canada to build a $660-million air traffic control system. The firm also represents General Motors.

McMillan Binch: 27 clients. This Toronto law firm represents a cluster of book publishers, including Penguin Books Canada and Prentice-Hall Canada.

Reduce nbrs to min.

Government Policy Consultants: 17 clients. A financial services specialist run by Jon Johnson, perhaps the most discreet lobbyist in Ottawa. Johnson balks at the label "lobbyist" and insists that his firm specializes in policy analysis and strategic advice. Nevertheless, his political contacts are hard to beat. A former Mulroney aide, Johnson is son of Manitoba's lieutenant governor and is Frank Moores' ex-brother-in-law. His staff includes, most notably, William Kennett, the former inspector general of banks. Among its major clients are American Express Canada, Citibank Canada and the Canadian Life and Health Insurance Association.

Lundrigan Consulting Services: 17 clients. Run by former Newfoundland Tory MP John Lundrigan, the St. John's firm lobbies for many companies based in the Atlantic provinces.

Intercon Consultants: 15 clients. Intercon is an Ottawa defence industry specialist with a client roster that includes General Dynamics Land Systems Division, Hercules Canada and MBB Helicopter.

These are only the busiest lobbying firms in Ottawa. Other notables include Bill Fox, Mulroney's former press secretary; Harry Near, the Conservatives' campaign manager in 1988 and a former aide to Energy Minister Ray Hnatyshyn in the 1979 Clark government; Simon Reisman, the former free trade negotiator for the Conservative government; and one of the city's most powerful lobbyists, Thomas D'Aquino, head of the Business Council on National Issues (BCNI). A lawyer from British Columbia and formerly assistant to Marc Lalonde, D'Aquino has made the BCNI, which represents CEOs from Canada's 150 largest corporations, into a major force in Ottawa. During the free trade debate, he spearheaded the creation of the pro–free trade Canadian Alliance for Trade and Job Opportunities. In the spring of 1991, D'Aquino masterminded a special meeting of 14 of the country's top constitutional experts at the government's Meech Lake conference centre to discuss Canada's future. The academics were commissioned to prepare papers for discussion by the BCNI, at a total cost of $100,000. The academics were joined at the session by Gordon Smith, then Mulroney's cabinet secretary for federal-provincial relations,and a number of other senior bureaucrats. The point of the exercise, D'Aquino explained later, was to get as much information as possible into the hands of federal decision-makers. The BCNI had no intention of playing hide-and-seek on constitutional affairs. It later issued its own policy paper.

Lobbyists are the human equivalent of zebra mussels, those pesky molluscs that have infested the Great Lakes. You can't get rid of them, so you just have to learn to live with them. Public opinion pollsters like Decima Research report that the majority of Canadians think that the government is usually more concerned about business than about the public's interest. Considering the pervasiveness of former politicos and bureaucrats turned lobbyists in Ottawa, the disenchanted majority are probably right.

The Opposition Leaders: Pretend Populists in Waiting

"I will not fail to remind any prince who has acquired a new state by the aid of its inhabitants that he soundly consider what induced them to assist him; if the reason is not natural affection for him, but rather dissatisfaction with the former government, he will find it extremely difficult to keep them friendly, for it will be impossible to please them."

Five centuries after they were written, Machiavelli's words have a special relevance to contemporary Canadian politics, where voters are likely to change governments out of contempt for their old leaders rather than for love of the new. By mid-1991, voter disillusionment with the Conservative government was so great that it appeared certain that the slogan "Anybody but Mulroney" would guide a good many voters in the next election. But were Canadians, like the fickle citizens Machiavelli described, simply setting themselves up for a new cycle of love and hate directed at the next incumbent of the prime minister's office? The leaders of the federal Liberal and New Democratic parties were trying to portray themselves as populists holding the people's will close to their hearts. A careful look at the leaders and their party policies, however, reveals them to be no answer to disgruntled voters' prayers. Despite their populist rhetoric, neither they nor their parties represent alternatives that would open up the power structures of government.

Jean Chrétien

"We Liberals believe that our society exists for the benefit of every one of its members, not just a privileged few," Jean Chrétien trumpets at party functions across the country. "None of us can truly flourish if the weakest individuals and regions among us are unfairly left behind." This sort of rhetoric has helped boost Chrétien into first place among the federal party leaders in numerous nationwide opinion polls.

Chrétien comes by his blunt and impassioned populism honestly. Across the country, he's known as the *p'tit gars* from Shawinigan, eighteenth child of a hard-working machinist, Wellie Chrétien, and a loving mother, Marie. He learned his love of politics from his father and his father before him; both were Liberal loyalists in the tradition of the Rouges, the nineteenth-century Quebec radicals who fought the power of the French-Canadian establishment and the Roman Catholic Church and formed the seeds of the Liberal party in Quebec. Chrétien studied law at Laval to gain the educational credentials for political life, but he learned his street-corner style from the Créditistes. In 1963, he won his first federal election as a Liberal using the potent popular style of his Créditiste opponents: he doffed his university polish for plain-spoken language that expressed the worries and aspirations of the people in simple imagery and ideas.

The remarkable thing about Chrétien is that he has held on to his *p'tit gars* persona ever since. He's clung to it through a political career that has included 17 years in cabinet in nine portfolios. He's maintained the pretence that he is just one of the little people, even though he's long since adjusted to living in well-appointed homes, hobnobbed with the rich and royalty and spent several years in the mid-1980s as a lawyer to the business elite with the law firm of Lang Michener.

But Chrétien's honest-as-a-boy-scout image is wearing thin lately. Voters are beginning to suspect he's just another obfuscating politician, given his recent dodging and equivocating on major national issues. Even the Liberals' chief financial officer, Michael Robinson, has argued that Chrétien's unwillingness to take a stand in the final days of the Meech Lake debate hurt his credibility. "The strength of Jean Chrétien was that people saw him as a cut above a politician," Robinson told *Maclean's* magazine in late 1990. "Now he is in danger of becoming just another politician." The problem was compounded by Chrétien's absence from the public stage for months after winning his party's leadership in June 1990. In September, when the public was focusing its attention on the government's GST legislation, Chrétien refused to say whether he would abolish the tax if he were elected prime minister. Finally, in October, Chrétien said he would do so. But a poll by Environics Research showed that almost two-thirds of voters didn't believe him; the doubters included more than half of those respondents who identified themselves as Liberal supporters.

In the public stands Chrétien *has* taken, he's clearly tried to stake out a left-of-centre political position. He has disavowed the free trade agreement, attacked the privatization of Petro-Canada, and come out against free trade with Mexico. However, his main political strategy has apparently been "what you don't say can't hurt you."

Yet telling the voters "what you see is what you get" won't be enough to win Chrétien the next federal election. He seems to have realized that and set two task forces in motion to generate policies: one on international trade strategy and another to find an alternative to the GST. Plans are also being made for a national party policy conference in 1992. Hammering out Liberal policies will be difficult, though, given party rifts over such issues as how to deal with Quebec, whether a devolution of powers to the provinces is advisable, and what stance to take toward the Mexico–American free trade talks.

Chrétien faces a huge hurdle to win political support in Quebec, where he trails the two other party leaders in popularity and where he is viewed with disdain by the francophone intelligentsia and na-tionalists. After all, Chrétien is the guy who gave Clyde Wells a bear-hug at the Calgary party convention in June 1990 to thank him for his role in killing the Meech Lake accord.

As of mid-1991, the most worrisome blind spot in the Liberals' policy agenda was any realistic policy on deficit reduction, a gap that reflected the dominance of welfare liberalism in the party. To talk about cost-cutting had become an act of heresy in Liberal circles. John Turner tried it for a time as leader but was gagged. Finance critic Roy MacLaren stressed the issue but was removed from his position. As journalist Jeffrey Simpson says: "This should be a Liberal hour when Canadians, tired of Tory ideology, hunger not for another ideology but for practical alternatives defined by a party that reflects the common sense of obvious limits. Instead, the Liberals shriek and consume themselves in parliamentary tactics, and are rewarded with middling poll results."

The biggest challenge the Liberals face is not to shake Chrétien's image as yesterday's man but to prove that they are not yesterday's party, marching straight into the past and espousing a return to big government engaged in interventionist policies the country can't afford. Canadians will be poorly served if, come the next federal election, they are offered a choice only between a vote for Big Government, as espoused by the Liberals and the NDP, or a vote for Big Business, whose interests the Conservatives unequivocally champion.

For voters looking for a more fundamental change in the political system, an opening up to more voices that better reflect the makeup of the electorate, Chrétien offers no real alternatives. The little-guy image is touching, and may win the votes of more gullible Canadians, but it is nothing more than a lovable act. It's the system itself that needs changing, not just the lead players.

Audrey McLaughlin

Federal New Democratic Party leader Audrey McLaughlin can match Jean Chrétien and raise him one in the populist rhetoric game any time. "A good leader has to see the world through many eyes," she says. "I know what it is like to be poor and what it is like to be comfortable. These are the worlds I want to pull together." McLaughlin's open face seems to back up her expressions of empathy with the people. She likes to talk about the "empowerment of the people" and insists that all sectors of society should be involved in decision-making. In Parliament, she accuses the Conservatives of paying too much attention to the views of business and devising a "corporate constitution" directed by the desire of business leaders for a more decentralized Canada.

McLaughlin, in short, is following an obvious political strategy: tell the voters what they want to hear. The NDP is acutely aware that the middle class is being hard hit by the recession and that the mainstream political parties are taking the blame. McLaughlin is marching lock-step with the majority of voters in her opposition to the GST, in her stress on environmental initiatives, in her opposition to the free trade deal (she's said she'd scrap it) and in her past opposition to the Meech Lake accord. (Although she accepts the idea that Quebec is a distinct society, she opposed the accord on the grounds that Meech Lake would have made it virtually impossible for the northern territories to become provinces, and left the First Peoples out of a constitutional settlement.) McLaughlin, the first woman in Canada to lead a national party, is a natural option for voters looking for a change from the norm. She's a mother and a grandmother, she's divorced, she's well educated, she's a social worker, and she's a transplanted northerner. How much more different from traditional Ottawa powerbrokers can you be?

Even McLaughlin's biography adds to her image as an outsider. When she talks about knowing what it's like to be poor, McLaughlin is referring to her childhood in Windsor, Ontario, and the nearby farming village of Essex. Shortly after Audrey was born in 1936, her mother was diagnosed as having breast cancer and was confined to hospital until she recovered. In those pre-medicare days, the family suffered financial hardship for 10 years while Audrey's father, a co-op credit manager, and mother paid off the hospital bills. They didn't even own a car. And when McLaughlin talks about being comfortable, she's referring to her life in the 1970s as a social worker in Toronto. In between her hard-up childhood and career success as a social worker were several ho-hum decades as a mink rancher with her first husband, Don McLaughlin. The couple split up in 1972 as Audrey grew more involved in her work with the Children's Aid Society and later as an executive director of the Canadian Mental Health Association. Meanwhile, Don settled into a job as a high school math teacher.

Other events in McLaughlin's life suggest a distaste for convention. In 1979, despite her blossoming social work career and active involvement in the NDP, McLaughlin sold her house and most of her possessions, bought a pick-up truck and drove 5,472 kilometres to Whitehorse in search of a new life. She was completely alone and unencumbered, her two grown children, David and Tracy, having moved out on their own.

Within a short time, McLaughlin had started a thriving social work consultancy business, serving clients such as native groups, battered women and the Yukon Status of Women Council. For five years she lived with Yukon judge Roger Kimmerly, working on his campaign for justice minister in 1985. When Kimmerly left her, McLaughlin, devastated, turned into a nomad once more, first working in Barbados as a consultant to women entrepreneurs, then taking off on a solo journey through Central and South America. She later described that trip as "probably the most dangerous thing I've ever done, a real test for myself." McLaughlin returned to Whitehorse to test herself in the political arena. In 1987 she won the Yukon federal by-election to replace retired Tory veteran Erik Nielsen. The next year she was sent to Ottawa in a landslide.

McLaughlin's life is inspiring for those who seek a politician for the people. But there are two factors that suggest she offers no sure-fire panacea. One is the identity crisis her party suffers; the other is the narrow power base that the NDP rests on.

First, the identity crisis. Two groups traditionally support left-wing parties like the NDP. In his book *The Silent Revolution*, political economist Ronald Inglehart calls these the materialists and the post-materialists. The former are the traditional left, the working class that for decades has formed the backbone of support for western social democratic parties and make up about half of the NDP's support. These workers are a conservative lot who believe in social order and the family and tend to be concerned about improvements in wages, working conditions, job security and union rights. The post-materialists are the so-called New Left. They are well-educated products of middle-class families who seek such goals as individual self-expression and the abolition of hierarchy.

The identity crisis of the NDP arises from the conflicting goals of these two major social groups among its followers. They clash on a whole range of issues, from gay rights, feminism and abortion, to the protection of the environment. For instance, environmentalists might call for the closure of polluting factories, which would throw workers out of jobs. As prime minister, McLaughlin would have to conciliate between the traditional left and the well-educated New Left, of which she is a member. Many of the NDP's more controversial policy stands, in fact, reflect New Left thinking. For example, McLaughlin supports the NDP policy to withdraw Canada from NATO. (That view is shared by only about 16 per cent of Canadians.) She also favours abortion as a woman's right. (Only about a third of Canadians favour abortion on demand.)

Another potential handicap of an NDP government would be the narrowness of its power base. The party's electoral strength currently rests on two distinct power blocs: the support of the big union bosses, like the CAW's Bob White, who are based in Toronto, and the west, which accounted for 32 of the 43 NDP MPs elected in 1988.

The clout of these two regional power groups was best illustrated in the 1989 leadership convention that elected McLaughlin as leader. A total of 1,979 delegates from riding associations were eligible to vote. The unions alone were entitled to 968 delegates. National labour leaders, provincial union chiefs and district presidents were entitled to 175 delegates, almost as many as the 180 delegates who were party MPs or members of the national council. The west also had a disproportionate share of power in the proceedings. That resulted from the party's policy of not giving ridings equal representation, as other parties do; instead, each riding is allowed one delegate for every 50 party members. Consequently, Saskatchewan, with only 10 ridings, had 405 riding delegates, compared with Ontario, which had 545 delegates representing 99 ridings. Three western provinces, British Columbia, Alberta and Manitoba, accounted for 56 per cent of the national total of delegates.

These factors suggest that Audrey McLaughlin and the NDP offer no easy solutions for alienated Canadian voters. No doubt the election of an NDP government in Ottawa would open up the legislative pro-

cess to a wider range of Canadians, with a diversity of career backgrounds and social perspectives, just as the changed makeup of the
NDP government in Ontario suggests. However, a McLaughlin-led
government could hardly turn its back on the interest groups that
have supported it in the past. Nor could it shuck off its left-wing
ethos. As Bob Rae, leader of the Ontario NDP, once commented,
the NDP without socialism would be like the Salvation Army without
salvation: "No salvation, no army." The federal NDP certainly offers
Canadians an alternative to the Conservative party's neoconservative
agenda. But the danger is that — just like the Liberals — the party,
once at the cabinet table, would exchange one lot of interest groups
for another.

Conclusion

Federal politics in Canada is the preserve of quarrelling interest
groups, lobbyists and mainly upper-middle-class lawyers and businessmen. The truly wealthy upper class aren't foolish enough to put
up with the harsh realities of political life — the long hours away
from home, the abuse from the media and the constant pressure to
compromise personal principals. The poor and the less privileged
in society haven't the money to run for political office even if they
did aspire to join the governing elite, which for them would be a
leap up the social ladder.

The political elite in Canada is, nevertheless, a meritocracy. Cabinet ministers are, with few exceptions, individuals who made it into
the ranks of the upper middle class by virtue of educational achievement, professional success and strong personal ambition. In this
sense, the political elite does offer upward social mobility for newcomers; it's an avenue to influence for aspiring social climbers. The
question is: Who is shut out from entry into the ranks of the political
elite?

Judging from the backgrounds of the major ministers, there is
a danger of drawing overly facile generalizations about the homogeneity of cabinet membership. After all, the Conservative ministers
I profiled arrived at the apex of political power from vastly different
directions. They and most other cabinet members are well educated,

extremely ambitious and had successful material and professional lives before entering politics.

Yet, as the survey results reveal, there are limits to the diversity the cabinet ministers represent. In happier political times, it might not be of the least concern to the general public that, for instance, so many cabinet ministers are male lawyers. The situation is nothing new. From Confederation to the Second World War, 60 per cent of federal cabinet ministers were trained as lawyers. In Trudeau's cabinet between 1974 and 1979, more than one-third of 42 ministers were lawyers. In Joe Clark's 1979 cabinet, half of 30 ministers were lawyers. And in happier political times, it might not cause the least concern that most cabinet ministers are men, of either British or French descent, and Protestant. But these, as everyone knows, are not ordinary political times. The mood of national distemper has never been greater; nor has the population's sense of alienation from the political process.

The makeup of the cabinet raises concern about its members' ability to represent the electorate. Arguably, the successful careers and social backgrounds of the ministers put them out of touch with the concerns of so-called ordinary Canadians. This is a difficult relationship to prove beyond a doubt. There has been very little study of the effects of social background on the attitudes of MPs to policy issues. But one revealing survey of federal MPs in 1975 found that the more upwardly mobile the MP, the greater the tendency to generalize his success to all Canadians. MPs appeared more hostile to welfare distribution than members of the electorate; MPs in every party but the NDP were more conservative on social policies than their own party members in the electorate. The survey also found that most MPs were somewhat out of touch with the economic situation of average Canadians: 95 per cent overestimated the economic wellbeing of Canadians, about 65 per cent by a substantial margin. Cabinet members were found to be even more conservative in their views on social issues. The study concluded that advancing age, former occupation and social origins were the most influential factors in determining the perceptions of MPs.[4]

It is interesting to theorize that the dominance of lawyers and businessmen in the Mulroney cabinet helps explain why most of the

Conservative agenda, especially regarding the issue of national unity, is cast as a search for economic wellbeing and material prosperity.

Bread-and-butter issues are the lowest common denominator in any political entity. They appeal to the physical needs of the populace, not the spiritual ones. When a government is reduced to casting almost its entire agenda in material terms, it reflects a profound poverty of spirit in a country, a dearth of more noble human aspirations, like compassion, tolerance and charity, or even national pride.

Should the cabinet be made up of a much more diverse group of ministers that better reflects the makeup of the electorate? Ideally, yes. At present, women and people from career backgrounds less lucrative than law or business and from minority and ethnic backgrounds are underrepresented in the cabinet and, for that matter, in the House of Commons.

At the very least, having cabinet ministers with broad backgrounds that better reflect the makeup of the electorate might go a long way to improve the tenor of parliamentary debates. It's hard to imagine a worse climate than that created by the lawyers and businessmen who now hold sway. Lawyers have become the bane of political life in Canada. Loquacious and schooled in adversarial tactics, they have turned Parliament into an arena for verbal jousting, sophistry and mock outrage that envelops the august chambers of Parliament each day like so much sulphurous flatulence. As they depart each daily sitting, smug in their contentment that they've scored points against a political opponent or deftly deflected an attack on their honour, nothing remains behind but noxious fumes. The public is left wondering — with good reason — what exactly was accomplished by their representatives.

The businessmen who join the fray — often in $800 suits — do nothing to quell the rancour. They may enter political life with no-nonsense demeanours developed while meeting a company payroll, but they are soon co-opted into the spirit of rancour. Women, too, soon learn the shoot-from-the-lip tactics required to hold their own in debate. Like all MPs, they have to show they have the aggressive instincts required to skewer opponents who slip up or have been rendered vulnerable by some political foible. Debates in Commons resemble nothing so much as a schoolyard fight over a game of marbles.

They would provide excellent fodder for anthropologists studying the belligerent nature of human beings because killer instincts, rather than reason, have become the prerequisite of survival. Style has long since displaced substance in parliamentary debates.

This unproductive atmosphere alone provides enough reason to argue that Parliament needs and deserves to be filled with people other than duelling lawyers and a smattering of former business executives and women who learn the tactics of verbal jousting. Imagine a Parliament comprised mainly of articulate university professors, school teachers, social workers, psychologists, nurses, doctors, an assortment of blue-collar workers and a good many more women. Conflict between opposing parties would certainly remain, but there would be much less narcissistic strutting, preening and mindless bombast. Without such a broadening of its members' backgrounds, the cabinet faces severe handicaps in representing the collective will of the electorate.

There are no easy cures, of course, for the highly centralized, overly exclusionary nature of Canadian politics. As we have seen, simply changing the party in power doesn't ease the disenchantment of voters. In fact, in one 1989 poll almost half of Canadians responded that none of the country's political parties "really stand for the things I believe in."

Senior Conservative ministers are not blind to this state of national distemper. However, from the vantage point of power, they are better aware than most of the difficulties of resolving the situation. "Our democratic institutions should be opened up more, there's no question about that," says Barbara McDougall. "We're in a bit of a dilemma right now in terms of how to capture the trust of the public." As McDougall points out, the public is of two minds about what it wants. "People want more say in the process," she says, "but they also want strong leadership. I would tend to opt for strong leadership, because I think we face some very real difficulties today, economically and socially."

McDougall also agrees that an essential problem facing the Conservative Party is that it has lost its collectivist appeal. "Traditionally, the Conservative Party has not been an elitist party in the sense that the Trudeau Liberals were. It has always been more a grass-

roots party, and I think to some extent we still are." In McDougall's assessment, it is now more difficult that ever for the government to discern the collective will of the people. "The collective interest has become very fragmented. Gun control is a good example. If you live in Toronto or Montreal, it's a crime-in-the-streets issue. If you live in northern Ontario or Alberta, they don't know what the hell you're talking about." She concludes: "There just isn't a collegiality of grass-roots interests. Regionalism is on the rise."

Don Mazankowski has come to similar conclusions. As minister of agriculture, as well as deputy prime minister, he's had to try to reconcile a hodge-podge of regional interest groups, like grain growers, poultry producers and dairy farmers, who often have conflicting priorities. "We're working very hard to maintain some semblance of a national agriculture policy," he says, "and that means working closely with the provinces and the various interest groups. "You're not going to satisfy them all." As far as Mazankowski is concerned, the only way to cope with the competing interests is to provide clear, decisive leadership. "People like bold leadership, providing it's transparent and above board, and providing they can understand your rationale.

In Mazankowski's view, the role of national parties is to forge policies in the national interest. "National political parties are one of the last remaining vestiges of consensus-building instruments," he says. "You have the input of members of Parliament from every region of the country and you function through a form of consensus. This is the only way we can overcome the special interest groups who zero in on specific items."

On the whole, there is very little enthusiasm in the ranks of the ruling Conservative Party for any substantial reform of the parliamentary process. The main changes to parliamentary rules proposed by the government in 1991 would reduce the number of days the Commons sits each year and shorten debates. Saying Canadians are disgusted with the circus-like atmosphere of the Commons, Government House Leader Harvie Andre said the new rules would help restore Parliament's prestige. But several opposition MPs pointed out, quite correctly, that the rules would "gag Parliament" and make it even more a rubber stamp for cabinet decisions.

Much more fundamental reforms of the parliamentary process are needed to help parliament more truly represent regional interests as well as the makeup of the population — by increasing the number of women, nonlawyers and minority ethnic groups, for example — and therefore better fulfil its goal of identifying and acting in the national interest. A full discussion of parliamentary reform is far beyond the scope of this book, but there are certain avenues that could be pursued. They are:

- An elected Senate with equal membership drawn from the following regions: the West, Central Canada (Ontario, and Quebec), and the East. Special seats would be reserved for territorial and aboriginal representatives. (More about this in Chapter 3.)
- Rules permitting government and opposition MPs more latitude to vote in their constituents' interests rather than along party lines, as is the practice in the United Kingdom.
- A stronger role for grass-roots party organizations to formulate party policy. At present, they have little say in the policy process once the party gains power.
- The fourth point is the most crucial. At present, money, just as much as talent, is required for running for political office. To encourage more women and people with career backgrounds less lucrative than business or law to enter politics, three steps could be taken: full public funding of candidates in nomination contests and elections; a relatively low limit on spending for nomination contests and a requirement that candidates reveal their sources of funds; and the outlawing of campaign contributions by corporations, something Quebec has done.

Such steps would not change the fundamental nature of federal politics. The government's needs to broker between the demands of various groups and regions would remain; so too would political patronage. They would, however, open up the legislative process to more players and redress somewhat our national disenchantment with the political system.

Chapter 2
The Federal Mandarins

"All government, in its essence, is a conspiracy against the superior man," wrote H.L. Mencken. If Mencken was still living, he would probably agree that the senior mandarins who run Ottawa are an exception to this rule. Superior in mien, education and intellect, they are the powers behind the throne who often conceive of, develop and implement major policies for the dilettantes who win political office every four years. Behind every strong cabinet minister is a powerful deputy minister. Their power ebbs and flows. Certainly, the golden era of the mandarins' influence, from the mid-1930s to the late 1950s, is long gone. In these days of fiscal restraint and of bureaucrat-bashing by politicians and the public alike, morale has never been lower in the federal civil service. One might even assume that the federal mandarins are becoming less influential as the Conservative government inexorably dismantles or reduces the web of national programs and Crown corporations that was created by the civil service in the decades after the Second World War. Not so. Since the Conservatives took power in 1984, amid a hail of antibureaucratic verbal fire, the senior mandarins have proven extremely adaptable to the changing political winds in Ottawa. They have not only adjusted psychologically to the Conservative agenda, they've devised it. Policies as diverse as free trade, the GST, Meech Lake and now the fight for national unity are all the products of a handful of supremely bright and powerful bureaucrats who are more than eager to throw off the Keynesian traditions of their forebears and adopt the economic and political philosophies of the ruling Conservatives.

This is the context within which recent assaults on the power of the bureaucracy must be viewed. Continued austerity measures aimed at reducing the size of the bureaucracy and increasing its efficiency have reduced its numbers to 1973 levels. Internal studies and bouts of self-analysis have produced calls for the civil service to take on a private-sector mentality that encourages performance and a greater sensitivity to serving public needs. Such measures have questioned the assumptions of the federal mandarins but arguably not reduced their influence, in any meaningful way, over government policies. They haven't made much of a dent in the pervasiveness of the civil service in Canadian life either.

The federal civil service is the biggest business in Canada. The chairman of the board is Paul Tellier, who as clerk of the Privy Council is the top civil servant. He oversees a mandarinate so large that it puts a multi-armed corporate conglomerate to shame. It embraces 27 deputy ministers of government departments (as well as dozens of appointees running Crown corporations and government agencies like the CBC and Telefilm Canada); below them are 14 associate deputy ministers and 343 assistant deputy ministers. Together these mandarins supervise a workforce of 217,860 people, whose salaries total almost $2 billion a year. These government employees make federalism work. They run airports and post offices, collect taxes and staff customs offices. They determine what you can't read by keeping a watch out for pornography and hate literature; they determine when it is necessary to raise or lower interest rates; they dole out billions of dollars in health and education funds, unemployment benefits, welfare payments and regional development grants; and they hand out contracts for work and supplies that keep thousands of private-sector companies in business.

The politicians grab the headlines and make the pronouncements, but it's bureaucrats who tell them what to say and run interference for them in cabinet committees and prompt them for the ordeals of Question Period in the Commons.

The most influential mandarins, such as Tellier, Fred Gorbet at Finance and Ian Clark, secretary to the Treasury Board, are part of the inner circle of decision-making power in Ottawa. They work in tandem with the most senior cabinet ministers, sitting on key cabinet committees and devising policies that govern the nation. Their rise to power in the postwar period has magnified the elitist nature of decision-making in the federal government and highlighted the degree to which ordinary MPs, cross-country party organizations and the official opposition are shut out of any significant influence on the creation and execution of policies. They have become part of a governing triad, made up of the cabinet, the bureaucracy and powerful interest groups. These three power centres interact in a mutually beneficial process, in which the politicians and bureaucrats seek to accommodate the wishes of the interest groups and use them as sources of information. The interest groups in turn compete with one another to put their concerns on the government agenda. Lunches, phone conversations and other informal meetings with the most powerful bureaucrats are crucial tools used by the interest groups and their lobbyists to exert influence over the policy-making process. "There's a lot more interdependence," says one veteran deputy minister. "The whole process of governing has become more complicated. In part because [people] understand that what governments do has a more pervasive influence now than before and because the business sector and special interest groups are more sophisticated in their understanding about how to influence government."

In this highly interdependent process, the way deputy ministers influence policy-making has changed, but the degree of influence they exert hasn't necessarily declined. Jean Fournier, under secretary of state, sheds some light on the issue. He argues that the influence of deputy ministers has not declined over the past two decades even though the conditions are much different. "Yes, the world is getting more complex. There are more interest groups, *à l'Americain*. There are more controlling agencies, the auditor general, comptroller general, and parliamentary committees. Yes, it is a more complex world, and because of that ministers have to turn to deputies even more so than in the past." A host of other deputies make similar comments, adding the proliferation of ministerial chiefs of staff and ministers of state to the list of new players.

In the recent past, the influence of deputies was severely undercut by the rapidity with which their political masters were rotating them through jobs. One important 1988 study by former mandarin Gordon

Osbaldeston, called *Keeping Deputy Ministers Accountable*, reported that in 1987, 50 per cent of deputies had been in their jobs for less than one and a half years; the average duration of a minister–deputy minister team between 1984 and 1987, was less than a year. One deputy minister reported to me that "the rapid rotation of deputies in recent years has made influence on specific policies less evident." But he added that on certain major policies their influence has been important. "Deputies' influence on major issues such as the National Energy Program, the Goods and Services Tax and the free trade agreement has been very substantial in the last few years."

At any rate, other deputies say the turnover problem has been corrected by the government and the typical tenure of deputies has been extended to four or five years. This is likely to reinforce the power of deputies.

The competence of Canada's federal mandarins is not in contention here. In fact the popular mythology that civil servants are underworked, overpaid and often incompetent has it all wrong. Canada has been served for decades by exceedingly bright, ambitious senior bureaucrats.

Admittedly this claim may seem surprising to readers familiar with the infamous Mashat affair of spring 1991. For two solid months, the news media were full of reports of how the bureaucracy mishandled the entry into Canada of Mohammed Mashat, the former Iraqi ambassador to the United States who actively supported his country's invasion of Kuwait. Amazingly, Mashat was given fast-track admission to Canada thanks to the efforts of middle-ranking External Affairs officials, without the prime minister or even the ministers of immigration (then Barbara McDougall) or external affairs (Joe Clark) knowing about it. In an ensuing public spectacle, the embarrassed politicians tried to lay the blame on the bureaucrats for not alerting them to the obviously sensitive case. Without doubt, the affair precipitated a crisis of trust between the politicians and their senior mandarins. Certainly, there was bungling involved. The clerk of the Privy Council, Paul Tellier, thought he had succeeded in making sure that Mashat didn't receive special treatment; the number-two man at External Raymond Chrétien, sent a memo on the case to Joe Clark's office that Clark never even saw. But the case was a startling departure from the normal state of relations between the legislators and the bureaucracy and, as such, it stands out as an exception that proves the rule.

The point here is that, largely because of their excellence, the mandarins have become part of the problem of elitist government in Canada. Their prominent role makes it all the more relevant to assess who has power in the mandarinate and who is shut out.

To shed light on this issue, I studied the backgrounds of the 27 deputy ministers in Ottawa who run full government departments. Seventeen answered detailed questionnaires in late 1989. Information on the remaining 10 was gathered from various biographical sources.

There's no doubt that the mandarins are an intellectual elite. All had attended university and 16 of them had earned postgraduate degrees. An additional eight had earned professional designations in law, engineering or medicine. The country's universities traditionally compete for the reputation as the breeding ground for Ottawa's senior mandarins, and the alma maters of the 27 provide an indication of which institutions are leading the race. The top two training grounds for the mandarins are Queen's University in Kingston and the University of Ottawa, with five graduates each. Next came the University of Alberta, with four graduates, and then the University of Toronto, the University of British Columbia, and Oxford, with three graduates each.

One of the more fascinating findings is that higher education was clearly a means of climbing the ladder from humble origins to the pinnacle of bureaucratic power. The majority of deputy ministers were born into modest, middle-class homes, judging from the occupations of their fathers, and therefore had no kinship ties or family connections to help them land jobs, as is the case of the business elite, for example.

But while the deputy ministers may be highly educated, their work experience doesn't tend to extend much beyond government. Most deputy ministers (14) went straight into the civil service after university; 22 had spent most of their career in the civil service. This sort of finding, of course, provides fodder for critics who say the civil service is out of touch with the country beyond the confines of Ottawa.

Other findings are more troubling. Judging from the survey, university degrees haven't been the only condition for getting ahead. A full 20 of the deputy ministers were male. Of the 23 deputy ministers born in Canada, 17 came from Ontario or Quebec. Six were from the west and none from the east. This is precisely the sort of Central Canadian dominance that infuriates residents of the west and the east.

The mainstream religions in Canada are fairly evenly represented among the deputy ministers. Of the 13 deputies who listed a religion in the questionnaire, five were Roman Catholic, three were United Church, two were Anglican, one listed Protestant and two were Jewish. However, the myriad of ethnic groups in Canada were not fairly represented. Of the 27 deputies, nine had at least one parent of British descent and nine had at least one parent of French descent. The remainder had other West or East European origins.

The conclusion is that women, regions outside central Canada and ethnic groups other than British, French and other Europeans are poorly or not at all represented in the highest ranks of the mandarinate.

A variety of studies in recent years have shown that similar problems exist in the federal civil service as a whole. The obstacles to advancement faced by women have received the most attention.[1] The most exhaustive recent study was "Beneath the Veneer," the April 1990 report of the government's Task Force on Barriers to Women in the Public Service. Initiated in late 1988 by Pat Carney, former head of the Treasury Board, the study showed that although women made up 43 per cent of public service employees in 1988, they held only 12 per cent of management jobs. Almost 60 per cent of female public servants held clerical or secretarial jobs. The study's authors concluded: "We have established that women in the federal public service are compressed into low levels of pay and status and confined to a few large occupational groups that provide poor access to promotion; . . . that if nothing changes, it could be another half century before anything approaching equity is achieved and that women do perceive gender-based barriers to advancement in the federal public service and can describe them clearly."

Listen to the comments that female deputy ministers made to me. Some encountered sexual bias when they approached the civil service for jobs in the 1960s: "I can remember being asked in an interview — I was engaged at the time — whether I planned to have children, and I said, 'I haven't got the faintest idea.'" For others, it was a matter of not being considered for promotions: "People who were in a position to put my name forward for advancement didn't do it and they didn't because they exercised their own judgment that I wouldn't be interested. Once I discovered this was happening, I spent a fair amount of time jumping up and down and saying explicitly to my bosses of the day, 'If an opportunity comes up, please ask me.'"

Even at the deputy minister level, being a woman surrounded by male colleagues can be difficult: "What I found the toughest and I think probably still is a problem is simply not knowing what to do when you travel. For example, there are five men and they want to go to a bar. Will they get embarrassed if you want to go? Will they feel insulted if you don't want to go?"

Diplomacy isn't free of discrimination either. "A person I know who was senior in the Canadian diplomatic service was overseas in a West European country and was asked to retire with the women after dinner. Well, this particular woman happened to be the senior Canadian at the event."

A Concordia University study for the National Advisory Committee on the Status of Women, published in late 1990, added more perspective to women's problems when it revealed that they are also big losers in the federal patronage sweepstakes. Examples: only 73 of 850 federally appointed judges are women; only 181 of 625 full-time positions with various federal boards, agencies, commissions and Crown corporations are filled by women.

Minority groups are even worse off than women. According to internal government progress reports, visible minorities made up 4.2 per cent of the public service payroll in September 1990 and held fewer than 1 per cent of management jobs. Disabled persons made up 2.25 per cent of the payroll and held 1.6 per cent of management jobs. Aboriginal people made up just over 1 per cent of the public service and held no management jobs.

The Superbureaucrats of the 1990s

Exclusivity and elitism in the federal mandarinate are nothing new. If anything, they have been much reduced in the past two decades. Between Confederation and the First World War, the civil service was little more than a collection of patronage postings that changed incumbents with every federal election. The first semblance of professionalism came in 1918, when Robert Borden's Union government called in teams of management experts from the United States to produce a rational system of bureaucratic organization. In 1924, Oscar Douglas Skelton, the first of the legendary Ottawa men, went to Ottawa to create a Canadian foreign policy and a department to run it for Liberal prime minister Mackenzie King. A professor from Queen's University, Skelton turned the Department of External Affairs from a conduit for dispatches from London into a professional policy-making outfit, with the help from the bright young men he hired in 1928: Lester Pearson, Norman Robertson and Hugh Keenleyside.

These men, along with such notables as Clifford Clark, Graham Towers, Jack Pickersgill and John Deutsch, launched the civil service into its golden age and deserve great credit for their uncommon intellects and energy. The most celebrated and prestigious department in the halcyon days of the civil service was External Affairs, whose members were the elite of the elite, a corps of pin-striped practitioners of diplomacy in the British tradition who defined a strong role for Canada as a middle power on the world stage.[2]

But the Ottawa men, as historian Jack Granatstein has called them, were few in number, tended to be educated at Queen's, the University of Toronto or Oxford, and were decidedly all male. It took until 1972 for a woman to be appointed deputy minister. "They were," writes Granatstein, "a remarkable group, a collection of friends and colleagues who looked, sounded, and spoke alike; lived close together; and to a surprising extent, socialized with each other during the work week and on vacations."

The mandarins' mantle has passed from Skelton and his disciples to the shoulders of a much larger and diverse group of successors.

But there are still remarkably few mandarins at the pinnacle of power in Ottawa. In the 1940s and 1950s, the truly influential mandarins numbered as few as fifteen. Today, there aren't any more than that, despite the enormous growth of the public service in the ensuing decades. The reason is that not all deputy ministers are created equal.

Those that excel are the human equivalent of pilot sharks, able to steer all but the most hammer-headed cabinet ministers away from hot water. This is not always possible, of course. Certain cabinet ministers are just impossible to direct. Defence Minister Marcel Masse, for instance, is legendary among the bureaucrats as a "difficult" man to get along with.

Such ministers aside, the best deputy ministers pride themselves on their malleability; they see their ability to adapt their personality to different political masters as a sign of professionalism. Anywhere else, this would be considered blandness. Not in Ottawa. Somebody has got to make sure the government machine proceeds on course.

In fact, blending in with the scenery, swimming with the school, as it were, is a prerequisite of success in the mandinarate. This entails a whole raft of career considerations, such as: never be seen dining alone; always compliment a peer on a promotion, whether you detest him or not; always deal with urgent matters, even if they aren't the most important ones, so as to keep the process moving; never admit your ignorance on a subject of conversation, just nod your head knowingly; never answer a question when you can ask one — that way you are sure to hold your own among the brightest of your peers. (It goes without saying that mandarins should not engage in socially questionable behaviour, which makes it the more surprising that one deputy minister was seen enjoying a table dancer's performance recently at an Ottawa strip joint.)

The most powerful deputies are those attached to the government departments and central agencies that are the most influential in setting the government's agenda: the Privy Council Office, Finance, External Affairs, the Treasury Board, the Federal-Provincial Relations Office, and Justice. Appointment to these posts is the sign of a bureaucrat whose star has risen.

The most powerful mandarin of all is Paul Tellier, 52, the clerk of the PCO, deputy minister to Brian Mulroney, secretary to the cabinet and, since June, 1991, deputy minister for federal-provincial relations. Tellier epitomizes the sort of bright, scheming, loyal civil servant with infinitely adjustable ideological convictions who gets ahead in Ottawa. Tellier is a retreaded bureaucrat from the Trudeau era who has returned from the wilderness to become the man whose job it is to keep the rivalry-ridden civil service functioning smoothly and who serves as the point man between the bureaucracy and the politicians.

For all his power, which is enormous, Tellier is getting mixed reviews these days. His loyalty to Mulroney is unquestioned. In June when the prime minister asked him to fire Gordon Smith from his post as deputy minister for federal-provincial relations, Tellier obliged swiftly and smoothly and, once again at the prime minister's bidding, added the portfolio to his own duties. Whether Tellier has shown the same loyalty to the civil servants under his sway is in doubt. Prominent civil servants were appalled when Tellier failed to defend the civil service during the Mashat affair. Instead he went along with a cabinet plan to sidestep political blame and pin it on a few bureaucrats.

Born in Joliette, Quebec, Tellier is a lawyer by training and taught briefly at the University of Montreal before joining the civil service in 1967. He rose to prominence in the mid-1970s as Prime Minister Pierre Trudeau's special adviser on Quebec. After the Parti Québécois came to power in 1976, Tellier became head of the semi-secret "Tellier Group" in Ottawa to prepare a federal strategy for dealing with the upcoming Quebec referendum. When Joe Clark's Conservatives took power in 1979, Tellier was thrown into political purgatory. Clark's circle was hostile to Tellier's group (they called it agit-prop), and, as prime minister, Clark immediately disbanded it. Tellier was shunted aside to become deputy minister at Indian Affairs and Northern Development. The aboriginals didn't like his frank style: Georges Erasmus, then Dene Nation president, described Tellier as "Public Enemy Number 1." After the Conservatives returned to power in 1984, Tellier was rehabilitated, becoming clerk of the PCO in 1985.

A shrewd man, with small, sharp eyes set in an angular face, Tellier has talents the Conservatives were wise to put to better use. Those who know him say he has a patina of charm and a sponge-like mind, in the sense that he seems to constantly ask questions rather than answer them. Mulroney relies heavily on Tellier's insights into Quebec politics. It was Tellier who drafted the Conservatives' national unity strategy unveiled in the fall of 1990 after the failure of Meech Lake. It's a matter of speculation how long he will stay in the post; he was rumoured to want out in mid-1990, but Mulroney convinced him to stay on.

A top bureaucrat with influence second only to Tellier is Fred Gorbet, 47, deputy minister of finance since 1988 and an influential force in the department through most of the 1980s. Like Tellier, Gorbet is a reconstructed Liberal who has been able to adapt to the economics of neoconservatism. Born in Welland, Ontario, Gorbet is the son of East European Jewish émigrés. He was educated in economics at York University in Toronto and Duke University in North Carolina. A specialist in economic and fiscal projections, he began his civil service career with the Bank of Canada and rose to prominence in July 1982, when he signed on with the Finance Department as an assistant to then deputy minister Ian Stewart, who was taking the fall for a disastrous budget tabled by Allan MacEachen. Working under succeeding deputies Mickey Cohen and Stanley Hartt, Gorbet put his stamp on every budget until 1988, when he became deputy himself.

Rumpled and informal, he copes well with the 14-hour days that go with the job. He's been a trusted advisor on budget packages that have grown progressively more tight-fisted in recent years. Colleagues say that, philosophically, Gorbet used to be considered soft on social policy by the Conservatives. If so, he's managed to adapt his thinking, like any good civil servant, to the views of his masters. The other premier public servants, as measured by prestige are:

Ian Clark, 45, secretary to the Treasury Board. Clark is a British-born career civil servant who was a Rhodes scholar at Oxford and earned a Masters in Public Administration at Harvard. As the bureaucracy's representative at Treasury Board, he's a crucial player in the government's attempts to cut costs in the public service.

John Tait, 46, deputy minister of justice. Tait is a blue-blood Montrealer whose father belonged to the corporate elite. With his receding hairline and clear-rimmed glasses, Tait resembles a cerebral grocer. He was educated at the best schools (Lower Canada College, Oxford, McGill and Princeton) and has spent his entire career with the federal civil service.

J.C. de Montigny Marchand, 55, under secretary of state for external affairs. A lawyer and stylish bureaucrat from St.-Jérôme, Quebec, de Montigny Marchand was last a major force in the civil service during the long Liberal reign. In previous postings, as deputy minister of communications and of energy, his career suffered from his abysmal relationship with Marcel Masse, his minister in both departments. De Montigny Marchand's appointment to the top job at External marks the rehabilitation of a veteran public servant. The question is can he rehabilitate External's sagging reputation in government circles.

Below the superbureaucrats are a host of bright, ambitious comers at or below the deputy minister level in a variety of departments. Those with the brightest prospects or most solid reputations include: Donald Campbell, who was appointed deputy minister for international trade in 1989 as a reward for dealing with the free trade issue for the previous three years; Jean Fournier, under secretary of state; Robert Fowler, deputy minister of national defence; Arthur Kroeger, at Employment and Immigration, an Albertan Rhodes scholar who holds the distinction of being the longest-serving deputy minister in Ottawa; Jeremy Kinsman, an assistant deputy minister in External Affairs, who earned a reputation as the *éminence grise* at Communications during a four-year tenure; and Michael Sabia, director of sales tax for the Finance Department.

The most powerful women powerbrokers are well educated high-achievers who have so far been largely confined to second-tier departments and agencies. None of them has reached the level of prominence of Sylvia Ostry, the government's former top GATT negotiator, who has now retired from the civil service. The new leading women are Jocelyn Bourgon (associate secretary for federal-provincial relations), Maureen Law (special adviser, External Affairs), Janet Smith (D.M., Privatization and Regulatory Affairs), Ruth Hubbard (D.M., Revenue Canada), Jennifer McQueen (D.M. Labour), Margaret Catley-Carlson (D.M., Health and Welfare), Huguette Labelle (chairperson of the Public Service Commission).

Other women on the outer rim of power are: Shirley Thomson, director of the National Gallery; Genviève Sainte-Marie, director of the National Museum of Science and Technology; and Paule Leduc, president of the Social Sciences and Humanities Research Council.

Dark Days on the Rideau

Since the Conservative government took power in 1984 with promises of slashing fat from Ottawa's swollen bureaucracy, a siege mentality has pervaded the mandarins' plush-carpeted office suites. A plotter's paradise at the best of times, the mandarinate has had more to worry about than simply who's getting ahead and who isn't. With few exceptions, the deputy ministers have had to contend with budget cutbacks and layoffs — a rude awakening for administrators who, by their own admission, have spent most of their careers spending money, not saving it. The austerity has helped sink the morale of their employees to record low levels, according to numerous studies. For example, a February 1989 study carried out for the Treasury Board surveyed 3,000 managers in all government departments and agencies. It revealed that 40 per cent of the government's senior executives believe there is a serious morale problem in their organization. One explanation, the report said, was that senior managers do not perceive any chance of getting ahead. The Public Service Commission's own studies confirm the problem. They blame the malaise on cutbacks that have left too many midlevel, middle-aged bureaucrats with no hope of promotion. It's not surprising that the PSC has found that few of the best and brightest university graduates want to joint the civil service these days.

During his 1983 campaign for the party leadership, Brian Mulroney promised to give civil servants in Ottawa "pink slips and running shoes." When the Conservatives won power the next year, Mulroney followed up by ordering 15,000 jobs cut from the civil service payroll. By late 1989, about 12,000 of those cuts had been achieved through attrition and retraining. In each of the four years since 1984, the government had reduced its spending on operations by more than

20 per cent, and the heat was still on all major departments to cut core budgets.

Late in 1989, Mulroney launched a massive internal review to study ways to modernize the civil service and prepare it for a "leaner and meaner" role in the next century. It was the first major stocktaking of the civil service since Liberal prime minister Lester Pearson launched the Royal Commission on Government Organization in 1960. As of 1991, the study, called *Public Service 2000* and headed by senior bureaucrat John Edwards, had spewed out 10 task force reports that essentially called for delayering and streamlining the civil service in the same way major private-sector corporations have done in recent years. The most crucial report, called *Service to the Public*, was the last. Produced by Bruce Rawson, deputy minister of fisheries and oceans, it dealt head-on with the sort of deep-seated attitudinal change needed. "We've got to change the *culture*," Rawson writes. "We've got to stop being a mute, self-interested, desk-bound bureaucracy, which won't admit mistakes, and become an open, responsive organization which makes Canadians feel *welcome* at our counters."

Already the emphasis on austerity and customer service has deputies talking tough, despite slumping morale in their departments. "Sure it affects people's lives, people's expectations, people's sense of self-worth," says one. "But I think people [employees] know that there's no free lunch. People know that taxes are too high and therefore better ways and means have got to be found for doing things. My sense is that there is an acceptance of the economic and fiscal realities." To which a member of the public might reply, seeing will be believing.

If the objectives of *Public Service 2000* are fulfilled, a more open, effective and publicly accountable civil service will result. That could help reduce the highly closeted, elitist way decisions are made at the highest levels in Ottawa — that is, by a closed circle of senior cabinet ministers, mandarins and interest groups. But further reforms would remain much needed. The civil service must progress toward making its powerbrokers more representative of the population at large, by sex, ethnic group and religion. And that progress must be coupled with more fundamental political reform, as discussed in the previous chapter, that opens up political power to ordinary backbenchers, parliamentary committees and party organizations.

Chapter 3

The Sulking Siblings

The last morsel of sugar pie has been finished, liqueurs are on their way, and the after-dinner conversation has begun. Inside Montreal's Club Saint-Denis, favoured hangout of the city's francophone elite, the mood is conducive to frank talk; this is, after all, the private club of my companions, multimillionaire businessman Guy St. Germain and two of his friends who are senior partners at a prominent law firm. The topic, this spring evening in 1990, is English Canada's opposition to the Meech Lake accord. Deep-seated emotions surface easily among these Québécois, all of whom voted against separation in the 1980 referendum. "Quebec is on a slope, drifting out of Canada," St. Germain says sadly. "Hearts have been broken," agrees one lawyer. "It will never be the same." The second lawyer adds: "We need a new arrangement, just like England and Germany have worked out a new arrangement. Given another chance, I would vote for separation." The comparison is stunning for an Ontarian who has never regarded French and English relations in such extremely war-like terms.

Shift the scene to another province and another gathering of a provincial elite. The occasion is a meeting of the Atlantic Provinces Young Presidents' Organization a few weeks later in a Charlottetown hotel. The highlight of the evening is an impassioned speech by PEI premier Joe Ghiz, easily the best political orator in Canada, on the merits of Meech Lake and Confederation. Afterward, I retire to the Confederation Room in Rodd's Classic Inn to discuss the state of the country with a handful of business leaders. There is talk of regional gripes: the federal government's imposition of cod quotas and the closing of the military base at Summerside. But the militant mood of Quebec has my companions befuddled. "There is a danger that the Atlantic provinces will become the Bangladesh of Canada if Quebec separates," says one.

A few thousand kilometres away and a year later in an Edmonton auditorium, about three thousand people have turned out for a rally of the Reform Party to hear party leader Preston Manning, the son of Ernest, Alberta's east-bashing one-time premier. In appearance and style, Manning is Canada's answer to Mr. Rogers, the avuncular children's television star, only his message is far from benign as he addresses the throng. The air is electrified as Manning hits all the right western chords: the foolishness and unfairness of bilingualism, with its assumption that Canada is built on two founding races; the sins of multiculturalism, which in these parts is viewed as anti-Canadian and a sop to immigrant-flooded central Canada. Three scenes. Three profoundly different sets of grievances and hopes. More than any agenda of a federal-provincial conference, they convey the deep divisions that plague Canada today.

At the root of these grievances is a sense of exclusion from the circles of power in Ottawa, which seem dominated by central Canadian elites. As the nation goes about its attempt to rebuild federation, a key goal should be to reform our national political institutions in a way that permits regional voices to be better heard. The present parliamentary system was designed to ensure that truly national policies that express the collective will of all Canadians could emerge. This is a laudable and necessary goal. But the regions outside Ontario and Quebec have tirelessly maintained that a whole torrent of decisions emanating from Ottawa has favoured central Canada at their expense and that national policies have come to mean policies, on everything from interest rates to transportation and language, that cater to the needs of Ontario and Quebec. It will be all the more galling for the regions if the present attempt to rebuild confederation focuses solely on the albeit more urgent demands of Quebec and excludes measures to make the west, the east and the North more equal partners in federation.

More than anything, the regions have come to resemble squabbling siblings with a variety of adolescent complexes. The western provinces are like prodigal sons who would rather argue than listen; the Atlantic provinces have an inferiority complex that comes from having to rely on allowances from dad (that is, federal transfer payments); Quebec is the black sheep, set in its rebellious ways; Ontario is the smug favourite son of Confederation; and the two northern territories are rather like adopted children, worried that they are not quite the equal of the others.

Like all adolescents, the siblings are growing apart as they become set in their ways. This is a natural process for a young country like Canada, a process that should be accommodated, not opposed.

Central Canadians find it easy to overlook the fact that the country has more than one distinct region. Quebec may be Canada's most distinct society, by virtue of its French-speaking majority, culture and separate legal system, but other regions of the country are also separate entities, based on their common political cultures, economic bases, ethnic makeups and, most often, shared contempt for the Toronto-Ottawa-Montreal power axis.

The West

The West, says Independent Edmonton MP David Kilgour in his insightful book *Inside Outer Canada*, "is weary of being dealt with as if it were Inner Canada's vast domestic colony. From John A. Macdonald to Brian Mulroney, Westerners have been treated mostly with polite indifference and subdued contempt by national governments." Opinion polls consistently back up Kilgour's assertion. A poll by Winnipeg's Angus Reid in November 1988 reported that two-thirds of the residents of the four western provinces believe that the Conservative government favours Quebec. A 1989 poll by Environics found that 85 per cent of westerners agreed with the statement that the West is usually ignored.

Westerners have long thought of the four western provinces as a distinct region. Manitoba, Alberta, Saskatchewan and British Columbia are hardly a homogeneous group. They embrace the Prairie populism of Saskatchewan and Manitoba and the conservativism of Alberta's Tories and B.C.'s Social Crediters. Yet they possess striking similarities that set them apart from the rest of the country. Most obviously they share a well-developed political consciousness, formed by their common frontier experience and physical isolation. Its main feature is a resentment of central Canada.

Economically, they all have resource-based economies in which manufacturing employs much less of their workforce than in the central or even the eastern provinces. Demographically, they have the highest proportion among the regions of residents of non-French and non-British descent. This has obvious implications for western views on Confederation. Most western settlers came directly from the United States or Continental Europe and were never imbued with the central Canadian notion that Canada has two founding racial groups whose interests somehow have priority over those of others. No wonder there is widespread western antipathy to federal bilingualism policies. In the same spirit, western residents who trace their origins to the U.S. West, Eastern Europe or the Ukraine consider how they assimilated into the common culture or their adopted homeland in past decades and wonder why they have to put up with federal multicultural policies that encourage the latest newcomers to do the opposite. This point is often missed by central and eastern Canadians, who dismiss such western attitudes as the product of bigotry.[1]

Politically, the western provinces have felt alienated from central Canada's power centres since Confederation. Here's a brief litany of the major gripes:

- Under Sir John A. Macdonald's National Policy of 1879, which protected Canadian industry through tariff barriers, Prairie farmers had to pay a 35 per cent tariff on machinery imported from the United States and Britain.
- In 1911, western farmers backed Liberal prime minister Wilfrid Laurier's campaign for limited reciprocity (free trade) with the United States. When Laurier lost the election, the West viewed his defeat as an example of the power of central Canadian business and political forces, who favoured tariff protection from foreign competition.
- Freight rates: The very phrase is almost a nationalistic rallying cry west of Winnipeg. For decades after Confederation, the CPR, with federal blessing, charged western grain farmers twice as much

to move wheat through the Prairies as it charged in Ontario and Quebec.

• Federal energy policies in the 1970s and 1980s proved once and for all to westerners, especially those in oil-rich Alberta and gas-rich Saskatchewan, that the federal government is capable of making decisions that economically devastate the west and favour consumers and companies east of Winnipeg. The trouble started in 1974, when OPEC began a concerted effort to raise oil prices from about U.S.$4 a barrel to the $20-plus range. Ottawa's Liberal government responded by imposing an export tax on oil moving from the west to the United States and froze the domestic price. Worse was to come. The National Energy Program of 1980 is probably the most overtly anti-western policy ever formulated by the federal government. A major feature was tax incentives for Canadian-owned companies, which encouraged them to move exploration and development activities from the west to the northern and coastal areas.

Disgruntled with Liberal-dominated Ottawa, the West threw its support and faith behind the federal Conservative Party, helping it to win in 1984 and 1988. (In 1988, for example, the west sent 48 Conservatives to Parliament, 32 New Democrats and only 6 Liberals.) But the sense of alienation soon returned. Some of the grievances are old — high interest rates designed to dampen inflation in the overheated economies of central Canada at the expense of underheated economies of the west, for example — and some are new: The CF-18 maintenance contract that went to Canadair in Montreal for political reasons instead of to a Winnipeg firm that entered a lower bid; the federal decisions to slash financial support to the OSLO tar sands plant in Alberta, kill Via Rail's Canadian line across the West, and scrap plans for a B.C.-built Polar-8 icebreaker. Even generous federal support payments to western grain farmers can't seem to soothe angry western brows.

As the growing popularity of the Reform Party attests, the anger is directed at the mainstream parties. Populist parties are nothing new in the west, where they have sprouted faster than new strains of wheat. Historically, westerners have expressed their sense of

alienation through new parties like the Progressives, the United
Farmers of Manitoba and Alberta, the left-wing Co-operative Commonwealth Federation (forebear of the NDP) and the conservative
Social Credit. More recently, the forces of alienation gave birth to
the Western Canada Concept,the Alberta-based separatist party of
the 1970s, and to the Reform Party of Canada (RPC). Formed in
1987, the RPC, in just two years, had become the federal party of
choice for 36 per cent of Albertans, 20 per cent of British Columbians
and 15 per cent of Prairie voters. It stood fourth among federal parties
nationwide. Across the west the RPC has federal and provincial parties on the run. A 1990 poll in Alberta showed that if the RPC
was to run provincially, it would have the support of 57 per cent
of the Alberta electorate. Preston Manning's explanation for this
rapid rise was simple. He told *Alberta Report*: "There's a feeling
out there that there's a great vacuum at the federal level. A feeling
that no one is offering substantive, systemic change on the big issues.
All the parties are high-spending parties, all the parties are locked
into this old French-English model of Confederation, all the parties
are distrustful of letting the public have more to do with constitutional
processes, with having public input. And so people are groping for
meaningful alternatives."

Whether Manning's idea of reform will catch fire in Central Canada, as he hopes, is another matter. Some aspects of his platform
are appealing. Examples: the federal budget must be balanced in
each three-year period or an election must be called; MPs should
be beholden only to their constituents, not to their party. Other aspects smack of close-mindedness that liberal-minded Canadians find
offensive. Examples: official bilingualism should be scrapped, official
multiculturalism must go.

It's not surprising, then, that the RPC is attracting all manner
of bigots and racists, a problem Manning himself acknowledges. He
thinks the solution is to add numbers to his party so that the more
virulent strain of bigotry is diluted by more mainstream views. His
chances of doing so are slim, at least in central Canada, where his
party already has a reputation as a haven for nutcases. But the message of profound discontent that his supporters bring should not be
dismissed or denigrated; neither should the need for western voices
to have more say in Ottawa.

Part of the problem, lately, has been the lack of western premiers with the clout to make Central Canadians sit up and listen. Alberta Premier Don Getty just doesn't carry the same credibility as his predecessor, Peter Lougheed, did in Central Canadian circles, where Getty is viewed as a good-looking intellectual lightweight. Saskatchewan's Grant Devine and Manitoba's Gary Filmon have had trouble enough building power bases in their own provinces let alone on the national stage. And poor British Columbia. Its long-time former premier, William Vander Zalm, evoked little more than chuckles in the environs of Toronto and Ottawa, where his peculiar brand of down-home religion, used-car salesman-style moxie and shoot-from-the-hip political pronouncements marked him as the premier of Fantasyland. He was a walking tragi-comedy for a province whose political influence in confederation doesn't match its economic contribution. British Columbia, for instance, accounts for about 12 per cent of the national GDP (1989 numbers), the highest percentage of the western provinces and greater than that of the Atlantic provinces combined. (Ontario and Quebec account for 65 per cent of the GDP). Rita Johnson, the new B.C. Social Credit premier, was a little-known community-based politician until she replaced Vander Zalm. She's likely to be a better spokesperson for B.C. than him; which isn't saying that much.

The Atlantic Provinces

In the fall of 1989, PEI premier Joe Ghiz carried a forlorn message to an audience in Toronto. His region, he said, "has a deep-seated feeling that we're not cared about, that policies made in Ottawa are insensitive to the region." As the Liberal leader of a province that elected four Liberals to its four federal seats in 1988, Ghiz might be dismissed as overly partisan in his outlook. But his viewpoint is widely shared throughout the four Atlantic provinces. The region elected 20 Liberal MPs and 10 Conservatives in the 1988 election. Only one province, Nova Scotia, has a Conservative premier, Donald Cameron. Ever since the election there has been a widespread fear that the federal government's policies have been intended to punish the region for its electoral sins. At present, and throughout Canada's history, the barometer of the region's relations with the federal government is Ottawa's largesse in doling out grants, contracts and megaproject funds.

The Atlantic provinces share a lot of traits that make them a distinct region. All four provinces rely heavily on primary industries, especially fishing, which accounts for 15 per cent of economic output in Newfoundland, 13 per cent in PEI, 11 per cent in Nova Scotia and 4 per cent in New Brunswick. They have higher unemployment rates than the national average, lower per capita incomes, and all four have suffered from serious emigration in past decades. Demographically, three of the Atlantic provinces have populations that are overwhelmingly of British or Celtic stock. The fourth, New Brunswick, has about one-third Acadian or French.

Political scientists often make other generalizations about the Atlantic provinces. Religion has exerted a stronger influence there. The people are generally considered less permissive on social issues and place more stress on thrift and self-reliance. Newfoundland, of course, is also a distinct society, with its own heroes, myths and historical accomplishments. The Atlantic provinces do more trade with the United States than the rest of Canada, a pattern that contributes to a sense of separateness.

But the overwhelming fact of life that shapes the region's sense of place is its dependence on federal funds. This dependent relationship can be shown by expressing federal transfer payments (comprising Established Program grants for health and higher education, equalization payments and the Canada Assistance Plan) as a percentage of gross provincial revenues. In 1987, federal transfer payments amounted to 47 per cent of Newfoundland's revenues, 46 per cent of PEI's, 38.5 per cent of Nova Scotia's and 40 per cent of New Brunswick's.

Little wonder that political debates in the region often revolve around Ottawa's actions. Regional politicians have fought Ottawa on everything from the fisheries to monetary, transportation and tariff policies that hurt local business. Before Clyde Wells came along to thumb his nose at Mulroney's Meech Lake accord, Brian Peckford was the most obstreperous premier in the region, especially when it came to the terms for development of the Hibernia oil project. But recently there have usually been unspoken limits to Atlantic intransigence in its dealings with Ottawa (with the exception of Wells) in tacit recognition that it is foolhardy to bite too hard the hand that feeds. This is most evident in the styles of New Brunswick's Frank McKenna and PEI's Joe Ghiz, who have shown they would rather reason with Ottawa (on Meech Lake and constitutional reform, for example) than rage against it.

This is not to say that the Atlantic provinces do not have major complaints on their minds. The region has been especially hard hit by recent federal budget cuts that led to cutbacks at Via Rail (60 per cent of the resulting job losses were in Atlantic Canada) and to the closing of the Canadian Forces base at Summerside, PEI. More recently, stricter cod quotas imposed by the federal government were seen as just another wrong.

Frustrated with its constant reliance on evidently shorter federal purse strings, the region is looking closer to home to solve its economic problems. As New Brunswick premier McKenna recently put it, "We know that we've got to become increasingly independent and become less reliant on Ottawa. The sooner we achieve that plateau the better." In pursuit of that goal, McKenna has been the leading force in creating a Maritime common market for New Brunswick, PEI and Nova Scotia. "The time has come," he says, "to create a single integrated market of over 1.5 million people and coordinate our strategic objectives so that we can speak with a single voice at national and international levels." Sometimes little guys have to shout in unison to be heard in Ottawa.

The North

Since they lack premiers to make their case in federal councils, the Northwest Territories and the Yukon Territory are often the forgotten siblings in Confederation. Their plight is not helped by their having a mere three seats in the House of Commons. In the 1988 election two went to the Liberals, one went to the NDP (Audrey McLaughlin).

The size of their population doesn't help their clout. Even though the territories account for about 40 per cent of Canada's land surface, they have just short of 79,000 inhabitants, which is only 0.3 per cent of the nation's total. As a group, they have very little political clout and no economic clout. Their economies are dominated by two major players: governments, both federal and territorial, and big-name southern resource companies. Apart from their shared geography and underdeveloped economies, the northern territories have other traits in common that affect their political concerns. In the NWT, about 58 per cent of the population are aboriginal peoples (Inuit, Metis, Indian and Dene). In the Yukon, about 21 per cent are aboriginal peoples. The whites in the region are made up of government employees, transient workers (mainly young males looking for adventure) and so-called bush-yuppies, who are well-educated southern whites wanting to experience the North for a while.

If the northern territories' diverse inhabitants have a common goal, it is to determine their political, economic and social futures according to their own agendas, not according to the whims of southerners with conflicting ideas. (For a good discussion of the North's aspirations, see David Kilgour's *Inside Outer Canada* published in 1990 by Lone Pine Publishing.) Given the large presence of aboriginal peoples in the North, the issue of land claims has long been a key priority in the region's dealings with Ottawa. On this score, some progress has been made. A number of tentative and final deals have been struck with Ottawa and the territorial governments, including a 1990 agreement in principle that gives the Council of Yukon Indians about 108,000 square kilometres of land. Another 1990 agreement in principle gives the Inuit about 2 million square kilometres within the NWT and gives the Inuit resource royalties, wildlife harvesting rights and a say in decision-making over the management of the land and environment. This is all good news for the aboriginal peoples of the region, who in several instances are still wrangling over certain aspects of the tentative agreements.

But major wrangles with Ottawa remain. For one thing, northerners were alarmed by the Meech Lake accord, which contained a constitutional amending formula that would have made it very difficult for them to acquired provincial status, and also failed to deal with aboriginal rights. Less crucial but nonetheless vexing, recent Conservative policies have hit the North hard. The GST increases the cost of transporting goods to the North, with the exception of food. But food costs have already soared anyway as a result of a Canada

Post decision, with the approval of cabinet, to eliminate cheaper rates for food transport to northern Canada. What can the North do about it? Not much, given its persistent lack of influence in Ottawa.

The Favourite Son and the Black Sheep

Ontario and Quebec are the targets of most of the venom that emanates from other regions. As far as just about everyone else is concerned, the two provinces of central Canada have had things their way for far too long. In the poor-cousin view of the residents of other regions, Ontarians are rich, arrogant and domineering, and Quebeckers have been spoiled rotten by federal governments eager to keep them happy. The complainers have a point.

Partial proof of Ontarians' smug contentment with Confederation lies in the province's failure to develop a political consciousness that can articulate political demands. This is because Ontario has long operated on the principle that what's good for Ontario is good for Canada. As political scientist Rand Dyck notes in *Provincial Politics in Canada*, "As long as the federal government was pursuing policies favourable to Ontario, or as long as Ontario equated its own interest with that of the country as a whole, there was little reason to develop a provincial consciousness." The result: Ontario premiers have been less vociferous than others in pressing for changes to federal policy, and Ontarians have traditionally identified most with the country rather than with their province. Only recently have the passions of profound political discontent awakened in the province, resulting in the election of a New Democrat government for the first time in its history. Whether Premier Bob Rae can hold on to his status as the champion of the discontented is in doubt, however, since the electorate voted for a new face when they elected him, not a socialist agenda. Already, Rae has had difficulty balancing the demands of his more militant followers with the sentiments of the electorate — to almost no one's satisfaction.

Ontarians are increasingly disgruntled with the policies of the Mulroney government as well. The bugbears have included the GST, free trade, high interest rates that, for once, hurt Ontario more than other regions in 1990 and the Meech Lake accord. (A spring 1990 Gallup poll showed that 42 per cent of Ontarians thought the Meech Lake accord would not be a good thing for Canada. Only 26 per cent thought it would be a good thing.) But these sore points are not seen as peculiarly regional concerns in the country's most populated province. Ontarians usually assume that their complaints are shared by all Canadians — with the notable exception of Quebeckers.

Quebec, as everyone knows, has grievances that are so serious they might lead the province right out of the country. Its history has been marked by often simultaneous demands for more autonomy and more funding from Ottawa. More than in any other province, politics in Quebec have been influenced by conflicts with Ottawa, usually over those seemingly contradictory demands.

There are two major, interrelated threads in the history of Quebec's relations with Ottawa. One is the record of Quebec premiers as champions of provincial rights; the other is the vast change in the political culture that occurred in the 1960s, when the political ethos of the province changed from *la survivance* (survival) to *rattrapage* (catching up) and later to *epanouissement* (expansion and growth).

Often, the tenor of relations between Quebec City and Ottawa has been set by the attitudes and demands of the provincial premier. Those relations have been on a nonstop roller coaster ride with never a dull moment. The ride started out fairly smoothly in the first few decades after Confederation; until Honoré Mercier gained power in the aftermath of the 1885 execution of Louis Riel. A Liberal, Mercier played upon Quebec's outrage at Riel's fate and forged a strongly nationalist governing party, based more on language, faith and race than on political principles. The next notable, though less bombastic, champion of provincial rights was Premier L.A. Taschereau, who fought with Ottawa on a slew of fronts between 1920 and 1936.

Then came Maurice Duplessis, who during an 18-year stint as premier seemed to fight Ottawa on just about every front. He opposed conscription and fought against the centralization of taxing powers in Ottawa. He objected to federal social programs like Unemployment Insurance and Old Age Security and fought against shared-cost programs like hospital insurance and the Trans-Canada highway.

When Jean Lesage replaced Duplessis in 1960, relations improved but were still tense, mainly because of Lesage's demands for more federal funding and the right to opt out of joint programs. In the decades since, Quebec's premiers have fought for greater Quebec participation in international francophone affairs, outright separation (in the case of René Lévesque) and more recently, under Robert Bourassa, for recognition in the constitution as a distinct society. As of 1991, Quebec's constitutional demands for this and other jurisdictional powers has boxed the province into an all-or-nothing approach to staying in the country.

This evolution in demands for provincial rights has taken place within the context of a deeper evolution in Quebec society. There has been a well-documented transition from the Quebec of the Duplessis era — when society was authoritarian, church-dominated, inward-looking and primarily concerned with cultural survival based on respect for tradition and boosting francophones birth rates — to the Quiet Revolution that began under Lesage in the 1960s. In that period of social upheaval, the government wrested from the church control over social and educational affairs, and in society at large the forces of modernization, urbanization and secularization took hold. The province's social and particularly economic progress since then has bred a powerful self-confidence that supports its apparent willingness to separate from Canada if need be. Bourassa is desperately trying to hang on to the helmsman's role, while Parti Québécois leader Jacques Parizeau grabs for the rudder.

The loud voices from Quebec City aggravate the resentment in other regions and add new urgency to their own demands for a fair deal in Ottawa. But do these regional demands that afflict Canada have any justification? Are the west, North and east justified in feeling shut out of decision-making that constantly favours central Canada? Who are the big financial winners in Confederation so far?

Who Has Clout in Ottawa?

As we have seen, the two most powerful power centres in Ottawa are the federal cabinet and the senior levels of the mandarinate. My surveys of these two groups show that the best-represented region is central Canada. While Quebec and Ontario account for about 62 per cent of the population, politicians born in those provinces hold 59 per cent of cabinet seats and about 63 per cent of deputy minister positions in the 27 major government departments I surveyed.

Separating the numbers for Ontario and Quebec is also revealing. With 26 per cent of the population, Quebec holds about 32 per cent of cabinet seats and 33 per cent of deputy minister positions. No room for resentment there. Ontario, with 36 per cent of the population, holds about 28 per cent of cabinet seats and 30 per cent of deputy minister jobs.

The west is not shut out of these two crucial power centres, but it *is* somewhat underrepresented. The four western provinces contain about 29 per cent of the nation's population, but westerners hold only 23 per cent of cabinet seats and 22 per cent of deputy minister positions.

The four Atlantic provinces, with about 9 per cent of the population, have about 13 per cent of cabinet seats. Amazingly, no one born in the Atlantic provinces holds a deputy minister's job in the major government departments studied.

No cabinet ministers or deputy ministers were born in the two northern territories, which have about 0.3 per cent of the country's population.

The conclusion: Quebec and Ontario have by far the most clout in the cabinet and deputy minister ranks, but the regions do have representation that roughly reflects the size of their populations. This, however, flies in the face of the notion, recognized in the 1982 constitutional amending formula, that the provinces are equal partners

in Confederation. Even when the representation of the east, west and North is combined, it doesn't equal that of central Canada. To resolve the situation parliamentary reforms need to be undertaken that increase the power of the less populated provinces and territories.

The dominance of central Canadians in Ottawa is further illuminated by David Kilgour (the disgruntled Edmonton MP who was expelled from the Tory caucus) in his book *Inside Outer Canada*. He looked at the makeup of the Prime Minister's Office in 1989 and found that of the 11 advisers in it, nine were born and educated in central Canada, and only one, Don Mazankowski, was a westerner.

There were no easterners or northerners. Kilgour also studied the place of birth and province of education of 220 of the most senior government executives. His findings: Only 10 per cent were born and educated in western Canada, 4 per cent in Atlantic Canada, and fully 70 per cent in either Ontario or Quebec. Another 8 per cent were born outside Canada.

On the whole, then, the regions outside central Canada don't have an adequate share of the most influential positions in Ottawa. As we have seen, Ontario has good reason for a smug contentment with the way things work in Ottawa. Quebec, with more power than any other province, has no reason to complain at all. This is especially true when the special role of the so-called Quebec lieutenant in Ottawa is taken into account.

Probably the most powerful Quebec lieutenant in history was Ernest Lapointe, the right-hand man to Mackenzie King. Grieving Lapointe's death in 1941, King declared, "But for him, I would never have been prime minister, nor would I have been able to hold office, as I had held it through the years." Indeed, King's political success owed a lot to his habit of always having a French Canadian as his closest adviser. He replaced Lapointe with Louis St. Laurent, who later succeeded him as Liberal leader and prime minister. Lieutenants like Lapointe and St. Laurent were far more than representatives of their province; the exerted special influence over the makeup of cabinet and hence over government policy.

Two anglophone prime ministers, R.B. Bennett and John Diefenbaker, didn't bother to find a Quebec lieutenant. Other prime ministers have been a lot shrewder. Pearson counted on well-respected francophones such as Frederick Monk and Guy Favreau. Pierre Trudeau's most notable Quebec strongman was Marc Lalonde. Brian Mulroney, despite overwhelming electoral support in Quebec at election time, has counted just as much on his own credentials as a Quebecker to keep the province in line as on any provincial powerbroker. That's a good thing, since his one-time trusted ally, Lucien Bouchard, quit his lieutenant's job and the party to form the separatist Bloc Québécois. Bouchard's replacement, Benoît Bouchard (no relation), is an able former education administrator and one-time Parti

Québécois member who is serving more as a troubleshooter than as a powerful provincial strongman in the tradition of his predecessors.

In many ways, 51-year-old Bouchard, minister of health and welfare, personifies Quebec's nationalist passions and its ambivalent attitude to Canada. He represents the riding of Roberval, his birthplace on the windswept shore of Lac St. Jean, 200 kilometres north of Quebec City. The area is so purely French, he says, that locals call it "a distinct society within a distinct society." Growing up in the area imbued Bouchard with a fierce loyalty to Quebec first. "I'm training myself to say I'm a Quebecker *and* a Canadian," he says amiably.

Bouchard isn't even a Conservative loyalist in terms of his background. His father, who ran a poultry business in Roberval, was a lifelong Liberal and friend of Pierre Trudeau. Son Benoît was never a member of any party until 1980, when he joined the Parti Québécois briefly during the referendum on separation. (He quit right after the yes vote failed because, although he was in favour of radical changes for Quebec in Canada, he didn't consider himself a true *independantiste*.) So what is this man doing a decade later as a Conservative fighting to keep Quebec in Canada?

"I'm a Mulroney man," he says. "I came to Ottawa in 1984 because of Brian Mulroney rather than because I was a Conservative." He took a lot of convincing, though. When Mulroney's then chief of staff Bernard Roy, first approached Bouchard to run, he turned him down flat. "I didn't want to hear about the Conservatives at first. Nobody was a Conservative in my region at all." Roy finally convinced him to run for election by accusing him of "not having the guts" to work for his province and country.

Bouchard's early cabinet postings were tumultuous. For example, at Transport he handled VIA Rail cutbacks, and at Employment and Immigration he was at the centre of the controversy that erupted over Canada's handling of refugees after Tamils landed in boats on the East Coast. Those trials were nothing, however, compared to his current role as troubleshooter for the fragile Quebec Tory caucus.

Since he took over as Quebec lieutenant in May, 1990, Bouchard's main job has been to keep the Quebec caucus from disintegrating.

The failure of the Meech Lake accord caused a clutch of French-Canadian MPs to leave the party, leaving 56 MPs in the Quebec caucus, and it profoundly challenged Bouchard's own commitment to federal politics. "I was devastated, just empty," he recalls. He remembers Mulroney being in the same state at the time. "His face was vacant, gone, empty." Rather than make a rash decision, Bouchard went back to Roberval to ponder his future and, after a few days, decided to stay on as an MP "I asked myself: 'If you leave, who is going to defend the interest of your people, who is going to stay there for Quebec?'"

Persuading other MPs to copy him was more difficult. "Many MPs wanted to leave at the time, many more than the six we lost." Mulroney depended heavily on Bouchard to keep caucus emotions under control. "If there was a problem with an MP," he says. "I'd get a phone call from the Prime Minister's office." He mimics Mulroney: "'Benny, we have a problem with that one, he's mad. Could you do something?'"

As Quebec lieutenant, Bouchard sees himself in a dual role. On one hand, Bouchard regards himself as a sort of conduit for federal views to his constituents. "I travel in a lot of regions of Quebec. I think I have transmitted what I have learned in Ottawa to rural Quebeckers. Ottawa may be a little less strange to them." On the other hand, there's little doubt he is the main spokesman for Quebec's interests at the cabinet table. As well as being close friends with Mulroney and Don Mazankowski, Bouchard sits on nine cabinet committees, including the most powerful: Operations, Priorities and Planning, Expenditures and National Unity. "I am the minister who speaks at the cabinet table for Quebec," he says.

The pleasurable part of that job is directing federal largesse to Quebec business ventures, such as the $18 million given to forestry projects in the province, or cultural projects. The tough part is defending federal positions in Quebec where his separatist adversaries have accused him of being a traitor. Bouchard is convinced that separation is no easy alternative for Quebec. "Sovereignty may happen in Quebec. But if it happens, it will be tough, it will be painful." As far as the fight for unity goes, he believes the ball is in English Canada's court: "Canada has to fight to convince Quebec to come

back because it is my impression that it has already left." Bouchard
is hopeful that the rest of Canada will be patient with Quebec's deep-
rooted sense of nationalism and inability to see Canada as a homeland. "A majority of Quebeckers would not be separatists, if they
are given time. They are saying to Canada: 'Give us time, give us
a chance to move to where you are in terms of identifying with Canada as a homeland.'" In the meantime, Bouchard will continue to
play his role as handholder and benefactor to his province and peace-
maker for the country. But whether he is ultimately successful will
have a lot more to do with the ability of the country to strike a
realistic constitutional compromise. Traditionally, the very existence
of a special emissary from Quebec in most federal governments has
been an ad hoc acknowledgement of Quebec's special place in Confederation and has often been a crucial ingredient in the formation
of a workable political community in Canada. At present, it provides
a much more tenuous link between the two solitudes.

Who Benefits Financially from Confederation?

Another way of assessing whether the regions are getting a good
deal in Confederation, and therefore are justified in grousing so much,
is to look at who contributes most to federal spending and who benefits most from it. A 1991 study by Vancouver's Fraser Institute provided a good snapshot of the winners and losers by calculating how
much the federal government spends in each province and then de-
ducting the total taxes paid by residents. Alberta, British Columbia
and Ontario have been the net financial contributors to Confederation. In 1988, Alberta paid $1,688 per person more in taxes than
the federal government spent in the province. Ontario's net contribution was $831 per person, and British Columbia's $645. The other
provinces have all been beneficiaries. (PEI topped the list with a
net gain of $4,315 per person, Nova Scotia gained by $3,758 per
person, Manitoba by $1,521, Saskatchewan by $1,854. Quebec was
ahead by a slim margin of $304 per person.)

Power-sharing in Canada has never been based on how much cash
a province or region brings to the table but the numbers show that

Alberta and British Columbia, two of the biggest net contributors, have added reason to resent the way central Canadian priorities often dominate policy-making in Ottawa.

Conclusion

There are essentially two ways to increase the influence of regional voices in the governing process in Ottawa. One, the most common approach, involves granting more power to the provinces. The other involves parliamentary reform.

Option One: Increasing Provincial Power

There is a free-for-all mood in Canadian politics in the early 1990s. Challenged by Quebec and the Mulroney government to rethink the nature of federation, the provincial premiers have adopted a me-first mentality. Task forces on constitutional reform have scoured each province, conducting public hearings like so many encounter groups in a psychiatric ward. More and more, academic experts, business leaders and media pundits are calling for a decentralization of power from Ottawa to the provinces.

Quebec, which seems determined to deal with Ottawa on an equal footing, has led the way. The Quebec Liberal Party's Allaire report, released in early 1991, put decentralization at the top of the agenda. It lists a whole range of areas, 22 in all, over which Quebec should have exclusive jurisdiction. They include health, agriculture, unemployment insurance, communications, regional development, energy, environment, industry and commerce, research and development, and income security.

Quebec's drive for a more powerful place in federation or else is understandable. A glance at history books confirms that Canada does have two founding cultures, despite the opposition of the west to the idea. As W.L. Morton observes in *The Kingdom of Canada*, safeguards for the rights of French Canada and of religious minorities were among the main features of the scheme of government laid out at the Quebec Conference in 1864, where the terms of the eventual

Confederation were negotiated by provincial delegates. The French
delegates, notes Morton, accepted the idea of union in terms of "coordinate sovereignty of the two Canadian peoples."

The rejection of the Meech Lake accord in 1990 by many English-
speaking Canadians (46 per cent in a March 1990 Gallup poll) and
the rejection of the idea that Quebec is a distinct society (by 68 per
cent of English-speakers in the same poll) was an affront to Quebec's
notion of its historical place in the nation. The province's belligerent
push for greater powers was an inevitable result. In response, the
other premiers are reconsidering how much power they want and
how much should be left to the federal government.

Trading powers back and forth between Ottawa and the provinces
is nothing new; they've been doing it since 1867. The country's founders designed it to have a supreme central government, responsible
for "the peace, welfare and good government" of the union, with
the provinces having jurisdiction over purely local matters. Taxing
powers were placed primarily in the hands of the federal government,
which paid subsidies to provincial governments and was responsible
for any debts they ran up. Over time, however, the division of powers,
mainly in the financial realm, remained fluid. By 1939, a hodge-
podge of federal and provincial tax regimes had evolved. To meet
the demands of the war effort, they were scrapped in favour of a
unified income and corporate tax administered by Ottawa. Later,
as the provinces assumed control of modern health care, welfare and
postsecondary education programs, new tax-sharing agreements
evolved with Ottawa.

A good deal of the discussion about decentralizing power from
Ottawa involves transferring to the provinces the power for making,
executing and financing programs now financed with Ottawa's help,
such as health and postsecondary education. But as most provinces,
with the exception of Quebec, have acknowledged, there are limits
to how much the federal government can be stripped of power. Whatever compromises are eventually struck, the national government
should have the power to set national standards in such fields as
health care and education, and not just take care of monetary, defence
and economic policy. Stripping the national government of its tax-
ation powers also risks jeopardizing its ability to make equalization

payments to the poorer provinces. Equality of economic opportunity within the regions should remain a basic building block of Confederation.

Option Two: Parliamentary Reform

A more effective way to increase the influence of regional voices in government would be to better adapt our parliamentary institutions and practices to take these voices into account. An elected Senate is needed, comparable in power to the German Bundesrat or the Australian Senate, with equal representation for the three following regions: The West, Central Canada (Ontario and Quebec), and the East. The guiding principles must be the need to give less populous provinces and territories greater representation than they presently have, while at the same time respecting aboriginal interests and the essential French/English duality of Canada. Therefore, the two northern territories should have a few seats reserved for them in the Senate. Special seats should also be reserved for aboriginal groups. To reflect the special concerns of these aboriginal groups as well as of francophones, special rules could be put in place that require the concurrence of their representatives on vital issues that concern them. These reforms, it should be noted, are in fundamental agreement with the principles of Senate reform agreed to by the premiers in the aborted Meech Lake accord.

The western premiers have traditionally favoured equal representation by province, but this would be a non-starter as far as Quebec and Ontario are concerned since it would see their representation in the Senate reduced from a current 23 per cent each to 10 per cent.

But something must be done to address the under-representation of the western provinces in the second chamber. As Queen's University professor Ronald Watts points out in his 1991 book *Options For Canada*, co-authored with Douglas Brown, each of the four western provinces have fewer senators than the less populous provinces of Nova Scotia and New Brunswick. As well, the two largest provinces, Ontario and Quebec are better represented in relation to their population than British Columbia and Alberta.

Although most provincial premiers have spoken in favour of Senate reform, the issue has now taken a back seat in provincial capitals as talk of a devolution of powers has risen to the fore. The premiers should not forget the merits of Senate reform in their rush to add to their own powers. (Making appointments to the Supreme Court a provincial prerogative would also be a step in the right direction.)

Another means of increasing regional influence in government would be to loosen up the tight party rules that virtually forbid MPs from breaking party ranks on legislation before the House. A third alternative, the increased use of referenda, requiring, say, a majority of support in most or all of the regions for a piece of legislation — such as abortion or the death penalty — is less attractive. Canada's system is based on representative democracy, not direct democracy. It would be better to empower elected representatives to speak for regions than to resort to rule by capricious referenda.

The litany of regional resentments and the evidence that certain regions are not fairly represented in Ottawa leads to the conclusion that, with or without Quebec, Canada has no hope of becoming a happy family of regions until all regions have equal influence in Ottawa's circles of power.

Part II
Business

Chapter 4

The Merchant Princes

Several decades ago, John Porter drew a rather alarming picture of the economic elite in Canada. Surveying the boards of the 170 largest corporations, the nine chartered banks and the ten largest insurance companies, Porter showed that the members of the economic elite tend to have a lot in common. The 760 directors in his sample were overwhelmingly British in origin, even though this ethnic group made up less than half of the general population in 1951 shortly before he did his survey. Only a smattering (6.7 per cent) were drawn from the French Canadian population, which made up one-fifth of the population at the time, and a negligible few (six persons) were Jewish. *only 1% of population*

The economic elite were predominantly Anglican, Presbyterian or United Church by faith. Just 10 per cent were Catholics, although Catholics comprised 43 per cent of the population in 1951. Most of the economic elite had a university education, and about one-third attended private schools. About one-third was born into the upper class, and most of the rest had middle-class origins. Porter estimated that only about 18 per cent made their way from the bottom rungs of the social ladder to the top.

Looking at those numbers in the 1990s, the average Canadian might react with mild scorn and believe that the situation is much different today. After all, the reasoning goes, religious and racial intolerance has declined in the past three decades, replaced by a passionate faith in the great leveller: consumerism. As well, the makeup of the country's population has changed immensely, and our universities have been churning out well-educated baby boomers of all races and both sexes at a quickening pace.

During my travels, the view I heard most often expressed by fast-rising young executives and veteran chief executives alike was that race, religion and social background don't matter in business any more, although no one disputes the notion that being male is an advantage. What counts most of all, say the majority, is performance. In other words, the widespread perception is that people get ahead by merit. Such assertions are nice to hear, suggesting as they do that the dream of social mobility for all is alive and well in Canadian commerce.

With these assumptions in mind, I set out to test just how open the economic elite has become. To represent the economic elite, I chose the directors of the country's largest corporations and banks in 1988. Detailed biographical questionnaires were sent to the 251 board members of the 20 largest corporations in Canada and the 181 directors of the five largest banks. In total, 94 corporate directors and 57 bank directors replied with completed questionnaires. That's not a bad response rate. But to complement it, my researchers delved into other biographical sources, such as the *Canadian Who's Who* and the *Financial Post Directory of Directors*, and came up with a broader picture. At the end of the exercise, information was assembled on 165 corporate directors, and 131 bank directors.

As a result, I could draw some reasonable inferences about class origins, ethnic background, gender, religion, schools and preferred clubs. Also helpful was my extensive knowledge of the two groups, picked up during my work as a business journalist for more than a decade. I have watched the business elite at play in their private clubs and watched executives of non-British origins mingle with the Old Boys in boardroom settings. I've had male CEOs tell me earnestly that women haven't got the stuff to make it in the corporate world and interviewed women directors who have faced prejudice in their careers. The survey results are, in many ways, in line with my subjective impressions. (See appendices for full survey results.)

The portrait that emerges of the typical business powerbroker of the 1990s is not all that different from that of the 1950s, long before multiculturalism and feminism gathered force in Canadian society. On many fronts, there has been progress, as the results summarized below show, but not enough to adequately reflect the changing demographics of Canada.

When high-school guidance counsellors are briefing idealistic youths on what it takes to make it to the top rungs of economic power in Canada, they should mention a few special requirements. Being male is almost a prerequisite. Only 9 per cent of the 251 corporate directors were women, and just 5 per cent of the 181 bank directors were women. Being Protestant, especially Anglican or United Church, is definitely an asset. Of the 117 corporate directors who listed a religious affiliation in their responses or other biographical sources, roughly 64 per cent were Protestant, mainly Anglican and United Church; 30 per cent were Roman Catholic, and 6 per cent were practising Jews. A total of 90 bank directors listed a religion, and about 78 per cent were Protestant. Another 15.6 per cent were Roman Catholic, and only three directors listed themselves as practising Jews. That compares badly with the religious affiliations of Canadians in the general population, where about 40 per cent are Protestant, 47 per cent are Roman Catholic and about 2 per cent are Jewish.

Most of the business elite hailed from the United Kingdom. Roughly 61 per cent of corporate directors and about 75 per cent of the bank board members who identified their ancestral origins had at least one parent of British descent. (By comparison, in the 1986 census, about 49 per cent of Canadians listed British among their ethnic origins.)

There has been some change in the ethnic background of directors, though. French Canadians have gained much greater access to the business elite in the past decades. About 32 per cent of corporate directors who responded claimed French Canadian origins, and roughly 18 per cent of bank directors did so. (In the 1986 census, 32.8 per cent of Canadians listed French among their ethnic origins.) In both groups, the remaining respondents claimed various European origins other than British. About 14 per cent of corporate directors and 18 per cent of bank directors listed various West and East European backgrounds, which compares well with their share of the population (16 per cent). Asians, native Canadians and other groups were nowhere to be found among the respondents.

The figures also show that, more than for any other elite studied in this book, it helps to have a father who belonged to the business elite before you, although the majority in both groups hailed from middle-class origins. And, just as guidance counsellors have always stressed, the right education is a big plus. Combine a private school or classical college education (Upper Canada College and Collège Jean-de-Brébeuf topped the list) with a university degree (preferably from the University of Toronto, McGill, Laval or Harvard) and you are a shoo in — if you are male, that is.

The findings of the survey suggest that there is a lack of openness in the most powerful boardrooms of the nation. This does not mean, however, that the business elite has been completely devoid of change for the past several decades. If you imagine all the powerful players in business assembled at an annual meeting, the head table would be dominated by the same old Establishment white male faces as ever. But the guests in the hall would be a polyglot group of entrepreneurs, ethnics and old money.

In the pages that follow, I profile the men I consider to be the most powerful businessmen in Canada. (Women, who have astonishing little power, are dealt with in the next chapter.) I am concerned only with the men who sit at the apex of power and who put power into practice. They are the main arbiters of deal-making in the country and the men who have mastered the art of political persuasion in order to further their own commercial interests. Wealth alone is not the criterion; power is irrelevant unless you use it. Being the chief executive officer of a large corporation is not enough to merit inclusion in this chapter, either. Many CEOs run a company for a few years, exercising little power beyond their corporate fiefdoms, then disappear into anonymity when they retire.

By looking at the top practitioners of power in person, it is possible to gain a better sense of the evolving nature of power in corporate Canada. The new faces in the chambers of power may be few in number, but these newcomers have been influential and represent a shifting of power's centre of gravity. Paul Reichmann of Olympia & York Developments has single-handedly broken up the hold of old money on corporate power. Then there are other one-man agents of change — erstwhile outsiders like Jack Cockwell and Jimmy Connacher — who have changed the way business is done in Canada. Entrepreneurs like Jimmy Pattison and Pierre Peladeau have proven that you can still make it to the top on ferocious ambition. Yet the same trait, run amok, helped former high-flying businessmen Robert Campeau and Garth Drabinsky fall from grace.

Some systemic changes must also be taken into account. The increased presence of several French Canadian entrepreneurs in the power elite attests to the transformation of the Quebec business establishment in the past decade. The wealthy Anglo business class that once ruled over commerce and society in Quebec has been supplanted by talented French Canadians. Says one leading member of the new francophone elite: "The old English families are cowering in the corner, sulking." *(They left Quebec !)*

There has also been a diffusion of institutional power at the top. The bankers now have to share their grip on the spigots that spew out cash with rival providers of capital, like the merchant banks. Without doubt the most powerful new forces in the capital and securities markets are the pension fund managers, who are emerging increasingly as activist investors.

The Political Influence of Business

The profiles that follow take into account two sorts of power wielded by top business leaders: power within the corporate community, as measured by deal-making clout, and power outside the community, as measured by the ability to influence politicians, not to mention the cultural and artistic leaders who rely on corporate donations.

Following the connecting webs of power between business and politics is like tracing the wispy filaments of a spider's web to the centre. How do you measure the effect on a politician's thinking of private phone calls from a business buddy? How do you measure the significance of a politician knowing that if he doesn't step on the wrong corporate toes, he can retire to a comfortable job in a business enterprise, or to a bevy of lucrative board seats? How do you measure the influence of political donations on public policy? Only an ingénue would think that politicians aren't mindful of who it is that finances their political careers. The bottom line in politics is staying in power, and that takes plenty of money.

Business influence in the political process has ebbed and flowed over the decades. The real heyday of business–government co-operation was during the reign of C.D. Howe, the federal minister of trade and commerce, in the 1940s and 1950s. Notes historian Michael Bliss: "For fifteen years and more, Howe's hand was visible in every major deal involving business and government in Canada . . . . Howe became 'our man in Ottawa' particularly to the people who had worked with him during the war, grown up with him in Ottawa, or, as it happened, had their careers advanced on his recommendations." Bliss points out that not only was Howe personal friends with the country's leading industrialists, "he unashamedly and personally dunned government contractors for contributions to the Liberal party, serving as political bagman and often handling large amounts of cash in bags and safety deposit boxes."

In the 1960s and 1970s, the influence of business leaders in Ottawa dissipated. Many of them found themselves in the ideological wilderness as the Pearson government built the welfare state and Trudeau's regime experimented with state intervention in the economy. The business community hunkered down into a siege mentality and couldn't — or didn't bother to — speak out with any degree of unanimity on issues of public policy.

In the late 1980s and 1990s, that has all changed. During the 1988 federal election, which was fought over the issue of the Mulroney government's proposed free trade deal with the United States, the business community emerged as a potent political force. Corporations organized themselves into the Canadian Alliance for Trade and Job Opportunities, a lobby group with a $5.24-million war chest. They conducted a $1.5-million newspaper ad campaign called "Straight talk on Free Trade" to reach voters, and otherwise rallied behind the cause in media comments and shop-floor talks with employees. They viewed the eventual Tory victory as their own.

The business community's influence over political affairs has probably never been greater than it is today. That is why the business leaders who have mastered the art of political persuasion merit inclusion here.

The Power Elite of Business

There is a power ranking among business executives in Canada that doesn't show up in any company annual reports or in any media listings of who has the most money or the most corporate assets. The ultimate criterion business executives use to determine whether someone matters is summed up in a single macho-sounding question: "Does he make things happen?"

To make things happen means to swing, stop, abet or veto deals, whether they be for takeovers, company startups or company bailouts. The powerful few at the top of this ranking get first look at whatever deals are going on. They can pick and choose among them like ancient potentates with the right to sample the kingdom's most beautiful virgins. When they want to raise a few million for this or that community cause, they call in favours and twist arms so effectively that their involvement is a virtual guarantee of success. Very often, their power is augmented by close ties to political leaders, which can be used to help win government contracts or influence the outcome of the legislative process. But these men are most powerful in the business arena, where they can make or break other businessmen simply by giving — or withholding — their seal of approval. Sounds Darwinian, doesn't it? It is. These men have seats on the most prestigious bank and corporate boards; they belong to the right private clubs; they run corporations with millions of dollars in assets; and they are active in the right charitable and philanthropic activities.

This section is not an introduction to the entire membership of the business establishment. That would take a book in itself. It focuses on the men who sit at the pinnacle of this privileged group, the men with national political and financial clout. Most of them sit in the office towers of Toronto and Montreal, the financial and deal-making centres of Canada. But a few regional powerbrokers have fought their way to the top rungs by force of their entrepreneurial personalities and consuming ambition.

The Top Deal Makers

Senator Trevor Eyton, chairman. Brascan Ltd., deputy chairman, Edper Enterprises Ltd.

The social ascent of Trevor Eyton from middle-class Montreal boy to business Brahmin and senator might at first seem unremarkable in a country where a baker (Garfield Weston) can found an international food empire and the son of a barber (Roy Thomson) can accomplish a similar feat in media. Yet Eyton's ascent adds a whole new perspective on how to make it into the ruling circles of business and politics in Canada. It defies comparison to the Horatio Alger–style careers of Canada's buccaneering capitalists. Men like Weston, Thomson, K.C. Irving and Sam Bronfman got ahead using their own growing pools of capital, exceptional business acumen and the acquisitive instincts of a great white shark.

Eyton has made it to the top by relying a great deal on other people's money; the indispensable business acumen of a business colleague, Jack Cockwell; and key mentors who schooled him in the social graces of the upper class. Always a quick student, Eyton learned his basic lessons, then turned the practice of power into an art form. He is to powerbroking what Toller Cranston is to figure skating: an original. Pity that powerbroking, per se, unlike true art forms, doesn't have any redeeming social value.

In appearance and manner, Eyton looks the part of the business tycoon and sober-minded senator he has become. At 57, he's grown a bit paunchy from all those dinners at Chiaro's, his favourite Toronto restaurant — where the food is a lot better than it is in the parliamentary restaurant. With his receding hairline and sagging jowls he has developed a look of Churchillian redoubtableness.

He has the power to match the image, too. Before becoming a senator in September 1990, Eyton held 24 corporate directorships, more than any other businessman, and was the most senior manager/ owner in the $100-billion Edper empire of Peter and Edward Bronfman. To free up time for his senatorial duties, he cut his directorships in half and gave up a few corporate titles, but the titles he retained, including deputy chairman of Edper, augmented his influence in the Bronfman conglomerate. In casual conversation, nevertheless, Eyton keeps his ego well hidden behind a patina of humility. He plays down his power and dismisses his numerous community involvements over the years with a humble: "I do what I can to help out." He's second only to Michael Wilson as a boring speech maker — they both have the same baritone drone — and would come across as a perfect Mr. Bland, were it not for his well-known penchants for telling corny jokes and admiring beautiful women. In deportment, Trevor Eyton has become, in short, the very model of a crusty member of the business elite and a budding statesman, to boot. But how this one-time middle-class lawyer made good is a tale that mixes a touch of *Pygmalion* with a dollop of *The Prince*.

There is nothing outstanding about Eyton's social origins. He was born in Quebec City in 1934, one of three children of Dorothy and John Eyton, an electrical engineer with Abitibi paper, whose Welsh forebears emigrated to Canada at the turn of the century. Soon after Trevor was born, his parents moved to a modest house in Toronto's Danforth and Broadview area. There is nothing especially outstanding about his adolescent years, either. Good-natured, tall and athletic, Eyton fitted in well with his classmates at Jarvis Collegiate and during undergraduate studies and law school at the University of Toronto. Football was his real passion for most of that time. He played at Jarvis and was first-string centre for U of T's Varsity Blues, where teammates such as Julian Porter, the noted libel lawyer, remember him as a hard-working, disciplined athlete. "He was not the fellow that you would have the concept of being a leader. But he was the leader, very quiet, with a good droll way about him," Porter recalled later.

Eyton didn't apply the same disciplined attitude to his studies until second-year university, after he married Jane Montgomery, a doctor's daughter from upper-class Rosedale. Motivated by marriage and the encouragement of his father-in-law, Eyton graduated with a gold medal in 1957 and went on to earn top honours at the University of Toronto Law School.

Like so many adolescents who pass in and out of the country's top universities, Eyton had no way of knowing that the friendships he formed at U of T would later become prominent in the business world. Besides Porter, scion of a fine old Ontario family (FOOF), Eyton's university circle includes the likes of banker David Lewis; investment expert Fred McCutcheon, son of a senator; and media mogul Allan Slaight, all of whom later joined him in a private investment club called the Canyon Beauport Club.

Eyton left law school and, in 1962, joined the prestigious Toronto legal firm Tory, Tory, DesLauriers & Binnington. He spent the next 18 years there, a time in which he learned not only law but also the behaviour standards of the business establishment. His teacher

on both scores was the very best: J.S. Tory, the grand old man of
the law firm. "I worked closely with J.S. Tory," Eyton remembers
fondly, "who I'm sure would have been on any list of the most prestigious and the most important businessmen in Canada. So I saw
much of that world and how it operated."

There's a well-worn career path from corporate law into full-time
business, and Eyton was one of the first of a slew of his generation
of lawyers to make the move. Starting in the late 1960s, Eyton's
legal clients included Peter and Edward Bronfman, who back then
were a couple of fledglings trying to make their own way after being
cut out of involvement in the Montreal distillery business run by
their uncle, Sam Bronfman. (Sam had the future of his own boys,
Charles and Edgar, to worry about.) Peter and Edward liked Eyton's
low-key manner and respectable image so much that, in 1979, after
Eyton advised them on the takeover of Brascan, they hired him as
CEO of the company. Initially, Eyton agreed to a two-year stint.
He liked it so much he's still there.

Eyton was remarkably successful as the human face of the burgeoning Bronfman fiefdom, which had grown into the largest conglomerate in Canada by 1990, with companies in just about every
sector of the economy. His slightly rumpled, unobtrusive public persona, which fit in so well with old-money Toronto, was a perfect
proxy for the Bronfmans — Jewish outsiders from Montreal — and
they relied on him to develop their business interests in the clubby
Toronto Establishment, even if they themselves never sought to be
part of it.

Eyton's open style also worked for at least a decade with the media,
allaying fears of the growing power of the Edper empire while his
colleague, Jack Cockwell, applied his financial brains to design innovative ways of spreading that power still further. Only at the end
of the 1980s did the efforts of this remarkable tag team flounder,
as evidence and accusations grew in the media and investment business that the brilliant strategies devised by Cockwell to create the
conglomerate and shuffle assets and cash within it were as compre-
hensible to investors as computer circuitry and didn't necessarily operate in their interests. (Bill L'Heureux, successor to Eyton as the
group's main public spokesman, could do little to stem the unravelling
of the public image.)

The truth is that Eyton himself, like the empire, has always been far more complex than his benign public image suggested. Certainly, his influence in the business and political world was unsurpassed, even before he added a seat in the Senate to his list of corporate board seats. The three words "Trevor likes it" became like a royal imprimatur for any business deal on Bay Street and beyond. His approval still carries the implicit promise that one of the Edper companies might take a piece of the action. Cockwell may be the major deal maker for the Edper Group, but it is Eyton who circulates at the places, like the Toronto Club, where deals often germinate.

Eyton not only has power, he knows how to use it, discreetly or bluntly, as required. Take the building of Toronto's domed stadium, for example. In 1986, relying on his extensive network of business contacts, Eyton single-handedly lined up 27 private-sector companies with $5 million each to chip in toward the construction of the sports stadium. It seemed like a good mix of public spiritedness and private gain for the companies — they got concession rights and private boxes in return — until it was later revealed that the consortium backed out of its plan to take over ownership of the stadium. They balked when they found out that the unexpectedly high construction costs of the Dome had left it with a $300-million debt and hefty interest payments that nixed its ability to make a profit, at least in this century. Rather than take ownership of the mess, the private companies decided to leave it in the hands of the provincial government, which had guaranteed the debt. Eyton was left to negotiate the matter with labour leader Bob White, who was appointed by Bob Rae to represent the province, to try to find a way out of the quagmire.

From his vantage point in the Commerce Court office tower, Eyton also has the sort of influence that can raise aspiring businessmen to the upper ranks of the business establishment, although he can't provide a guarantee that they'll stay there. Eyton's consummate networking skills have backfired badly only once — in 1986, when he got caught up indirectly in the publicity surrounding the Sinclair Stevens scandal. In 1986, Stevens was forced to resign his post as federal industry minister in the Conservative cabinet amid conflict of interest allegations after his wife, Noreen, negotiated a $2.6-million loan for a family company from a co-founder of Magna International, the auto parts company. The trouble was, Magna had received development grants from Stevens's department. There was no solid connection between the two-way flow of money, but it didn't look good. The company that needed the Magna loan was York Centre, a financially troubled operation that ran Sinclair Stevens's various business interests in a blind trust.

Eyton's name came up in a judicial inquiry into the Stevens case; it was revealed that Eyton had tried to help Noreen and York Centre in their efforts to raise money for the company on Bay Street. At the time, Eyton was also dealing with Sinclair Stevens as a board member of the Crown-owned Canada Development Investment Corporation, which was busy selling off federal assets to the private sector. In late 1987, the judge in charge of the Stevens inquiry concluded that Eyton was not involved in any conflict of interest — Stevens was not so lucky — but the episode was publicly embarrassing for Eyton. Such are the perils of trying to lend a hand to powerful friends in need.

Members of the media have experienced a more blunt version of Eyton's powerbroking. Journalists who write uncomplimentary stories about him or his friends are liable to receive a scathing letter from Eyton expressing his disappointment. Since the early 1980s, Eyton and other Edper/Hees executives have been extremely displeased, not infrequently, with the *Globe and Mail*'s coverage of Edper-owned companies. In one incident, a Hees executive actually visited the newsroom to complain. There was no discernible effect on coverage, however.

Eyton's relationship with federal politics has always been a lot more fruitful and is a good example of how the circles of power between business and politics overlap in mutual self-interest. Eyton, like any good senior executive, has made it his business to keep track of what federal politicians are up to, since their actions can have great effect on the myriad operations of the Edper Group. A loyal Conservative fund raiser, Eyton has long maintained close personal ties with Prime Minister Mulroney. "Trevor is the most powerful man [in business] when it comes to influencing the federal government," comments a close friend, the CEO of a major Toronto investment dealer. Interviewed before his appointment as senator, Eyton acknowledged that he had to spend an increasing amount of time keeping track of the government's agenda. "My predecessors in business would spend maybe 5 per cent of their time thinking about government," he said. "I spend probably 35 to 40 per cent of my time dealing with or thinking about government."

Eyton's loyalty to the prime minister has been second to none, except perhaps Mila's. In 1988, at the request of the prime minister, he and businessman John Bitove spearheaded a Toronto area fund-raising drive that raised $7 to $9 million for the Tory war chest. In 1989, Eyton personally chipped in a meagre $1,250 to the Conservative party, but Brascan Ltd., a key Bronfman holding company where Eyton serves as a senior executive, contributed $24,299.

Considering Eyton's track record of financial support and, more importantly, his philosophical support of such Tory issues as free trade and the Meech Lake accord, no one was surprised in the least when the prime minister appointed him a senator in 1990. From this vantage point Eyton can keep better watch than ever on the legislative agenda for his corporate interests — with limits, of course. Conflict of interest guidelines stipulate that senators can't vote on any subject in which they have a vested interest or become a member of any Senate committee studying such a bill. There's no doubt that Eyton is motivated in large part by his sense of public duty and deep convictions about how to promote the country's economic and political well being. It would be churlish to suggest otherwise. But in taking up his seat in the Red Chamber while maintaining strong links to the corporate world, Eyton continues a time-tested, overlapping relationship between the spheres of politics and business.

Other examples of switch-hitting senators: Liberal Sidney Buckwold was, at one point, also a director of Mutual Life Assurance Co. of Canada; Liberal Michael Kirby is a director of Crownx Inc., the financial services company; Independent Michael Pitfield is vice-chairman of Power Corp., the Montreal financial conglomerate; Conservative Claude Castonguay is chairman of Laurentian Group, another Quebec financial conglomerate; Liberal Leo Kolber has long been a key operator and director of companies owned by the Montreal Bronfmans.

For Eyton, the Senate appointment was the result of a steady, prudent and pragmatic rise to the top. It finished off a remarkable case study in how to make it to the top — without *looking* like you're really trying.

Jack Cockwell, executive vice-president and chief operating officer, Edper Investments Ltd., chairman and director, Hees International Bancorp Inc., president and chief operating officer, Brascan Ltd., Toronto.

When the average Canadian buys a home from Bramalea Ltd., picks up a case of Labatt's Blue, takes out an insurance policy from London Life, opens an account at Royal Trust, buys lumber hewn by MacMillan Bloedel or watches the Toronto Blue Jays play baseball, the name Jack Cockwell doesn't spring to his or her mind. Those who avidly read the newspapers might be able to connect the Bronfman name to ownership of some of these companies or several hundred other corporations in the ambit of the largest conglomerate ever to emerge on the Canadian scene. But Jack who?

As far as Cockwell is concerned, that anonymity is just fine. But it is vanishing fast. Trouble is, his name has been appearing regularly in the financial pages for a year or so, and more often than not the context has been controversial. Investment advisers are saying they won't invest in the Edper-Hees-Brascan group of companies because they can't fathom the complexity of its inner workings; minority investors are worried that their interests are getting short shrift in intra-empire dealings that seem beyond the comprehension of anyone on the outside.

There's no doubt that Cockwell, the South African–born accountant who created the intricate financial neurosystem of the Edper empire, is unsurpassed as a deal maker who makes things happen; the problem is that a lot of people don't like the way those things are happening.

Cockwell is the Lee Marvin of Canadian finance; he's a stone-faced hombre who rides his associates hard. Cockwell excels as a taskmaster; he's been known to pin notes of reprimand to the chairs of underlings who aren't at work early enough. But he's as stiff as a wooden soldier at the social events his wife Wendy drags him to. Still, it's Cockwell who has built the family dynasty of Peter and

Edward Bronfman from a $40-million nest egg into its present size. Now 50, Cockwell has been the *éminence grise* at Edper since 1968, when he joined. His influence extends far beyond his role as the financial architect and overseer of the Bronfmans' affairs. Cockwell's management style and inventive financial mind have transformed the way business is done in Canada.[1]

Cockwell's impact on the sleepy Canadian business establishment has been the equivalent of a Scud missile delivered without warning. There are two important traits in the man's background that help account for his success. First, he hails from a country that seems to produce as many shrewd, parsimonious deal makers as there are canny Scots. Second, he has been honing his number-crunching skills since his youth — no search for the meaning of life in *his* biography. It's as if he always knew his purpose in life was to figure out ever more innovative ways of making money.

The man who would become the gunslinger of Canadian business was born in 1941 in East London, a farming community in Boer country outside Capetown. Life on the family farm and at the British-style boys' schools he attended was strictly no-nonsense. "South Africa is a country where you are taught very early to think about survival," he once said. At the tender age of 18, he realized that accounting, not farming, was the kind of survival he was looking for. In 1959, he signed up with the international accounting firm Touche Ross and, apart from some time off for undergraduate and graduate studies at the University of Capetown, he worked for Touche Ross until 1967. A year before he left the firm, it sent him to work in Montreal.

That's where he met Peter and Edward Bronfman, who hired him away to work as chief operating officer of Edper Investments, the investment vehicle for their part of the family fortune, which at the time amounted to a modest $50 million or so. Thereafter, Cockwell masterminded the Bronfmans' expansion through acquisitions into just about every nook and cranny of the Canadian economy.

But Cockwell's more lasting legacy will be the way he upset the status quo on Bay Street and transformed the ossified attitudes of Canadian commerce. From the outset, Cockwell was disgusted by the Old Boys' network of investment dealers, which operated as a closed club when underwriting new share issues. He had a point, since the major firms divvied up deals and reaped profits at very little risk to themselves. During the 1980s, as the Edper empire and its need for new share issues grew, Cockwell became fed up with paying millions of dollars worth of commissions to investment middlemen who took very little risk themselves. In reaction, he and his associates dreamed up the now ubiquitous bought deal, in which brokerage houses compete to buy share issue outright and then sell it, instead of acting as middlemen who sell new shares to the public for a commission. The man who made Cockwell's wishes a reality was Jimmy Connacher, head of Gordon Capital and a close adviser to the Edper Group. Connacher did the first bought deal — with the Royal Bank — in 1983. In the next few years, Connacher perfected the art of the bought deal, and the rest of the investment industry begrudgingly followed suit.

Cockwell also devised highly lucrative strategies for preferred shares, using them to raise cash and buy stakes in companies in ways that attracted little tax for Edper companies. The idea caught on so well in the investment industry at large that a whole new market in preferred share issues developed — until the federal government effectively scuttled it with tax rule changes in 1987.

Cockwell also vastly expanded Edper's influence in the capital markets when he created a merchant bank, Great Lakes Group, in 1984. Overnight, Great Lakes became a giant in the investment industry, with four times the capital of any other dealer at the time. The Edper Group generated so many share issues that Great Lakes Group was assured success. Typically, it took a piece of the action in these myriad offerings, along with outside investment dealers. (Subsequently, in one of the frequent rearrangements of the Edper companies, Great Lakes' investment duties were passed to Trilon, another Edper financial subsidiary.)

Through Hees International Bancorp Inc., Cockwell and his financial disciples have become the busiest workout specialists in Canada. Their modus operandi is to buy stakes in floundering companies, return the companies to health and — in many cases — take over ownership of the rejuvenated assets themselves. This technique usually involves asset grabbing in return for money Hees-related companies have pumped into the troubled company in the form of loans or investments.

The almost forgotten significance of Jack Cockwell's handiwork at the Edper Group is that, in one sense, his revolutionary ideas and obsessive working style proved that industrial enterprises can grow to mammoth proportions without suffering bureaucratic entropy. Until Cockwell came along the accepted thinking in North America was that mature industrial enterprises of the second half of this century would be great hulking bureaucracies, run by highly specialized technocrats trained in the science of modern management. American multinationals such as IBM and General Motors were the models of this brave new organizational world. Cockwell and the dozen or so crackerjack managers he developed as his lieutenants single-handedly proved that big does not necessarily mean slow or bureaucratic. They created a multi-armed conglomerate without sacrificing a fast-moving, lean entrepreneurial style, in which decision-making is never encumbered by layers of management or bureaucratic inertia. Decisions are made by a small group of managers personally picked by Cockwell or Eyton. They are: Bill L'Heureux, a lawyer from Eyton's old firm, Tory Tory, Manfred Walt, Brian McJannet, Michael Cornelissen, Timothy Price, Timothy Casgrain, David Kerr, Kenneth Clarke, George Myal and Norman Gish.

Like piranhas in a goldfish bowl, they scared the investment community out of a somnambulent existence that paid big dividends for a little work over lunch at the club or in a well-appointed corporate dining room. The Edper Group's expansionary designs created a multifaceted conglomerate that, along with budding conglomerates such as the Laurentian Group in Quebec, helped pressure regulators into overhauling financial services rules on cross-ownership, related party transactions and the like. Ultimately, however, this penchant for stepping on well-polished toes, for pushing the rules and regulations to the limit, generated criticisms that Cockwell and his crew were guilty of being too clever by half. Their entrepreneurial image wasn't looking so good to investors by 1991 after 12 months of recession had battered the share values of major companies in the empire. Investors who did their homework found that the annual average increase in market value of Royal Trustco was a meagre 0.4 per cent in the preceding five years. Brascan Ltd.'s was 4.6 per cent, John Labatt's was 6.3 per cent, and Hees International Bancorp scored a slightly better 7.2 per cent annual increase. An investor could have done better investing in Canada Savings Bonds. This state of affairs led one leading business journalist, David Olive, to argue that the Edper managers were right to maintain that Edper does not represent a dangerous concentration of power. Instead, wrote Olive, "it represents a wasteful concentration of power."

Cockwell's influence helps explain why his competitors on the street have come to fear and resent him. "Cockwell is a very tough, mean son of a bitch. He's a financial wizard and he lets everyone know it," says a Bay Street veteran. Another major financial executive is kinder. "That group is a bit controversial. The group is widely feared, but it may be just envy."

The publicly stated goal of the Edper Group has always been to "add shareholder value," yet by the late 1980s, critics were asking which shareholders and what value. The Edper experts had proven themselves masters at moving around cash and assets within the empire and acquiring the assets of outside companies in creeping take-overs without triggering public disclosure requirements or takeover laws that would force them to pay minority shareholders a premium for their shares. Their dealings have become so complex that some major investment managers, such as Montreal-based Stephen Jaris-lowsky, who oversees about $11 billion in pension funds, avoid investing in Edper Group companies.[2]

Cockwell and his team of managers, all large investors in Edper Group companies, were by no means immune to the investing public's disenchantment. It was a strange sight indeed when, in 1990, Cockwell and several managers took to the road in a dog-and-pony show to explain their methods and motivations to select audiences of investment professionals. After one lengthy question-and-answer session at a brokerage house, Cockwell was asked what he and his team had learned from their troubles. "To be more humble," he replied.

The challenge facing Cockwell and his team for the 1990s is to restore the investing public's confidence in their management. That will be tough. Public appearances have never been Cockwell's forte. After he made a testy appearance before a House of Commons sub-committee a few years ago, committee chairman Don Blenkarn remarked: "They should keep that guy in the back, back room." Blenkarn's advice aside, Cockwell will have to get out of the back rooms and into the public eye a little more to reverse the Edper Group's sliding image. It won't be easy for him, But then, he's always been a quick learner.

Paul Reichmann, president, Olympia & York Developments Ltd.

Devout, principled, reclusive, highly strung: many adjectives and nouns are used to describe Paul Reichmann, but powerbroker isn't usually one of them. That's because the man who runs the world's largest private real estate development company likes to operate behind the scenes, far from the prying eyes that corporate chiefs at publicly owned companies have to put up with. Reichmann has cultivated his image as a recluse the way other people cultivate their taste in fine wines. He talks to the media only when it suits him, when he wants to sway public opinion about his company's affairs, and even then it is usually only on background. Media insiders chuckle when they see an article on O&Y quoting a "high-placed company executive." They know it's Reichmann who's talking. In rare on-the-record interviews he is a picture of humility. He brushes off the notion that he is one of the most powerful businessmen in Canada. "It's one thing to have a position of influence; it's another to use it," he told journalist Dianne Maley. "We influence the companies in which we have an interest, but other than that, we do not bring our influence to bear on either business or government."

Insiders in the deal making universe that centres on Bay Street know differently. They say that Reichmann's vast pool of capital ensures that anyone looking to make a deal takes the proposal first to one of two people: Reichmann at his First Canadian Place office or Jack Cockwell at Commerce Court. For most of the 1980s Reichmann was on the buying end of those deals. These days, with Reichmann retrenching after a diversification binge, he is most likely to be on the selling end of deals. But the traffic to his office is busy, just the same.

Unlike Cockwell, Reichmann hasn't changed the way business operates in Canada, but he's had immeasurable influence on the business scene in another way. A devoutly religious man who reads the

Talmud daily for insights into business, Reichmann has irreversibly altered the Anglo-Protestant nature of the business establishment. While the Edper Bronfmans never really bothered to fit in and the Belzbergs are still looking for acceptance, Reichmann has simply been too powerful and successful to ignore.

He sits on the boards of the Canadian Imperial Bank of Commerce and Hollinger Inc., the centre of Conrad Black's media empire, and is a regular at Black's fêtes at the exclusive Toronto Club. Money helps, of course. Sixty-one-year-old Reichmann and his brothers, Albert, 62, and Ralph, 58, were personally worth about $10 billion at last count. Through Toronto-based Olympia & York they run a diversified real estate, energy, newsprint and transportation empire worth about $25 billion, give or take hundreds of millions depending on economic cycles. Their better-known real estate holdings include the World Financial Center in New York, First Canadian Place in Toronto and Canary Wharf in London, England, where they're trying to turn a run-down patch of dockland on the Thames River into Europe's largest collection of office and retail buildings. Apart from real estate, they control well-known giants Gulf Canada Resources Ltd, (oil and gas) and Abitibi-Price (newsprint), and they own large chunks of numerous other companies.

Unlike some of Canada's wealthiest men, the Reichmanns don't sit back and watch their assets grow under the supervision of managers. Although they rely on trusted aides such as Lionel Dodd in Toronto and John Zuccotti in New York, the Reichmanns are both owners and operators. As president, Paul takes a lead role at the company, handling the financial and political negotiating for O&Y's projects, while Albert supervises construction details. Ralph, the other brother, runs the Toronto tile business where the family empire got started a couple of decades ago.

How much real power does Paul Reichmann have? Even power in repose can have a deterrent effect on others. Consider the testimony of a business executive at a 1990 Ontario Energy Board hearing into O&Y's plan to sell Consumers' Gas to British Gas PLC. Warren Hurst, a former executive with Consumers', described how investment dealers shied away when he approached them with his plan to make a counter offer for the Reichmann-controlled company. "I encountered reluctance to be seen opposing Reichmann family interests," said Hurst. For example, Hurst said the Toronto-Dominion Bank indicated that it would organize a banking consortium to finance his bid but only with approval from the Reichmanns and the OEB. That testimony provided a rare glimpse into how power works in Canadian business.

Despite his disclaimers, Reichmann has shown little reluctance to use power overtly to achieve his ends. In 1987, he launched a $102-million lawsuit against *Toronto Life* magazine for what he considered a defamatory article by Elaine Dewar on his family and its origins. The suit became a battle of bank balances. Reichmann spent $3.1 million to hire private investigators to trace Dewar's research. *Toronto Life* spent about $1.5 million on legal bills before the suit was settled out of court. As part of the settlement the magazine ran a full-page abject apology and made an unspecified contribution to charity.

Tall, urbane and soft-spoken, Paul Reichmann is far from gentle, however, with the underlings at work who must deal with his high-strung, demanding presence. Lieutenants who aspire to break into the tight family circle at the top invariably fail.

Reichmann also knows how to court politicians when his business interests are at stake. At the Canary Wharf development, Margaret Thatcher, an unabashed Reichmann fan, sank the first concrete pile. Prime Minister Brian Mulroney was treated to a tour of the development with Reichmann as his personal guide. When the World Financial Center opened in 1988, then New York mayor Ed Koch was among the glittery array of celebrities who attended the ribbon cutting.

The circles of friends Reichmann moves in these days are a social universe away from those of his nomadic youth. Shortly after Reichmann was born in Vienna in 1930, his family fled Hitler's armies, bouncing from France to Spain, then to Morocco, where Reichmann and his four siblings grew up. In 1956, Reichmann and his wife, Lea, emigrated to New York, but finding the New York lifestyle manic, they soon moved on to Toronto, which he later described as being a quiet little town like Birmingham. Brother Ralph was already in Toronto, and Paul teamed up with him to start a small tile business. Albert and the parents, Samuel and René, joined them in 1958.

From those humble beginnings, the Reichmanns grew into North America's wonder boys of real estate. They first came into the public spotlight in 1965, when they bought a package of land in the Toronto suburb of Don Mills for $25 million and paid for it by selling off parcels they did not intend to develop. Their international reputation was sealed in 1977, when they purchased a clutch of New York office towers for the bargain-basement price of $400 million. At the time, New York was on the skids and other developers viewed the properties as dogs. Less than a decade later the buildings were worth about $2 billion. Their next major international coup was the building of the World Financial Center in a run-down portion of Manhattan. They turned the development into a financial success despite skeptics who doubted they could attract tenants away from the financial heart of Manhattan.

Through the 1980s, the family used its burgeoning cash flow to extend its reach beyond real estate. But the keen sense of timing and market judgment that made them such a great success in real estate wasn't easily transferred to other arenas. In 1985, Reichmann paid $2.8 billion for a controlling interest in Gulf Canada, then sold off most of its refineries and service stations to Petro-Canada and kept the exploration and production operations. Reichmann then rolled another newly purchased company, Abitibi-Price, into Gulf to form one large diversified concern. He added Hiram Walker Resources in 1986. Reichmann was adamant that he would form another great Canadian conglomerate, like Canadian Pacific, even though the investment community doesn't like conglomerates because they are large, unwieldly and hard to make sense of. Reichmann persisted. Investors balked. Reichmann relented and unbundled the companies.

That was only mildly embarrassing compared to Reichmann's involvement with Robert Campeau, the Toronto real estate developer who accumulated a $10-billion-plus debt load while taking over prestigious U.S. department stores before his debt got the better of him. Reichmann backed Campeau's purchase of Federated Department Stores in 1988, and when Campeau missed his debt payments a year later, Reichmann bailed out Campeau Corp. by buying a 36 per cent stake in return for a dominant say in its management. Alas, no turnaround was forthcoming, and Reichmann ended up with about $500 million of his money mired in a financial imbroglio.

Now all eyes are on Canary Wharf, where Reichmann has plans to transform 28 hectares of dockland into a busy financial centre by 1992. Renting office space in the development has proven a hard sell for Reichmann, who has had to resort to price slashing to attract tenants. There's no doubt Reichmann overestimated the short-term demand for office space in London, but he has time on his side, especially now that he's arranged bank financing for the construction project rather than relying on O&Y's cash flow.

For Reichmann, like other developers with exposure to the real estate bust in North America, cash flow has become the number-one concern. No one knows how much Reichmann was squeezed by falling office rents and property prices in the 1990–91 slump, since O&Y is a private company, but there were some indications. In 1990, the company put 20 per cent of its U.S. commercial real estate portfolio up for sale — and found no takers in the property-glutted market. Elsewhere, O&Y was busy planning to sell major companies in a drive to reduce long-term debt. Reichmann talked publicly about getting back to two core businesses — real estate development and oil.

If nothing else, Reichmann's business record has gone from miraculous to mixed. He spent the past two decades looking like he had the smartest eye for real estate since Moses found the promised land — until his investments in Campeau Corp. and initial setbacks at Canary Wharf nixed that idea.

Reichmann built his empire by buying property cheap and watching its value soar. These days he's trying to sell at the bottom of the market just like everybody else. Since the 1980s his offices in Toronto have been like Grand Central Station for would-be deal makers, but Reichmann isn't the one listening — he's the one with something to sell.

Bank Power

Bank boards have lost little of their traditional cachet for aspiring powerbrokers. An invitation to join the board of one of the large chartered banks is still an invitation to take a prestigious ringside seat at the arena of business. After all, together the Big Five (the Royal, the Bank of Montreal, the Canadian Imperial Bank of Commerce, the Bank of Nova Scotia, and the Toronto-Dominion) control more than $400 billion in assets.

But the banks no longer have a monopoly on the best seats in the house. Their financial clout has been eroded in the past two decades by several major developments. Most importantly, rival sources of capital have sprung up that have deprived the bankers of their veto power over deals and careers in the broader business community. Institutional investors such as pension funds, life insurance companies, trust companies and mutual fund companies now command more than $1 trillion in assets. Foreign banks are crowding into the Canadian marketplace, vying with the domestic banks for the lucrative commercial lending market. And once-loyal corporate customers of the banks are taking advantage of alternative sources of funding. The Reichmanns, for instance, now prefer to arrange their long-term financing with insurance companies and pension funds.

Increasingly, big corporate customers are bypassing bank loan officers and raising money by selling debt securities to investors in Canada and abroad. In an effort to keep up with the competition, Canadian banks have belatedly jumped into the investment business. In the past few years, five chartered banks have bought investment dealers with well-established investment banking expertise.[3] Another, the Toronto-Dominion, started its own investment operation.

But now there is too much capital chasing too few deals. The banks are competing among themselves for deals as well as with veteran Canadian players like Hees International Bancorp, Trilon Financial, Gordon Capital and sharp foreign interlopers like Citibank, HongKong Bank of Canada, Barclays and BT Bank of Canada.

So bank chairmen are no longer the unchallenged arbiters of business deals they were just a couple of decades ago. But there is one bank chairman who stands out from his counterparts thanks to his ability to keep his bank at the forefront of change in the deal-making universe. Ask almost any business leader in Canada to name the best banker in Canada, and the answer is virtually unanimous: Dick Thomson, chairman and CEO, the Toronto-Dominion Bank.

Most weekdays, 58-year-old Dick Thomson takes a break from work at 11:30 a.m. and heads over to the Cambridge Club, in the nearby Sheraton Centre. There, he has a light work-out and then a sandwich at a communal table with a few other regulars. By big-business standards, this is not power dining. The Cambridge is open to anyone who can put up the $3,000 initiation fee — with the notable exception of women.

Thomson doesn't go in for the trappings of power and wealth. Even though he earns more than $1 million a year, he still lives in the modest north Toronto home he bought 20 years ago with his wife, Heather, and their four children. His office on the eleventh floor of the T-D Centre is modestly furnished considering his post. There's a cherry credenza, a chrome and marble desk, a few Inuit carvings and little else. The simplicity reflects Thomson's low-key personality. An engineer by training, he's a man of few words and he abhors financial excess.

Since he became chief executive in 1977, Thomson has paid attention to innovation, not ostentation. He's combined the parsimony of a good branch manager with strategic innovations that have made the T-D Bank the most profitable in Canada for years, with the exception of 1990 when the bank's exposure to Ontario real estate loans dampened its profits. Thomson has won ungrudging admiration in the business community. Says the head of a competing financial conglomerate: "There's a lot of respect for his ability to run his bank. He's highest on the list of bankers. Very intelligent."

Thomson was born in Winnipeg in August 1933, the son of Harold Thomson, a local bank branch manager. Harold was a high-school dropout who spent decades with the bank and eventually worked his way up to vice-chairman by the time he retired in 1971. Eldest son Dick became a career banker like his dad, but not before getting an outstanding education. Dick Thomson earned an engineering degree at the University of Toronto and followed it up with a Harvard MBA. Inspired by his father, Thomson eschewed more glamorous jobs and joined the T-D in 1957, just two years after it was formed by a merger of the Bank of Toronto and the Dominion bank. Thomson began as a ledger clerk at an east-end Toronto branch, a job that seemed like financial oblivion to the newly minted Harvard grad. But he was rescued from obscurity in 1963, when Allen Lambert, then T-D's president, asked Thomson to become his assistant. Thomson obviously shone in his new job. He was made chief general manager at head office in 1968, became vice-president and director in 1971 and just a year later, at age 39, was named president.[4]

Thomson has carried out two revolutions at the bank. He began his first revolution in the early 1970s when he hired young, well-educated MBA grads like himself as managers. For customers, he began courting emerging industries. For the past decade, the T-D has outperformed all Canadian banks and most American banks. Although the T-D was a big lender to Dome Petroleum, the energy albatross, it kept its exposure to less developed countries (LDCs) lower than most banks, then moved aggressively to boost its reserves against loan losses and slash back its LDC loan portfolio by selling bad loans to other banks and corporations.

While other banks were saddled with more traditional authoritarian leaders, like Russ Harrison at CIBC and Bill Mulholland of the Bank of Montreal, Thomson was distinguished for his team approach to management. Together with Robin Korthals, his indispensable president, Thomson today runs a lean team with few layers of management. Unlike the other big banks, there has been no outpouring of management talent from the T-D, thanks to Thomson's management style. There is one problem, however: Thomson and his senior managers are closing in on retirement age together, with no obvious successors. The next level of managers are young turks in their 40s.

Currently, Thomson is in the midst of his second revolution. As the traditional loan business of banks declines, Thomson is leading the T-D into the investment banking and insurance fields. Overall, his strategy is to reshape the bank into a giant North American merchandiser of custom-designed financial services. "If we can devise a more efficient way of serving the customer, that's how we are going to grow," Thomson has said. "You either grow and prosper or you die."

Pension Fund Power

Ask the average Canadian to name the country's top business powerbrokers and he or she would likely rhyme off names like Bronfman, Thomson, Weston and Irving. The family business dynasties have certainly received the most coverage in the media and in business books. but there is a little-known group of men who surpass Canada's business dynasties both in financial assets and in influence in the capital and stock markets. They are the managers of Canada's huge pension funds. At the end of 1989, trusteed pension funds had $175 billion in assets, more than three times the total net worth of Canada's 50 richest families. The funds own big chunks of just about every sizable publicly traded company in Canada, and in many cases are the largest shareholders. About 28 per cent of their assets, or $50 billion, is invested in Canadian stocks. By comparison, the total value of the shares listed on the Toronto Stock Exchange was only $168 billion at the end of 1989. Experts estimate that by 1994, the value of pension fund assets could grow to about $350 billion.

More than any other force, pension funds, which invest money for thousands of Canadians, have rearranged the configuration of power in Canadian business. They have become the only players with enough influence to protect the interests of the little person against irresponsible actions by corporate executives.

This phenomenon has occurred only in the past decade or so. Traditionally, pension fund managers have been regarded as third-rate talents who passively invest cash. Recently, however, they have become active investors who are willing to challenge the managements of the companies they invest in. A man who runs one of the largest pension funds in Canada is Robert Silcox, director of investments for the Ontario Municipal Employees Retirement System (OMERS). From his downtown Toronto office, Silcox oversees about $12 billion worth of investments on behalf of 200,000 fire fighters, police officers and other municipal workers across Ontario.

Head of OMERS since 1988, Silcox has had no choice but to become an outspoken opponent of management behaviour that hurts his fund's interests as a shareholder. "We don't like to get involved in the boardroom," he says, slouching his six-foot frame into his chair, "but we see things happening that hurt our rate of return."

Silcox has spent a lot of time lately fighting so-called poison pill plans put in place by more than 50 Canadian corporations. Management calls them shareholder rights plans because, typically, they are corporate bylaws intended to fight off hostile takeover attempts. Often, they strip would-be acquisitors of voting rights on the shares they hold, or entitle other shareholders to buy stock cheap if a raider buys up a big chunk of stock. Silcox thinks they are intended to protect management more than shareholders. "They're a whole bunch of weasel words put together by the legal fraternity and the investment banking fraternity to keep management in place," he says.

Big pension fund managers like Silcox, Tullio Cedraschi, president of CN Rail's $6.9-billion fund, Peter de Auer, director of Ontario Hydro's $4.1-billion fund, and Montreal investment counsellor Stephen Jarislowsky, who invests well over $10 billion for several pension plans, have taken on managements with increasing frequency since 1988. That was the year the pension fund industry was galvanized into action by Canadian Tire's owners, the Billes family, who made a deal to sell 49 per cent of the company to a group of Canadian Tire dealers at a hefty premium over the market price. The problem was that the offer excluded nonvoting shareholders. "It was the first time that institutional investors really had to take a stand," recalls Silcox, who was at Metropolitan Life at the time. The institutions fought back before the securities regulators and won.

Since then, most of the fights have been over poison pills. OMERS has voted against almost every poison pill plan introduced in Canada since Inco began the trend in 1988. "Alcan, CP and all those others, we voted against them," says Silcox. "Very often those boards and managers have owned practically no shares. They're not owners." In most cases, OMERS managed to have the poison pill watered down.

In 1990, OMERS went so far as to take a company to court to protect its interests. OMERS filed personal suits against the directors of Xerox Canada because it objected to the company's plan to swap voting shares for nonvoting shares that would then be convertible into shares of the U.S. parent. OMERS saw the plan as a thinly veiled takeover by the parent company. In court it contended that the conversion price was too low and was not subjected to a proper fairness test by either independent directors or outside experts. The case was eventually settled out of court. The plan went ahead.

Pension fund managers like to play down their role, even though the managers are becoming increasingly influential. Silcox, a former U.S. Navy lieutenant who went on to be an investment specialist at the Bank of Montreal and Metropolitan Life before joining OMERS, is typical. He'd prefer to be a wallflower than a public pundit; he sees himself as a humble fiduciary whose job is to earn top returns for pension plan members. "I'm a free enterpriser with no hidden agenda," he says.

There are limits to the power of pension funds like OMERS. By law they can't organize themselves into groups to fight managements. Instead, they rely on outside investment counsellors and stockbrokers to orchestrate shareholder revolts, which they then join. Another law limits their investment in any one company to 30 per cent of its shares. This means they have to band together with other shareholders to win a vote against management. But since most Canadian companies are closely held by a controlling shareholder, there are few where disgruntled shareholders can assemble a majority vote. Nevertheless, as the country's capital and stock markets become the exclusive playground of large investors, it's nice to know that someone is going to bat for ordinary Canadians.

Wheeler-dealers, but not stealers

There are numerous ways to make it to the top in business. There's the take-no-prisoners school perfected by the Irvings in New Brunswick; or the shout-until-they-give-in method that helped make Garth Drabinsky a movie house mogul for a time. Other tycoons have got ahead by hiring good help or by wooing politicians for government contracts. It's rare to find business successes who have got ahead on pure business skill — and have gained the often begrudging respect of their peers for it. Here are the men who've managed it.

Peter Bentley, chairman and CEO, Canfor Corp., Vancouver is a good example. From his West Coast headquarters, Bentley runs a sizable forest products company, which is one of the world's largest producers of pulp and paper and provides most of the wood panelling bought by Canadians. Yet he is more than just another regional forestry executive. In Vancouver circles he's regarded as a gracious aristocrat. He's tapped in to central Canadian powerbroking by virtue of his seat on the board of the Bank of Montreal. And his international connections are just as sound. He sits on the International Advisory Board of Chemical Bank in New York.

Bentley's polar opposite in personality is *Jimmy Pattison*, the 63-year-old owner and CEO of the Jimmy Pattison Group, B.C.'s largest private company. Pattison has built the company from a used-car dealership into a money machine with operations in grocery retailing, broadcasting, magazine distribution and electric signs. As brash as he is energetic, Pattison busted his way into the Vancouver Establishment by becoming too influential to ignore. He was the one-man dynamo behind Vancouver's Expo 86, but in the process of making it a success, earned a reputation for having an ego second to no-one. A Christian fundamentalist, Pattison plays the trumpet and loves to eat at McDonald's. Pattison likes to fly in such notables as Ronald Reagan and Margaret Thatcher to give pep talks to his staff. But he wouldn't be caught dead in the Vancouver Club, even though it relented a few years back and made him a member. He attended once to celebrate the event, then never showed up again. Yet for all his bluster, he's earned a reputation as one of Canada's few successful modern-day entrepreneurs. He has seats on the boards of the Toronto-Dominion Bank and Crown Life Insurance.

You have to travel east to Winnipeg to find corporate bosses to match Bentley and Pattison in terms of success, and survival instincts. One such is *George Richardson*, president and managing director, James Richardson and Sons Ltd. and chairman, Richardson Greenshields Securities Inc. Richardson is the great-grandson of company founder James Richardson and since he took over as head of the family grain business in 1966 he has expanded it by purchasing rival elevator operators and building terminals at the Lakehead and on the West Coast. In 1989 he tried to sell the family investment company, Richardson Greenshields, but there were no takers. For decades

Richardson has been the most powerful businessman in Manitoba. He is now 67, and his influence is fading somewhat. But he still sits on the boards of Inco, Canada Packers and Du Pont Canada.

The other Winnipeger with a profile to match Richardson's is *Jack Fraser*, chairman and founder, Federal Industries Ltd. Fraser is known in business circles across Canada as the man who took a sad collection of money-losing companies and turned it into a profitable conglomerate. He took over at Federal Industries in 1978 and immediately began building the company in his own image. He ditched money losers and expanded into steel distribution, consumer products, electrical manufacturing, trucking and bookselling. He remains based in Winnipeg but he carries clout in central Canada, where he spends much of his time attending board meetings of Thomson Corp, the Bank of Montreal and Air Canada. By the early 1990s, however, he was spending most of his time trying to revive the sagging stock market fortunes of his conglomerate, which, like other conglomerates, had fallen out of favour in the investment community.

While it's hard to find a top-ranked tycoon in Montreal who made it to the top without sweetheart government deals, Toronto's doyens of dealmaking range from the rough hewn to the refined.

Probably no one has less time for corporate niceties or protocol than *Jimmy Connacher*, chairman and CEO, Gordon Capital Group. A university dropout, Connacher began his brokerage career at Wood Gundy and later joined Gordon, where he established his reputation as a maverick with no patience for the time-honoured ways of doing business on Bay Street. Connacher was shut out of the clubby circle of investment dealers who had a monopoly on lucrative underwriting deals for major corporate clients. In response, he pioneered the bought deal, in which Gordon bought new share issues outright and then resold them. He's been helped along by his tight ties with the Brascan group of companies, which are always buying or selling some company or issuing new shares. Those who have worked for Connacher say he can be as irascible as a bear after hibernation. One rookie trader was upbraided for being too pleasant to clients on the phone. "He told me I'd make it if I tried being less nice," she recalls.

His legendary moxie has kept him at the heart of the deal-making universe.

Jack Lawrence, chairman and CEO, Burns Fry Ltd., is just as tough, but uses the velvet glove approach. A low-key, backroom operator in the investment community, Lawrence made his name as a money market specialist. His political links are strong. Most notably he influences national fiscal policy through personal contacts with Michael Wilson as well as with Finance Department officials. His rating on Bay Street soared after his 1987 deal to sell 30 per cent of Burns Fry to Security Pacific, the U.S. banking giant. The deal was viewed as the best in a rash of broker/bank marriages on Bay Street because Burns got a good price and kept a high degree of independence. Since then, the marriage has shown signs of strain. Lawrence doesn't like taking orders from anybody.

For old Toronto attitudes it's hard to beat *Hal Jackman*, chairman and president of E-L Financial Corp. Ltd. Known for his sagebrush eyebrows, eight-inch cigars and the perpetual twinkle in his eye, Jackman is an outspoken doyen of the Toronto business establishment. He inherited his wealth from his stockbroker father, but he's established his own track record building up his trust and insurance interests into a $1.8-billion conglomerate. Jackman is known for his willingness to shoot off his mouth whenever he feels like it, usually at bankers. He spends most of his time these days working for arts and cultural committees, and almost single-handedly led the campaign to finance a new ballet-opera house in Toronto, which fell apart when governments reneged on funding plans. But that was a reflection of the mood of austerity, not Jackman's prowess at pulling purse strings.

Jackman's equal in the profile/clout rankings in Toronto is *Allan Taylor*, chairman and CEO of the Royal Bank of Canada. As head of the country's largest bank, Taylor is consulted by politicians and courted by business tycoons, no mean accomplishment for a guy who began his career at 16 as a bank clerk in Prince Albert, Saskatchewan, and never went to university. Unlike his more voluble predecessor, Rowland Frazee, Taylor exerts a quiet influence in government and business circles. He sits on the boards of some of Canada's largest corporations, including General Motors of Canada, Canadian Pacific Ltd. and TransCanada PipeLines Ltd. In addition, he exerts influence on the world economy through his role as a director of the International Monetary Conference.

The East Coast businessman who has earned the least blemished respect, nationwide, is *Harrison McCain*, chairman, McCain Foods Ltd. of Florenceville, New Brunswick: Harrison and his brother Wallace, president of the company, set up a frozen french-fry processing business in the late 1950s and have since turned it into a flourishing international player. McCains is now the world's largest french-fry producer, with plants on three continents. They have also expanded into microwave breakfasts, orange juice and pizza. The company has captured 90 per cent of the french-fry market in France and has a major share of the markets in Britain, the Netherlands, Belgium and Australia. Yet the McCain brothers have never been tempted to relocate from the town where they were born and raised.

The Hired Guns: The Lawyers

Any assessment of who makes deals happen in Canadian business has to include the middlemen — the securities, tax and corporate lawyers who move silently in the boardrooms of the nation advising the owners of capital on how best to deploy it during expansion binges, corporate dogfights and takeover wars.

Until he left Davies Ward and Beck in 1990 to run the Canadian merchant banking arm of Rothschilds Bank, Garfield Emmerson, lawyer to the Reichmann family, was considered the leading securities lawyer in Canada. Now the mantle is up for grabs among Peter Beattie (McCarthy Tétrault), James Baillie, (Tory, Tory, DesLauriers & Binnington), Ed Waitzer and John Stransman (Stikeman Elliot) and William Howard (Howard, Mackie in Calgary).

The top practitioners of corporate and commercial law in the country are Jim Tory, (Tory, Tory, DesLauriers & Binnington), Eddie Goodman (Goodman & Goodman), Morley Koffman (Freeman &

Co. of Vancouver), John Elder (Fraser & Beatty), William Mingo (Stewart McCain, Covert in Halifax), Francis (Frank) Murphy (Farris, Vaughn Mills and Murphy in Vancouver) and Claude Ducharme (Desjardins, Ducharme of Montreal).

The most sought after corporate tax lawyers are Arthur Scace (McCarthy Tétrault) and David Ward (Davies Ward and Beck), who is the chief legal adviser to the Reichmanns.

Outside counsel is handy for corporate chiefs, but loyal, well-trained right-hand men are still better. Over time these lieutenants can acquire power second only to the wealthy bosses who hired them. Take John A. Tory, right-hand man to Ken Thomson for example. A lawyer by training, Tory has served as Thomson's able administrator, strategist and sometime executioner for so long it's hard to tell who is more responsible for the success of the enterprise. In the process, Tory has expanded his family's blue-blood legal tradition into the corporate realm as well. A member of the business establishment in his own right, Tory sits on 12 boards.

Senator Leo Kolber, also a lawyer, has served much the same role for the Montreal Bronfmans as chairman of Claridge Inc., the family investment vehicle. That role has helped vault him into board seats at the Toronto-Dominion Bank and several Bronfman companies. Unfortunately, however, he also helped get the family's money tangled up in Garth Drabinsky's ill-fated adventures at Cineplex Odeon, the theatre chain. Tsk, tsk.

Another trusty power behind the throne is Lionel Dodd (actually an MBA, not a lawyer), who serves Paul Reichmann as chief operating officer, Olympia & York Enterprises. The Reichmanns acquired Dodd when they bought control of Gulf Canada, and he's risen in influence ever since, although even he couldn't do much to help the family out of its disastrous investment in Campeau Corp. As reclusive and religious as his bosses, Dodd oversees the family's equity interests while the Reichmann brothers search for new real-estate opportunities in Europe and Asia.

Power Shifts:
The Old and New Regional Kingpins of Finance

"They say," wrote Byron, "that knowledge is power. I used to think so, but I now know that they meant money."

Money is no easy taskmaster. Capturing it requires devotion, mental discipline and single-mindedness bordering on obsession. Keeping it is almost as tough, and losing it takes no effort at all. The men and women who toil for cash think and talk about deals the way ordinary folk discuss daycare or baseball scores. Some hide their obsession better than others; they affect a studied disregard for capital even as they ponder how to make more of it. There's no such thing as part-time work in the money-spinning business. Take your eyes off it and it'll be in someone else's pocket before you know it.

The fastest way to make money for yourself is to do deals using other people's money. Here's a roundup of the doyens, old and new, of money making in Canada's three major centres of finance, as well as a list of the rising stars of the discipline, whose power flows from their access to someone else's cash.

Vancouver: The city that celebrates cash is still home to investment veterans like Peter Brown (LOM Western Securities Limited), promoter Murray Pezim and back-from-the-dead real estate impresarios Nelson Skalbania and Jack Poole. The future belongs to such newer deal makers as Larry Lunn, CEO of Connor, Clark & Lunn, a fast-growing pension fund manager in Vancouver; James Cleave, CEO, Hongkong Bank of Canada; and Asian imports like Victor Lee (real estate), David Ho (soft drinks) and Ron Shon (real estate).

In Toronto and Montreal, there are still plenty of Old Guard bank and trust company chiefs with their hands on money spigots. They are:

The bankers: Matthew Barrett (Montreal), Cedric Ritchie (Scotia), Don Fullerton (CIBC), Dick Thomson (T-D), Allan Taylor (Royal), André Berard (National).

The Trust bosses: Michael Cornelissen (Royal Trust), Leonard Ellen (Central Guaranty Trustco), Peter Maurice (Canada Trust),

Brian Mehlenbacher (National Trust), Robert Gratton (Montreal Trust), and Maurice Myrand (General Trustco).

Then there are investment industry veterans: Leighton McCarthy (McCarthy Securities), Latham Burns and Peter Eby (Burns Fry Ltd.), Tony Fell (RBC Dominion), Chuck Winograd (Richardson Greenshields), Austin Taylor (ScotiaMcLeod), Garrett Herman and Peter Cole (Loewen Ondaatje McCutcheon), Jack Lawrence (Burns Fry), Bill Allen (Allenvest), André Charron and Pierre Brunet, (Lévesque Beaubien Geoffrion).

The rising stars of the investment industry are Lawrence Bloomberg (First Marathon Inc.), Brian Steck (Nesbitt Thomson Deacon), Gordon Cheesebrough (ScotiaMcLeod), Eric Sprott (Sprott Securities), Irwin Michael (I.A. Michael Investment Counsel), Paul Bates (Marathon Discount Brokerage).

Several investment managers and counsellors also rank in the upper echelons of deal-making. They are: Andy Sarlos (Sarlos and Associates), Bob Foster (Capital Canada), Stephen Jarislowsky (Jarislowsky Fraser), Austin Beutel (Beutel Goodman), Ned Goodman (Dynamic Capital), Jean Claude Delorme (Caisse de Dépôt).

But as more and more Canadians opt for mutual funds over direct stock market investments, the fund managers have risen to prominence. Among the best: Alex Christ (Mackenzie Financial), Robert Krembil and Arthur Labatt (Trimark), Mitchell Bourke, Robert Jones and Jean-Luc Landry (Bolton Tremblay), Frank Mersch (Altamira), Harold Hillier (Talvest), Don Reed (Templeton Management) John Embry (RoyFund Equity), Patrick Foster and Richard Wernham (Global Strategy Financial), Brian McDermott (Cundhill Value Fund).

Masters of Political Persuasion

Paul Desmarais, Power Corp.
Paul Desmarais is the godparent of French-Canadian businessmen. The Sudbury-born phenomenon ranks as the country's wealthiest

French Canadian, worth about $500 million. He's the architect and CEO of Power Corp. of Montreal, a $2.3-billion conglomerate with financial services holdings in Canada and Europe, including Great-West Life Assurance and the Investors Group of Winnipeg. Power Corp.'s publishing arm includes *La Presse*, one of the largest French-language dailies in Montreal. At 64, Desmarais is the longest-standing member of Canada's business elite. He was at its pinnacle when Peter Newman first chronicled the business establishment in 1975, and he remains at its pinnacle today. "He's a legendary figure," says Stephen Jarislowsky, the prominent Montreal investment counsellor, who observes that Desmarais has shown other French Canadian entrepreneurs that they have what it takes to "play in the big leagues."

What's less well known about Desmarais is that he is a political junkie who has made a career of nurturing political contacts that can assist his business objectives. Desmarais's political tactics aren't likely to be taught in any commerce course at university, but they arguably have played a crucial role in his success. Traditionally, Canada's corporate tycoons have taken the attitude that the only good politician is the one who leaves them alone. For much of his career, Desmarais has been Canada's most prominent exception to the rule.

Initially, of course, he wasn't the sort of player who could even get politicians to answer his phone calls. His journey to the top began in Sudbury, Ontario, where he was born in January 1927 to Lebea and Jean, a local lawyer and businessman. After earning a commerce degree at the University of Ottawa, Desmarais began his business career at age 25 as the head of the family's nearly bankrupt Sudbury bus line. His father wanted to sell the company, but when Paul asked to buy it, his father gave it to him. Managing the bus line, a fore-runner of Voyageur Colonial, was a struggle at the start. Finances were so tight that Desmarais did maintenance himself on its 19 buses and sometimes paid his drivers with bus tickets. Bounced payroll cheques and showdowns with local bankers over loans were not uncommon.

Then Desmarais got a break. Inco, the local mining giant, gave him the contract to operate a bus service between Sudbury and a mine in Copper Cliff. (Inco also threw in the money to launch the service.) With the cash flow from the Copper Cliff service, Desmarais was able to pay off his $380,000 debt load and get into the black.

By the 1960s, he was able to buy another bus line in Montreal. Once on his feet, he didn't waste any time building a conglomerate. By 1965 he had assembled 15 companies into an operation called Trans-Canada Corporate Fund. In 1967 he branched into publishing by forming a partnership that bought eight small newspapers. In 1968, Desmarais made the most crucial move of his career. He took control of Power Corp., a cash-rich holding company, by rolling his assets into it in return for 50 per cent of Power Corp.'s shares. Along with Power Corp., Desmarais picked up control of the corporate gems in its stable, which included Canada Steamship Lines and Consolidated Bathurst, the giant newsprint maker.

Desmarais's next major strategic move came in 1969, when he bought control of Great-West Life, one of the country's largest life insurance companies, after a takeover battle with Peter and Edward Bronfman. In 1970, he acquired control of Investors Group, the highly profitable Winnipeg-based mutual fund and financial services company. By the mid-1970s, Desmarais was sitting on top of a corporate empire with about $7 billion in assets.

Today although Desmarais has sold off several major Power Corp. subsidiaries, including Canada Steamship Lines, Consolidated Bathurst and Montreal Trustco, his corporate commonwealth remains one of the largest in Canada. Power Financial, Power Corp.'s major subsidiary, controls Great-West Life Assurance ($19 billion in assets) and Investors Group ($2 billion in assets) and holds a 23 per cent stake in Pargesa Holdings S.A., a huge Belgian financial and industrial company.

Desmarais may not have built his empire using political connections, but once it was established, its reach was so diverse that it made good business sense to keep on top of political developments that could hurt his interests. Tall, shy and afflicted with a stutter, Desmarais is hardly a social butterfly, but he loves to mingle with the powerful, particularly prime ministers and other politicians. "He simply likes to hang around with other powerful people," says a Montreal friend.

Desmarais's parties are more like parliamentary reunions than social gatherings. In 1983, he threw a New Year's Eve bash at his Palm Springs villa that drew Brian Mulroney, Pierre Trudeau, Trudeau confidant Jim Coutts, Ontario premier Bill Davis and several Liberal and Conservative senators. They mingled with celebrities like Estée Lauder and Douglas Fairbanks, Jr. The 1984 wedding of his daughter Sophie attracted Trudeau, Mulroney, Jean Chrétien, governor general Jeanne Sauvé and businessmen Conrad Black, Charles Bronfman, George Richardson and Jean de Grandpré.

Desmarais is intensely loyal to his political friends. He was a strong supporter of Trudeau during the 1980 Quebec referendum on separation and has remained a friend of Mulroney even when the popularity polls were showing the Tories at new depths. Desmarais was one of the few who stuck behind Quebec premier Robert Bourassa during his unpopular first term in office. "He even supported Bourassa when others gave up on him," says a friend. That support, of course, proved prescient, since Bourassa came back from the political wilderness to win the premiership again.

Sometimes, Desmarais's eagerness to court politicians, no matter what their stripe, has lead to difficulty. In 1982, he teamed up with the Parti Québécois to attempt a takeover of Canadian Pacific. But under pressure from his blue-chip business confrères, he later did an about face, dropped the bid and left the PQ dangling.

When Desmarais is not meeting politicians at parties, he likes to bump into them in the hallways of Power Corp.'s offices at Victoria Square in downtown Montreal. He's long made a habit of hiring out-of-work politicians. Observes a Toronto investment counsellor: "When a national politician is looking for a job, Desmarais is there. Look at the Trudeau Liberals. Many of Trudeau's cabinet ended up working for Desmarais. If Mulroney were defeated, the same thing would happen. That's what gives businessmen the most influence."

Consider Desmarais's present and past payrolls. Power Corp. vice-president John Rae, brother of Bob, the Ontario premier, was an executive assistant to Jean Chrétien in the late 1960s and later became Chrétien's national campaign chairman. That's just fine by Desmarais. He and his wife, Jacqueline, are close friends of Chrétien and his wife, Aline. Desmarais's second son, André, married Chrétien's daughter France in 1981. Power vice-chairmen include Senators Michael Pitfield, former clerk of the Privy Council for Trudeau, and former senator John B. Aird. Power Corp.'s directors include former

Ontario premier Bill Davis, now a lawyer with Toronto's Tory, Tory, DesLauriers & Binnington, and William Simon, former U.S. treasury secretary. Power Corp. also has a prestigious international panel of advisers, which includes Trudeau, Sheik Ahmed Zaki Yamani, former U.S. Federal Reserve Board chairman Paul Volcker and former West German chancellor Helmut Schmidt.

Previous Power Corp. employees include Bryce Mackasey, a Trudeau cabinet minister; Paul Martin, Jr., a Liberal leadership contender in 1990 who ran Canada Steamship Lines for Desmarais before acquiring it himself; multi-talented Maurice Strong, whose political connections span the globe; and Tony Hampson, who went on to head Crown-owned Canada Development Corp. Former board members include Jean-Luc Pepin, ex-minister of industry, trade and commerce in the Trudeau government; John Robarts, former premier of Ontario; and Jean-Paul Gignac, then president of Sidbec, the Quebec-owned steel company.

Desmarais rarely takes public stands on political issues. For instance, during the showdown over the Meech Lake accord in 1990, Desmarais was one of the few major Quebec businessmen who didn't speak out in favour of the deal. Privately, though, he was deeply troubled by the strife it caused. He backed Mulroney's desperate attempt to win the support of Newfoundland Premier Clyde Wells by journeying to St. John's for a private dinner at the premier's residence — to no avail. (Later in the spring of 1991, Desmarais finally spoke out in favour of a united Canada.)

Desmarais is slowing down his work pace these days, as he prepares to pass control of his empire to sons Paul, Jr., chairman of Power Financial, and André, an executive with Gesca Ltée., Power Corp.'s publishing arm. But friends say his influence has never been greater in Ottawa, which at least assured him input into the federal government's new legislation governing financial services. His pull in Montreal hasn't slipped, either: "We would not think of doing something important in Montreal without consulting Charles Bronfman and Paul Desmarais," says Lavalin chairman Bernard Lamarre.

Politics is a dangerous sport for any businessman to engage in. But Desmarais has avoided being caught on the losing side by spreading money and moral support to both Liberal and Conservative politicians. That should stand him in good stead in the next election, when good buddy Mulroney runs against Desmarais's old family friend Jean Chrétien, the Liberal leader. A wily businessman should never get caught backing only one political horse.

Laurent Beaudoin, Bombardier Inc., Montreal

As CEO of a $900 million transportation and aerospace conglomerate, Laurent Beaudoin specializes in transporting people, whether that be on the company's transit cars, Challenger jets or snarling snowmobiles. Whether they know it or not, Canadian taxpayers have been generously paying part of the fare for decades. A good many of the major contracts the Montreal company has won have been subsidized by taxpayers' money.

Beaudoin, 53, sits on prestigious boards, including those of Alcan Aluminium, BCE Inc. and T.C.C. Beverages, otherwise known as Coca Cola Canada. He frequents the Ritz Carlton dining room, favoured lair of Quebec businesspeople, and is a vice-president of the Boy Scouts of Canada. But Beaudoin is not known as a glad hander who constantly mingles with politicians. He has a couple of ex-politicians on his board — former Liberal cabinet minister Jean Pierre Goyer and former Alberta premier Peter Lougheed — but he doesn't publicly support any one political party. That strategy has paid off, judging from his unsurpassed record at winning financial favours from governments of all stripes.

For instance, the Quebec government helped Bombardier make the transition from Ski-Doos to transit vehicles. After Bombardier's 1975 acquisition of a Montreal locomotive manufacturer went sour, the provincial government bailed out the company with a $6.8-million rescue package.

The federal government has always been there for Bombardier to lean on, too. In 1982, the Export Development Corporation helped Bombardier win a landmark $1-billion contract to make 825 subway cars for New York City by offering the buyer U.S.$750 million in loans at 9.5 per cent. (At the time, interest rates for the rest of us topped 20 per cent.) In 1986, Bombardier bought Crown-owned Canadair Ltd. for a mere $120 million after Ottawa absorbed $2.2 billion in debt and development expenses incurred by the aircraft maker.

That same year, Bombardier's clout in Ottawa helped it to win the maintenance contract on Canada's CF-18 fighter, even though Winnipeg's Bristol Aerospace made a technically superior, lower-cost bid.

Bombardier's sweet-talking ways have won it concessions from the British government, as well. In 1989, Bombardier bought Short Brothers PLC, a Belfast commuter-jet maker, from the U.K. government for $60 million. In return, the government gave Bombardier $200 million in grants and underwrote $1.3 billion in debt financing.

This is not to negate Beaudoin's business skills, which are considerable. Born in Laurier Station, in Quebec's Eastern Townships, he earned a Masters of Commerce degree from the University of Sherbrooke in 1960 and qualified as a chartered accountant in 1961. Beaudoin joined Bombardier in 1963, four years after marrying the daughter of company founder Joseph-Armand Bombardier. After his father-in-law's death in 1965, Beaudoin took over as president, and in the following years he transformed Bombardier from a floundering snowmobile company into a flourishing multinational with annual sales approaching $1.5 billion, 80 per cent of which are earned internationally. Beaudoin has sold urban transit vehicles to New York City, Boston, Amtrak and Disney World in Florida. He's also bought stakes in French, Belgian and Austrian railway and urban transit makers to exploit the European market. A quiet-spoken hard-driving guy, Beaudoin is well liked, both at work and after hours at the Mount Royal Club. "He did some intelligent planning and shrewd manoeuvres to build his company into an international player," says a Montreal businessman. Beaudoin has said that the secret of competing worldwide is "to choose your niche, then exploit it by motivating your people through a highly decentralized organization." Judging from his track record, that's only the half of it.

Bernard Lamarre, Consultant, SNC-Lavalin, Montreal

Lamarre, the 60-year-old former CEO of Lavalin Ltd. of Montreal, a once-proud engineering multinational, makes Beaudoin look like a wallflower when it comes to massaging political egos. "Lamarre is the most political animal I've ever met in my life," says a Montreal investment executive. Lamarre openly admits that he courts politicians. "I don't belong to any party, but I know all the politicians," he says with an irrepressible grin. Personal charisma and contacts helped Lamarre build his privately owned company into an international operation with 6,000 employees and annual revenues of more than $1 billion.

A key strategy was to hire out-of-work politicians. Some examples: Marcel Masse spent a reprieve from politics with Lavalin before going on to become a federal Conservative minister; Yves Bérubé, former Parti Québécois minister of natural resources, is another political refugee hired by Lamarre. Bérubé became president of Lavalin's engineering unit.

Nurturing political ties is a wise strategy for a company like Lavalin, which relies on government contracts for its livelihood. In Canada, Lavalin's record included hefty engineering contracts for the 1976 Olympic site and the massive James Bay Development project. Abroad, Lavalin had to deal with everything from Communist bureaucrats to military potentates to win projects in more than 100 countries.

A native of Chicoutimi, Quebec, Lamarre is one of 11 children born to Emile Lamarre and his wife, Blanche. Like his father, Lamarre became an engineer, earning a civil engineering degree at Ecole Polytechnique de Montréal and a Masters in engineering at the University of London. While at school he met his wife, Louise Lalonde, and later joined her father's construction firm. He went on to change it from a modest schoolhouse builder into a worldwide construction company. CEO from 1972 to 1991, Lamarre recently merged the company with rival engineering company SNC and remains a consultant to the new firm. He's also a leading social light in Montreal, where he chairs the high-profile Montreal Museum of Fine Arts and frequents the Mount Royal Club and Club Saint-Denis.

A back-slapper in public, Lamarre was a butt-kicker at his company, where he ran an autocratic show. He saves most of his charm for arm-twisting politicians. "He has the ability to make everyone think they are his best friend," says a business peer who has watched Lamarre work a room. "He must have been a masseur in his previous life."

The irony is that Lamarre's cajoling did not work on his bankers. It was pressure from his lenders, including the National Bank which was owed $100 million, that forced him to give up control of the company he had built.

Desmarais, Lamarre and Beaudoin take top honours among businessmen for mastering the political game. But they are by no means alone. Many business executives forge strong ties to political leaders, often by serving on government task forces or commission or by working as fund raisers. Many former mandarins and politicians find refuge in friendly corporations, as the lists below demonstrate.

Honourable Mentions
— businessmen with the most political clout

Trevor Eyton, CEO, Brascan Ltd., Toronto: Has strong ties with Brian Mulroney but also got along well with former Ontario premier David Peterson. Sits on the international trade advisory committee of the Business Council on National Issues.

Hal Jackman, chairman, E-L Financial Corp., Toronto: A longtime Conservative fund raiser, riding association executive and one-time Tory candidate for Rosedale riding in Toronto.

E. Leo Kolber, chairman, Claridge Inc., Montreal: Longtime fund raiser for federal Liberals. Appointed to the Senate in 1983.

Gerry Schwartz, CEO, Onex Corp., Toronto: Former national chairman, Revenue Committee, Liberal Party of Canada.

Elvio Del Zotto, president, Tridel Enterprises, Toronto: A life-long Liberal, Del Zotto lost a race for a provincial seat in 1979 but was elected president of the federal Liberal Party's Ontario wing in 1988.

Arthur Lundrigan, chairman, Lundrigans-Comstock Ltd., Corner Brook, Newfoundland: Lundrigan is the most powerful businessman in Newfoundland. He is a construction baron with intimate ties to Newfoundland Premier Clyde Wells.

Brian Flemming, CEO, CanEast Capital Ltd., Halifax: Assistant principal secretary and policy adviser to Prime Minister Pierre Trudeau, 1976–79. Flemming ran as a federal Liberal candidate for Halifax in 1974 and 1979. He is unsurpassed as a Liberal powerbroker in Atlantic Canada.

Conrad Black, chairman and CEO, Hollinger Inc., Toronto: Black has excellent access to his old friend Brian Mulroney.

Allan Taylor, CEO, the Royal Bank of Canada, Toronto: Taylor runs the country's biggest bank and has the most clout of any banker in Ottawa.

Edward (Ted) Newall, CEO, Du Pont Canada Inc., Mississauga: Newall has served on three important committees for Mulroney. He was chairman of the Advisory Committee to the Prime Minister on Business Government Executive Exchange, a member of the federal advisory committee on international trade and a member of the advisory group on executive compensation in the public service.

Arden Haynes, CEO, Imperial Oil, Toronto: Haynes is a member of the Policy Committee of the Business Council on National Issues, and a member of the federal Advisory Committee on Business Government Executives Exchange.

Ken Harrigan, CEO, Ford Motor Co. of Canada, Oakville, Ontario: Harrigan's memberships include the policy committee, Business Council on National Issues, the Ontario Business Advisory Council, the Automotive Advisory Committee of the government of Ontario and past member of the federal advisory committee on international trade.

Politicos Turned Business Powerbrokers

Bill Davis, former Ontario premier, counsel, Tory, Tory, DesLauriers & Binnington, Toronto: Davis holds eleven powerful directorships, including the Canadian Imperial Bank of Commerce, Ford Motor Co. of Canada, Honeywell Ltd. and Hemlo Gold Mines.

Peter Lougheed, former Alberta premier, law partner, Bennett, Jones, Calgary: He sits on boards of 16 major companies, including Brascan Ltd., the Royal Bank, Maclean Hunter Ltd. and Northern Telecom.

Darcy McKeough, former Conservative MPP and cabinet minister in Ontario: Currently chairman and CEO, Redpath Industries: McKeough holds 10 major board seats, including CIBC, Noranda Mines and Union Gas Ltd.

Brian Smith, attorney general of British Columbia, 1983–89; currently chairman, Canadian National Railway: A lawyer by training, Smith spent 20 years in elected office, first in municipal politics, then as a Social Credit MLA. He left the B.C. cabinet after accusing Premier William Vander Zalm of interfering in his office. His old friend Brian Mulroney stepped in and offered him the job of boss of the Crown-owned railway.

Gerald Regan, premier of Nova Scotia, 1970–78; currently president, Hawthorne Developmental Services: After a career as a provincial Liberal politician, Regan is a director of Provigo Inc., Roman Corp Ltd., Sceptre Resources Ltd. and United Financial Management.

Other notable ex-politicians with powerful board seats: Pierre Trudeau (Power Corp.); Marc Lalonde (Citibank Canada, Coronet Carpets Inc., and Steinberg Inc.); Donald Johnson (BCE Inc.).

Bureaucrats Turned Business Powerbrokers

Grant Reuber, deputy chairman, Bank of Montreal; deputy minister of finance, 1979–80: An economic researcher at the Bank of Canada and the Finance Department during the 1950s, Reuber spent most of the 1960s and '70s teaching at the University of Western Ontario, where he rose to dean of social science and vice-president, academic.

Michael Pitfield, Liberal senator and vice-chairman, Power Corp.: Clerk of the Privy Council and secretary to the cabinet, 1975–79, 1980–82. Pitfield, a Montreal lawyer, started his illustrious 25-year career in Ottawa in 1959 as an administrative assistant to the attorney general and joined the Privy Council Office in 1965. As a business-man, he sits on seven powerful boards, including those of Power Corp., Great-West Life Assurance, Montreal's *La Presse* and Investors Groups Ltd.

Marshall (Mickey) Cohen, CEO, the Molson Companies: Deputy minister of finance, 1982–85. A tax lawyer by training, Cohen joined the federal revenue department in 1969. In 15 years as a bureaucrat, he served as deputy minister of energy, then industry, trade and commerce, and finally, finance. He left Ottawa for Bay Street in 1985, when he became president of Olympia & York Enterprises. He joined Molson in 1988.

Allan Gotlieb, publisher, *Saturday Night* magazine, chairman, Canada Council, Canadian ambassador to Washington, 1981–89: A bright, aggressive mandarin of the Trudeau era, his government posts included deputy minister of communications, and deputy minister of manpower and immigration and under secretary of state for external affairs. Since leaving civil service in 1989, Gotlieb has accumulated corporate board seats rapidly. They include Alcan Aluminium Ltd., Macmillan Inc., Hollinger Corp. and Burston-Marsteller, one of the world's leading communications and consulting firms. He also serves on the advisory board of the Bank of Montreal and Investment Co. of America.

Gordon Osbaldeston, fellow, School of Business Administration, University of Western Ontario; Clerk of the Privy Council and secretary to the cabinet, 1982–85: He began his career in External Affairs, but rose to deputy minister, Consumer Affairs, deputy minister, Industry, Trade and Commerce, and under secretary of state for external affairs. Osbaldeston now sits on the boards of Canada Packers Inc., Du Pont of Canada Inc. and the Molson Companies Ltd.

Conclusion

The picture emerges of a Canadian business establishment inhabited by key powerbrokers with exceptional personal influence. Their orbits often extend into the political arena, in relationships nurtured through personal friendships, fund-raising efforts and the activities of such lobby groups as the Business Council on National Issues. The overlapping relationship between the business and political spheres is cemented by a largely one-way flow of ex-politicians and bureaucrats onto corporate boards and management teams. (Traffic the other way, through formal executive exchange programs where private sector executives do a stint in the federal bureaucracy, has been too limited to have much effect.)

In view of the business elite's influence in Canadian commerce and politics, it is all the more important that it not be a closed club. How much progress the business establishment has made opening up to newcomers is a matter of debate.

Trevor Eyton has watched the mores and makeup of the business elite evolve over the past three decades. The days are gone, says Eyton, when business success was determined by a person's family name. "Birthright used to be 75 per cent of the game," he says. "It's a tougher game today. It's more competitive, partly because the world is much more open in every sense, partly because of the press and partly because investment analysts are tougher." Toronto is a good example of the new openness, he says. "The city has more than 700,000 people of Italian descent. There are at least 100 contractors who are richer than E.P. Taylor ever was. And yet nobody knows their names." Ira Gluskin, a Toronto investment manager, puts it another way. "The barriers to power have been thrown open to French Canadians, Jews and renegades," he says. More than ever, entrepreneurial abilities are respected in the business community. Just a few years ago, to call somebody an entrepreneur had all the social cachet of calling him a used-car salesman. In the 1990s, it has become the highest form of praise. Entrepreneurship is the new buzzword of business; it's taught at MBA school, and corporations are trying to inculcate it into their managerial ranks.

Yet as the results of my surveys suggest, the attributes of the entrepreneur — brains, ability and dynamism — are rarely enough to gain someone admittance into the upper echelons of power. When you knock on the doors of the Toronto, Vancouver, Mount Royal or Halifax clubs, it is still who you know that counts.

The fact remains that no Jew has ever become chairman of a chartered bank and isn't likely to in the near future. The Jews who have entered the power elite of business have arrived there via routes that were once considered to be on the outer fringes of business respectability.

A blue-chip Toronto businessman, who asked to remain anonymous, explains the situation: "When I was growing up, I don't say business avenues were closed to them but they were not in, let's say, investment banking. They didn't work for big firms. They didn't work for the chartered banks. They didn't work for Dominion Securities. They went into real estate, which was something Anglo-Saxons shied away from because they said, 'Oh, well, that's sort of speculative.' Well, obviously it was a great mistake because that's where all their money was made and that's why they're so wealthy. A lot of them used the money that they made to get into other things . . . . But then again there is something about the Jewish people. They wouldn't admit this themselves when you talk to them, they've always been reluctant to put themselves at the mercy of Gentiles.

"In other words, they say, 'Why would you go and work for the Royal Bank of Canada?' when it's not theirs. And so they tend to be individual entrepreneurs. I think you could say that about a lot of non-WASP groups. That sort of disqualifies them from being the top corporate leaders, heads of big public companies, because they didn't want to be. That is certainly changing. Both the Toronto and the York clubs have Jewish members now. But they are underrepresented certainly to their strength in the elite or business community, but that will change." Perhaps.

In the following chapters, the makeup of the business elite is examined from two other perspectives: the extent to which it is closed to women, and the dominance of family dynasties in Canadian business and the difficulty of maintaining those dynasties from one generation to the next.

Chapter 5

Women in Business

A Tale from the Land of Nod

If there are advanced life forms on other planets, they would no doubt have some form of management consultants. After all, what intelligent society could exist without them? As soon as businesspeople on earth heard of this exotic new breed of expert, they would undoubtedly hire one of them to do a management study. I like to think that the alien consultant would be appalled by what it found and would tell the following tale in its report to earthly businesspeople.

There was once a kingdom known as the Land of Nod. The most powerful corporations there had been ruled for many years by a wealthy group of several hundred women. These were like-minded women. The most powerful of them tended to be of the same age — in their fifties and older. They had learned about the privileges and responsibilities of power on their mothers' knees and had honed their minds at the best schools in the kingdom. They lived in large homes and enjoyed a good cigar now and again at their private clubs. They viewed themselves as the natural ruling group by virtue of their genes, their upbringing and their sex.

They got together every few months to talk over the state of business at a kingdom-wide association called the Women's Business Coucil on National Issues (WBCNI). They talked mostly about production runs and how the politicians were screwing up the economy. But one year they decided to discuss what they should do about the growing demands of men for equal opportunity of entry to the highest ranks of business.

The problem was that men were not like them. All their lives they had viewed men as helpful supporters who kept house for them or brought them coffee at work. Men were just too aggressive and tempestuous to be trusted with serious decision-making. Worst of all, men were physically different. Their bodies were not aesthetically pleasing to the eye, as women's were, and everyone knew that under their pants they had unsightly appendages dangling between their legs. Certainly this made them good for reproduction, but not much else.

We pick up the discussion at the meeting of the WBCNI.

"I'm just not sure that men have the emotional temperament to lead," proffers one CEO. "They can't be trusted to make balanced, tough decisions about business."

This seems reasonable to another member of the corporate elite, who has her own observation to add. "We have a man on the board of my corporation," she says. "I must admit, I find his presence disconcerting. I'm accustomed to talking to men in the bedroom, not across a board table."

The talk is all very agreeable to a third CEO, who is the chair of a major chartered bank. "The problem is, there just aren't enough qualified men around to serve on our board. There are plenty who work well as tellers, but I'll be damned if I can find many that merit a seat on my board."

Our fictional consultant would draw conclusions about the economic damage caused by shutting out some of the kingdom's brightest minds from leadership roles.

The tale is absurd, but only because it is about women power-brokers. Substitute males as the corporate rulers in the Land of Nod and we're left with a reasonable portrayal of attitudes that remain widespread in the male-ruled upper echelons of Canada's corporate elite.

If you think that assessment unfair and simplistic, consider this real-life quote from the chief executive of one of Canada's largest corporations: "Women may be uncomfortable about some of the things required of a chief executive. They may want a more balanced life. They may also not be as cold in some of their decision-making. I'm not saying that is good or bad." This man doesn't realize that his words would enrage a self-respecting female manager.

In 1977, Royal Bank chairman Earle McLaughlin claimed that he couldn't find any women who were fit to sit on his board. Today, the bank has three well-qualified women directors on its board, which is an improvement. But progress for women in the corporate world has been extremely slow. As my survey revealed, women held only 5 per cent of directorships at the five largest chartered banks and only 9 per cent of directorships at the nation's 20 largest corporations. There never has been a female CEO of a chartered bank, nor is there likely to be one in the foreseeable future, since all but a handful of the senior executive positions are held by men. [1]

Elsewhere in Canada's largest corporations, women have made it to the vice-presidential level but they've been shut out of the CEO jobs. (This is true in the nation's 150 largest corporations.) Only a handful of women run lower-rung companies that could be considered large. The business elite contains fewer women than any other elite group with the exception of the Roman Catholic Church. It will be 10 to 15 years at least before a women ascends to the top job at the largest corporations in the country.

Discrimination against women extends throughout the Canadian economy. Ask a well-informed, well-meaning Canadian male to name examples of human rights abuses around the world and his response would likely include acts of racial and political discrimination in South Africa, Iraq or El Salvador. It is ironic that socially concerned Canadians can become so vocal about wrongs committed elsewhere while ignoring sexual discrimination at home. The limits placed on women's upward progress in Canada's economic system are more subtle, yet just as pernicious, as whites-only buses and segregated washrooms.

Women have flooded into the workforce in recent decades. Statistics Canada surveys tell us that between 1981 and 1986 alone, women accounted for 75 per cent of the growth in the labour force and 94 per cent of new jobs. The 1986 federal census revealed that the percentage of women working or looking for jobs had climbed from about 20 per cent in the 1950s to more than 56 per cent.

But the same census showed that women are still concentrated in traditionally female work, such as clerical and service jobs. And even though more women than ever are landing professional and managerial jobs, they are paid less than men in the same positions. Consider these disparities.

On average, full-time female doctors earned less for curing earaches and performing surgery than males ($57,126 for women versus $90,562 for men). Female judges were paid less for their wisdom than males ($61,094 versus $78,402 for men). And you'd think drilling a molar would be worth the same regardless of the driller's sex but female dentists earned an average $46,777 versus $79,346 for men. Female managers, scientists and engineers also took home much less than their male counterparts, on average. In short, women in the Canadian workforce earn about two-thirds of the money men earn for performing the same jobs.

Then there is the problem of making sure women are paid the same as men for different work of comparable worth. Federal and provincial pay equity laws are trying to correct glaring inequities. Why should female nurses, for instance, be paid far less than male garbage collectors? Figuring out the inherent value of a job is a challenging, often subjective task, and opponents of pay equity say it is a distortion of the free market system.

The price of labour, say the free market purists, should be determined by the preferences of society, just as the price of any other commodity is determined by supply and demand. But unfortunately, despite its many merits, the free market system has no social conscience and cannot right social wrongs.

At any rate, the problem of discrimination against women is not the fault of the free market system. It is the fault of the male decision-makers who pass over female job candidates, even though it is arguably in their economic interest to promote the brightest and best managers regardless of their sex.

It takes exceptional abilities for a woman to succeed in a man's world. The career of Jeannine Guillevin-Wood of Guillevin International reveals how one woman made it to the top.

The Rise and Rise of a Female CEO

Jeannine Guillevin-Wood is as wary as a jaguar. Sitting serenely at a breakfast table at the Four Seasons hotel in Toronto, the 61-year-old businesswoman talks sparingly. She conveys an elegant coolness in her black suit, cream-coloured silk blouse and stylishly short silver hair. Her watchful eyes meet yours directly, sometimes narrowing into suspicious slits as she constantly assesses your motives. She obviously doesn't give people the benefit of the doubt on first meeting. Life has taught her to be stoical about hardship and suspicious of other people's intentions. It's a potent mix that has carried Guillevin-Wood further ahead in the world of business than almost any other woman in Canada.

Guillevin-Wood is the chief executive officer of Guillevin International of Montreal, the country's second-largest distributor of electrical supplies, which sells wires and gadgets like switches and security systems to business customers across Canada. Since 1965, Guillevin-Wood has expanded a small, one-store operation in east-end Montreal into a nationwide company with about 1,300 outlets and $400 million in sales. She has also picked up eight corporate board seats — a number matched only by Mona Campbell, chief executive of Dover Industries. And in 1989, Guillevin-Wood became the first woman member of the Business Council on National Issues, the most prestigious association of business leaders in Canada. She also sits on umpteen charitable and cultural boards. In Quebec, Guillevin-Wood is known as the Godmother of Business.

The lives of leading business figures usually follow one of several predictable models: the plugger, who makes a long, slow rise up the corporate ladder; the inheritor, who walks into a corporate sinecure; the Old Boy, who goes to the right schools and mixes in the right circles; and the entrepreneur, who builds a corporate monument to himself with a combination of gall and talent.

Guillevin-Wood fits none of these models, and her career is therefore one of the more fascinating in the Canadian business scene. Guillevin-Wood didn't even think about a business career until she was 35. Her father didn't hand her a fortune, nor did she attend a school favoured by the Old Boys in the business elite; in fact, she has no education past high school. And she doesn't fit the hard-driving, scrambling mould of the entrepreneur, either.

If it were a movie, Guillevin-Wood's story would fit the woman-against-the-odds genre represented by such box office hits as *Places in the Heart*, in which Sally Field plays the resourceful wife of a dirt farmer who keeps the farm going and her children fed after her husband dies. But aspects of Guillevin-Wood's life are too harsh to be believable on celluloid. She grew up in Maisonneuve, a French area on the east side of Montreal. She never knew her father — he died when she was four — but her mother was an inspiration. "I had a mother who went through a lot in her life. She was very strong. She taught us discipline, how to work." Family life improved after her mother married a man who worked as an industrial supervisor. "It was a very nice family. Even if my parents were not rich, we were brought up as a very close family."

Guillevin-Wood is not given to self-promotion, but, when prodded, admits that she's always been the leader type. "In public school, I was the leader of my group of boys and girls," she recalls. "I'd be the one to say 'Let's go dancing. Let's organize a party' — things like that." The same trait showed up in high school. "Even in my teens, I was the organizer. You know how you always have a leader? It seems that I was the leader. When I talked to friends and my sister, I was like a mother."

Guillevin-Wood seemed assured of a comfortable, relatively wealthy existence when, at 19, she married François Guillevin, who was 13 years her senior. François co-owned F.X. Guillevin & Son Ltd., a small electrical wholesaler founded by his father in 1906. A wistful smile creeps across Guillevin-Wood's face as she recalls the ease of her life as a housewife. "I spent three months in Florida every year at a nice resort," she says with a chuckle, allowing her wall of reserve to fall a little.

A series of personal tragedies abruptly changed Guillevin-Wood's circumstances in the mid 1960s. "My family disappeared over a period of two and a half years," she says quietly. Almost everyone who mattered most in her life, with the exception of her daughter, died for unrelated reasons. Her husband, François, slipped coming out of a swimming pool, suffered a concussion and died. Her son, who suffered from cerebral palsy, died of his illness. Her grandmother died of old age. Her brother-in-law, and co-owner of the electrical company, died of a stroke. Her sister-in-law lost a battle against cancer. "My daughter and I woke up and we were by ourselves," she says. "Maybe that gives you character."

Many spirits would have been crushed, but Guillevin-Wood managed to survive psychologically intact. "Pride got me through," she concludes. She talks in quiet, even tones, betraying none of the emotional strain of the period twenty-five years before. She describes herself as a fatalist. "Maybe my life was preparing me to run a business."

The financial crisis that followed the death of her husband certainly didn't give her time to withdraw into an emotional shell. She faced an immediate decision: sell the business or take it over herself. The first option would have meant paying taxes. The second option involved stepping into a man's role in a man's business. A woman just didn't run a company in 1965, especially not an electrical distribution company.

For a woman of Guillevin-Wood's innate competence, there really was no question. "I said to myself, 'I'm going to give it a try. If I lose money, I'm going to lose it myself.'"

Her husband's funeral was on a Friday, and on the Monday she called the three senior executives of the company to a meeting in her home. To their surprise, she announced that she was stepping into her husband's job. "They told me later that they never believed me," she says.

The company that Guillevin-Wood took over was financially sound, with no debt, but it was a sleepy, single-store operation with about $1.5 million in annual sales and 35 employees. "My husband never liked the business. He did it for his father. So he didn't grow the business. He was more interested in the stock market. He made more money there."

Her first task as CEO was to apply for a hefty loan at the Royal Bank. The company needed the loan because it had used up its cash paying succession duties. "The family had never borrowed, and I had to borrow $50,000. I was shaking. Mr. Chabot, an accountant, came with me because back then banks didn't loan money to a woman." The bank made the loan, which was as fortunate for the bank as for the company, since Guillevin International has used the Royal as its main bank ever since.

Within two years, Guillevin-Wood faced a crisis at the company — a major supplier threatened to take his business elsewhere. "One

of the suppliers of industrial electrical products gave me a shock,"
she recalls. "He told me, 'We're going to take our line away from
you. You're not doing the job.'" His complaint was that Guillevin
was concentrating too much on selling small household appliances,
which at the time accounted for about two-thirds of Guillevin's product line. Guillevin-Wood saved that relationship by making a personal
visit to the supplier's head office in Toronto. But the episode helped
her to quickly decide to get out of appliances, a no-growth area,
and concentrate exclusively on the more obscure — and more lucrative — business of supplying industrial customers with toggle
switches, wires, plugs, receptacles and lighting supplies.

From the start, Guillevin-Wood concentrated on corporate strategy
and left the details to the stockroom boys. "I know our product,
the transformers, the distributors, but don't ask me this number, that
number. I never bothered about that because in distribution you don't
do the manufacturing, you just buy and sell. So it's important for
you to know the people at the top, to be good at negotiations."

Even in negotiations with suppliers, though, Guillevin-Wood didn't
come on like a Queen Boadicea. "I let the purchasing people do
most of the talking; I explained the company philosophy."

In subsequent years, Guillevin-Wood's negotiating skills were responsible for the expansion of her company into an industry giant,
which enjoyed 26 years of profits. She has led the company through
more than a dozen acquisitions. Her biggest was the $64-million pur-
chase in 1987 of Steetly Distribution, the Canadian subsidiary of
Steetly PLC of the U.K. That purchase doubled Guillevin International's size overnight.

The company's financial results are the final measure of Guillevin-
Wood's success in business, but they reveal nothing of the obstacles
she faced as a woman in achieving them. Her experiences as the
only female CEO in a man's business should be required reading
for anyone, male or female, who plans a career in business. Guillevin-
Wood recounts the incidents without anger, but with the wry humour
of a woman who was too competent to be put down because of
her sex.

In the 1960s, the feeling that business was the domain of men
was much more entrenched than it is today. Take Guillevin-Wood's

experience at the first big convention of the Electrical Distributors Association, held in Niagara Falls. "It was in 1966. There were about 200 men and I was the only woman.

"At those conferences," she continues, "there is always a man at the door to watch who comes in and who goes out. The man at the door took one look at me and said, 'You're not coming in here this morning, the sightseeing for wives is over there.' I laughed and said I was a regular member from Quebec. He laughed, too." Once inside the hall, Guillevin-Wood was asked to take a seat at the side. She chose a seat front and centre. "Twelve years later, I was named president of that association," she says, enjoying the irony.

Success in any kind of commerce depends to a great extent on personal relationships with business colleagues. But in the late 1960s such relationships were exceedingly difficult to develop for a female. To avoid gossip, she says, "men would phone me for business reasons but never leave their names." Having a lunch meeting was even trickier. Back then, a man met a woman for lunch only for three reasons: she was his wife, she was his sister or she was his mistress. In 1969 Guillevin-Wood travelled cross-country to found Copel Inc., a national marketing organization for independent electrical distributors. One prospective member of the organization was a successful businessman in Saint John, New Brunswick. "Naturally, you have to meet somewhere and you have to go for dinner," recalls Guillevin-Wood. "This gentleman was very religious. He would never have thought of being seen with a woman in a restaurant. We ended up in the hospital accompanied by one of his sisters, who was a nun, eating in the dining room."

Guillevin-Wood is glad that era is over. But she adds that she was very comfortable challenging the old customs. "Let's just say I was contrary."

Until very recently, Guillevin-Wood was not permitted to join any of the exclusive clubs that serve as homes away from the office for established businesspeople — a noticeable disadvantage for anyone trying to pass muster in the upper circles of business. She remembers going to the St. James Club in Montreal in 1967 to discuss a deal with two General Electric executives. One was Keith Wood, whom she was dating at the time and who would later become her husband.

When she arrived at the club, Wood was flustered. "He didn't know how to tell me that I couldn't use the front door. He said, 'I'll go with you. We have to use a special door.'"

Being forced to use a side door because she was a woman was a revelation for Guillevin-Wood. The same thing happened again at the Mount Royal Club in 1977, when Guillevin-Wood had to be spirited in a side door to attend a meeting of the Nabisco Brand's board. Today, the St. James Club is open to both sexes. The Mount Royal Club is not. (Guillevin-Wood belongs to the Club Saint-Denis, the favoured club of the French Canadian business elite.)

At 61, Guillevin-Wood is an accepted fixture in the rarefied, clannish circles of big business. She works at least 60 hours a week like the rest of the workaholics who rule business and spends much of the year on the road doing deals and attending board meetings. She has also reaped the material rewards that generations of male executives have sought. With her husband, she has an Outremont apartment and a large home in the Laurentians and takes a regular 10-day vacation at the family's "small place" in the Bahamas.

Twice during her career she was named "Man of the Year," first in 1974 by the Electrical League of Montreal, then in 1976 by the *Revue Commerce*, a magazine funded by the Montreal Chamber of Commerce. In 1990, *Le Journal de Montréal* named her one of the most influential businesspeople in Quebec in the past decade. She has become a sought-after director and sits on the boards of such major companies as the Laurentian Bank, Royal Insurance, Sun Life, Provigo, BCE Inc. and Quebec Hydro. She has also been involved in charitable and cultural affairs and sits on the boards of the Museum of Fine Arts, L'Hôpital du Sacre-Coeur de Montréal and the University of Montreal. In her opinion, her outside involvements have been important in attracting invitations to sit on boards, as if somehow working with top businessmen in fund raising and the like proves to them that she can fit into their milieu.

Does this mean she has finally gained acceptance in the business world? Hardly. Guillevin-Wood says she still encounters cold pinstriped shoulders at board meetings. "You still feel when a man is antiwoman when you enter a room." She corrects herself: "No, antiwoman is too strong. They are not ready to accept that a woman could lead the same life as they do. So I never have anything to do with those people."

Guillevin-Wood's eyes narrow as she talks of her boardroom strategies. "If I join a new board, I'm very quiet. I don't talk sometimes for 10 meetings before I give my opinions. After that, when they see what you can do, that you can talk the same language, they accept you." That suspicious, patient strategy might not be one that would appeal to an ardent, vocal feminist, but it's taken Guillevin-Wood to the top of the heap.

The Most Powerful Businesswomen in Canada

Powerful males behave in peculiar ways when they assemble in groups of two or more to talk business. At a typical board meeting of a large corporation, money power is on display in its most blatant form. Money is the arbiter of rank: control over it, personal possession of it or access to it puts a hint of a swagger in a person's stride. The thought of it is enough to bring a glazed look to ageing male eyes, just like the sheen in a lover's eyes in the afterglow of sex. The directors sitting around the board table are likely to be chairmen of large financial institutions and large corporations. Often, they have the flat, unidimensional personalities that you wouldn't want at your next dinner party. But that doesn't matter if they have a job title that carries financial heft. Money power can imbue even the most boring old curmudgeon with mystique. (Certain bank chairmen, past and present, come to mind.)

Breaking into this very male atmosphere is acutely difficult for women. Since most male directors are approaching 60, or act as though they are, they are a generation too old to have first-hand familiarity with modern women. For them, women are the gals who serve as secretaries and bring coffee to the meeting or the wives who are busy organizing fund raisers and practising interior design.

A woman sitting across the boardroom table is still a strange, slightly exotic presence who has to prove that she's not going to upset the personal dynamics of the group. Fortunately, overt sexual harassment is a non-issue in the boardroom. The social breeding of the men present militates against it. While open lust for money is permitted in the boardroom, overt lust for a female across the table is not.

The women who rise highest in the corporate elite are those who tend to understand the peculiar male social milieu of business and, like Jeannine Guillevin-Wood, fit into it in a nonthreatening way. This is not a commendable situation, but it will be decades before women are accepted on their own terms.

The most powerful women in Canadian business are those who serve on the boards of the largest corporations and the big five banks, or they are the CEOs of medium-sized corporations. There are not many of them. It is a sad commentary on the state of business that I can list these women in just a few pages. By studying their backgrounds and social connections, it is possible to draw some conclusions about what it takes for a woman to crack the top rank of business.

- The vast majority are brighter and better qualified than most of their male directors.
- Most are 60 years old or more.
- With few exceptions, they have kinship ties to the corporate elite — father or husband.
- In the few instances where women have become CEOs or directors without kinship ties to the elite, they have done so with truly formidable talent and often with outstanding academic qualifications.

The Old Guard

Mona Campbell, president and director, Dover Industries Ltd: Campbell is, at 72, the *grande dame* of Canadian business. She is the daughter of Toronto financier Frederick Keenan, who was a director of the Bank of Toronto, a predecessor of the T-D Bank, and is married to Lt. Col. Kenneth Campbell. She has been a director of Dover Industries since 1954, was one of the first women on a bank board (the T-D) and serves on the boards of seven other companies, among them Rothmans Inc., Churad Properties Ltd., the Capstone Investment Trust, National Sea Products Ltd., and Canada Development Investment Corp.

Outside business, her involvements rival those of any member of the male corporate aristocracy. She is a governor of Dalhousie College and University, which has honoured her with a doctorate; she is vice-chairman of the Advisory Board, Dalhousie School of Business Administration. Her social connections are impeccable. Campbell is a life member of the Toronto General Hospital Auxiliary and a life member of the Toronto Zoo. ("Zoo Do's", otherwise known as fund raisers, are currently trendy among Toronto's society wives.) She is also a founder of the Royal Ontario Museum. With so many credentials, Campbell is probably overqualified to sit on a good many corporate boards.

Jean Casselman Wadds: Daughter of William Earl Rowe, a politician, businessman and corporate director, Wadds is a scion of the elite. If she had been born male, she probably would have been either a chief executive of a major company or prime minister, judging from her track record. At 71, she is at the pinnacle of success permitted a woman of her generation in the business world. She sits as a director of Bell Canada, Canadian Pacific, Celanese Canada Inc., Royal Trustco Ltd. and Air Canada. A former Progressive Conservative MP for Grenville-Dundas, she also served as Canadian high commissioner to Great Britain from 1979 to 1983. Wadds has four honorary doctorates and was appointed an Officer of the Order of Canada in 1982. Is it any wonder men are intimidated by the women on their boards?

Pauline M. McGibbon: From humble beginnings in Sarnia, Ontario, where her father, Alfred Mills, was a local merchant, McGibbon rose to become one of the most gracious and competent lieutenant governors any province has ever had. Her late husband, Donald W. McGibbon, spent his career at Imperial Oil, rising to vice-president, and was treasurer from 1974 to 1975. McGibbon established a string of firsts in her career. They include first woman member of Toronto's National Club, first woman governor of Upper Canada College, first woman chancellor of the University of Toronto and the University of Guelph, and first woman director on the boards of IBM Canada, George Weston Ltd. and Imasco Ltd. Now in her eighties, McGibbon is a director of George Weston and Mercedes-Benz Canada Inc. The list of her charitable and religious involvements is extensive.

Dawn Rue'ann Campbell McKeag: Born in Portage la Prairie in 1927, McKeag trained as a nurse in Winnipeg. She is the daughter of former Manitoba premier Douglas Campbell and wife of W. John McKeag, lieutenant governor of Manitoba from 1970 to 1976. Her list of directorships is impressive. It includes the Royal Bank of Canada, Hudson's Bay Co., Assiniboine Travel Service and Goodyear Canada Inc. Her community work ranges from the Manitoba Heart Foundation to the Royal Winnipeg Ballet and the Winnipeg Art Gallery.

Sonja Bata: Born in Zurich in 1926, Bata had the good fortune to marry Tom Bata, who emigrated to Canada in 1938 and built the shoe company he founded into a worldwide multinational. But Bata has long since emerged from her husband's shadow to become a corporate player in her own right. She holds directorships at Bata Ltd., Canadian Commercial Corp., Alcan Aluminium Ltd., Canada Trustco and the Council for Business and the Arts in Canada. She's also prominent in Toronto's social affairs. She is vice-chairman of North York General Hospital, a former governor of York University and a former trustee of the Art Gallery of Ontario.

Mary Alice Stuart, chairman and CEO, CJRT-FM Inc: Stuart, 63, is the daughter of Edgar Gordon Burton, and her talents and pedigree could have propelled her much further had she been born male. Stuart ranks as one of the most accomplished women in Canadian business. She sits on the boards of the Bank of Montreal and S.C. Johnson and Son, Ltd. of Brantford. She recently headed the $100-million Breakthrough Campaign for the University of Toronto and has worked for many major charitable and arts organizations, including Massey Hall, Roy Thomson Hall and the National ballet. She's also president of the Burton Charitable Foundation.

Mitzi S. Dobrin: The 62-year-old daughter of Sam Steinberg was a lot more powerful before the family sold off Steinberg Inc., its grocery and real estate empire, in 1989. She lost her post of chairman of Steinberg, but she still has clout thanks to her board seat at the Royal Bank of Canada and her post as governor of the University of Montreal. With the family fortune to fall back on, Dobrin will never be poor, but she'll likely never be as powerful as when she was chairman of the family firm.

Wendy McDonald: The owner-operator of B.C. Bearing Engineers Ltd. took over the bearing and transmission distributor from her first husband in 1950 after he died and left her with a family to feed. Since then, she's built the company into an operation with about $60 million in sales. She's also served as vice-president of the Vancouver Board of Trade and is a director of Westcoast Transmission. "Wendy's very comfortable in a male atmosphere," says a local businessman. "She's got all the gags and lines."

Anne R. Dubin: Dubin is the wife of Charles L. Dubin, chief justice of Ontario, but she has her own legal credentials to commend her. Daughter of a fur broker, Dubin, 65, studied law at the University of Toronto and earned a partnership at Tory, Tory, DesLauriers & Binnington, the high-powered Toronto law firm. She is a director of Central Guaranty Trustco Ltd. and Petro-Canada and is a former governor of the Toronto Stock Exchange. She's a trustee of the Toronto General Hospital foundation and serves as vice-chairman of the board of governors of York University.

Jeanne Estelle Lougheed: In the *Canadian Who's Who*, Lougheed is listed as an arts patron. In business circles, 63-year-old Lougheed is known as the wife of Peter, former Alberta premier, and a dependable choice for corporate directorships. Educated at the University of Alberta, where she obtained a B.A. in 1951, Lougheed serves on the boards of Sears Canada and Northwestern Utilities Ltd. She is a former member of the Canada Council and has served on numerous local, provincial and national arts organizations. She is an honorary governor of the National Ballet of Canada and a member of the board of the Banff International Television Festival.

Margaret Southern: A former elementary schoolteacher, Southern is married to Ronald Southern, chief executive of Calgary's Atco Ltd. Southern, 62, sits on the boards of Shell Canada, Royal Trustco Ltd. and Woodwards Ltd. But her first love is the Spruce Meadows Equestrian Centre, one of the finest show-jumping facilities in North America. Southern is co-chairman of the facility, which was set up with her husband's money but relies on corporate donations to fund four annual tournaments that attract the best riders in the world.

Lucille Johnstone, president of Rivtow Straits Ltd. of Vancouver, a heavy-equipment supplier: Now 65, Johnstone has spent her entire career at the company. She doesn't own it, but she was the driving force behind her company's decision to buy the North American licence for Komatsu heavy machinery and made it the main rival to Caterpillar in North America. She's known for her disregard for appearances — she used to roller skate to work — and her tenacity. "She's tenacious and inquisitive," says a colleague. "She's like a pit bull with a pot roast. Once she's got her grips on something she doesn't let go." Johnstone also served on the Expo 86 board.

Barbara Rae, president and CEO of Office Assistance (Canada) Ltd., a temporary office help business she founded in the mid-1950s: Born in Prince George and educated at Simon Fraser University (MBA, 1975), Rae is known as a small-town girl who made good. She ranks with Johnstone and McDonald as the top West Coast businesswomen. Named B.C.'s Entrepreneur of the Year for 1986, Rae holds important corporate directorships (B.C. Telephone, Seaboard Insurance Co.) and is a member of the Royal Trust advisory board and the Judicial Appointments Committee of B.C. She has served as chairman of the Vancouver United Way and Salvation Army fund raisers. Most recently, she was named chancellor of Simon Fraser University.

The New Guard

Helen Roman-Barber, chairman and chief executive, Denison Mines: Daughter of the late Stephen Roman, Roman-Barber, 43, took over at the mining company after her father's death in 1988. At the time, Denison was the country's 153rd largest (measured by profits) company. Since then she's been wrestling with losses that have forced the company to sell off assets, and it has fallen to 996th spot. Described as domineering, smart and aggressive by her colleagues, she'll have to be all of that to keep the empire her father built from unravelling further.

Martha Blackburn, chief executive, the Blackburn Group Inc., chairman and publisher, London Free Press Printing Co. Ltd., chairman, CFPL Broadcasting Ltd., president, Kilbyrne Investments Inc.: Blackburn, 47, inherited the London, Ontario, media empire on the death of her father, Walter Blackburn, in 1983. She replaced her husband, Peter White, at the helm after they separated in 1986. Since then she has revamped the *Free Press*. So far, she's been overlooked by the blue-chip corporate boards and serves as a director for Blackburn Holdings Ltd., CKNX Broadcasting Ltd., Compusearch Market and Social Research Ltd., Netmar Inc. and the Walter Blackburn Foundation. What does a woman have to do to get noticed in Toronto, anyway?

Heather Reisman, managing director, Paradigm Consulting, Toronto: Reisman is the wife of Gerry Schwartz, chief executive of Onex Corp. Strong Liberals, they rank as one of Ontario's power couples. Reisman, 43, is said to have had easy access to former premier David Peterson's ear. She backed a loser in politics and her board directorships have been just as unlucky. They include Financial Trustco Capital Ltd., Magna International, Morgan Financial Corp. and Suncor Inc.

Anna Porter, publisher, Key Porter Books. President, McClelland-Bantam Inc. (Seal Books): Outstanding business connections and fierce determination have made Porter the risen star of Canada's publishing world (for more information, see pp. 415.)

For young women considering a career in business, there is some hope. Many of the women in the old guard have had their careers limited by their sex. But the women in the new guard are not willing to accept the same fate. New female players in the business world like Marie-Josée Drouin, a director of the CIBC, and Sherry Atkinson, chief economist at Burns Fry, the investment dealer, are equally smart and aggressive and aren't about to sublimate their personalities to protect sensitive male egos. More power to them.

Chapter 6

Business Blood Lines

Over the next decade, some very powerful family patriarchs in Canada will decide who gets to control a couple of hundred billion dollars worth of companies involved in just about every aspect of Canadian life. By a coincidence of history, many of the great family-owned business dynasties are preparing for the passing of power from the second to the third generations at the same time. They include well-known names like Reichmann, Thomson, Desmarais, Bata, Irving, Belzberg and Sobey. In some cases, the successor has already been chosen; in others, more than one sibling is vying for the title. In a few instances, like the Toronto Bronfmans, the Eatons, the Jackmans and the Southams, there is no inheritor ready or qualified to take over the family birthright, and power might pass outside the family to professional managers.

These family fiefdoms are the breeding ground for Canada's wealthy upper class, whose members possess at least second-generation vested wealth and do not have to rely on a salary to make ends meet. Income from family trust funds and stock market investments worth hundreds of millions of dollars throw off plenty of cash for the trappings of the upper-class life.

For many families that are now considered blue-chip, their business exploits have taken them from the bottom of the social ladder to the top, often in the space of two generations. Roy Thomson, founder of the Thomson publishing empire, was the son of a Toronto barber. George Weston was a Toronto baker before he began building the international food conglomerate now run by his grandson Galen. Sam Bronfman, founder of Seagram's, the world's largest distiller, was a bootlegger during Prohibition. Kenneth Irving, now in his nineties, got his start with a single gas pump and went on to build or acquire most of the business infrastructure of New Brunswick. Samuel Reichmann was an egg exporter and currency trader who loaned his sons $40,000 to start Olympia & York Developments. The Wolfe family, which runs the Oshawa Group food distribution business, are descendants of two Lithuanian immigrants, brothers Max and Maurice, who got their start selling hay to the cavalry in World War One.

More recent history is also replete with examples of remarkable social ascents. The most powerful businessman in Newfoundland, Arthur Lundrigan, got his start working with his father in a small sawmill and lumber business. Paul Desmarais built Power Corp. on the crumbling foundations of his father's near-bankrupt Sudbury bus line. British Columbia's Jimmy Pattison got his start as a used-car salesman. Jean Coutu is a Quebec pharmacist who expanded his single corner drugstore into a huge chain. Quebec publishing mogul Pierre Peladeau bought his first newspaper company with $1,500 borrowed from his mother. Toronto's Paul Phelan built a catering giant, Cara Operations Ltd., from a single lunch counter.

Canada's second-generation inheritors come in two types. First, there are those like Desmarais, the Reichmanns, the Lundrigans, the McCains and the Belzbergs, whose inheritance amounted to little more than a grubstake. They deserve all the credit for multiplying thousands of dollars into millions and billions. Second, there are those who had a much better head start, who took millions generated by their forebears and turned them into billions. They include Ken Thomson, czar of Thomson Corp.; both the Montreal and Toronto branches of the Bronfman clan; financier Henry (Hal) Jackman; publishing executive Conrad Black; Ray Wolfe; the Eaton brothers; George Richardson, of grain and investment business fame; Tom Bata, shoemaker to the world; the Steinbergs; the Sobeys; and the McCains.

Across the nation, the third generation is being groomed to take over the family empires.

At their best, these corporate successions will be miserable affairs, fraught with sibling rivalry. At their worst, they will become modern-day replays of the Jacob and Esau blood feud. After all, money and power are at stake. At the Oshawa Group, son Jonathon is the anointed successor to Ray Wolfe, the eldest of five brothers who built the business. At Power Corp., Paul Desmarais's eldest son, Paul, Jr., is the frontrunner, ahead of André. At Thomson Corp., eldest son David, who has worked as an executive at Zeller's and Simpson's, is the clear successor. At Olympia & York, the race is on between Albert's son Philip, a senior vice-president, and Paul's son-in-law Frank Hauer, who is earning his spurs helping to oversee the family's Canary Wharf project in London. They lead the pack of 14 children.

The losers will keep their stake in the family fortune, which is no small consolation prize, but they must strive to give their life meaning in other endeavours. Charles Bronfman, for example, found his feet as owner, until recently, of the Montreal Expos after brother Edgar took the lead role at Seagram's. In turn, Edgar's son Edgar, Jr., has become the third generation's heir apparent instead of his older brother, Sam. Some inheritors, like Nancy Jackman, sister of Hal, and Phyllis Lambert, sister to Charles and Edgar Bronfman, opt for philanthropic activities and find meaning through social and cultural causes. Others try to prove themselves in new careers. Hal Jackman's siblings include a psychologist and a cleric.

Traditionally, blood lines have been about the best qualification possible for ascending into the ranks of the corporate elite. In the past, this tendency to promote kin has been mostly associated with white Protestants of mainly British descent who built many of the nation's first corporate empires. As the chart shows, however, this desire to keep the business in the family and the corporate outlook the same is just as common among relative newcomers of diverse ethnic groups who have built their fortunes in the past several decades.

Successions that work are rare in business. History is littered with the names of once-proud families that have faded from relevance. The names Koerner (forestry), Rogers (sugar), Prentice (forestry) and Woodward (retailing) are examples from the west. Taylor (Argus empire), Gooderham (booze), McLaughlin (cars), Heintzman (pianos) and Steinberg (grocery stores) have become part of business lore in central Canada.

Experts estimate that the life of the average family corporation is only 24 years. A major reason for that is the difficulty of handing

The Top 10 Successions

Company and Controlling Shareholders	Contenders
Edper/Brascan empire Peter Bronfman (1989 assets of companies controlled or owned: $110 billion)	Top nonfamily managers and Bruce Bronfman (Peter's son)
Olympia & York Developments Ltd. Paul, Albert and Ralph Reichmann (1989 assets: $25 billion)	Philip (Albert's son) and Frank Hauer (Paul's son-in-law)
Power Corp. Paul Desmarais (1989 assets of companies controlled or owned: $45 billion)	Paul, Jr., and André (sons of Paul, Sr.)
Seagram Company Ltd. Edgar and Charles Bronfman (1989 assets: U.S. $10 billion)	Edgar Bronfman, Jr. (son of Edgar, Sr.)
Irving Oil Ltd. Kenneth and sons James, Arthur, John (1989 assets: $10 billion est.)	Jim, Jr. (son of James) Kenneth and Arthur, Jr., (sons of Arthur) John, Jr. (son of John)
Thomson Corp. Kenneth Thomson (1989 assets: $8.24 billion)	David Thomson (son of Kenneth)
First City Financial Corp. Ltd. and other companies Samuel, Hyman and William (1989 assets: $6 billion)	Brent (son of Hyman)

Quebecor Inc.   Erik and Pierre-Karl (Pierre's sons)
Pierre Peladeau
(1989 assets: $1.9 billion)

James Richardson & Sons   Hartley and David (sons of George)
George and James III   Roydon (son of James)
(1989 assets: $1.7 billion)

Empire Company Ltd.   Frank C. and Karl (sons of William)
Donald, David and William Sobey   Paul (son of David)
(1989 assets: $1.3 billion)

The Second-Tier Successions:

**Company and Controlling
  Shareholders**   **Contenders**

Oshawa Group   Jonathan and Elizabeth (children of
Wolfe family   the late Ray Wolfe)
(1989 assets: $954 million)

Dylex Ltd., Toronto   Lynn, David, Wendy (children of
Wilfred and Irving Posluns   Wilfred)
(1989 assets: $741 million)

Guillevin International   Top nonfamily management
Jeannine Guillevin-Wood
(1989 assets: $153 million)

power from one generation to the next. Often the offspring of the founder don't possess the founder's drive and dynamism. The first succession is tricky, but it sometimes works. The next step, passing power to the third generation, which usually involves cousins, is much more difficult.

Experience shows that successions are most likely to work when there is only one heir apparent, a crown prince who is selected from the brood for his character and abilities. Successors are still mainly male, although there are two notable exceptions: Martha Blackburn, who now runs the London, Ontario, media empire founded by her father, Walter; and Helen Roman-Barber, who succeeded her late father, Stephen, as chief executive of Denison Mines in Toronto.

To complete this section, here are the tales of two third-generation inheritors, one who was cut out from corporate power in the family succession shuffle and one who emerged as the crown prince.

The Outcast

Paul Bronfman accelerates his Saab as if it were a Formula One contender entering the stretch. Between each smoothly executed gear shift, he takes the tachometer to the limit; the engine howls from the depths of its high-performance lungs before it settles into cruising speed in fourth. Sailing down the Gardiner Expressway, the 34-year-old scion of the Toronto Bronfman clan is talking about Comweb Corp., his private $30-million foothold in the film business. "I'd like to grow and expand in the entertainment business," he says. "But I don't want the company to become unwieldy. It doesn't turn me on to try to create an Edper."

Bronfman seems to have everything it takes to run the $100-billion Edper conglomerate built by his father, Edward, and uncle, Peter. He's got the qualifications: a commerce degree from the University of Toronto and a strong track record so far in business. He has the character, too: an outgoing personality that stops just short of being overbearing. The catch is, the Edper empire will never be his to run. Paul Bronfman is the perfect example of an heir without a power base to inherit. Why this is so has to do with two factors: the family's past experience with the pain of generational successions and the way Paul Bronfman has dealt with the burden of having a last name associated with enormous wealth.

Bronfman is a great-nephew of Sam Bronfman, the one-time bootlegger who died in 1971 after building the Seagram distillery business into one of Canada's first true multinationals. An autocratic, intimidating man with the personality of a grizzly bear, Sam excelled at the distillery business in all its aspects, from blending to marketing, at least when it was needed after Prohibition ended. But Sam's lack of parenting skills would horrify a reader of *Psychology Today*. He had little time and few words of praise for his sons, Edgar and Charles, who toiled thanklessly at the company until his death. Eventually, both men shook off their upbringing and went on to become respected businessmen, Edgar as the main mover at the family company and Charles as owner of the Montreal Expos, which he eventually sold.

But probably nothing illustrates Sam's ruthless character better than his treatment of his in-laws, Allan Bronfman, his brother, and Allan's two sons, Peter and Edward. "Mr. Sam," as he was known, let Allan work at the company, but in a secondary role. Allan served as the company's polished, university-educated front man. As recounted in *The Brass Ring*, a 1988 best seller on the Toronto Bronfmans by Patricia Best and Ann Shortell, Sam surprised Allan's offspring by cutting them off from involvement in the family company without compunction in 1952. Edward and Peter, in their twenties, were thrown out of their Seagram offices with little business experience between them.

What happened next is part of business lore. The two young ingénues dabbled in investments for a decade without much success. But starting in 1962, the Bronfmans had the good fortune to hire a string of top-ranking investment advisers, Austin Beutel, Ned Goodman and Neil Baker. All spent time working with them at Edper in the 1960s before going on to become major business figures in their own right.[1] Things really took off at Edper, however, with the arrival of Jack Cockwell and later Trevor Eyton.

Long before Edper grew into a realm, Edward and Peter had taken steps to ensure that their offspring would not be put through the painful experience they went through at the hands of Mr. Sam. In the 1970s they agreed that Peter's children would eventually have control of Edper. In 1989, they lived up to the agreement. So that Edward and his family could cash out, Edper Enterprises reorganized and went public. The senior managers, Cockwell, Eyton and others, became Peter's partners and part owners in the conglomerate. On Bay Street there is now plenty of speculation about who will eventually control Edper, the managers or Peter's children, Linda, 36, Brenda, 31, and Bruce, 33. Of the three, Bruce is the only one working in the family business. But Bruce has a long way to go to prove himself a capable leader in the mind of the investing public. In his mid-twenties, he went through a rocky emotional period, which ended when he successfully completed treatment at an addiction centre in Minnesota.

For Paul Bronfman and his siblings, David, 31, and Brian, 27, there never has been any doubt that they'd have to make their own way outside the Edper realm. Asked if he ever wished he could take over at Edper, Paul answers slowly and deliberately: "Never, never, never. I never had any desire to work at Edper, and the business there never really interested me. I read the annual reports and that's about it." Paul wants to cut his ties with Edper entirely. "I certainly have no intention of hanging on to my Edper shares. I don't think my brothers do, either."

The most surprising thing about Paul Bronfman is that he seems so *normal*. He's happily married with children, goes to synagogue regularly and has a job he likes. Bronfman has none of the personality traits that often characterize the offspring of the super rich: the ennui, the listlessness, the lack of direction that come from growing up in a world where reality is distorted by enormous wealth and by enormous pressure to be a success. "People will always make presumptions about who you are and what you should be because of your name," he says. "For me it was a big negative for many years. I must admit it was a chip on my shoulder. I had to prove not only to myself but to the world that I had merits in my own right — that I could hold a job, pay my own rent and didn't have to take money from Daddy or anyone else. Once I became confident enough in my abilities to strike out on my own I felt a lot better about myself."

For Bronfman, the music business became the avenue to independence at an early age. Born in Westmount, "the Anglo bastion of Montreal," as he calls it, Bronfman joined his first rock band at age 12. The Lords of Power, as the group was called, was a teenybopper salute to the music of the 1960s. With Bronfman singing lead and playing rhythm guitar, they performed music by the Doors, Jimi Hendrix, Jethro Tull and Led Zeppelin for their classmates at Westmount Junior High. "That was a ball," he recalls. "But I realized quickly that I wasn't cut out to be a guitar player." By the time he was 16, he concluded that he could make better money playing other people's music. Riding the disco wave, he became a disc jockey in what he billed as a "mobile discotheque." Bronfman and the buddies who helped him played birthday parties and bar mitzvahs for cash. "We invested $500 and over two years we took in five grand," says Bronfman. Even then, he was determined to earn money himself rather than taking handouts.

In 1975, he enrolled in a communications course at Concordia University but dropped out after a semester. "I quickly found out that the program was great if you wanted to become a cameraman or a creative talent. But they didn't teach the business side." Instead, Bronfman signed on as a roadie with the legendary Montreal rock promoter Donald K. Donald. Bronfman's parents were predictably horrified. "Imagine the phone call," he says. "Hi, Mom. The good news is I got a job. The bad news is I quit school."

Bronfman's move was understandable, in a way. Working for a rock band is probably one of the best ways for a scion of wealth to conceal his origins. Sporting shoulder-length hair and a gold earring, Bronfman looked anything but a child of privilege as he toured the country with bands like April Wine and The Stampeders. As part of the crew, he worked six or seven days a week loading and unloading equipment in the middle of the night, snatching three or four hours of sleep a day at most. "It was rough, but good training," he says. He was later promoted to production manager for Donald's tours.

In 1978, Bronfman opted for the film business, signing on with Pathé Sound in Toronto, a sound and post-production film studio owned by Astral Bellevue-Pathé of Montreal. Connections helped

Bronfman land the job. His father, Edward, is a longtime friend of Harold Greenberg, entertainment mogul and owner of the Astral empire. Edward also has a small stake in the company. But Paul can claim full credit for his subsequent rapid rise in the company.

Apart from a three-year break, from 1981 to 1983, taken to earn a commerce degree at the University of Toronto, Bronfman worked for most of the next decade at Astral companies. He helped reverse the declining fortunes of Astral's First Choice pay-TV with smart promotions campaigns and later helped Bellevue Home Entertainment, Astral's video distribution business, which was losing a few millions a year, climb back into the black.

In Bronfman's view, Greenberg handed him each job to test him. The boss was apparently pleased and, in 1987, Bronfman, then 30, was appointed vice-president of development for the parent company Astral Enterprises.

But it was only a matter of time before Bronfman struck out on his own. Astral is very much a Greenberg family company, and there were three young Greenbergs with a better shot at the top job than Bronfman.

In 1988, Bronfman quit and, with money borrowed against his shares in Edper, set up Comweb (short for communications web) as a management company with about $30 million worth of investments in the film industry. Comweb owns just under half of North Shore Studios, Canada's largest motion picture and television production complex, based in Vancouver. Bronfman also owns half of William F. White, Canada's largest supplier of lighting and grip equipment to the film industry. He is also trying to establish himself as a film producer.

Perhaps the strangest thing about this tough-talking, confident man who conceals any self-doubts below a skin as thick as a pachyderm's is that he is the son of one of Canada's shyest, most retiring tycoons. Edward has always been the other Toronto Bronfman. Before their partnership in Edper ended in 1988, Peter was always an involved overseer of Edper's operations, while Edward never claimed to have more than a passing interest in business.

While he was no whirlwind as a businessman, Edward gets high marks as a father. Paul praises his dad for never pressuring him about his career. "He's been a good father. I was lucky because he never gave me any pressure to get involved with the family business. He basically said, 'Do what you feel you can be happy at, successful at.'" Paul says he and his father don't even talk business when they get together. "He's not interested in business. He prefers to spend his time on charitable activities."

At the gala opening of North Shore Studios in Vancouver in 1989, politicians, celebrities and even "Entertainment Tonight" showed up. As co-owner, Paul gave a speech as the cameras clicked and the champagne corks popped. Standing off to one side, Edward was all smiles. "He was very proud, as any father would be," says Paul fondly.

The Crown Prince

Family empires tend to fly apart by the third generation. As we have seen, Paul Bronfman turned out to be a loser in the corporate inheritance sweepstakes. By contrast **Brent Belzberg**, who runs First City Financial Corporation, a $5-billion conglomerate based in Vancouver, has emerged as an inheritor. In 1991, Brent, 40, succeeded his uncle Sam as chief executive of the parent company and its major subsidiary, Toronto-based First City Trustco. The mantle went to Brent even though Sam's son Marc was also in the running. Only Marc's abrupt departure from the board and the family firm signalled the intense competition that had existed between the contenders behind the scenes.

Brent is the grandson of Abraham Belzberg, a Polish-born fish-monger who emigrated to Calgary in 1919 and built a modest real estate business on profits from a used furniture store. Abraham had three sons, Hyman, Sam and William, who had various roles in building First City into a continent-wide operation involved in the trust company business, real estate development, merchant banking, commercial lending and, until 1990, corporate raiding in the United States and Great Britain.

Sam, 63, the former financial brain and one-time chairman of the parent company, operates out of Vancouver, where he's pursuing personal deals, Hyman, 66, runs a used-furniture business in Calgary, and William, 58, spent the last few years running a struggling savings and loan company in Los Angeles.

The Belzbergs brought several of their offspring into the family business in the same collegial spirit that helped them build their empire. While Hyman's sons, Brent and his younger brother Murray, ended up working at the trust company in Toronto, Sam's boy, Marc, chose New York. As head of first City's Manhattan merchant banking operation, he was a key enthusiast and strategist in many of the family's corporate raids. As it turned out, however, the road to power lay not in the swashbuckling excitement of raiding but in the more banal business of loans and ledger sheets that Brent pursued.

Brent has forged a conservative career, first in law, then finance, that has gained him the acceptance by the corporate establishment that has eluded the rest of the family. He acts and thinks like old money: he's low-key, staid and great at schmoozing with the Old Boys, who have chats instead of conversations, girls instead of secretaries, and prefer to accumulate money quietly, not grab it by the wheelbarrow-full in greenmail plays that attract international headlines.

Yet Brent, like his more flamboyant cousin Marc and his uncle Sam, is very much a product of his upbringing and of the very different influences of his two grandfathers. As Brent tells it, his paternal grandfather, Abraham, gave him his love of business. Brent recalls how his grandfather would come around on Sunday mornings and wake up him and his brother, Murray, who shared a basement bedroom in the family's Calgary home. "Every Sunday, from the time I was eight years old, there would be a tap on the basement window, and my brother and I would get dressed and we'd get into his big old Cadillac and we'd go out and look at land — farms and buildings. He owned a trailer court and he'd collect some of the rents. Then we would collect the quarters and dimes out of the washers and dryers he owned and deposit them at the bank."

In truth, Abraham was known as a slum landlord, whose holdings included low-rent buildings and two used-furniture stores. More kindly, Brent describes his grandfather as "a true entrepreneur, the most aggressive type of cattle country westerner. He bought and he didn't care about how things were taken care of afterward. He had no operating skills at all. My father always tells the story of how my grandfather would buy a house but would never go to collect the rent. He never worried about the taxes or the upkeep or the zoning."

Yet Brent says he was even closer to his maternal grandfather, which may help explain how he differs in personality from his more aggressive, deal-doing kin. "His name was Abraham Lapvin. He had a real impact on my life because he was a real humanitarian. He was a farmer who weighed 275 pounds and had arms as big as your thighs. He never cared about money and he hated people who cared about money. He was almost a communist, and he was always doing good deeds for people. We'd see a bum on the street and he would bring the guy home for lunch and give him a bowl of my grand-mother's soup. I care about people a lot, and he was responsible for that in a lot of ways."

But if Abraham Lapvin planted a seed of humanitarianism in Brent, it was Abraham Belzberg who planted a knack for cutting deals in the rest of the family. By the 1950s, Abraham Belzberg had become prosperous buying and selling used buildings and had opened a used-furniture store. That store he gave to Hyman, his oldest son. William, the youngest, dropped out of school to run a family pet food business. Sam didn't need any such help. By 19, he had com-pleted a commerce degree; shortly thereafter, he made his first fortune leasing oil and gas properties in Alberta.

Brent offers some insight into how a cooperative relationship de-veloped between his father and uncles. Certainly, he says, Sam pro-vided the financial acumen that built the family financial empire, but it was by no means a one-man show. "My dad [Hyman] is the eldest brother and really the patriarch. Dad remained in Calgary and took care of his small business. He is the guy who helped put the others through school and bought them their first car and things like that. He sacrificed his own life in a lot of ways to ensure the success of the others. Everybody in the family recognizes that during the initial periods the cash flow from my dad and his business was very instrumental in the foundations of the company. So they treat themselves as absolute equals and they share everything."

In Brent's upbringing, there was a strong sense of family loyalty and devotion to hard work. The eldest of three children, he never had more possessions than any other kids living in the Mount Royal area of Calgary. "If my parents had money," he says, "they never showed it. We didn't go on holidays. We lived in a nice area but it certainly wasn't the nicest house on the street. I went to school at the end of the street."

While his mother, Jenny, took care of the family, father Hyman worked arduous hours at the furniture store. "My father worked from seven in the morning until ten at night, seven days a week."

Brent got his first exposure to business working after school for his father. "From the time I was 11 years old, I worked for my dad on the truck and dusting in the store." The rest of the time Brent spent doing charity work at the local synagogue. He found he excelled at sales. "I was the top salesman on the floor and I was earning commission. So I made enough money to pay for my first year at university."

Equipped with an Oldsmobile presented to him by his father, Brent went to Queen's University in Kingston, where he earned a degree in commerce in 1972. He placed near the top of his class with an average in the high 80s. Then it was off to law school at the University of Toronto, where he completed his law degree.

Afterwards, Brent joined the blue-chip Toronto law firm Tory, Tory, DesLauriers & Binnington. The Belzberg family name certainly wasn't an asset in securing the position. At the time, there was widespread cynicism in the business community about Sam's recent sale of Western Realty Projects Ltd., the Calgary real estate company the family controlled. The Belzbergs walked away with cash and debt while minority shareholders were obliged to accept an inferior stock swap.

Working at the law firm was a crash course in the manners and mores of the Toronto business establishment for the young recruit from Calgary. Belzberg speaks with particular reverence of two senior partners he assisted. "I worked with John Tory and Bill DesLauriers on the Thomson family reorganization. I spent every third week in London. They are the two most ethical, moral people I have ever met in my whole life." Nevertheless, by 1979, Belzberg felt compelled to spend some time working for the family in Vancouver. That summer, with his new bride, Lynn, he moved there to become an executive assistant to Sam at First City Financial. It was not a pleasant experience. "I'm not too good at the executive assistant kind of role. It was just following him around learning and picking up pieces."

But Brent could hardly move into a management role at the trust company. "You couldn't take a 29-year-old kid who didn't know anything but practising law and put him into a formal management structure like First City Trust," he says. "The only thing that was embryonic was the real estate group, so I went there to do a few transactions." That's when his education at the hands of Sam began. "I sat in the office two down from Sam. I was learning from him daily. What Brent was learning was how not to get caught in a real estate collapse. By 1981, interest rates were heading into the 22 per cent range and real estate markets were collapsing. Sam foresaw the problem and got out of the market early. "I basically headed up the disposition of our real estate assets during that period," says Brent. As the market picked up after the recession, so did Brent's activities in the real estate group. "At that point most of the real estate deals were in Los Angeles, San Francisco, Boston, Dallas and Toronto. I was in the air from Sundays to Thursdays every week." With a young family at home, he decided it was time for a change in work style.

His solution was to move to Toronto in 1986 to develop the family's business interests in the east. He also took over as head of the trust company and moved its headquarters to Toronto with him. "In 1986 in Vancouver things were generally quiet," he explains, "and all the growth in the trust company was coming from Toronto."

Under Belzberg, First City Trust began specializing in serving mid-market corporate customers. First City also has a large equipment leasing operation and offers a full range of RRSP products to individual investors.

Brent is generally highly thought of in Toronto business circles and has all the credentials for acceptance into the often stuffy and sometimes anti-Semitic Toronto Establishment. He leads a quiet life, jogs, lives in Forest Hill and tends to socialize with a small circle of friends. "I'm not a clubby person," he remarks.

The only thing he has going against him is his last name. The Belzbergs are a controversial family in North American business. During the 1980s, they gained an infamous reputation as corporate raiders in the United States, where they worked closely with Michael Milken, the now disgraced architect of Drexel Burnham's junk bond business. The Belzbergs made more than U.S. $300 million by launching hostile takeover bids on companies, then selling out their stakes for a profit. This tactic is better known as greenmail, and although the Belzbergs have always claimed that they never launched a takeover bid with greenmail in mind, the fact is that they repeatedly took payoffs from frightened managements at the target companies or from so-called white knights; third parties who came along to rescue the target companies from their clutches.

Marc Belzberg, who ran the New York arbitrage operation suffered the added ignominy of being convicted, under a civil suit, by a New York court for illegally "parking" stock with a friendly broker during the family's 1986 raid on Ashland Oil.

By 1990, the Belzbergs had given up their raiding ways in the United States. The junk bond market had collapsed, Drexel Burnham had declared bankruptcy, and Michael Milken had been convicted of securities fraud. The family's last attempt at a hostile takeover — on Armstrong World Industries, a Pennsylvania floor and ceiling tile maker — failed miserably. In the aftermath, Sam was back in Vancouver mumbling about profits in the takeover business not being what they use to be. Even the *Wall Street Journal* had declared the Belzbergs "toothless raiders" in coverage that typified the U.S. media's hostile reaction to the Canadian family.

Brent feels the family name has been unfairly tarnished by the media. "I've never seen anything in our organization other than fair treatment of people," he says. How does he cope with the criticism? "I react to it by keeping my nose to the grindstone and by running my business as best I can." He wants people to learn that "his word is his bond. I'll bend over backwards to never alter a deal. I'll always do what's right and what's fair."

It was the juxtaposition of Marc, who was clearly identified with 1980s-style corporate raiding, and Brent, who has a reputation as a solid, conservative financial executive, that ultimately settled the succession race at First City Financial.

For the 1990s, the parent company needs a conservative fixer like Brent at its helm, not a deal maker like Marc, or for that matter

Sam. The 1980s left the Belzbergs with more than a controversial reputation as raiders. Brent's biggest problem when he took over leadership was a looming debt at the parent company in Vancouver. While the $300 million in profits from corporate raiding were nice, they were overshadowed by the matter of $150 million worth of junk bonds issued by a subsidiary that were due and couldn't be paid. There was also another $250 million in Swiss franc and dual currency bonds held by foreign investors, maturing between 1992 and 1994. Where do you come up with that kind of fast money when the corporate raiding game is over?

If that weren't enough of a headache, Brent had to cope with mounting losses at First City Trustco in Toronto. As a result, he was spending most of his time as the new czar of the First City Empire cutting costs, slashing staff and refinancing debt to avoid a cash crisis that would force him to sell off assets at fire-sale prices, or fail at the hands of creditors.

In short, Brent inherited more a mess than a fiefdom. It's not a mess he had a hand in creating and it will take years for him to clean up. There are no windfall profits worth hundreds of millions of dollars in the basic loan business. But if Belzberg can survive long enough, there's plenty of respect.

Conclusion

For those who fear the extent of corporate concentration in Canada, the succession problems faced by the families at the centre of most of the major corporate empires offer some needed perspective. The fact is that many of the dynasties that seem so all-powerful today are likely to be consigned to the history books within a decade. It's doubtful, for instance, that the Edper-Hees-Brascan conglomerate will survive in its present all-embracing shape, since there is only one young, inexperienced Bronfman hankering after control and at least a dozen owner/managers. The Southam publishing empire faces a similar problem: no interested family heirs and plenty of would-be corporate acquisitors on the prowl. The Eatons and the Jackmans will soon face the same problem. Meanwhile, the Richardsons would dearly love to sell off their investment company to the highest bidder, but when they tried to do so recently, they had no bidders. Jimmy Pattison is proud that his offspring won't get a helping hand from him.

Canada's business dynasties tend to be impermanent constructs of one man's ambition. They rise and fall every few decades. This is laudatory in one respect: it lets new, hard-driving entrepreneurs and acquisitors have a shot at grabbing the brass ring. But this gradual turnover in who holds corporate power doesn't change the essential fact that great wealth is concentrated in very few hands.

Part III

THE SOCIAL

ESTABLISHMENT

Chapter 7

Fairy-tale Lives

You've just won a game show called "Socialite for a Season." As the big winner you collect the sensational grand prize: a trip for you and a companion through Toronto's upper-class social scene. From September until March, the two of you can attend every big gala and ball in the social calendar. Money is no problem: the prize includes free tickets, a chauffeur-driven Jaguar, a selection of drop-dead ball gowns and a couple of sleek black tuxes with trimmings. All you need to bring is a good deal of gall.

The season begins pleasurably enough. Your first event is the Symphony Ball in September, a fund raiser with an Oriental theme put on by the symphony's Women's Committee.

Your chauffeur drops you off at the Royal York Hotel at 6 p.m. sharp for cocktails, champagne and sushi. By 8:30 you're sitting down to a sumptuous feast: consommé and a main course of lamb, chicken teriyaki on bamboo sticks and Oriental vegetables. Afterward you and other guests mingle around a towering "Dream Tree," surrounded by glittering packages filled with jewellery, designer clothes and other trinkets. You are all invited to bid on the items, with proceeds going to the symphony. Some lucky bidder wins a chance to conduct the symphony for an evening. You're glad you passed on that one. Then it's on to Roy Thomson Hall, where you foxtrot to the strains of the Toronto Symphony. A magical evening, one that leaves you anticipating the next big event.

It comes before your calf muscles have fully recovered from the dancing. A week later you're whisked to the Opera Ball at the Inn on the Park. As you pull in, a dozen violinists are there to serenade you. Maidens dressed in baroque gowns shower you with rose petals. Inside, you are surrounded by the old-world grandeur of eighteenth-century Italy. You sample the antipasto served from a real Italian gondola before sitting down to an Italian feast served by waiters wearing white gloves. Over there is Hilary Weston with her husband, Galen, the grocery store tycoon; and there are Sonja and Tom Bata and a smattering of politicians and diplomats. There's an ambience that is intoxicating. Dashing men in white tie flirt with glamorous women in gowns designed for maximum impact on the senses. They feature breast-baring necklines and thigh-revealing slits that suggest their price is inversely related to the amount of material used. You're not sure whether your ego or your libido is getting the most stroking.

The social whirl becomes dizzying. You reread your F. Scott Fitzgerald to maintain the mood between events. There's the star-studded opening of *Phantom of the Opera*; more dining and dancing at the Herbie Mistletoe Ball, an annual fund raiser for a special children's program of the Hospital for Sick Children. then there's the Snow Ball gala, put on to raise money for psychiatric patients, and the annual Ireland Fund luncheon, organized each year by Hilary Weston to raise money for her home country.

But it's the Brazilian Ball in February that gluts your senses like too much crème caramel. It's a taste of Brazil in the deep of Toronto winter that would make Vincent Massey choke on his port. There's more flesh on display than on the Riviera; assorted corporate heavyweights and politicians check their public personae at the door to cavort under flashing laser lights. Costumes range from the gaudy to the bizarre. You're surrounded by a blur of Carmen Miranda feathers, sequined masks and diaphanous dresses. Dancers imported from Brazil set the tone with a grinding, thigh-to-thigh lambada. Door prizes range from two $15,000 Rolex watches to a $25,000 shopping spree at Holt Renfrew. You stagger home exhausted.

By March you've attended three or four more galas and the novelty has begun to wear thin. You notice that you seem to see the same faces at every event. You don't get the same kick anymore from the party favours for him and her, wrapped in pretty packages, that await you at your table. The string ensembles and girls' choirs hired to serenade you all begin to sound the same. The rich food has added inches to your waistline. The $500 tickets have begun to seem exorbitant. You wake up at night with a chill, dreaming you've just been invited to another gala. You decide you'd rather watch "Hockey Night in Canada" than dance the lambada one more time.

This imaginary escapade is not so far-fetched as it might first appear. Such a profusion of galas took place in the 1989–90 social season in Toronto and left hundreds of socialites feeling just as fatigued as our fictional party goers.

Over the past decade, Toronto's upper classes have raised partying to dizzying new heights, as if they want their revelries to be just as world class as their city. In the process, Toronto has become the unrivalled social playground of Canada, a city with imperial pretensions in the social sphere that match its power as the ecomonic centre of Canada.

These revelries attract important personages from Montreal and Ottawa, but mainly they are venues for the moneyed classes of Toronto to indulge in self-admiration. In one sense they signal a vast opening up of the city's social establishment. At any given gala, the crowd is drawn from the Establishment families of Rosedale and Forest Hill, who mingle with new millionaire developers, investment executives and CEOs from Don Mills. An Italian or Hungarian name is no longer a barrier to the upper-class social scene.

But in pursuit of worthy causes the gala fund raisers have become the victims of their own excess. To attract the crowd that counts — those who can afford $500 tickets or $10,000 corporate tables — the gala impresarios have had to offer bigger and better shows. Laser lights, chamber orchestras and beribboned party favours no longer impress the jaded crowd. Like cocaine addicts, they seem to need a bigger fix each time. The feverish revelry fills the senses and pumps up the ego, but it leaves the soul as flat as a deflated party balloon.

The soaring grandeur of public galas has been matched by the rising ostentation of private entertaining. Caught in the upward spiral of party goers' expectations, hostesses in Rosedale and Forest Hill can no longer impress with a simple dinner party. The top hostesses think nothing of spending $4,000 on an evening for a dozen friends, featuring imported spring flowers in February, a gaggle of musicians and a professional chef. The social scene may include more people with more money than ever, but their eagerness to flaunt wealth has turned Toronto into a more openly stratified society.

In some ways, the social establishment hasn't changed all that much in the past century. It still rather clumsily mimics the aristocracy of Great Britain. This emotional connection with England is manifested most openly in the plummy, mid-Atlantic accents that the wives of leading lawyers and businessmen take pains to cultivate, despite their humble origins in, say, Orillia or Renfrew. At a deeper level, it is reflected in the instant credibility given any member of the upper class whose connections extend to members of the British royal family or aristocracy. Canadian citizens can no longer accept knighthoods from the Queen, but the same yearning for the trappings of class that motivated Lord Beaverbrook and Lord Thomson to seek peerages still imbues the hearts of latter-day colonials.

Yet in other ways, the manners and mores of the Toronto social elite have been irrevocably changed by the influx of hundreds of new millionaires into its ranks, and by the passage of time.

In the early 1900s, when the descendants of the Family Compact began building mansions in Rosedale, they expressed their desire for status in the magnificence of their homes. But their social habits were serene by today's standards. The social affairs of families like the Masseys, the Jarvises, the Powells, the Ridouts and the Oslers tended to centre around ladies' visiting days, say, every second Wednesday, and around tea dances and embroidery. In many well-to-do homes, Protestant values were the order of the day. Successful businessmen like Timothy Eaton, the department store tycoon, A.E. Ames, E.R. Wood and J.H. Gundy, all three founders of investment houses that bore their names, and Sir Joseph Flavelle, who made a fortune in the bacon business, were also devout Methodists who gave generously to charities. They followed a creed of thrift, sobriety and hard work.

Certain standards of the founding families have been passed down to the current generation of Toronto's upper class. They are:

1. Never make a show of money;
2. Never wear tight, flashy clothes;

3. You may buy a sports car, but your family should also have some old car, like a Jaguar or a Jeep;
4. Preferably live in Rosedale; although, as everyone knows, the Westons and Eatons live in Forest Hill;
5. Always have a property in the country — Muskoka, the Thousand Islands or Georgian Bay;
6. Don't get your name in the paper;
7. If you do, pretend you didn't want it to appear;
8. Marry someone from a respectable family.

In some cases, the mores of the founding families have been passed on as well. Take the case of Robb Heintzman. Today a 39-year-old law partner with Fraser Beatty, Heintzman has blue blood on two sides of his family. He is a great-grandson, on his mother's side, of Sir Joseph Flavelle. On his father's side, his great-great-grandfather built the now defunct piano-making business that bears his name. In many ways, Heintzman grew up in a life of privilege. He attended Upper Canada College, a private school in Switzerland, then Queen's University in Kingston. At home he was brought up according to the upper-class standards of the day. Even on weekdays, he was expected to dress for dinner, at which his parents might ask him to lead a discussion on some current event. When he was young, his grandmother, Clara, daughter of Joseph, was still alive. "Every Sunday after church, Grandmother Flavelle had us over for lunch at her place, or at the Granite Club."

Heintzman speaks admiringly of the values espoused by Flavelle, originally a poor boy from Peterborough who was reputedly second to none in his desire to help out the less well off and gave handouts to every pauper who knocked on the door of his mansion.

"For Joe Flavelle, making money was less important than working hard," says Heintzman. He credits Clara Flavelle and his own mother, June Barrett, for passing on a good value system to him. They taught him, he says, "that it mattered what you were, not who you were." Discretion is a must, he adds: "When you do something you don't do it for the acclaim. You do it well, quickly and with dignity."

Heintzman has no time for the snobbery that often afflicts scions of the upper class. It was one of the aspects of life at Upper Canada

College that he didn't like. "It inculcated the wrong values. It made people think their name was more important than their contribution. I remember one time an old boy addressed us in the prayer hall. He told us that because of who we were, we were likely to succeed."

Overall, however, standards have slipped in the Toronto upper classes. There's still plenty of stress on good breeding and a good education, but families no longer get dressed for formal dinners on weeknights; and religious devoutness, whether it be Protestant, Catholic, Judaic or Muslim, is no more common than it is in the rest of society. Many members of the upper class still give generously to charities, but increasingly the fund raising galas aimed at the rich are relying on the lure of a good time and door prizes not generosity of spirit, to loosen purse strings.[1]

The Blue Book: The Leading Lights in Toronto's Social Establishment

Whether they be from old money families or the newer ranks of millionaire entrepreneurs and professionals living in Don Mills, the people on the following lists are widely recognized as the social elite of Toronto.

The Old Guard

The Westons: Galen Weston and his wife, Hilary, stand at the apex of the social establishment in Toronto, thanks to their personal charm, wealth and connections to British royalty. Galen is the billionaire chairman of George Weston Ltd., one of the world's biggest food companies, with North American revenues surpassing $11 billion. Canadians know the company by its store names (Loblaws, Zehrs, Econo-mart and Superstore) and by its products (Neilson's chocolate bars, Clover Leaf tuna, White Swan bathroom tissue). Brother Garry runs the family's U.K. operations, such as Fortnum and Mason.

Galen is the son of W. Garfield Weston and grandson of George Weston, the Toronto baker who founded the family dynasty in 1882. Hilary is convent educated, a former model from the Irish seaside town of Dunleary. Together, they set the social standards for Toronto from their mansions in the Forest Hill district of Toronto and London, England, where they sometimes entertain Canadian friends along with good chums Prince Charles and Princess Diana. In the summer of 1989, Galen organized a fund raiser attended by Canadian couples, who flew on the Concorde to London and were hosted by the Prince and Princess of Wales. Reputed cost: $30,000 a couple. The money went to Lester B. Pearson College of the Pacific, of which Galen is chairman.

The Westons' London residence is a 24-hectare estate, Fort Belvedere, in the Great Park of Windsor Castle. It's where the Duke of Windsor courted Wallis Simpson, just a short drive from the Guards Polo Club, where Galen captains his own team, the Maple Leafs.

But Toronto has been their main address since 1972, when Galen moved back from England to oversee a turnaround at Loblaws. The Westons "came out" in Toronto society in 1986. "It used to be that they didn't get involved in public events, but Hilary got bored," says a Rosedale socialite. "They started going to lots of social events after Galen bought Holt Renfrew."

The Thomsons: "Ken and Marilyn Thomson are extremely shy," says an acquaintance. "They don't throw their money around." The Thomsons generally pass on the glitzy pastimes of their party-going fellow residents of Rosedale. Their names rarely appear in society columns, and overall, their social habits are a throwback to traditional Rosedale — old money all the way. Worth roughly $7 billion, Ken, 68, owns and runs the Thomson Corp., a publishing and retailing empire founded by his father, Roy, that includesmore than 300 newspapers, including the *Globe and Mail*, in North America and Britain. In retailing, his holdings include the Hudson's Bay Co., parent of the Bay, Simpsons and Zellers.

Ken is a practising Baptist, and his idea of a good time is walking his dog in the neighbourhood around his 23 room red-brick Georgian home in Rosedale, or venturing downtown to stroll around his stores on a Saturday. Otherwise he's happiest collecting paintings and other works of art — in contrast to his acquisition-minded father, who was a self-professed rube when it came to the fine arts. Marilyn

Thomson hails from more modest circumstances in Toronto. A former model for Eaton's and a Miss Cheerleader of Toronto, she is now much sought after as a social companion by the Rosedale ladies-who-lunch set. Her presence on the organizing committee of a Zoo Do, for the Metro Zoo, assures its financial success. But her more catty friends suggest that she is just as highly prized for her ability to get coverage for the do's in Thomson-owned newspapers. The Thomsons' social standing is also boosted by Ken's peerage, inherited from his father. There's nothing like having Lord Thomson of Fleet at your party to add the touch of class so many seem to seek so desperately.

The Eatons: In some ways, Upper Canada College never lost its influence on Fred Eaton, 53, the most sociable of the four Eaton brothers who inherited the department store chain that carries their name. At black tie events, Fred is liable to be the one having a boisterous good time with a few buddies. He's still a bit of a jock with a salty sense of humour and enjoys a good laugh with his business peers. Fred shares the hard-working habits of his famous great-grandfather, Timothy, who founded the company in the late 1800s, but he didn't inherit Timothy's very staid Methodist piety. Worth more than $1 billion, the Eaton brothers have divvied up responsibility for running their business concerns, which are centred on the department store but also include a majority stake in Baton Broadcasting, the largest CTV affiliate in the country.

As chairman of T. Eaton Company, Fred is the hands-on manager of the nation wide chain. Eldest brother John, 54, serves as chairman of the parent company, Eaton's of Canada Ltd. Younger brothers Thor and George play more limited roles in the company. They all lead comparatively private lives of affluence and comfort. When he's not stepping out with friends like Conrad Black or the Bassett boys, Fred likes to drive from his Forest Hill mansion to his country house in Caledon or fly down to his place in Lyford Cay. John has always had a fascination with politics and keeps in close touch with Ontario Tory circles. The two younger brothers are loners. Neither is listed in the *Canadian Who's Who*. Thor's main love is horseback riding in Caledon. George spent seven years as a successful Grand Prix racing driver. All four brothers maintain the family's very generous rcord of giving to charities, mainly through the Eaton Foundation. But John spends more time than his siblings on charitable activities. He's active on the board of the Salvation Army in Toronto, the Canadian Hearing Society Foundation and the Canadian Council of Christians and Jews.

Sometimes the boys appear at social affairs with their redoubtable mother, Signy. When they do it's Toronto's version of a command performance.

The Bronfmans: For all their wealth and power, the two Toronto-based Bronfmans, Peter and Edward, are humble, likable guys. Critics say the operations of their Edper Enterprises, which controls more than $100 billion worth of the North American economy, are menacingly large. But in person, they are as menacing as a couple of puppies. On social occasions, Peter, 62, is the more outgoing of the two and has an easy-going, engaging manner that can put even the most nervous social climber at ease. Edward, 64, is much more shy. Together, the two brothers are worth a little more than a billion dollars.

In keeping with Toronto old money mores, the two lead quiet, private lives. When he's not at work, Peter plays tennis and supports several community organizations. Edward's favourite philanthropies include the Canadian Psychiatric Research Foundation, Hebrew University and the Canadian Council for Native Business. Remarkably, neither brother is a member of the Toronto Club.

Other Prominent Old Money

The McCutcheons, James and Fred, millionaire sons of the late Senator Wallace McCutcheon, one of the founders of Argus Corp.;

Mr. Justice William Howland, former chief justice of Ontario, a direct descendant of a Family Compact family;

Mr. Justice Joseph Potts, Ontario Supreme Court judge, son of Maj. Gen. A.E. Potts of Saskatoon;

Julian Porter, leading libel lawyer, son of former chief justice Dana Porter. His wife Anna, a publisher, easily matches him in prominence;

The Honourable John Black Aird, lawyer, former chancellor of the University of Toronto;

Henry (Hal) Jackman, chairman, Empire Life Insurance;

Donald Webster, Helix Investments.

George Gardiner, Scott's Hospitality

New Money: The Fund-raising Corps

They are ostentatious, in their mid-forties, married to rich men, and they are formidable fund raisers for cultural organizations like the Toronto Symphony and the Canadian Opera Company and various medical causes that have become reliant on their fund-raising ability.

Nancy Anne Raeburn Paul: Like so many upper-class wives, Paul calls herself an interior decorator. She is also the founding force behind the Canadian Women's Breast Cancer Foundation. Social columnist Rosemary Sexton calls her "the Queen of Toronto socialites." She was born in Midhurst, Ontario, where her father worked for the CNR. Today she is married to accountant Vincent Paul and lives in an Old Yonge Street mansion. She combines a knack for showmanship with top people-managing skills, and has a self-confessed passion for New York–style fund raisers with plenty of pomp and circumstance.

Carole Grafstein: The wife of Senator Jerry Grafstein, she has spent more than three decades working for causes ranging from the Toronto Hadassah-WIZO to Mount Sinai Hospital to the Canadian Opera Company. She has become the link between old money Rosedale and the newer Jewish fortunes of Don Mills. Otherwise known as the Energizer, Grafstein is noted for rescuing the 1989 Herbie Mistletoe Ball, a fund raiser for a children's program at the Hospital for Sick Children. She's easily the most socially respected of the fund raisers, although that's not saying a lot.

Patricia Appleton: A Grafstein protégée, Appleton was the key organizer at the 1989 Opera Ball, which netted more than $400,000 from 650 guests. Married to lawyer Michael Appleton, she operates from her Bridle Path mansion, where she has a well-equipped office to work in and a swimming pool and Renaissance-style gardens to relax in. She grew up in a modest Jewish section of Toronto.

Anna Maria de Sousa: Wife of investment banker Ivan de Sousa, she is the one-woman dynamo behind the annual Brazilian Ball. The first event was held in the basement of a Portuguese church in 1966. In 1990, the ball netted more than $500,000 for the Hospital for Sick Children. Her event now ranks with the Opera Ball as the most sought after invitation in Toronto.

Catherine Nugent: Wife of business executive David Nugent, she reigned until recently as the queenpin of Toronto soicalites from her Glen Road home in Rosedale. She used to chair as many as 10 functions a year until she scaled back to give herself time to raise three children.

The Social Impresario

Conrad Black: Worth between $300 and $400 million, Black is in a social category all by himself. He is chairman and CEO of Hollinger Inc., a publishing empire that owns such prominent publications as London's *Daily Telegraph*, the Jerusalem *Post* and Canada's *Saturday Night* magazine. But he's just as well known in Toronto circles for arranging top-drawer social events that attract a wide cross-section of influential people.

In manner, Black seems to be acting the part of a businessman he read in a Charles Dickens' novel. He's so starchy, he could be a breathing replica of a tycoon in Madame Toussaud's wax museum. He is an ardent conservative who dresses like a merchant banker and speaks in polysyllables. He has a wicked wit, however, and is well known for his tirades against journalists, which seem primarily designed to produce drawing-room chuckles from his less outspoken peers. Nevertheless, Black has an allure that attracts other social heavyweights to him like flies to honey. Black's immediate circle of male buddies includes Fred and John Eaton, Doug Bassett, Dixon Chant, John Findlay and David Radler. But Black's pull reaches into all sections of Toronto society.

He uses his social skills to make his annual Hollinger dinners at the Toronto Club big draws for the city's black tie set. He understands the importance of having a big name to pull in the cream of society. In June 1988, at the fifty-seventh annual Hollinger dinner, Black's guest of honour was British Prime Minister Margaret Thatcher, who received a standing ovation from 170 guests even before she spoke. In 1989 Black's guest of honour was former U.S. president Ronald Reagan. As usual Black's event drew even the most retiring billion-aires, like Ken Thomson and the Reichmann brothers, and there was the usual array of intellectuals, cultural mavens and businessmen. The wittiest comment of the evening came from *Saturday Night*'s editor, John Fraser, who had a suggestion for the next year's speaker: "Deng Xiaoping shouldn't charge too much a year from now," he quipped.

The Social Elite of Toronto at a Glance

The A List (blue bloods in pecking order):

Galen and Hilary Weston; Ken and Marilyn Thomson; Henry (Hal) and Maruja Jackman; John and Liz Tory (John is president of the Thomson Corp.); Frederick and Catherine Eaton; Peter and Lynda Bronfman; Tom and Sonja Bata; Albert and Paul Reichmann; Beverly Matthews (lawyer, McCarthy Tétrault); George and Mary Heintzman.

The B List (in pecking order):

Marlene and Elvio Del Zotto (she's an active fund raiser, he is president of Tridel Enterprises and president of the provincial Liberal organization); Senator Jerry and Carole Grafstein (he's chairman of the board, O'Keefe Centre, and she's the doyenne of fund raising galas); Catherine and David Nugent (she's a one-time fund raising dynamo, he's president of the Riviera Group); Patricia and Michael Appleton (she's the fund raiser, he's a lawyer); Anna Maria and Ivan de Sousa (she created the Brazilian Ball, he's an investment banker who helped pay for it); Sally and Steve Stavro (he's president of Knob Hill Farms); Ronnie and Martin Richman (he's president of the Richman Group); Brenda and Leighton McCarthy (he's a stock-broker); Susan and Art Scace (he's a lawyer with McCarthy Tétrault). Conrad and Shirley Black; Julian and Anna Porter; Joey and Toby Tanenbaum, philanthropists; Allan and Sondra Gotlieb (he's chairman of the Canada Council and former ambassador to Washington, she's a columnist and author); June Barrett; Dr. John and Gay Evans (he's Allelix Inc. chairman); Richard Currie, president of Loblaws; Judge Rosalie Abella and husband Prof. Irving Abella; Paul Godfrey, Toronto *Sun* publisher and his wife, Gina; Bluma and Bram Appel, philanthropists; Eddie, a lawyer, and Suzanne Goodman; George and Susan Cohen (George is the fun-loving head of McDonald's Restaurants); Peter Munk, chairman of American Barrick Resources Corp., and wife Melanie; Gerry Schwartz, president of Onex Corp., and his wife, Heather Reisman, a management consultant; Mickey and Judi Cohen (he runs Molsons, she's president of the board of directors, National Ballet of Canada); Rudy and Cathy Bratty (he's a multimillionaire developer and partner in HCI Holding with Fred DeGasperis and Marco Muzzo); Arthur Gelber, patron of the arts and president of Gelber Realty and Investments; Jane and Trevor Eyton (he's chairman of Brascan Ltd., she's active in charity fund raisers like the Snow Ball for the Canadian Psychiatric Research Foundation); Allan Waters, president of CHUM Ltd., and wife Marjorie; Allan Slaight, head of Standard Broadcasting; Emmett Cardinal Carter (former Roman Catholic bishop of Toronto); Roy and Lee MacLaren (he's a former Liberal MP and media owner; Raymond and Shirley Matthews (he's a surgeon); Donald C. Webster, Helix Investments; Douglas Bassett, president of Baton Broadcasting Inc., and Susan, who helps organize the Brazilian Ball; Pauline McGibbon, former lieutenant governor of Ontario and now chancellor of the University of Toronto; John Black Aird, former lieutenant governor of Ontario and former chancellor of the University of Toronto; Bernard and Sylvia Ostry (he's chairman, TVOntario, she's an economist and public servant); Mary Alice Stuart, chairman, CJRT-FM Inc.; John Bassett, Sr., chairman of the executive committee, Baton Broadcasting, and wife, broadcaster Isabel Bassett; Peter Herrndorf, publisher, *Toronto Life*; Adrienne Clarkson and mate John Raulston Saul; Arthur Gelgoot, accountant to the media; Nalini Stewart, Ontario Arts Council.

The Montreal Social Establishment

The evidence is everywhere, from the croissant shops on rue Ste. Catherine to the Eaton's department store, where English matrons once resolutely spoke English to store clerks who answered them with French accents. The French language and culture have captured the soul of the city. The Scottish, English and Irish economic czars who once dominated the city have become ghosts of another era. Such tycoons as Sir Herbert Holt, Samuel Bronfman and J.W. McConnell once dictated the city's economic and social agenda from their offices on St. James Street and their homes in Westmount. Today, the street is called rue St. Jacques, and on the leafy thoroughfares of Westmount, you can often hear French spoken.

The English private clubs, like the St. James and St. Stephen's, have lost their status to the Club Saint-Denis, favourite haunt of the new French Canadian business lords. Even the Mount Royal, still Montreal's most prestigious club, where the annual fee tops $2,000, the membership is roughly banlanced between English and French.

The retreat of the English upper class that began in the 1970s has turned into a rout. There has been no war, just a bout of hostile events: the October Crisis of 1970; the election of a separatist government in 1976; after which landmark companies like Sun Life Assurance, the Royal Trust and even the Bank of Montreal moved their head offices out of the province; the enactment of the French language law; and, most recently, the passage of the sign law, which ruled that exterior signs must be in French only.

There has been a social revolution in Quebec that has thrown a new entrepreneurial class of French Canadian businessmen to the top of the economic and social order. Remnants of the English community reign, but they have vastly reduced influence in the affairs of the city and province. Names like Molson, Birks and Webster don't carry the clout they used to. The corporate heads of the big multinationals, like Bill Stinson at CP Ltd., Purdy Crawford at Imasco and Claude Taylor at Air Canada, quietly go about the business of running their companies and don't play a dynamic role in the city's affairs. Charles Bronfman is the only anglophone left with enormous clout. There is a certain mingling at social events — the old family anglophones are still big benefactors of Montreal's cultural life. and both French and English cut deals over breakfast at the Ritz Carlton. But otherwise, the English gather quietly in their homes, or perhaps for a game of tennis at the Hillside Club while the French play at Laval Golf and Country. The English play golf at the Royal Montreal, the French at Laval-sur-le-lac or Richelieu Valley.

The numbers tell the same story. At the Board of Trade, once a bastion of English dominance, operations are now fully bilingual and half the organization's 2.700 member companies are run by francophones. Throughout the province, francophone control of business has been steadily growing. They provided 61.6 per cent of jobs in 1987, up from 54.8 per cent in 1961.

The latest census data show that 53 per cent of Quebec's anglophones are now bilingual. Yet ethnic anxieties are still high in Montreal because only 60 per cent of its residents are francophone — compared with 90 per cent outside the metropolis — and the number is falling. Hence the province's fixation on developing its own immigration policies separate from Ottawa. Before and after the Meech Lake crisis in 1990, the attitude of Quebec's new French business rulers toward Confederation turned radical. For the first time, these innately conservative executives spoke openly about the possibility of outright separation, or at the very least a complete rethinking of Quebec's constitutional relationship with Canada. Most of them voted against separation in the 1980 referendum, but the reluctance of many English Canadians to accept that Quebec is a distinct society jaundiced their views toward the rest of Canada.

Whatever its future political status, Quebec society is more distinct than ever; little wonder that the passions and play of the upper class have more than ever taken on a French flavour. For high society, that means a social whirl of elegance and sophistication in keeping with the city's European style. The social establishment's flair was on full display at the 1989 gala for the Musée des Beaux-Arts de Montréal — the Museum of Fine Arts. the theme for the evening was la Belle Epoque. Society ladies in ball gowns of every hue sat down with black tie escorts at gold-covered tables decorated with centrepieces of grapes and lilies. They dined on scallop mousse wrapped in smoked salmon, sliced duckling and crêpes suzettes. The 625 gala goers represented a good cross section of the city's business and political elite, French and English. There were business czars: Paul Desmarais of Power Corp. attended with his wife, Jacqueline; Jonathon Birks of the venerable Henry Birks & Sons escorted his wife, Maria, co-chairman of the event; Bernard Lamarre, the gregarious chairman of the museum and CEO of Lavalin, was there with his wife, Louise. There were politicos, including former prime minister Pierre Trudeau and Marcel Masse. And there were philanthropists: Phyllis Lambert, daughter of the late Sam Bronfman, founder of Seagram Co., added a dash of old money cachet to the crowd.

Montreal's establishment is now dominated by the entrepreneurial class, which has captured the imagination of the province's youth. In an exaggerated way, they have become the new heroes of Quebec society. The city's social estabishment thus contains a large number of newly rich French businessmen, lawyers and accountants. The English form a shrinking rump.

The French Contingent

Paul Desmarais: Desmarais, 68, has been a role model for young Quebeckers for decades. (See pp. 146). He's slowing down and passing the reins to sons Paul, Jr., and André, but his influence in Montreal has never been greater.

Bernard Lamarre: The former CEO of engineering giant Lavalin Ltd., (see pp. 152.) Lamarre, 60, has pushed the Musée des Beaux-

Arts to new heights of prominence. A ubiquitous presence in downtown Montreal, he spends his time at the Beaver Club, in the Queen Elizabeth Hotel or at the Ritz.

Raymond Cyr: Cyr, 57, inherited the CEO spot at BCE Inc., which owns Bell Canada, from Jean de Grandpré and has been undoing his predecessor's diversification splurge beyond telephones ever since. For this, he is earning respect at the Mount Royal Club.

Michel Bélanger: The former CEO of the National bank, Bélanger is known for his unflappable disposition and his entrepreneurial talent. He transformed the bank from a dog to a star. He spent his early years as a bureaucrat. Most recently, he co-chaired Bourassa's committee on the future of Quebec's place in Confederation

Laurent Beaudoin: An accountant turned entrepreneur, Beaudoin, 53, is the CEO of Bombardier Inc., (see pp. 151.) which he turned into a flourishing multinational maker of subway trains and planes.

Claude Castonguay: The chairman of the Laurentian Group, a financial services and insurance conglomerate, Castonguay, 63, is a no-nonsense actuary who shares the spotlight with Desmarais as mentor for Quebec business.

Philippe de Gaspé Beaubien: Beaubien, 63, is chairman of Telemedia Inc., a magazine publishing and radio broadcasting company that controls more than two dozen radio stations in Quebec and Ontario and publishes *TV Guide*. He divides his leisure hours between the Mount Royal Club, Club Saint-Denis and the Virgin Islands.

Bertin Nadeau: Nadeau, 51, is the chairman of Unigesco Inc., a multifaceted conglomerate involved in food products, hardware and building materials nationwide. Son of a New Brunswick pig farmer, Nadeau built Unigesco from a small holding company involved in insurance into a national force.

Others

André Chagnon (Groupe Vidéotron operates Télé-Métropole and Vidéotron cable, Canada's number-two cable company); Jean Coutu (CEO of drugstore owner Groupe Jean Coutu); Marcel Dutil (chairman of steel-products maker Canam Manac and grandson of Edouard Lacroix, once one of Quebec's most powerful industrialist-politicians); Paul Ivanier (CEO, Ivaco Inc.); Claude Beland (head of the 4.6-million-member Desjardins credit union group); André Saumier (investment executive); Pierre Peladeau (a nondrinking publishing tycoon who riled Jewish Montrealers in 1990 with what they perceived as anti-Semitic remarks); Camille Dagenais (director, the SNC Group); Bernard Lemaire (president, Cascades Inc.); Jean-Claude Delorme (chairman, Caisse de Dépôt, the $35-billion investment fund.)

The Anglophone Contingent

By far the most influential anglophone in the city is Charles Rosner Bronfman, 60-year-old co-chairman of Seagram Co., the world's leading distillery. His clout ranks with Desmarais's within the business community and in his case the Jewish community as well. Worth about $1.5 billion at last count, Bronfman is the youngest son of Sam Bronfman, the hard-driving founder of the booze empire who died in 1971, finally leaving Charles and his older brother, Edgar, 62, to flower without his overbearing presence. Charles was considered the wimp of the family until he decided to launch the Montreal Expos in 1968. "The Expos helped give me a sense of confidence," he once said. "It was the first time I ever got out from under my father and it was very important in the making of me as a person in my own right."

Bronfman works out of the medieval-style fortress that is the Seagram building in Montreal. (Edgar runs its international headquarters in New York.) He belongs to both the Mount Royal Club and the Club Saint-Denis and is fluently bilingual. He's generally well liked by French and English alike.

Bronfman divides his time between running Claridge, a vehicle for his personal investments, and Seagram's affairs. He sits on the boards of Power Corp., the Montreal Symphony and the Museum of Fine Arts. In 1990, he decided to sell the Expos. (Apparently, now that he's in his sixties, he feels he has grown up.)

The English-speaking community that remains influential in Montreal breaks down into two groups:

The Corporate Heavyweights (in random order):

David Morton (CEO, Alcan); Purdy Crawford (CEO, Imasco); Claude Taylor (chairman, Air Canada); Bill Stinson (CEO, CP Ltd.); George Petty (CEO, Repap Enterprises Corp.); William McKenzie (CEO, Memotec Data Inc.); Harold Greenberg (chairman, Astral Bellevue Pathé Inc.); Leonard Ellen (majority owner with Reuben Cohen of Moncton in Central Capital, a $17-billion financial services conglomerate); Stephen Jarislowsky (Canada's most powerful investment counsellor, invests a portfolio in excess of $10 billion for more than 200 pension funds. Of German descent, Jarislowsky moves easily between the French and English communities in Montreal); Nathanael Davis (big holder of Alcan stock, worth more than $100 million); Liberal MP Paul Martin, Jr. (former CEO, Canada Steamship Lines. Unlike many of his Montreal peers, Martin speaks French.)

Wealthy Anglophone Families (in random order):

The Birks (worth $70 million; George is company chairman, son Jonathon is CEO, son Thomas is president); the Molsons (worth about $93 million; Eric is chairman, the Molson Companies Ltd.); the Cummings (worth at least $50 million; Jack and Steven run Maxwell Cummings & Sons Holding Ltd. The family made its money in real estate and selling CCM bicycles); the Reitmans (worth about $65 million; Jack, Jeremy and Stephen own the chain of clothing stores); the Steinbergs (worth about $175 million; former owners of the food store chain, which they sold after a messy family squabble over which family member would run it); the Krugers (worth more than $300 million; run Kruger Inc., a vast international newsprint company, and other operations); the Kanebs (worth about $40 million; Wilfred and son Mark run Olco Petroleum Group); the Timmins (made their money in Noranda Mines, worth more than $100 million, now invested out of Toronto); the Nesbitts (Aird and Arthur; worth at least $60 million; owned Ogilvy's. Nesbitt Thomson, the investment dealer, is the family company); the Clarkes (Stanley, retired, and Brock, a lawyer; the family made its money through Clarke Transport; worth more than $60 million).

Prominent Lawyers and Accountants

Nothing much happens in Montreal, socially, politically or commercially, without these ubiquitous middlemen:

Georges Pouliot (lawyer, Pouliot, Mercure, Lebel); Claude Ducharme (lawyer, Desjardins Ducharme); André Monaste (lawyer, Stein Monaste Pratte and Marseille); Claude Pratte (lawyer, Stein Monaste Pratt); Neil Phillips (lawyer, Goodman Freeman Phillips and Vineberg. Son of Lazarus, the trusted adviser to Sam Bronfman, spends most of his time in New York office); Peter Blaikie (Heenan Blaikie); Serge Saucier (accountant, Raymond, Chabot, Martin, Paré, Quebec's largest accounting firm).

Vancouver: City of the Forever Young

Ever wonder where the jocks and cheerleaders you met in university ended up? Well, those who didn't settle in Calgary moved to Vancouver, the home of the tan, the Ferrari and the trophy wife. The city is a bit like a yuppie who won't grow up. The libido is as strong as ever but the blue jeans are beginning to fit a little too tight and the party animal image is getting tiresome. It's not that the city hasn't had time to pass through adolesence. Vancouver has some serious second- and third-generation money — the scions of the lumber, mining, sugar and investment barons who built vast fortunes there in the last century. But the old money mores are swamped by each new tide of arrivistes and rule busters who come seeking Lifestyle with a capital L.

For refugees from the cruel, cold parking lot with buildings on it that is Toronto, Vancouver is a sensuous lover waiting just beyond the Coast Mountain range for a purely physical relationship with no strings attached. For emigrants from the busy streets of beautiful Montreal, Vancouver is a destination that has Florida beat ten times over, if they have the air fare. And for the Asian investors who are arriving by the jet load at Vancouver Airport, the city is a sponge for all the cash they can pour into it.

Vancouver is imbued with a sense of physical permanence. To the northwest, there's the spectacular, lasting beauty of the Coast Mountains; to the southeast, there's the faintly exotic allure of the Pacific waters that lap in Burrard Inlet. Little wonder the city and surrounding coastline is a magnet for nature lovers, writers and artists of all types.

But for all its natural grandeur, Vancouver is not a city for aesthetes. It's a city of conspicuous consumption; of cars, lovers, houses and all the sporting thrills nature has to offer. From the garden-frilled homes of Kerrisdale to the cabins at Whistler and the 40-foot boats moored at the yacht club beside Stanley Park, Vancouver is a city with a fixation on toys, halter tops and net personal wealth. Count cars on Georgia Street and you'll see more Jaguars, Porsches and BMWs than you can see on Toronto's Avenue Road at rush hour. Sit in a trendy restaurant in False Creek on a summer day and you'll see as much star material as you can at a Hollywood film gala. It's a city where short skirts never went out of style and business suits, whether for men or women, mark the wearer as an interloper from Toronto. In Vancouver, clothes are meant to show off year-round tans; forget the cool formality of Toronto fashion and the elegance of Montreal chic. Unfortunately, it's also a city that has trouble keeping serious culture alive — witness the recurring financial crises endured by the Vancouver Symphony and Ballet British Columbia. People are evidently too busy throwing parties on boats or whisking themselves off to Whistler to listen to a sonata.

In the business district, a hodgepodge of post-modernist architecture dominates the cityscape. From the glass and steel of the Bentall Centre and the Hongkong Bank buildings to the fascist-style concrete fortress of the old MacMillan Bloedel offices, even the buildings seem arriviste. Older buildings, like the decaying Woodward's department store or the beautifully restored Marine Building, just can't compete with the brashness of the newer edifices.

Vancouver is unlike any other city in Canada. Its motto is *carpe diem*: live for today. But it sure is a lot of fun.

The self-perpetuating frontier mentality has a positive side. Vancouver's vibrant social establishment is open to just about all comers. Big money is more important than old money, even if you're Asian or Jewish. New money defines the mores of the city, despite the efforts of the Vancouver Club, a bastion of upper-class pretension, to keep newcomers in their place.

The stalwarts of the city's social elite are a rainbow of diversity. There are just a few old family names and many more wealthy financiers, business executives, lawyers, doctors and academics who have risen to the top in the past decade or so. In Toronto, Montreal or Halifax, many of them would be considered nouveau riche.

The Authentic Old Guard

Anyone who doubts the transitory nature of Vancouver's social establishment should consider the almost complete disappearance of the city's founding families from its ranks. Names like Koerner, Pemberton, MacMillan, Prentice and Spencer have vanished; their fortunes have scattered across the continent through dozens of heirs. Old guard, in Vancouver's lexicon, includes first-generation wealth.

The Bentalls: Clark Bentall, 76, and his brother Bob, 69, still run the construction and real estate empire founded by their father, Charles. A devout Baptist, Clark runs Dominion Co., the construction operation that has poured concrete in just about every major western city. Bob runs Bentall Developments, the real estate wing of the family business. Clark's son David, 36, is executive vice-president of Dominion. Their lifestyle is old money as quiet as Hush Puppies.

Peter Bentley: Bentley, 61, is the CEO of forestry giant Canfor Corporation, the company founded by his father, L.L.G. (Poldi) Bentley, and John Prentice, Poldi's brother-in-law. Bentley lends aristocratic charm to an otherwise crass town. (See p. 139.)

Frank Griffiths: Chairman, WIC Communications. At 75, he's become the most powerful broadcasting mogul in the west and a rival power centre to the eastern broadcasters. He achieved that status in 1990, when he added the broadcasting operations of Dr. Charles Allard to his stable. From his floating office, an 87-foot launch called the *Feline*, Griffiths oversees a $350-million empire of radio and television stations from Vancouver to Toronto. He has owned the Vancouver Canucks since 1974. WIC CEO Doug Holtby, 43, minds the empire while Griffiths indulges in his favourite pastime, fishing off Alaska or in the Gulf of Georgia.

Edgar Kaiser, Jr.: The 49-year-old scion of the Kaiser Steel Corp. family is chairman and CEO of Kaiser Resources Ltd., but he spends most of his time on his favourite charity, the Kaiser Substance Abuse Foundation. He raised eyebrows in Vancouver when he sold control of his coal company to British Columbia Resources Investment Corp., which eventually had to write off its entire investment. He also presided over the deteriorating fortunes of the Bank of British Columbia before it was sold to the Hongkong Bank.

Norman Keevil, Jr.: He's the CEO of Teck Corp., the mining giant that snapped up Cominco, a mining gem, in 1986 when CP Ltd. put it on the auction block. An engineer by training, Keevil is a stalwart at the Vancouver Club and the Shaughnessy Golf and Country Club.

The First-Generation Old Guard

Sam Belzberg: On Wall Street, Belzberg, former chairman of Vancouver-based First City Financial, is known as an infamous corporate raider who made more than U.S. $300 million in the past decade in the arbitrage game. In Vancouver, he's become known as a major philanthropist. He founded the Simon Wiesenthal Centre at Yeshiva University in Los Angeles, started the Dystonia Medical Research Foundation and is a generous benefactor of Simon Fraser University, which gave him an honorary degree. He's clearly aware of the value of a reputation for philanthropy, and if he keeps up the benificence, he's bound to earn the social respect he craves.

Larry Bell: The former chairman of B.C. Hydro, Bell is a widely respected businessman and has been a major fund raiser in Vancouver for the past 25 years. He's known in business and politics as a tough straight shooter.

Peter Brown: A stockbroker, Brown, 50, built Canarim Investment Corp. from a bucket shop promoting penny stocks into a respected firm that generates as much as 25 per cent of the VSE's activity. In 1989, he merged his creation with Toronto's Loewen Ondaatje McCutcheon; it's now called LOM Western Securities Ltd.

Robert Lee: A major real estate developer in Vancouver since the 1960s, Lee is president of the Prospero Group of Companies. He's been busy attracting Asian investors to Canada since the 1960s. The company manages a real estate portfolio worth $350 million and bought Montreal's landmark Place Victoria for $85 million in 1981.

Wendy McDonald: In 1990, McDonald became the female chairman of the Vancouver Board of Trade — the first in its 104-year history. McDonald earned her credentials as CEO of B.C. Bearing Engineers Ltd. She took control of the ball-bearing and transmission distributor from her first husband when he died in 1950 and has since expanded it into 24 branches in western Canada and 10 in the United States. She also has 10 children from three marriages.

Jack Poole: Now the president of VLC Properties Ltd., Poole has ridden the roller-coaster real estate business since 1964, when he founded Daon Development with Vancouver businessman Graham Dawson. Caught in the real estate squeeze in the early 1980s, Daon became BCE Development Corp. when it was bought by BCE Inc. Poole resigned as CEO of the foundering company in May 1989 to begin his current operation. As *Equity* magazine noted: "He is the only private developer building significant amounts of rental housing in Vancouver."

Barbara Rae: Chancellor of Simon Fraser University, Rae, 60, is president of ADIA Canada Ltd., an employment placement business she joined in the 1950s. Named B.C.'s Entrepreneur of the Year for 1987, she is a director of B.C. Telephone, Seaboard Life Insurance and Microtel Ltd.

Milton Wong: This 52-year-old longtime Vancouver resident made a name for himself as the gregarious chairman and CEO of M.K. Wong Associates, a major pension fund manager that invests a portfolio of about $2 billion. Wong's enthusiasm got the better of him before the 1987 stock market crash, which caught him heavily invested in equities. He's been fighting an uphill battle to restore client confidence ever since. He spends a lot of time on community projects.

The New Guard

Victor Li: The 28-year-old son of Li Ka-shing, reputed to be Hong Kong's richest citizen, Victor Li became a Canadian citizen in 1983 and has served as a conduit for an outpouring of his father's money into the country. He is the senior vice-president of Concorde Pacific, a company that will, over the next 15 years, develop Vancouver's Expo site into Pacific Place, a mixed-use development with hotels, apartments, condominiums and shops. With substantial holdings in B.C., Alberta, Saskatchewan and Ontario, the Li family is already a major force in Canadian business. Its holdings include Toronto's Harbour Castle Westin Hotel, a 43 per cent stake in Husky Oil and a 10 per cent holding in the Canadian Imperial Bank of Commerce. Li sits on the board of the Vancouver General Hospital and is an avid supporter of the annual Dragon Boat festival at False Creek. His younger brother, Richard, 24, has a stake in Toronto's Gordon Capital Corp.

David Ho: A newcomer from Hong Kong, 39-year-old Ho is an heir to the Hong Kong Tobacco Co. fortune. He crashed onto the Vancouver scene in 1987 with his $400-million purchase of Gray Beverage Inc., western Canada's largest soft-drink bottler and distributor. He followed that up by purchasing a 75 per cent stake in the University

Golf Club. His first job was loading tobacco for the family business in Hong Kong. Now he oversees 1,000 employees and drives a custom-built Ferrari.

Ron Shon: One of Vancouver's most successful real estate developers, Japanese-born Shon runs the Shon Group of Companies. His biggest gem is Cathedral Place, which will replace the Georgia Medical Dental Building. It will include a 900-square-metre art gallery with three lion sculptures flanking the entrance. At 38, he's already a member of the Vancouver Club and is active on the boards of the Vancouver Museum Foundation, the Vancouver Symphony Orchestra and the Canadian Cancer Society.

Mohammed Faris and Joe Houssian: The two Lebanese-born cousins run Intrawest Properties. They've been a team since 1976. Their first big deal, in 1984, was the $3-million purchase of Lonsdale Quay on the north shore of Burrard Inlet; it's a multi-use development replete with retail space and a 57-room hotel. Better yet was their 1986 deal that gave them a foothold in Blackcomb Mountain Properties. Today they control Blackcomb, which features year-round glacier skiing and rivals Whistler as the most popular skiing location in B.C.

Other Leading Social Lights:
The Executive Contingent (in random order):

Joe Segal (retired founder, Mr. Jax fashion); Ray Smith (CEO, Mac-Millan Bloedel, B.C.'s largest forestry company); Ian Donald (CEO, Fletcher Challenge Ltd.; has taken the Vancouver Establishment by storm since he arrived in 1985 from New Zealand); Michael Phelps (president, Westcoast Energy; one-time adviser to energy minister Marc Lalonde, he joined Westcoast in 1982 and has forged a national reputation since); John and Tim Kerr (own and run Lignum Ltd.); Hassan Khosrowshahi (president, Inwest Investments); Paul McElligott (CEO, B.C. Rail); Bob Hallbauer (president and CEO, Cominco Ltd.); Dick Whittall (chairman, Placer Development Ltd.); Daniel Jarvis (CEO, Intrawest Development Corp.); Rusty Goepel (Goepel Shields & Partners); Murray Pezim (stock promoter); Harry Moll (stock promoter); Peter Cundill (mutual fund manager).

The B List (in random order): Volunteers, Fundraisers and Philanthropists

Ron Longstaffe (former Canfor and Lignum Ltd. executive, currently CEO, 1994 Victoria Commonwealth Games); Frank Murphy (lawyer, Farris, Vaughn Wills and Murphy); Bob Wyman (former CEO, Pemberton Securities); Dr. David Strangeway (president, UBC); Tom Rust (former CEO, Crown Forest Industries, currently chairman of Vancouver Foundation, a philanthropy that distributes $20 million a year to various groups); Bill and Sharon Wright (he's Vancouver Opera president and a partner in Davis and Co.); Craig Lahmer (Arthur Anderson & Co.); John McCutcheon (president, Ark La Tex Industries Ltd.); Bernie Magnan (philanthropist); Lydia Suderman (past president, Vancouver Opera Guild); Barrie Innes (president, Vancouver Opera Guild); Eric and Jo Moncur (members, Vancouver Opera board executive).

The C List (in random order):

Gerri Marshall (founded the Emerald Ball in 1988 to raise money to fight schizophrenia); Dr. Cliff Harris and his wife, Louise (she's an organizing dynamo behind the Emerald Ball); MLA Carol Gran and her husband, John; geneticist Dr. Michael Smith; Anthony Petrina (senior vice-president, Placer Development Ltd.); Brandt Louie (chairman of the board of trustees, University Hospital, and director of the Vancouver Symphony Society); Hugh Main (chairman, University Hospital Foundation); Tom and Caleb Chan (recent Hong Kong immigrants, they donated $10 million in 1990 to a new arts centre at UBC; Caleb is president of Burrard International); Rob Heffron (chairman of the Ballet B.C. board).

Winnipeg

Winnipeg is a wealthy dowager clinging to what's left of her former prestige and living in splendid isolation in a mansion on the Assiniboine River, where she can remain untainted by the grasping types from Toronto and the barbecue-loving boys from Alberta.

Winnipeg is a city of refined social sensibilities, a legacy of the proud history that saw it develop from a bustling boom town at the turn of the century, when the CPR linked it to the east and west, to the grand days of the tycoons who built vast fortunes buying and selling grain. The grain trade was a gold mine for merchant families like the Richardsons, the Gooderhams, the Patersons, the Parrishes and the Heimbeckers — at least until 1935, when the Canadian Wheat Board, a federal marketing agency, took over from the private, freewheeling Winnipeg Grain Exchange, where the grain barons wielded their influence.

There is a widespread perception that Winnipeg has produced more than its share of influential people in all walks of life over the years. And it's probably true. Beginning with Sir Clifford Sifton, minister of the interior for Wilfrid Laurier and a publishing tycoon who built an empire based on the Winnipeg *Free Press*, the city has issued federal political movers, for example, Jack Pickersgill, Mitchell Sharp, Claude Isbister, James Coyne and the Axworthy boys, Tom and Lloyd.

Today, Winnipeg has a strong sense of its past but a less certain sense of its future. The great grain families have vanished from the scene, with the notable exception of the Richardsons, who are still the region's dominant family, socially and economically. The city derives its economic vitality from insurance and financial powerhouses like Great-West Life Assurance and the Investors Group (both controlled by Power Corp. of Montreal) and Federal Industries, a multi-armed industrial empire forged by Jack Fraser, who remains based in the city as a matter of pride, not convenience. There are the old rich, who prefer to live in the mansions along Wellington Street not far from the centre of town, and the new rich, who opt for executive-style homes in the affluent Tuxedo district. Together they form the social establishment of the city, a rather discreet group with old money mores and a passion for the arts that has made the Royal Winnnipeg Ballet a national gem. They go in for galas, but not with the manic compulsiveness of Torontonians.

The Royal Winnipeg Ballet's fiftieth anniversary gala in October 1989 was a showcase event that drew most of the social elite of the region. About 750 guests turned out at the Centennial Concert Hall to watch the ballet's Evelyn Hart and Steven Hyde dance Marius Petipa's *Paquita*. Then it was off to the Westin Hotel for a dinner of tiger prawns, mangoes, filet of lamb, watercress salad with pine nuts and, finally, berries Romanoff. Digital Equipment and Great-West Life Assurance funded the event, and the local business heavy-weights were out in force — George Richardson and his sister Katherine, an RWB board member; Great-West's Kevin Kavanagh and his wife, Else; and Gendis Inc.'s Albert Cohen and his wife, Irena, both RBW board members. Toronto couldn't have done it better.

The Winnipeg Establishment

George Richardson and brother James (inherited James Richardson & Sons Ltd., a grain and investment empire founded by their great-grandfather); Margaret Richardson (sister of George and James, honorary president of the Royal Winnipeg Ballet); Albert and Irena Cohen (he's founder of Gendis Inc., an import-export business that won exclusive rights to distribute Paper Mate Pens and Sony products in Canada, she's a Royal Winnipeg Ballet board member); Jack Fraser (president, Federal Industries); Kevin and Else Kavanagh (he's president and CEO, Great-West Life Assurance); Izzy Asper (CEO, Canwest Capital, chairman, Global Communications); Art Mauro (president and CEO, Investors Group Inc.); Arni Thorsteinson (president, Canadian Holdings Ltd., board director and number-one fund raiser for the Conservatives in Manitoba); Rod Zimmer (president of the Royal Winnipeg Ballet and director of marketing, Manitoba Lotteries Commission); Louise Soubry (vice-president, Royal Winnipeg Ballet).

The Prairie Paladins

It is an axiom of political science that a nation or region will always develop a strong sense of identity if it faces an external threat to its wellbeing or integrity. (Israel is the example most often cited.) The same reasoning holds true for the prairie provinces, which have been fending off the supposed machinations of eastern powerbrokers in one form or another since they entered Confederation. Opposition

to the east has fostered a strong regional identity in the western provinces and a relatively close-knit Establishment.

For uninformed or uncaring reidents of central Canada, the words
Establishment and *West* might seem contradictory. Central Canadians think that advanced civilization stops at Winnipeg and begins
again on the other side of the Rocky Mountains, in Vancouver. Nothing could be further from the truth.

There are important differences, though, between the western social
elite and those in eastern capitals. Whether in Calgary, Edmonton
or Regina, entry into elite circles depends more on your achievements,
abilities and often, corporate title than on your father's or grandfather's last name, as it does in Toronto or Halifax. In the west,
the social establishment is dominated by oil barons, a few industrialists and the lawyers who do their deals for them. Social life in
Calgary revolves around the old money Ranchmen's Club, the new
guard's Petroleum Club and the 400 Club, which caters more to the
oil service and supply crowd. But Calgary also has a fancy arts centre,
the Spruce Meadows show jumping extravaganzas and the Alberta
Ballet. Edmonton, the provincial capital, is not only the home of
bureaucrats and oil field workers but also boasts the prestigious Citadel Theatre. Regina's Establishment hang-out is the Assiniboia
Club.

Mind you, westerners do have a taste for the unconventional when
it comes to high-society functions. A popular event in Edmonton
is the Mad Hatter's Ball, an annual fund raiser for a local community
college. In 1989, city heavyweights turned out in bizarre headgear
of various descriptions to dine on fine food and bid on items such
as Mark Messier's hockey stick, a submarine ride at the West Edmonton Mall and a bottle of Château Mouton Rothschild. Former
Edmonton mayor Terry Cavanagh turned up in a hat bearing a replica
of the Stanley Cup. Another guest wore a battery-powered drummer
boy on his head.

Sometimes, one wonders if all sense of social decorum stops at
the Calgary city limits. Recently, a group of central Alberta ranchers
and investors put on black ties and tuxedos for a gala livestock auction. They wined, dined, then bid on the livestock on display. Llamas
went for as much as $50,000 a piece.

The Western Establishment (in random order):

Calgary

Jeanne and Peter Lougheed (he's the former premier, now a sought-after corporate director and a law partner with Bennett Jones Verchère in Calgary); Jim Palmer (lawyer with Burnet, Duckworth and Palmer in Calgary); Fred Mannix and sons Frederick and Ronald (own and run the Loram Group, a Calgary coal empire that has branched into oil exploration, pipelines and construction); Jack Singer (the founder of a real estate fortune who began in the business with cousin Abraham Belzberg and now has holdings in the U.S. and Canada); Ron and Marg Southern (he's the dynamo behind Calgary's ATCO Ltd., a construction trailer supplier, she's the dynamo behind the Spruce Meadows horse ranch, whose annual competitions have become a major social event for Canada's horsy set).

The Oil Men

J.C. Anderson (Anderson Exploration Ltd.); don Barkwell (Poco Petroleums); Jim Gray (Canadian Hunter Exploration); Dick Guzella (formerly Sceptre Resources); Bill Hopper (Petro-Canada); David O'Brien (PanCanadian Petroleum); John Pierce (retired boss, Ranger Oil); William Siebens (son of Harold Siebens, who made a fortune by selling the company he built, Candor Oil & Gas, for $160 million in 1978); Don Stacey (Amoco Canada Petroleum).

Edmonton

Margaret Zeidler (CEO and Vice-Chairman, Zeidler Forest Products); Lila Lee (runs the Clifford E. Lee Foundation, a charitable trust that funds cultural and social welfare causes); the Ghermezian family (reclusive Lebanese immigrants who built the ghastly West Edmonton Mall, a sprawling testament to the mall mania that has swept North America); Pat and Connie Harden (he's the publisher of the Edmonton *Sun*); Allan Olson (president of Stuart Olson Construction; he and his wife, Fran, are big supporters of the Holly Ball, an annual fund raiser for the Edmonton Art Gallery); Robert Stollery (the multimillionaire who owns and runs PCL Construction).

Regina and Saskatoon

Ken Dickhoff (CEO, Saskatchewan Trust Company); Frederick Hill (the richest man in Saskatchewan, he's the owner of Regina's McCallum Hill Ltd., a conglomerate that invests in real estate, broadcasting and oil and gas; son Paul is now president of the company); Herb Pinder (chairman, Saskatchewan Oil and Gas Corp.); Trevor Shepstone (president, Saskatoon Credit Union); Donald Stankov (chairman, Saskatchewan Power Corp.); Garfield Stevenson (president, Saskatchewan Wheat Pool).

Cultural Icons

Ruth Carse: Carse, 74, is Alberta's first lady of ballet. She's the founder and driving force behind the 26-year-old Alberta Ballet Company. Edmonton-born, she was trained as a dancer at the Canadian Ballet School in Toronto, the Royal Academy of Dance in London, England, and Copenhagen's American School of Ballet. During 50 years as a dancer with the National Ballet of Canada and as instructor and administrator at the Alberta Ballet, she received many awards, including the Queen's Silver Jubilee Medal. At a ceremony in 1990, 600 of Alberta's social elite turned out to honour Carse as she received the Dance Canada Award. Her comment at the time: "It meant more to me than all the others because it is a national award. The rest of the country is finally taking notice of what we're doing in this province." Carse's award was a morale booster for ballet in Alberta. A few months earlier, the struggling Calgary City Ballet had been forced to merge with its stronger cousin in Edmonton, the Alberta Ballet.

Joe Shocter: The whole country, not just Alberta, owes Shocter a debt for founding Edmonton's Citadel Theatre 26 years ago and remaining its impresario ever since. Now 69, Shocter founded the theatre in a Salvation Army Building and has overseen every stage of its growth. He's raised money, run its board, even directed plays. The Edmonton-born son of a Russian-Jewish immigrant junk dealer, Shocter is a lawyer and a real estate developer whose first love has always been the stage. More than anyone else, he's helped to turn Edmonton into a thriving theatre community. It now has more than a dozen theatre companies for a population of less than 750,000.

The Social Establishment of the Atlantic Provinces

The four Atlantic Provinces have a near-feudal social hierarchy, where ruling families operate business empires from the small towns in which they were born. Wealthy families like the McCains of Florenceville, N.B., and the Jodreys and Sobeys in Hantsport and Stellarton, N.S., still espouse the small-town values espoused by their forebears: prudence, humility and modesty. As noted regional writer Silver Donald Cameron has put it, "Hidden fortunes have been built on the humble belief that money is personal and should be held close to home." Of course, you don't have to flaunt your wealth if you're a regional economic lord with enough financial might to convey your clout without words. Whether the rich are summering in the mansions of Chester on the Nova Scotia coast or dining at the Halifax Club, they talk softly and carry fat wallets.

The social establishment in the Atlantic Provinces is more ossified than anywhere else in Canada. The old guard is ancient, by any other region's standards, and the new guard tends to be locals in their fifties who've worked for decades in the area.

Halifax

In Halifax, the social elite is much smaller and more tightly knit than in Toronto or Montreal. The opportunities for staging events, whether to benefit charity or to satisfy the whims and egos of the social elite in general, are not as frequent. Those who form the Halifax elite say the atmosphere is much less competitive, much more tranquil and relaxed, than in the bigger centres.

The Old Guard

Donald McInnes: An 88-year-old lawyer with McInnes, Cooper and Robertson, McInnes is the patriarch of one of the most influential legal families in the Maritimes. Donald was, for many years, the reigning prince of the Halifax social elite, hobnobbing with senior provincial and federal officials and serving as a loyal friend and benefactor to the Tory party.

Henry Hicks: A lifelong Liberal, Hicks, 77, has had a remarkably varied and influential career. He has been a lawyer, educator, university administrator and senator, and was premier of Nova Scotia in the mid-1950s. After his government's defeat, he remained leader of the opposition until 1960. In that year, he was named president of Dalhousie University, where he oversaw the institution's physical expansion in the south end of Halifax. He was called to the Senate of Canada in 1972. He resigned his post at Dalhousie in 1980. Hicks, who served as a member of the Canada Council between 1963 and 1969, spent much of his career shmoozing with others of his ilk at every important social event in the life of the city.

Bruce Oland: A 73-year-old master brewer, he is the oldest surviving member of the Oland clan in Halifax and still a fixture around old Halifax society. His nephew, Derek, operates Moosehead Breweries in Dartmouth. The elder Oland has been active in both the business and the cultural life of Halifax. Currently, he is president of Culverwell Holdings Ltd., Oland Investments Ltd. and Seahorse Investments Ltd. Despite his age, he still plays squash and sails, but now concentrates on the more sedate pursuits of numismatics and philately at his Marlborough Woods home, which he calls The Anchor.

Arthur Cooper: A former justice of the Supreme Court of Nova Scotia, Cooper, 83, ranks as another grand old man of the Halifax

Establishment. His activities, cultural and otherwise, have dwindled over the past few years, and the old judge leads a quiet life now. One of his biggest contributions to Halifax, in fact, is his son George, who is a partner in one of the most successful law firms in the country, McInnes, Cooper and Robertson.

Desmond Piers: Rear Admiral (retired) Piers, 79, is a reminder of Halifax's glorious past as a navy base. A career military man when the Canadian Navy was a force to be reckoned with, Piers now lives in Chester, N.S., playground of the Maritime rich, with his wife, Janet. His activities and responsibilities during World War Two marked him as one of the Allied Command's most valuable assets. He was the commanding officer of HMC *Algonquin*, which sailed with the British Home Fleet from Scapa Flow. He participated in the invasion of Normandy and ran convoys to northern Russia. After the war, he held a variety of important Canadian military posts, including chairman of the Canadian Defence Liaison Staff in Washington, D.C., and agent general of Nova Scotia in the U.K. and Europe. His landlocked social activities have been almost as numerous as his professional distinctions. He belongs to the Halifax Club and Halifax Golf and Country Club but spends most of his time at his Chester home, well known to older members of the Halifax Establishment as The Quarter Deck.

The New Guard

Brian Flemming: Only in the Atlantic Provinces could a 51-year-old lawyer be known as new guard, but then changes in the region's social scene tend to be measured in half centuries, not decades as they are in the rest of Canada. Although he trained as a lawyer, Flemming is founder and president of VGM Capital Inc., a venture capital company. He was born and raised in Halifax, so his is not exactly a new face on the social scene. But his growing influence constantly redefines his position in the elite corps. He was instrumental in establishing both Symphony Nova Scotia and its predecessor, the Atlantic Symphony Orchestra. In addition to his seats on a handful of prestigious business boards in the Maritimes, he is a member of a dozen international legal and political associations. Once a principal secretary to Prime Minister Pierre Elliott Trudeau, his ties to the federal Liberal Party remain strong. He lives with his wife and children in one of the most historic houses in Halifax, The Bower — once the residence of Sir Brenton Haliburton, the judge who tried Joseph Howe for slander and treason.

Dr. Richard Goldblum: Aside from being a nationally recognized expert in pediatrics and children's diseases, Goldblum, 67, is an active and visible member of the rising social elite in Halifax. What has kept him in the public eye is his dedication to a dizzying variety of cultural and artistic activities. He is always ebullient and outgoing, and his friends include politicians, educators, lawyers, businessmen and members of the arts community. He is the recipient of the 1978 Queen's Jubilee Medal, and in 1987 he was named an Officer of the Order of Canada.

Derek Oland: The 51-year-old president of Moosehead Breweries Ltd. and a noted philanthropist, Oland was born in Saint John, N.B., and now operates out of Halifax and Dartmouth. He defines the current generation of Olands, who have dominated Halifax social life since the nineteenth century. He sits on a dozen business boards but still finds time for an extraordinarily active life of charity and good works. He is a member of Dalhousie University's Business Advisory Board for the School of Business Administration. As well, he is a member of the board of Rothesay College, one of the more exclusive private schools in the Maritimes.

Stuart McInnes: McInnes, 55, was a minister of public works in the 1986 Mulroney government and is currently a law partner in McInnes, Cooper and Robertson in Halifax. His political affiliations are unparalleled among his Maritime peers, and he carries on the McInnes membership in the highest ranks of the local Establishment. He is also a former provincial squash champion and is a provincially ranked tennis player.

George Cooper: Also a partner in McInnes, Cooper and Robertson, Cooper, 51, is the son of old Halifax denizen Arthur Cooper. George maintains very close links with both provincial and federal Conservatives. He was a member of Parliament for Halifax and served as parliamentary secretary to the minister of justice and attorney general of Canada. He is also a member of the board of Canadian National Railways Ltd. and CN Explorations Ltd. But he spends more time on his charitable causes, such as fundraising for Dalhousie University. When he relaxes, it's over lunch at the Halifax Club or playing tennis at the Waegwoltic.

Allan Shaw: Shaw, 49, is president and general manager of L.E. Shaw Ltd., a construction and transportation company in Halifax. He is conceivably the only capitalist in the Maritimes with a strongly developed socialist instinct. His company, which offers a variety of profit-sharing schemes and competitive wages even during slumps, is one of the happiest shops on the East Coast for workers. As a result, organized labour has never been able to gain a foothold at the company. A tennis fanatic, he is also one of the most popular members of the social establishment, although he would likely gracefully decline membership if it were ever officially offered.

Donald Sobey: Sobey, 58, is chairman and chief executive officer of the family dynasty, Empire Co. Ltd., Stellarton, N.S. Although he lives and works in a town some 150 kilometres northwest of Halifax, Sobey's influence in Atlantic Canada's largest city makes him a member of the area's social establishment. Through his various interests, he has built at least 50 per cent of downtown Halifax's commercial property over the past two decades. Moreover, the heir to the supermarket and real estate conglomerate that ranks as one of Canada's top 50 companies is active in social and cultural events. Unfortunately, Sobey shocked his peers in 1991 when he entered a guilty plea to charges that he sexually assaulted a male acquaintance. He was fined $750.

Robert George: A rear admiral and current maritime commander, Atlantic Region, George, 52, is new to the Halifax Establishment. But he is a member of the elite corps by virtue of the historical importance of his position to the life of the city and his recent efforts to support charitable causes. According to locals, he is friendly and helpful in assisting various fund-raising events, such as the annual Kermesse, around the city.

The Lawyers

Fred Dickson (Patterson Kitts): Dickson has the closest ties of any lawyer to the provincial Tories. He is not a bagman, but rather a dedicated adviser.

Dennis Ashworth (Patterson Kitts): He's known to be very influential in provincial bureaucratic circles and has a reputation for unfailing instincts for which way the political winds blow.

Gerry Godsoe (Stewart, MacKeen and Covert): A loyal Liberal, he was the executive secretary of the MacDonald Royal Commission on the economy.

Bill Mingo (Stewart, MacKeen and Covert): Extraordinarily powerful both in and out of Halifax, Mingo is a high-powered federal Conservative with ties to many international governments. He is a high-ranking director of the World Bank.

Don Oliver (Stewart, MacKeen and Covert): One of few black members of the Establishment, Oliver is very close to Mulroney and has served on the Royal Commission on electoral practices.

John Dickey (McInnes, Cooper and Robertson): A devoted Liberal, his influence extends into international circles. He was once the Canadian representative on the Social and Economic Council of the United Nations.

Fund Raisers and Benefactors

Ruth Goldblum: Ruth Goldblum is the most successful, energetic campaigner in Halifax on behalf of a dozen good works in the area. Among her activities: community advisory board of the Junior League of Halifax Inc.; member of the Halifax Foundation; regent,

Mount Allison University; vice-chairman, Halifax-Dartmouth United Way; and member of the board, Canadian Council of Social Development. She is the recipient of a number of awards recognizing her community service, including the Human Relations Award, Canadian Council of Christians and Jews, 1978, and Volunteer of the Year Award, Centre for the Advancement and Support of Education, Washington, D.C. She is married to Dr. Richard Goldblum.

Dale Godsoe: Currently chairman of the board of governors, Mount Saint Vincent University, Halifax, Godsoe is a successful fund raiser for a variety of charitable organizations. Her primary area of interest, however, is higher education.

Robbie Shaw: A vice-president of National Sea Products Ltd., Halifax, Shaw is a former vice-president of Dalhousie University. He has devoted much of his time and energy to university and charitable fund raising.

Diane Campbell: Campbell has been chiefly involved in the Art Gallery of Nova Scotia campaign, but recently became a very effective back-room fund raiser for the Victoria General Hospital in Halifax.

Dean Salsman: A company executive and dedicated fund raiser for the provincial Liberal Party, Salsman is also involved in charitable works, and he devotes much of his time to fund raising of a less political nature.

Newfoundland and Prince Edward Island

As might be expected, islands tend to produce tightly knit social establishments. Tiny PEI spent most of this century dominated by absentee landlords, which, combined with the province's small size and heavy reliance on federal government equalization payments, has militated against the emergence of a moneyed aristocracy. Wealthy families have emerged, however, in potatoes (the McKays and Willises), contracting (the Schurmans) and food processing (the McLeans).

Newfoundland, by contrast, has a social aristocracy to rival any region in Canada. There are numerous fine old Newfoundland families, whose names still carry social cachet years after their fortunes were started on Water Street. They include the Lundrigans, the Crosbies, the Perlins, the Collingwoods, the Outerbridges, the Monroes, the Lakes, the Bells and the Pratts. Members of several of these powerful families are still dynamic businessmen, including Arthur Lundrigan, Henry Collingwood, Peter Outerbridge and Harold Lake, all of whom sit on the board of the Newfoundland Telephone Co. The most active Perlin still on the island is John, president of Newfoundland Publishing Services Ltd. The legacy of Chesley A. Crosbie is carried on by Andrew Crosbie, a real estate executive and brother of federal cabinet minister John Crosbie. John's son, Chesley Furneaux Crosbie, is a noted lawyer in St. John's. The most influential members of the Newfoundland wealthy aristocracy are:

Arthur Lundrigan: A 70-year-old industrialist, Lundrigan is the son of William Lundrigan and chairman of Lundrigans-Comstock Ltd. of Corner Brook, Newfoundland. Aside from building almost every major road and sewer system in Newfoundland, he has been a valuable member of many Maritime business boards for decades. His purely cultural activities on the Rock are negligible, but his political influence is unsurpassed. He is the businessman most listened to by Premier Clyde Wells.

Miller Ayre: Miller Ayre is the son of Lewis Ayre, who built up a powerful retailing business on the island with brother Fred. At 50, Miller Ayre is chairman of Ayres Stores Ltd. and a director of numerous island companies. He also leads one of the most socially involved lives of anyone in St. John's. He is past chairman of the Newfoundland Medicare Commission and a former member of the St. John's Municipal Council, and has served on the advisory boards of Memorial University, St. John's, and the city's School of Business Administration. As well, he is a past chairman of the Retail Council of Canada. Outside Newfoundland, he is vice-chairman of the National Theatre School in Montreal and the Canadian Chamber of

Commerce. He is also a director of the Canadian Council of Christians and Jews.

Ewart Pratt: Pratt is the son of late senator Calvert Coates Pratt. The family fortune is centred in Steers Ltd., a merchandising business established in 1924. Now 72, Pratt sits on the boards of major Newfoundland companies, including Newfoundland Light and Power, but his influence extends beyond the island. He is a director of the Canadian Imperial Bank of Commerce and is a member of the Mount Royal Club (Montreal), the Granite Club (Toronto) and the Canadian Club (New York).

New Brunswick

New Brunswick has produced family dynasties that rank with the most powerful in the country. Their current members are:

Kenneth Colin Irving: Irving, 92, is one of the richest men in the world, with assets of nearly $10 billion under his control. His personal net worth is unknown. He leads an extremely private existence, granting interviews to no one. His economic influence in Saint John and most of New Brunswick is inestimable, not to mention controversial because of its pervasiveness. When people speak of New Brunswick's economic base, they speak of Irving. He is known to have few social entanglements, and he rarely ventures out of his apartment suite in downtown Saint John. His three sons, who run the far-flung conglomerate's daily operations, are only slightly less hermetic in their ways.

Kenneth Cox: Cox, 69, is chairman of Bruncor Inc., the main subsidiary of the New Brunswick Telephone Co. Ltd. A dedicated businessman, he also sits on the boards of almost a dozen other New Brunswick and Nova Scotia firms. His financial influence extends throughout the Maritimes. His volunteer activities appear limited to municipal development projects in Saint John, where he resides.

Gilbert Finn: Finn, 72, was an active member of the Acadian business community before he became lieutenant governor of his native province in 1987. He was the founding chairman of the Conseil économique acadien du Nouveau-Brunswick, 1980–82, and a trustee of Les Presses francophone du Nouveau-Brunswick, 1984–87. He is the recipient of numerous honorary degrees and has served as a director on the boards of more than two dozen companies throughout the province. As lieutenant governor, his residence is an obvious gathering place for the social elite of Fredericton, Saint John and Moncton.

David Ganong: The heir to a grand old chocolate-making tradition, Ganong, 49, is president and chief executive officer of Ganong Bros. Ltd., established in 1872. The candy maker is dominant in the small social network of St. Stephen, N.B., about 100 kilometres southeast of Saint John. He sits on a number of boards in New Brunswick and Nova Scotia.

Harrison and Wallace McCain: The two brothers, 65 and 62, run one of the world's largest food-processing operations, McCain Foods Ltd. Together with their wives and children, they dominate the social fabric of Florenceville, N.B., and the surrounding area. Harrison's nonbusiness activities include directorships of the Beaverbrook Art Gallery in Fredericton, the Izaac Walton Killam Hospital for children in Halifax and the Agricultural Institute of Canada.

Philip Oland: The 82-year-old patriarch of the younger Oland clan in Halifax, N.S., Philip is chairman of Moosehead Breweries Ltd. His social activities are largely restricted to Saint John, N.B., where he resides. He is governor of St. Thomas University and honorary president of the New Brunswick Youth Orchestra and the New Brunswick Army Cadet League.

Patrick Rocca: Born in Sambiase, Italy, Rocca, 50, arrived in Saint John as a child. He later mastered the building trade and became one of the region's most successful real estate and commercial property developers. But he has also spent much of his spare time working to improve the social life of the city. He is past president of the

Saint John Board of Trade and a member of the Atlantic Provinces
Economic Council.

Reuben Cohen: Cohen, 70, is a lawyer and founding partner of what
has become, in recent years, the massive Toronto-based financial services company Central Capital Corp. He is a successful businessman,
worth millions, but also a community-minded citizen of Moncton,
N.B. He received the Order of Canada in 1979. He is a trustee of
the YMCA Retirement Fund, a member of the Moncton Rotary (he
is also past president), a member of the Moncton Barristers' Society
and a member of the Friends of the Moncton Hospital Foundation
Inc. He lives quietly, determined to avoid the public eye as much
as possible.

Conclusion

For the majority of Canadians, the meaning of wealth is poorly
grasped. It is a fantasy world whose geography is drawn by the set
designers of "Dallas," or the global meanderings of Robin Leach
on "Lifestyles of the Rich and Famous" or by the money-dripping
prose of novelist Dominick Dunne. These glimpses of the rich tit-
illate, entertain and provide diversion for the masses of viewers, yet
the wealthy people portrayed are, in the end, no more real than the
romantic heroes of a Harlequin romance.

Thanks to foreign-dominated media fare, when Canadians think
of truly wealthy lifestyles, they think of people somewhere else —
in Manhattan or Hollywood, or in the polo-playing circles of the
British aristocracy. The super rich in Canada for the most part keep
to themselves, operating in close-knit circles in well-defined neighbourhoods. Ordinary Canadians know where these neighbourhoods
are, or have heard of them — Westmount, Kerrisdale, West Vancouver, Forest Hill, Rosedale, Chester, Tuxedo and the like. But Canadians have little comprehension of who these people are and the
opulence they live in, because they have never experienced it first-
hand or even seen fictionalized representations of it on television.

The rich in Canada keep to themselves. Their networks of friends
don't reach down the class structure, only across it. They operate
in isolated social enclaves that are connected by family, corporate,

private club and friendship ties with other enclaves of the super rich across the country. They mingle at extravagant society weddings. Example: When investment dealer Chuck Loewen's son John was married in 1989, Chuck threw a party at the Royal Canadian Yacht Club that featured an African band and African dancers. The African theme was picked because John works for an investment dealer in South Africa and his bride, Jacquie, was born there. Following African custom, John Loewen had a truckload of farm animals delivered to the front door of the bride's father, who lives in Vancouver. The festivities didn't end there. The wealthy McCutcheons threw a party for the couple at the 54th Club, atop the T-D Centre in Toronto, where the "older folks" jived to '50s music.

The rich entertain each other in homes that would make suburbanites drool if they were ever invited inside. The Eatons have just built a 2,200-square-metre mansion in the hills of Caledon, near Toronto, for their mother, Signy. Designed by a French architect, the house has ten bathrooms, a billiard room, tennis courts, a private pond, a helicopter pad and a compact disc player capable of handling 290 CDs that can be operated from any one of dozens of rooms.

Even the run-of-the-mill homes of the rich in Toronto are temples of affluence. Dr. Morton Shulman, a crusading coroner turned financier, lives in a $4-million stone mansion on Russell Hill Road. It sits on a one-hectare arboreal retreat filled with the natural splendour of mature trees, wisteria and rhododendrons. Inside, a centuries-old Belgian tapestry covers one living-room wall, and nooks and crannies display Shulman's prize collection of antique clocks. The house also has an indoor swimming pool and a master bedroom featuring a round bed so large it looks as though it could sleep 16. A TV with a one-metre screen dominates one bedroom wall. Morty clicks it on at six each morning to hear the gold quotes from London, which are picked up by a satellite dish on the roof.

The vacation retreats of Canada's rich tend to be second to none. Bermuda is a favourite getaway destination. Michael DeGroote, who made a fortune in waste management and school buses, owns an $8-million island at the mouth of Riddell's Bay in Southampton that housed a series of U.S. millionaires before he bought it in 1990. Built in 1937, it was one of the most grand and palatial properties in its day, with a main house that includes servants' quarters, seven bathrooms, five bedrooms and a large commercial kitchen. The doors, made of thick Bermuda cedar, open to sprawling lawns, two swimming pools, a wading pool, a greenhouse, a skeet-shooting range and a tennis court, all encompassed by a jogging track.

Money isn't enough to guarantee acceptance into the social circles of the upper class, but it is the main prerequisite. It is the one thing all the leading lights of the social establishment have in common. Earlier in the book, I pointed out that the upper class is made up of Canadians with substantial second-generation wealth. It's possible to be more specific. Having millions is not enough to let you join the ranks of the rich. After all, there are now 425,000 families in Canada with net worths that top $1 million. To lead the life of the rich takes a net worth of at least $5 million. To even aspire to live the lifestyle of the upper class, one needs an income of about $300,000 a year. This explains why the country's social establishment, from Vancouver to Halifax, is dominated by business inheritors, executives of major corporations or professionals with incomes in that range or well above. The income of the average Canadian family ($46,185 in 1988) wouldn't begin to cover the basic living costs of the rich, who typically spend up to $22,000 a year in after-tax dollars just to send one child to private school (school trips and uniforms included). Joining an exclusive private golf club typically costs about $50,000. Initiation fees at the most prestigious private business clubs range from $4,000 (the Vancouver Club) to $10,000 (the Toronto Club, the York Club and the National Club). Then there are annual dues ranging from $1,000 to $2,000 to worry about.

Canadians who can consider this type of expenditure include lawyers and accountants at big-city firms and a few medical doctors. Businessmen have the best chances of joining the upper class quickly, thanks to their hefty salaries. For example, in 1989, Arden Haynes, chairman of Imperial Oil, made $1.2 million; Raymond Cyr, president of BCE, pulled in the same.

Private schools are the breeding ground of the upper class, and private clubs are their meeting place once they've arrived. The most prestigious private schools in Canada are:

- Upper Canada College, Toronto: boys from Grades 4 to 13; cost, about $16,000;
- Crescent School, Toronto: boys from Grades 4 to 13; cost, $7,800;

- Havergal College, Toronto: girls to Grade 13; cost, about $16,000;
- Lower Canada College, Montreal: boys from Grades 3 to 12; cost, about $7,000;
- Branksome Hall, Toronto: girls to Grade 13; cost, about $16,000
- Bishop's College School, Lennoxville, Que.: coed from Grades 7 to 12; cost, about $16,000;
- Appleby College, Oakville, Ont.: boys from Grades 4 to 13; cost, about $16,400;
- Ridley College, St. Catharines, Ont.: coed from Grades 5 to 13; cost, about $16,500;
- Lakefield College School, Lakefield, Ont.: boys Grades 7 and 8, coed Grades 9 to 12; cost, about $16,600.

Other notable private schools include: St. John's-Ravencourt, Winnipeg; St. George's School, Vancouver; Collège Jean-de-Brébeuf, Montreal; Trinity College School, Port Hope, Ontario; Bishop Strachan School, Toronto; Halifax Grammar School, Halifax.

In recent years, some private schools opened their doors to students from a variety of ethnic backgrounds; some now offer bursaries to deserving students without the economic means to attend. However, families generally need incomes well over six figures to even consider applying.

In the private clubs of the rich there has been even less loosening of the requirements for entry, which traditionally have meant that the aspiring member must not only be well off and well connected, he (for most are open only to males) must be well liked and respected and must fit in effortlessly with the other members of the club, all of whom vote on each new application. Little progress has been made in recognizing women as suitable members.

The top clubs that permit women members are the St. James's Club of Montreal, which has elected a female chairman; the Albany Club of Toronto, which began admitting women in the late 1970s; the Calgary Petroleum Club; the Calgary Desk and Derrick Club; and the 400 Club, also of Calgary. A motion to admit women to the Saskatoon Club died in 1989 after a deadlocked vote.

For most Canadians, entry into the social establishment is out of the question. Their dreams of social mobility must remain confined to middle-class goals: perhaps a vacation in Barbados, a VCR, a sun deck in the back yard. Abraham Lincoln commented that God must love the poor because he made so many of them. Considering Lincoln's words, writer H.L. Mencken countered: "God must love the rich because he spread so much *mazuma* among so few of them." Only Canada's rich know how right Mencken was.

Part IV

THE

RELIGIOUS

ELITE

Chapter 8

The Pulpit

Anyone who thinks that east coast fishermen face a serious problem over declining cod stocks should consider the lot of the nation's clergy. The fishers of men have never had a poorer harvest of souls. This is the distressing context for any discussion of who has power in Canada's religions and how they use that power. Empty pews are nothing new for God's fishermen, but empty churches are.

It won't come as a surprise to anyone who has been in a half-empty place of worship lately that, in the decades since the Second World War, the number of Canadians who regularly attend a church or synagogue has fallen. Gallup poll figures show that in 1946, 67 per cent of Canadians had attended church or synagogue in the week before they were polled. In 1990, only 27 percent had. This shows a massive exodus from organized religion that no ecclesiastical authority can regard with equanimity. There are, however, signs that the exodus may be ended. According to the 1988 *Yearbook of American and Canadian Churches*, 85 Canadian religious bodies reported total membership of 16,615,094 people in 1986. That represented a 0.5 per cent increase over total membership in 1985. (Apparently observing the Christian principle that every lost sheep counts, the organization doesn't round off its tallies.)

Other numbers contain good news and bad news for Canada's religious bodies. According to Prof. Reginald Bibby, a Lethbridge University sociologist and author of *Fragmented Gods*, a 1987 analysis of religion in Canada, polls show that about 84 per cent of young Canadians aged 15 to 24 and 83 per cent of adults say they believe in God. The bad news for religious leaders is that very few young or old Canadians are expressing that belief by going to church, except, of course, on special occasions, for example baptisms, marriages and funerals. The sheep are running lost in the pasture, to borrow from the New Testament parable, and the shepherds are having little luck bringing them home.

The decline in church attendance over the decades has not been spread evenly through various denominations. On the contrary, there has been a major realignment among the denominations in terms of how many Canadians are affiliated with each one. The Roman Catholic Church is now dominant in Canada. This was made clear in a Statistics Canada study of religious affiliation that used figures from the 1981 census.

The study offered some fascinating insights into religious trends in Canada. It noted that, historically, most Canadians have been either Protestant or Catholic. In the 1871 census, 98 per cent of the population was affiliated with one of these two groups. At the time of the 1981 census, the figure was 89 per cent. (Note that *affiliation* means simply the denomination people identify with; it doesn't mean they are practising Christians or have membership in a church.)

During the same period the Roman Catholic Church overtook its Protestant cousins. Through the late 1800s and the first few decades of this century, notes the report, Protestants clearly outnumbered Catholics. But the proportion of Protestants dropped from 54 per cent in 1931 to about 40 per cent in 1981. Meanwhile, the proportion of Roman Catholics rose from 41 per cent to 47 per cent between 1931 and 1961, and remained at that level in both the 1971 and 1981 censuses.

There is a major qualification to be made to the dominance of the Roman Catholic Church in Canada. Although it has the largest number of affiliates, it holds the majority in only two provinces: Quebec, where 88 per cent of people called themselves Roman Catholic in 1981, and New Brunswick, where 53.9 per cent of the population did so. In all other provinces, Protestants form the majority.

There are, of course, many other faiths in Canada's religious mosaic. The 1981 census, the last one with results on religious affiliation available, revealed that 362,000 people were affiliated with the Christian Eastern Orthodox denominations; 300,000 with Eastern religions such as Islam, Hinduism, Sikhism and Buddhism. As well, there were 296,000 people of the Jewish faith, or 1.3 per cent, down from 1.5 per cent in 1951.

No discussion of religious affiliation can ignore nonconventional spiritual groups, ranging from the practitioners of New Age faiths to aboriginal groups practising the oldest spirituality on the continent. The census revealed that 13,450 people classed themselves as followers of the Inuit or Native Indian faiths, as well as religions like New Thought–Unity–Metaphysical, Pagan, Fourth Way and Theosophical.

The Statistics Canada study, a treasure trove of information, went a step further and revealed that religious affiliation reflects important underlying social differences between Canadians. Protestants, on average, were older, had more years of schooling, higher average incomes and lower unemployment rates than did Roman Catholics. Persons of Jewish faith had the highest median age, the most schooling, the highest average annual income and the lowest unemployment rate. Interestingly, the group with the second-highest median income was made up of those who claimed no religious preference.

Religion and the Ruling Elites

The churches' temporal influence can't be measured only by *how many* people claim religious affiliation; it also matters *who* claims affiliation. From the surveys carried out for this book, it's strikingly clear that most members of the ruling elites are affiliated with a church and they're overwhelmingly Protestant.

In the federal cabinet, which is constantly dealing with value-loaded issues from abortion to social welfare policies, almost two-thirds of 39 ministers I surveyed claimed a religious affiliation. And although several of the most powerful ministers are Roman Catholic (Brian Mulroney, Joe Clark, Don Mazankowski and Benoît Bouchard) only 15 per cent of the total belong to that religion. Most ministers (72 per cent of those listing a religion) are Protestant, primarily Anglican and United Church. (One cabinet minister is Jewish.)

Federal deputy ministers aren't quite so religious. About half of those surveyed adhered to a religion, and of those, 46 per cent were

Protestant. Another 38 per cent were Roman Catholic and about 15 per cent were Jewish.

The members of the corporate elite are more religious than either the politicians or the bureaucrats, and once again they're mainly Protestant. About 71 per cent of 165 corporate directors on whom information was compiled claimed a religious affiliation, as did 69 per cent of 131 bank directors. Protestantism (mainly Anglican and United Church) is the faith of choice for most corporate directors (64 per cent) and even more bank directors (79 per cent).

Only 30 per cent of corporate directors and 16 per cent of bank directors were Roman Catholic; only 6 per cent of corporate directors and about 3 per cent of bank directors were Jews.

In the media elite, most newspaper editors (73 per cent) and publishers (79 per cent) claim religious affiliation. In both cases almost all are Protestant, primarily Anglican and United Church.

The overall conclusion is that Canada's ruling elites are a bastion of Protestantism, despite the fact that Roman Catholicism has become the dominant religion in society at large. Among the Protestant churches represented, the Anglican and United churches are overwhelmingly dominant. While poorly represented in the ruling elites, Judaism is represented in rough proportion to its share of the population. Other minority religions are not represented.

Of course, it does not follow from the religious affiliation of the members of the ruling elites that the churches have great influence over their decisions. Religious faiths, particularly Protestantism, Roman Catholicism and Judaism, provide the ethical underpinnings of Canada's mix of capitalism and social welfarism, but beyond that generality it is difficult to ascribe direct influence to churches. As we shall see, religious leaders are divided on whether political leaders are paying heed to the public pronouncements and private overtures of church leaders.

In the following pages, I examine the power structures of three churches to shed light on why their influence is declining and discuss the main challenges they face in increasing their flocks. Both the Roman Catholic and Anglican churches have hierarchical power structures that permitted extensive surveys of their leadership ranks. In the case of the United Church, there is no formal governing hierarchy of clerics that could be surveyed, but there is a ruling bureaucracy that plays an increasingly controversial role in the church's affairs.

By focusing on Canada's three largest denominations, the Anglican, United and Roman Catholic, I intend no slight to other branches of God's family. But this book is about power, and these three churches have the most potential influence over the lives of Canadians and the country's social, economic and political agendas.

The Anglican Church of Canada

The Anglican Church is Canada's second-largest Protestant denomination (it loses by a whisker to the United Church), and it is one of Canada's oldest. The first service of the Church of England (as it was then called) in Canada took place in 1578, just a few decades after the first Roman Catholic mass was celebrated in 1534. But in its dotage, the Anglican Church is suffering from the afflictions of old age. It's being dogged by a faltering sense of purpose, shrinking membership rolls and dwindling influence in societal affairs. The church still has a potent cachet among those Canadians who aspire to the social establishment, especially in Ontario. It is a branch of the Church of England and has long been a home away from home for those whose spiritual antecedents can be traced back to England. But this upper-class respectability and social cachet will not be enough to make it a vibrant church into the next century.

Power is centred in the hands of the primate of the church in Canada, Michael Peers, and 42 assistant bishops, bishops and archbishops. There is one step between them and God, however: the Archbishop of Canterbury, leader of the 70-million-strong worldwide Church of England.

When Peers was elected as the eleventh primate in 1986 (his was one of five names nominated by his peers; the names were then submitted to a synod of 250 lay people and priests and 40 bishops for a vote), a very middle-of-the-road clergyman became head of a very middle-of-the-road church. In view of the turmoil the United Church has suffered over the issue of the ordination of homosexuals, many Anglicans don't consider the middle of the road a bad place to be.

Considering that he left the church in his youth, it's ironic that Peers, 57, has become primate, a post he will hold until mandatory retirement at 70. Born in Vancouver in 1934, Peers was still a boy when he quit the church — for good, he thought. He walked out after he was asked to leave a service because the pew he was sitting in was not his. Peers didn't return to church until he was 18.

Peers did a B.A. in Slavic studies at the University of British Columbia, then studied languages in Heidelberg, Germany. (Besides English, he can speak French, German, Russian and Polish.) In the late 1950s Peers returned to Canada to study theology at Trinity College in Toronto. He was ordained in 1960 and three years later married a minister's daughter, Elizabeth Bradley of Ottawa. Together they made a steady ascent into the church's highest circles. After serving as a university chaplain in Ottawa, Peers left for Winnipeg, where he became rector of St. Bede's Church. In 1974 he was appointed rector of St. Paul's Cathedral, Regina, and dean of the Diocese of Qu'Appelle. He became bishop of that diocese in 1977, and in 1982 became archbishop of the Ecclesiastical Province of Rupert's Land, which covers Manitoba, Saskatchewan and most of the Northwest Territories.

As primate, Peers has become known for a laid-back style that belies his tendency to be a workaholic. "He's a consensus builder," a friend of Peers told journalist Michael Tenszen. "That doesn't mean that he won't make a decision or take a stand. He dislikes waffling."

True to style, Peers has well-thought-out positions on contentious social issues that he's prepared to state plainly. The positions tend to be slightly liberal and very much in line with mainstream Anglican thinking. Examples: Peers views abortion as a choice between two conflicting things — the life of the child and the health of the mother. The challenge, he has said, is to determine in each case whether abortion is or is not the lesser of two evils. As for the role of women in the church, another very divisive issue within the Anglican congregation, Peers hopes to see Canada's first female bishop elected soon. (Women have been ordained in the Canadian church for more than 10 years. Two have stood for election as bishops but lost.)

The elite of the Anglican Church consists of its bishops and archbishops. To get a sense of who these people are, what sort of backgrounds they come from and the ethnic groups they represent, I sent detailed questionnaires to the 43 clerics who led the church in 1990.

Twenty-one responded; less complete biographical information was compiled on five more church leaders for a total of 26. This response level provides a worthwhile though not complete picture of the makeup of the Anglican Church elite.

The men who hold the highest offices in the church (there are no women) tend to be well past middle age. (Of 24 whose age is known, only two were younger than 50.) They also tend to be born in Canada rather than England, and they represent the regions of the country reasonably well.

Their British ethnic backgrounds were not surprising, perhaps. Except for one cleric with German ancestors, most reported that both or at least one parent were of British ancestry, making the leadership of the Anglican Church probably the strongest bastion of British heritage in Canada.

Rather surprisingly, however, the leaders of Canada's only truly upper-class church came from very middle-class backgrounds, judging from the occupations of their fathers. Although four of 21 were the sons of clergymen and one was the son of an engineer, the rest had fathers who held white-collar or blue-collar jobs. Obviously, the respondents were a socially mobile group, rising to the elite of the church in one generation. The route for all of them, aside, presumably, from a strong faith, was an excellent education. Almost 40 percent had postgraduate degrees.

The Anglican Church, then, is a largely white, middle-class church with leaders of mainly middle-class origin. This poses problems for the church, as one Anglican minister, Reginald Stackhouse, a former Tory MP, has pointed out. Stackhouse says that the church's membership of a little more than 800,000 is ageing faster than the population of Canada as a whole; that it has an ethnic and class character that gives no indication of a broader appeal to minority groups; and that its membership is made up mainly of women. "As in the days of colonial settlement," says Stackhouse, "the Anglican Church of Canada is not renowned for the energy and creativity of its outreach to the lapsed, the apathetic and the unbelieving."

The Anglican Church has not shied away from taking stands on controversial public issues. It has spoken out for native rights, against surrogate motherhood, against economic policies that worsen the plight of the poor and enrich the wealthy, and it has undertaken to fight violence against women.

Yet the bishops surveyed revealed that they had no illusions about the sway the church has on societal values. Of the 21 respondents, 17 said that the church's influence on societal values had fallen in the past 20 years. None thought it had risen. "The church is no longer seen as a significant part of our society," commented one cleric. Others blamed the decline on factors like the secularization of society, materialism and the glorification of science over spirituality. The Right Reverend Ronald Ferris, bishop of Yukon, noted that the Anglican Church is "more outspoken on social-moral issues. But Anglicans are a small percentage of the population, so have less influence on personal morality." The Right Reverend Eric Bays, bishop of Qu'Appelle, was among a minority who thought the church's influence had stayed the same. He didn't see shrinking rolls in the churches as necessarily a bad thing. "While active Christians are fewer in number," he said, "they are more ready to stand up for distinctly Christian values."

All but one bishop felt that the church still had some influence over government policies. "Yes, it does," said the Right Reverend Stewart Payne, archbishop of western Newfoundland, "in that church people are involved with framing social and economic policies. Also, in many instances, the governments do listen to what the church says regarding issues." But more than half (12) thought that the church's influence over government had decreased in the past 20 years. "The church is no threat to the ballot box," opined one cleric. Five bishops thought it had risen, three said it had stayed the same and two said they didn't know. Said one Ontario bishop: "The church does a lot of lobbying, some of it very well, for example, on South Africa, native affairs, Latin America, religious education in public schools. Who knows the extent to which it influences a politician's personal views on the policies that emerge?"

The Anglican Church may not have lost its drive to speak out forcefully on public issues, and has a deserved reputation for defending the disadvantaged. But the main challenge it faces lies within its ranks. It must to reach out to save new souls, whether disadvantaged or advantaged, and not just comfort old ones.

The United Church of Canada

Walter Farquharson, a small-town Saskatchewan minister, is the spiritual leader of the United Church of Canada, the country's largest Protestant denomination, with about 850,000 members. Farquharson, 55, was elected moderator of the church in 1990 and completes his term in 1992. But how much power does he really have? And if he doesn't have it, who does?

Farquharson is in many ways an inspiring man. A hymn writer and former elementary school principal, he is pastor of a three-church charge in Saltcoats, 25 kilometres southeast of Yorkton, Saskatchewan.

Beefy, with receding grey hair and friendly eyes behind clear-rimmed glasses, Farquharson has spent his entire life on the Prairies. He was raised on a Saskatchewan seed grain farm and has 30 years' experience as an ordained minister, including 13 years working outside the church as a high-school and elementary school teacher.

From the start of his tenure, he has made it clear that the environment is a priority for the church. "I believe that if the United Church is to be faithful to the gospel within the context of the 1990s, we must learn to hear the lament being sung by the earth, the waters, the plants and the animals of this planet," he said at a news conference after his election.

The moderator's emphasis on the environment issue caused a massive sigh of relief among church members across the country. At last, after two years of tearing ourselves apart on the issue of homosexual ordination, the thinking went, we can work on an issue we can agree on.

This is what United Church moderators do best: raise the sights of the flock to higher ideals and play down petty power struggles and theological battles. It has worked in the past, but in the last two years, the deficiencies in the organizational structure of the United Church have been laid bare for all to see. The moderator's role has been reduced to chief spiritual cheerleader, while the real power seekers fight it out.

The power structure of the United Church is, to say the least, fluid. Its ruling body, the General Council, meets every two years in various cities; then a different group of almost 400 clergy and lay people, elected from across the country, gather to vote on church policy. In any political legislature, this would classify them as grossly inexperienced. In theory, their redeeming feature is that they are open to the Spirit of God as He moves through the deliberations of the General Council.

At the council, these commissioners are divided into working committees, which assess accountability reports from "civil service" divisions, which are responsible for carrying out directives from earlier councils. The rest of the time, church business goes on in a highly decentralized fashion.

The moderator is elected by the General Council every two years. He or she may or may not be well versed in church politics or have sophisticated skills for dealing with them. The Reverend Farquharson, while no doubt an exemplary Christian, arguably falls short on both scores.

On one hand, this willingness by the church to pick outsiders is a refreshing feature. On the other hand, when combined with the moderator's short tenure, it severely limits the potential of the moderator to exert a powerful or long-lasting influence on the direction of the church.

In theory, this attempt to avoid an ossified power structure in the United Church leaves its highest courts open to the will of God rather than the will of any one titular head of the church or any group of all-powerful clergy.

The structure works exceedingly well at times. But the problem is, it is tremendously vulnerable to domination by salaried staff members from the church's national office in Toronto, who have accumulated experience and consistent influence in the church's highest deliberations.

Arguably the most powerful person in the United Church is not the moderator but the most senior member of the General Council's executive, general secretary Howard Mills. Known as Howie to everyone, Mills, 56, is the social opposite of Farquharson. The son of a prominent churchman and Toronto lawyer, Mills grew up in the affluent Rosedale area of the city. He has an outstanding academic record. He attended the academically exclusive University of Toronto Schools, the University of Toronto (B.A. and D.D.) and Emmanuel College, where he won the gold medal on graduation with a Master of Divinity degree. A seasoned minister and university professor, Mills rose to his present position in 1987. His term is indefinite. Mills works out of the church's national office in downtown Toronto, which houses the church's "civil service." He heads the General Council's executive, which is made up of 75 people from across Canada. The other powerful staffers are the general secretaries of the national office's five major divisions, Communication, Finance, Ministry Personnel and Education, Mission in Canada, and World Outreach. These general secretaries oversee a lot of work, including implementing the directives of the General Council to create various studies and task forces. In one recent year, there were 141 standing committees, task forces and ad hoc committees active at the national office level.

Whether United Church members approve or disapprove of the power of 85 St. Clair Ave., as head office is known, depends almost entirely on whether they are liberal or conservative in their approach to theological issues. Mills's friends and foes alike agree that he and the head office staff are leading the church in a liberal direction, as exemplified by the controversy over the ordination of homosexuals that erupted again in 1988. Mills spoke strongly against more conservative forces that viewed practising homosexuality as a sin and an obstacle to ordination.

The United Church was pushed out of the closet on the issue when, in 1978, a candidate for the ministry in the Hamilton conference declared herself to be a lesbian. The conference asked the General Council to adopt a national policy. The issue was first debated at the 1984 General Council meeting in Morden, Manitoba, which affirmed the ministries of gay and lesbian persons currently in the church but called for further study on the question of fitness for ordination.

The Morden General Council instructed two divisions at the national office, the Division of Ministry Personnel and Education and the Division of Mission, to study and "attempt to understand

homosexual orientation and practice as well as a theological understanding of marriage and creation."

With the approval of the General Council executive, the two divisions appointed a committee, called the National Coordinating
Group (NCG), to prepare the report (with contributions from local
workshops and study groups throughout the church) in time for the
1988 General Council meeting.

Unfortunately, the members of the NCG, appointed by the church
hierarchy, did not represent the membership at large. They were,
as they later acknowledged, all liberals and/or gay. This was un-
intentional, according to then moderator Anne Squires, who said at
the time: "I was on the committee responsible for selecting these
members. We had no idea where they stood on this particular issue.
We chose them because of other gifts, such as open-mindedness and
the willingness to dialogue."

When the committee met, its members realized that there wasn't
a conservative among them. A sole conservative voice was added
later, but it didn't redress the imbalance. It should have come as
no surprise to anyone that the committee produced a report that
gave the church leaders in Toronto the liberal findings they were
looking for.

In the uproar that followed, the debate over the report immediately
polarized into two camps. On one side, there were the conservatives,
led by two groups, the Community of Concern, and the Renewal
Fellowship, made up of ministers and lay people. On the other side
were liberal church members and the national leadership of the
church, led by the Reverend Mills. The silent majority sat in-between,
baffled by the invective and, according to various polls, disapproving
of the ordination of homosexuals.

The 1988 General Council accepted the NCG report, then consigned
it to the archives. It made it clear that the report does not represent
official church policy, but went on to adopt several statements based
on it. Essentially, these statements on homosexuality were an attempt
to cool down the fires of controversy. They included a mea culpa:
"We confess before God that as a Christian community we have participated in a history of injustice and persecution against gay and
lesbian persons in violation of the Gospel of Jesus Christ." They

also included an indirect statement on homosexual ordination: "That all persons, regardless of their sexual orientation, who profess faith in Jesus Christ and obedience to Him, are welcome to be or become full members of the Church," and further, that, "All members of the Church are eligible to be considered for Ordered Ministry."

With these statements, the General Council intended to make clear that it wasn't prepared to ban a whole cross-section of people from the ministry. But it was an interpretation of the standards for ministry that left thousands of church members bitter. Many members decided to leave rather than fight. In 1988, 36 ministers and 37 congregations quit the church over the issue. Church membership dropped by 15,000 over the year, though how much is attributable to the fight over the ordination of homosexuals is unclear.

The leadership role taken by the Reverend Mills, the church's senior staff person, as a proponent of the report only cemented the impression of dissidents that the "civil service" of the church had become a power unto itself and had forgotten the church's tradition of encouraging unity in diversity.

Botched from the start, the whole process split the church in a schism that hasn't healed nor soon will, led to an exodus of clergy and lay people and resulted in a witchhunt mentality that caused untold suffering for homosexuals among the clergy.

Unfortunately, this issue has obscured many of the United Church's laudable initiatives on social, economic and political issues. Controversy is nothing new to the church. It became embroiled in the issue of female ordination in 1936, just 11 years after the church was formed. Today, more than 250 of its 4,000 ministers are female; women make up more than half of the students in its theological colleges. In recent years, General Council or various task forces have spoken out on a host of issues, from the government's relations with South Africa to abortion and free trade.

But the flaws in the way the church conducts its own affairs need to be addressed. Demands for reform of the church structure are nothing new. In 1985, a five-member church task force warned bluntly that the church was beset by problems that were thwarting its mission. Among the problems listed were a complex structure that breeds distrust among ordinary church members, and resentment caused by the perception that real power lies in the hands of a few people. The report called for participatory democracy at the local level and a bureaucratic structure at the administrative level that was designed along the lines of a major secular corporation. The General Council set up a study group to examine the recommendations. But in 1988 the report was rejected as inappropriate.

However, recent controversy has highlighted problems caused by the present church structure and sparked renewed calls for reform. It is clear that more checks and balances must be put in place to counter the influence of the bureaucrats at head office. (I say this although I am a liberal member of the United Church.) The fastest and most effective way to do this would be to lengthen the tenure of the moderator to, say, five years. As it is, the church is in the habit of changing leaders every two years like new hats that come in and out of fashion. That leaves power to the head office bureaucrats by default.

The Roman Catholic Church

"The most educated, best informed people must endure total secrecy, lack of accountability, no choices, no elections. We have seen in John Paul II's pontificate a centralization of power that is breathtaking, an imposition of one man's will on the universal Church which is creating havoc literally all over the world." So wrote Ted Schmidt, a journalist and member of the *Catholic New Times*. As his comment suggests, never before have so many devout Roman Catholic Canadians, from lay people to clergy, had so much reason to question the infallibility of Pope John Paul II. While the United Church has lurched into the vanguard of liberalism and the Anglican Church has stayed middle-of-the-road, the Roman Catholic Church has been headed straight to the conservative past. Many Canadian bishops and lay people have been dragged along kicking and complaining.

At stake, worldwide, is nothing less than the progress the Roman Catholic Church made at its Vatican II Council from 1962 to 1965. At the time Pope John XXIII called for an "Aggiornamento," an updating of the church for the twentieth and twenty-first centuries. He spoke of "opening a window for the Holy Spirit." Today, as Tom

Harpur, a respected Anglican priest and journalist, has commented, "Rome seems to be doing everything it can to dampen down the fires. John Paul II, who will soon complete a decade in office, has not just run a 'tight ship'. He has waged a relentless campaign of retrenchment." It seems, added Harpur, that the Pope is determined to return "to a view of the church that is not just pre-Vatican, but almost medieval."

The Pope's conservative bent has been seen in his insistence on celibacy for priests, his refusal to consider women suitable for the priesthood, his strong action against dissident theologians, and most pervasively his habit of putting conservative-minded bishops in place around the world, passing over popular local choices. The Pope has been busy moulding a very conservative and highly centralized church.

This agenda has enormous implications for the Roman Catholic Church in Canada, where many church leaders are genuinely struggling with the shrinking freedom of thought permitted them. It's also a jolting change for the Catholics who have long been disenchanted with church teachings in such areas as birth control, celibacy, the role of women in the church and so on. As it heads toward the next century, the country's largest religious denomination, with 11 million people claiming affiliation (no actual membership count is released), has one foot stuck in the future and the other foot stuck in the past. And the strains are showing. It falls upon the country's cardinals, archbishops and bishops to calm down a religious flock that seems headed in all directions.

To compose a biographical picture of the church leaders in Canada who face this daunting task, I sent detailed questionnaires to the church's 123 bishops, archbishops and cardinals. (It should be noted that the Catholic elite is not centred in a national church body in Canada, as is the case with most other main religions. Collective opinions of the leaders, however, are expressed through the Canadian Conference of Catholic Bishops and the Assembly of Bishops of Quebec.)

The results of the survey were illuminating about who speaks for the Catholic Church in Canada. I was able to compile biographical information on 59 of the church's leaders.[2] Here are the most interesting results.

They are probably the oldest group of religious leaders in Canada, on average. Six are older than 80 (two have died since the survey was completed), 15 are in their seventies and 21 are in their sixties. They are overwhelmingly Canadian by birth (only four were born outside the country) and come from the full range of regions. The highest number (23) were born in Quebec. (Most Quebec-born serve French-speaking dioceses.) The dominance of French, at least among those who completed the survey, also showed up in the ethnic origins of the church leaders. Of the respondents, 33 had at least one parent of French descent.

Roman Catholic leaders hail from humble backgrounds. In 26 cases, their fathers worked at blue-collar occupations, from farmers and carpenters to labourers. As was the case with Anglican Church leaders, the route into the religious elite for these men was higher education. (See appendix for more details.)

The picture that emerges is of a Canadian church being led by a group of well-educated, elderly gentlemen of mainly humble origins, ministering to a multicultural flock that tends to have lower incomes and less education than their Christian cousins in the mainstream Protestant churches.

Yet there is a lot of burning dissent within the Canadian Catholic Church, and it's occurring at two levels. At the top, many bishops are grumbling publicly about the conservative, secretive ways of Rome. For example, the Canadian Conference of Catholic Bishops has complained about numerous Vatican policies. It has questioned the validity of a new Vatican oath of fidelity that would require those who take it to "adhere with religious submission of will and intellect to the teachings" of the Roman pontiff or the college of Bishops. The council has publicly criticized a tough new Vatican stance on the requirements of the priesthood that precludes married priests as being "more centred on power than on service within the People of God." A leading bishop has also blasted the Byzantine ways of Rome. In 1987, Moncton Archbishop Donat Chiasson commented on returning from the Synod of the Laity: "Bishops hoping for meaningful dialogue found themselves lectured to by the Vatican bureaucracy. . . . The synod's message to the world's Catholics is paternalistic and laced with platitudes."

But the bishops aren't the only ones with complaints. The criticisms being directed at them from below are similar in tenor. In the wake of widely publicized sex-abuse scandals, most notably at the Mount Cashel orphanage in St. John's, laity have organized a broadly based challenge to church structures and power. In response to the scandals, in 1989 a grassroots action group sprang up called the Coalition of Concerned Catholics. The gist of its challenge was contained in a letter it sent to the Canadian bishops. It read in part: "As long as lay people are excluded from real input into decisions and pastoral planning takes place behind closed doors, as long as women are barred from full participation and equal opportunity, and as long as the preservation of existing structures rather than urgent contemporary issues of justice appears to be its main preoccupation, then many young people and adults will remain cynical about the vitality of the church."

The dissidents are raising a forceful new challenge to the church's power structure at a time when its influence over society is already on the wane. In the survey, most Roman Catholic leaders (24) expressed the view that the influence of the church over society's moral values had fallen over the past two decades. Nowhere is this more apparent than in Quebec, where church influence has fallen steadily since the 1960s. "The Catholic Church is passing through a difficult period and its influence on moral values has decreased," says Bishop André Gaumond, of Sainte-Anne-de-la-Pocatière in Quebec. "Man has become secular and quasi-atheistic." In the view of Marius Paré, bishop (now retired) of Chicoutimi, this decline in influence is attributable in large measure "to the enormous influence of the mass media: television, radio, film, newspapers, books and magazines."

Many other bishops across Canada share that view. "Society is more permissive," says Monseigneur Fernand Lacroix, of Quebec City. "The voice of the church is covered by many other voices — the mass media in particular." In the view of Bishop J. Edward Troy, of Saint John, N.B., "The media — radio, TV, the press and cinema — and those with access to the media have now taken on the role of moral guide for most people."

Other Roman Catholic leaders attributed the decline to factors such as the laicization of education, the "breakdown of respect for all authority," the rise of personal self-centredness, of relativism and secularism.

But there were also Roman Catholic leaders who believed that their church's influence over society has risen, at least outside Quebec. Most Reverend Charles Halpin, archbishop of Regina, attributed this to the influence of the Second Vatican Council, greater collaboration on the ecumenical front and "the more aggressive role played by the Canadian Conference of Catholic Bishops." Says Halpin: "The church has a much deeper notion of solidarity with the poor and oppressed."

The Roman Catholic leaders were much more optimistic on the question of whether their church's influence over government policies has risen or fallen over the past two decades. Of the 41 leaders who responded, all but one thought the church still had some effect on government policies. Fourteen thought its influence had fallen, while 13 felt that it had risen. A handful of others felt it had stayed about the same.

Paradoxically, while Quebec-based bishops were despairing of their church's role in forming societal values, several said their influence over governments had risen. "The indirect influence of the church over federal and provincial government social and economic policies in Canada has increased," said one. "I say indirect because it is through study documents, participation in public debates, inquiries [and] consultations that the church has her influence in such matters." Adds Monseigneur Lacroix, "At least they [politicians] consult us and we participate in a lot of commissions, in the presentation of reports frequently in common with other churches." It also helps to have political leaders who are members of the church, says Most Reverend Maxim Hermaniuk, archbishop of the Ukrainian Catholic Church in Winnipeg.

Most Reverend James Hayes, archbishop of Halifax, however, is among those who think the church's influence over government policies has fallen. "Over the past 20 years we have seen a massive erosion of the public conscience that was an overarching influence on many aspects of our society. By that I mean that most Christians, clergy, laity, Christian legislators and policy makers had a common idea of what was right and wrong, and our laws reflected that," he says. "There were common principles such as the value of human life, the horror of using another person for individual convenience or gain, the idea that the value of life did not depend on whether someone else wanted it to continue or not." Today, he says, that has changed. "The great emphasis currently given to the rights of individuals, the lack or absence of a commonly held public morality, the tendency to accept as facts everything presented by the news media . . . has radically changed the relationship between the churches and governments."

Hayes is right in linking the church's influence over government policies to a general weakening of religion's influence in society at large. The most important question for the Roman Catholic Church in the future will be not whether it has the ears of politicians, but whether it has the ears of a growing membership.

Conclusion

Joining the clergy was a route to the prestigious ranks of a ruling elite for church leaders in the Anglican and Roman Catholic faiths. Most of the bishops, archbishops and cardinals came from lower- or middle-class backgrounds rather than from the upper classes with whom they now associate as princes of the church. A prerequisite of advancement in most cases was high academic achievement. Although this degree of social mobility is welcome, it does have ethnic overtones.

The Roman Catholic Church is led mainly by clerics of French Canadian and Irish descent; the Anglican leaders are mainly English and Scottish. Stereotypes of the kindly grey-haired Irish or French Canadian father are based on more than screen writers' imaginations, considering the makeup of the Roman Catholic Church leadership. Likewise, the image of the Anglican vicar holding a cup of tea at a ladies' garden party is not far off the mark, judging from the ages and backgrounds of Anglican bishops and their middle-class flock.

The United Church prides itself on not being ruled by a hierarchy of the clergy. Yet it does have a bureaucratic hierarchy that affords considerable prestige and de facto power to the top bureaucrat, the general secretary, whose term of office is indefinite. Moderators in recent years have been chosen as symbols of the openness of the church — but they are mainly that, symbols. Farquharson is a Saskatchewan farm boy. His predecessor, the Reverend Sang Chul Lee, is pastor of a South Korean church. Before him, Anne Squire, a former teacher from Ottawa, symbolized the equality of women in the church at its highest levels. But the membership of the church tends to be drawn from the vast white, relatively prosperous middle class.

All three churches are engaged in efforts to stay relevant in a society that doesn't pay much attention to religious teachings. They have become more outspoken than ever on social issues through public pronouncements and submissions to government policy makers. But this effort to speak out in pursuit of the collective good of society, while laudable, has been a way of compensating for the diminishing influence of the church in forming the values of individuals. That power has been usurped by the mass media, to which we now turn.

Part V

THE MEDIA

Chapter 9
The News Media

Value Factories in the Age of Technology

It's no coincidence that two of the world's greatest communications scholars were Canadians, inhabitants of a huge land with dispersed population groupings separated by vast distances. Both Harold Innis and Marshall McLuhan saw communications as providing the foundations for society. A University of Toronto economics historian who died in 1952, Innis developed a theory that distinguished between oral, literate and electronic societies. McLuhan, his colleague at the university, carried on the work and became an internationally recognized specialist on the effects of the electronic age. Much of what McLuhan wrote before his death in 1980 is still crucial to our understanding of the influence of the electronic age on our lives.

"After three thousand years of specialist explosion and of increasing specialism and alienation in the technological extensions of our bodies," he wrote in *Understanding Media*, "our world has become compressional in dramatic reversal. As electricity contracted, the globe is no more than a village. Electric speed is bringing all social and political functions together in a sudden implosion [that] has heightened human awareness of responsibility to an intense degree. It is this implosive factor that alters the position of the Negro, the teenager, and some other groups. They can no longer be *contained*, in the political sense of limited association. They are now *involved* in our lives, as we are in theirs, thanks to the electric media."

McLuhan is best known for his notion of the global village. He did not suggest that in this global village familiarity would breed harmony; he meant rather that our expanding information-gathering capacity would make us intimately aware of people, places and events around the world. For example, we may be involved in the situations of some oppressed groups like blacks in South Africa to the extent that they make the nightly news, but that doesn't necessarily lead to conviction or action. On the contrary, the flow of bad news — of violence, crime and injustice — is so great that viewers become numbed; they must switch off their ethical sensibilities to retain mental stability. This, too, McLuhan foresaw.

It's intriguing to think what Innis or McLuhan would think of the state of Canada's media today, of the effects on society of the profusion of television and radio signals, newspapers, magazines, films and books that Canadians watch, hear and read every day. Some things haven't changed. We're still caught between the literate and the electronic ages. Even though daily newspaper readership has been falling for 20 years, the printed word is still a dominant information medium in our society, a refuge for the mind amid the plethora of network, cable and specialty TV channels available to viewers. With the exception of newspapers, our media are also still dominated by American-produced fare, whether that be in television signals and programs, magazines, films or books. We're still caught up in a media revolution and we're still trying to understand it. What we *do* understand leaves no room for complacency.

Every society has its wizards, priests and mythmakers. Ours is no different. But instead of shamans or clerics, the mass media have become our arbiters of truth. Increasingly, that truth is revealed to the flock through the images that fill our television screens, magazine and newspaper pages and advertising billboards. These images, of everything from politicians and soap opera stars to national revolutions, serve as signposts in a mind-boggling torrent of more information than we could ever possibly digest. They shape our political, social and cultural values the way the church did in more religious times.

The most powerful message of the images is this: Consume. All it takes is enough cash and you too can have the right look, the right attitude, just like the role models you see in ads and on TV. Even the word *consumer* has replaced the word *citizen* as the most-used descriptive for ordinary people.

The media, and especially television, have become the primary source of ideology in our technological society. Studies show, for example, that people who watch a lot of TV have an exaggerated notion of how violent the world is. As well, the news media play a crucial role in determining our political outlooks; the experiences of TV serial stars, not clerics, provide our training in situational ethics; we're more likely to develop our idea of the good life from watching "Street Legal" than from reading Thoreau.

Considering the role that the media play as the dominant value-factories in our society, it's crucial to know who the most powerful people in the media are, where they come from, how they wield their influence and to what ends.

Allies or Adversaries of the Powerful?

"It must be the worst of all possible times to be a politician," says Barbara Frum, host of CBC's "The Journal." "I don't think it's ever been tougher, unless you're one of the favoured ones who is granted an endless honeymoon just to prove that the press isn't against all politicians . . . . There are an awful lot of people who say, 'I'm not going to lift my head above the trench, in any field, it's not safe.'"

Frum is talking about a mood of negativism among journalists and, she stresses, the population as a whole, in which everyone seems to be saying, "Gosh, why don't we see how many screws we can unscrew and how many holding clips we can unclip before this place falls apart." Her view is shared by several leading figures in the news business.

Jeffrey Simpson, Ottawa columnist for the *Globe and Mail* has worried in print about an "exceptionally disturbing" trend in contemporary journalism. It is "an increasingly pervasive cynicism about government that goes beyond the healthy scepticism and endemic tensions that have always existed — and should exist — between politicians and the fourth estate."

Elly Alboim, Ottawa bureau chief for CBC-TV, is concerned that relations between the government and the media are more "poisonous" than he's ever seen them. "It's horrible. It's almost impossible to work." Alboim believes that the Ottawa Press Gallery is "acting as an agent for an alienated population. It's really quite destructive." The views of Frum, Simpson and Alboim represent one school of thought about what's wrong with the media. They identify an important threat to the media's integrity, insofar as journalists should prevent themselves from adopting a shoot-from-the-hip cynicism. It takes a lot less work and experience to react to news with a cynical sneer than to do the heavy research required to truly weigh the merits of complex government policies or simple news events.

There is a second school of criticism of the media that is the antithesis of the journalists-are-too-negative school. Other media insiders (invariably on the left of the political spectrum) argue that the media have become the mouthpiece of the ruling elites, including the economic elite that owns them. "I think that increasingly the media does not inform the public about what is really happening in society," says veteran *Globe and Mail* investigative reporter Jock Ferguson. "Essentially what we do is reflect and regurgitate the interests of the ruling elites." Ferguson says that the battle for healthy media, fought in newsrooms everywhere, is being lost. "In every area of the media in this country there is a very, very substantial narrowing of who are the dominant voices — the government and the institutions in this society increasingly dominate what's covered. People with views that are alternative to the mainstream find it more and more difficult to get access to the mainstream media, and if they do gain access their views are often belittled or buried in the back of the paper. It's leading to a tremendous disenfranchisement of vast sections of the population. We're very much returning to nineteenth-century traditions, where only the elites mattered in society."

Ferguson's view is shared by leading left-wing academics. In his book *The Canadian Corporate Elite*, Toronto academic Wallace Clement writes: "The conclusion must be drawn that, together, the economic and media elite are simply two sides of the same upper class; between them they hold two of the key sources of power — economic and ideological — in Canadian society and form the corporate elite." Two American left-wing intellectuals, Edward Herman and Noam Chomsky, write in their 1988 study of the U.S. media, *Manufacturing Consent*, that the media, through their choice of topics and sources, the way they frame issues and by keeping debate within the bounds of certain acceptable premises, "inculcate and defend the economic, social and political agenda of privileged groups" that dominate life in America.

Both these opposing criticisms of the media suggest that the media are falling short of their ideal role in society, which is to hold up the actions and motivations of the powerful to objective scrutiny on behalf of the public. In this role journalists are inveterate seekers of the truth, devoted to the facts and to the reader. But which line of criticism is right? Have the news media become too antagonistic and cynical or are they undergoing a temporary bout of pessimism about the elites they serve? Putting the question another way, is the media elite a sphere of power bouncing like a yo-yo on strings held by the other ruling elites? Or is it more accurate to describe it as an independent circle of power whose interests and goals sometimes overlap with those of other ruling elites and sometimes conflict with them?

It's a question that leading editors in Canada have strong opinions on. Asked whether newspapers should be in conflict or cooperate with other ruling elites, William Thorsell, editor of the *Globe and Mail*, says: "It's both. We reinforce elites at the same time as we aggravate them, bring them down. We're part of the Establishment at the same time as we're burrs in the side of the Establishment. Obviously a paper with a good strong newsroom will, at the same time as it serves its readers who happen to be members of the Establishment, know instinctively that it has a role to describe the Establishment's failures." John Fraser, editor of *Saturday Night* magazine, sees the relationship between the media and other ruling elites in pragmatic terms. He uses relations between the media and government as an example. "The media has got to cooperate with government and the government with media, but it's not a particularly loving relationship. It's got an element of self-interest on both sides. And yet it is symbiotic: a newspaper without a hot political story is not worth much, and a government or a politician that can't get some public display doesn't feel like they're taking part in anything."

Kevin Doyle, editor of *Maclean's* magazine, rejects the idea that the relationship between the media and other ruling elites should be characterized as either adversarial or cooperative. "I don't think it's either," he says. "I think the role of a major news organization is to explain, to analyse, to uncover, as far as is humanly possible, the truth about an event that it judges to be of significant interest to its audience. If your object is to be adversarial, then more often than not you'll be biased, by definition. And I still believe that a news organization can report in an unbiased way. What comes out in the end may be less than objective, and quite often is because we're all human and can't see around every corner. But it won't be biased."

The picture emerges of a media in which the principles of journalism are alive and well. Notably, Thorsell and Fraser acknowledge the symbiotic relationship between the news media and other ruling elites, but they also assert the media's role as independent critics of the powerful. Their comments would never satisfy leftist commentators, however.

The fact is that major news organizations in Canada all operate within the boundaries of liberal-democratic traditions. Newspapers in particular are usually known for the political stripe of their editorials, a legacy of the days when interventionist publisher/owners founded media organs to espouse their political points of view. It's true that newspaper editorial pages still come in political hues. For example, everyone knows that the Toronto *Star* has taken a predominantly Liberal editorial stance since Joseph Atkinson ran it between 1899 and 1948. The *Globe and Mail*'s editorial line has been generally Conservative since its creation from the *Globe* and the *Mail and Empire*. In the west, the Vancouver *Sun* became known as a Liberal paper soon after it was founded in 1912. Likewise, the Winnipeg *Free Press* traditionally supported the Liberal Party, especially after 1898, when Liberal politician Sir Clifford Sifton bought control and appointed John W. Dafoe to a tenure as editor that lasted for the next 43 years. In Quebec, *Le Devoir* is traditionally federalist and pro-Catholic while *Le Journal de Montréal* is nationalist. The country even boasts a staunchly pro-monarchist paper, the Halifax *Chronicle-Herald*. But there isn't a mass-media outlet in the land, in print or broadcast journalism, that the left, or even NDPers, can call their own.

Simply pointing out that the news media operate within mainstream ideological parameters is not terribly illuminating. To find out whose interests the news media serve and represent — the ruling elites, the relatively powerless in the population at large, or both — we need to take a closer look at who owns the media, who runs the newsrooms of the nation and who works for them. Ferguson's charge that fewer and fewer voices are finding expression in the media is a serious one. To what degree are these owners, managers and journalists a homogeneous group that poorly represents the population at large? To what degree are the media open to those who are iconoclastic in temperament and intellect?

Power within the media exists at three levels. At the top are the business tycoons who have carved the Canadian media market into national and regional fiefdoms. The high concentration of media ownership in a few hands is, on balance, a constricting force on diversity of thought and opinion. These owners have the power to hire and fire the publishers, editors and programming chiefs who form the second tier of power. Normally selected for their compatibility with the owners, these employees decide, in turn, what is news and how it is covered. A third level of power exerts a countervailing force against the two upper tiers: the working journalists in the newsroom who, at their best, can pride themselves on their objectivity and independence.

The Owners: Media Concentration

The last major publication to profile Ken Thomson was the *Financial Post*. You could hardly expect the *Globe and Mail* to do the same, since Thomson controls Thomson Corp., which owns the *Globe* and 40 or so other newspapers in Canada. The reason is simple: it's a no-win situation for a journalist to write a profile of her ultimate boss. Even if the subject merited a positive article, the journalist would put her reputation at risk by writing it. At best her judgment would be suspect because of the conflict of interest; at worst, her peers would accuse her of toadery.

So tearing apart or toasting Thomson is a job only a journalist at a rival chain would take on. By the same token, don't expect to see a penetrating profile of John Fisher, boss of the Southam printing and publishing empire, in any of the chain's 18 papers. Among them: the Montreal *Gazette*, the Ottawa *Citizen* and the Vancouver *Sun* and *Province*. Conrad Black, owner of the Hollinger Inc. publishing group, is fair game for the *Globe and Mail* but less so for his *Saturday Night* magazine or the *Financial Post*, in which he has a minority stake.

This mild form of self-censorship engaged in by the minions of the media czars illustrates one small ramification of media concentration in Canada. Business tycoons have long known that the best way to cut down on uncomplimentary coverage is to buy the outlets. This and the fact that newspapers in one-paper towns can be made to spew out cash like slot machines has led to a remarkable degree of concentration in Canada's newspaper and magazine media. In 1970, monopoly newspaper chains put out 58 per cent of all copies of newspapers in Canada. By 1980, it was 77 per cent.

Today, two chains, Thomson and Southam, control about 48 per cent of English-language daily newspaper circulation. Torstar's Toronto *Star*, the country's biggest daily, accounts for another 10 per cent of the market all by itself. The other central Canadian giant is Maclean Hunter Ltd., whose $2 billion or so in assets includes ownership of leading magazines *Maclean's*, *Chatelaine* (French and English versions) and *L'Actualité*, as well as the Toronto Sun Corp. stable of daily tabloids and the *Financial Post*.

Conrad Black's Hollinger has also become part of the print power club in recent years. With assets of more than $1 billion, it owns a growing collection of newspapers and magazines in Canada, the United States and Britain. *Saturday Night*, London's *Daily Telegraph* and the Jerusalem *Post* are its most prestigious publications.

In Quebec, Philippe de Gaspé Beaubien has made his Telemedia into the largest publisher of consumer magazines in Canada. Among them are *Canadian Living, TV Guide* and its French equivalent, *TV Hebdo, Equinox* and *Harrowsmith*. The biggest-circulation French-language dailies are also members of conglomerates. Paul Desmarais's Power Corp. owns *La Presse*, Pierre Peladeau's Quebecor owns *Le Journal de Montréal*.

Every year more proud independents are sold to the chains. Two of the most recent independently owned papers to pass into

Southam's orbit were the highly respected Kingston *Whig-Standard*, previously owned by Michael Davies, and the Kitchener-Waterloo *Record*, previously controlled by the Motz family. For the most part, the newspapers across Canada not owned by these central Canadian giants are part of smaller, regional powerhouses. These include the Irvings in New Brunswick, who control all five English-language dailies in the province and a slew of TV and radio stations. Graham Dennis in Nova Scotia runs the two dominant papers in Halifax and region, the *Chronicle-Herald* and the *Mail-Star*, as though they were his personal fiefdom, which they are. They've been in the family for generations. The most powerful female media owner in Canada is Martha Blackburn, of London, Ontario, whose Blackburn Group owns the London *Free Press* as well as the city's major television station and AM and FM radio stations.

Attempts to decrease concentration of ownership in the media have been abject failures. In 1981, Tom Kent's Royal Commission on Newspapers identified increasing concentration of ownership as the major problem of newspapers in Canada. (The Kent Commission was set up by the Liberal government after one major newspaper chain, Southam, shut down the Winnipeg *Tribune* on exactly the same day as another major chain, Thomson, shut down the Ottawa *Journal*, leaving each with a monopoly in those two cities.)

In his findings, Kent's essential argument was that concentration of ownership leads to a "rationalization" or centralization of expenditures. This, he said, leads to a centralization of content development, budgetary procedures that ensure profit to the neglect of the news, and generally a denigration of the historical function of newspapers, which is to inform readers of important events and to provide a range of interpretation of those events.

The only response to the Kent Commission report was the Trudeau cabinet's passage, in 1982, of an order-in-council discouraging a greater degree of cross-ownership between newspapers and broadcasting. The Irvings, who were a target of the directive for their cross-ownership of newspapers and TV and radio stations in New Brunswick, took the government to court over the directive, challenging its legality. Before that case was settled, the order-in-council was rescinded by the Tories, in June 1985. In any case, the CRTC had not been single-minded about not allowing new cross-ownership.

But the Kent Commission did serve notice to the media conglomerates that further expansion in Canada, especially if it entailed cross-ownership of different outlets in the same market, would become increasingly difficult. Since then, the big chains have moved their acquisition hunts to the United States and Europe, where a greater supply of independent papers is up for grabs.

The only worrisome threat of an even greater concentration of ownership in Canada's print media arises from the joint-ownership relationship between Torstar Corp., owner of the Toronto *Star* (as well as Harlequin Books), and Southam. In 1985, Beland Honderich, then publisher of the Toronto *Star*, and St. Clair Balfour, boss of Southam at the time, hatched a defensive alliance to enable Southam to fight off a hostile takeover bid. Torstar got a 23 per cent voting stake in Southam and, in return, Southam got a 30 per cent nonvoting stake in Torstar. A stand-still agreement between the two companies expired in 1990. Media pundits are watching to see if Torstar moves to acquire control of Southam — regulatory officials should be too, since the acquisition would vault Torstar into first place among newspaper owners, with the Toronto *Star* and 18 more city dailies in its stable.

If the print giants have the Canadian market divvied up like a luscious peach pie, there are still a lot of squabbling contenders for pieces of the broadcast industry. As in the newspaper and magazine industry, central Canadian companies are the dominant players, nationwide, in the television and radio business. There are only two nationwide networks, the CBC and the CTV Television Network, whose largest member is Baton Broadcasting of Toronto. Other Ontario-based broadcasting empires include Rogers Communications, the largest cable operator in Canada; Maclean Hunter, which operates cable systems in 16 Ontario centres plus a TV station in Ottawa; Toronto's CHUM Ltd., run by Allan Waters, which has a couple of dozen radio stations across the country as well as a handful of television stations, including ATV in the Maritimes, CITY TV in Toronto and the pay-TV services MuchMusic and Musique Plus; and Allan Slaight's smaller Standard Broadcasting, which owns seven radio stations, including its flagship CFRB in Toronto and three cable systems.

Quebec has a few broadcasting powerhouses, most notably André Chagnon's Télé-Métropole Inc., which operates a regional network. Chagnon's major Montreal-based competitors are CFCF, a CTV affiliate that owns Télévision Quatre Saisons, a fledgling pay-TV service; Radio-Canada, French-television arm of the CBC; and Radio-Québec, the province's smaller entrant in the field.

The central Canadian broadcast empires do not dominate the market the way their print cousins do. The broadcasting world is still populated by numerous smaller players, like Michael Sifton's Saskatchewan string of TV stations, Moffat Communications' clutch of Prairie TV stations, Edmonton-based Shaw Cablesystems, and the more recent Alberta Television Network, run by Wendell Wilks. The biggest challenge to the supremacy of central Canadian station owners comes from two western companies with nationwide aspirations, WIC (Western International Communications, owned by Vancouver's Griffiths family) and CanWest Communications, of Winnipeg, whose flagship, Global Television, is one of the most successful stations serving southern Ontario.

The Media Czars and Their Top Lieutenants

The owners who hire and fire the publishers and station managers and therefore have indirect control over the contents of news pages and broadcasts fall into two groups: the silverspoons and the bootstrap brigade. The silverspoons were born into inherited wealth and used it to build or expand their media holdings. They include Ken Thomson; John Fisher; Doug Bassett, son of John Bassett and the man who runs Baton Broadcasting for the Eatons; Conrad Black; Martha Blackburn, who inherited her London-based holdings built by her grandfather Josiah and father, Walter; Graham Dennis; the Irving boys, sons of the mighty K.C. Irving; and Michael Sifton, scion of the once-mighty Sifton media clan.

Yet running an inherited media conglomerate is no sinecure for faint-hearted dilettantes, and none of the above could be described as such. Either global competitors are waiting for you to make a misstep, as in the case of Ken Thomson, or the challenge is to keep the company from crumbling beneath you, as in the case of John Fisher.

Ken Thomson: By far the most powerful newspaper owner in Canada, Thomson, 68, is heir to the $7-billion newspaper, specialty publishing and travel empire built from scratch by his father, Roy. In Canada, Thomson's 40 or so newspapers, led by the flagship *Globe and Mail*, account for 20 per cent of total newspaper circulation. Thomson also owns about 150 dailies and weeklies across the U.S. and a string of newspapers and TV stations in the United Kingdom. Ken's low-key personal style and concentration on the publishing business means he doesn't rank as the sort of top deal maker portrayed in Chapter Four. He's not one to revel in the power of words, like fellow publisher Conrad Black, but he knows all about the power of the presses; power to make money, that is.

One of the most perceptive portraits of Ken Thomson was done by accomplished Toronto writer David Macfarlane in a 1980 issue of *Saturday Night*. He describes meeting Thomson in his art-and-collectible-strewn office in Toronto: "There is nothing of the mystery of power about him. His flat, Ontario accent is without the smoothness that Scott Fitzgerald called the ring of money. His sense of humour is unbarbed. His public image, what little there is of it, is possessed of the same happy dullness that characterizes a Hallmark Christmas card. But privately, up close, there is a surprising warmth and simplicity."

Thomson's modest style, which I witnessed in my six years at the *Globe and Mail*, is baffling when set against the arrogance, brashness or rudeness disguised as bluntness that characterizes so many better-known businessmen of the age. In his style Thomson is an anachronism, a throwback to a generation of empire-building, churchgoing Protestants who really did believe that "pride goeth before destruction." To be sure, Thomson's public reticence is partly a product of growing up under a domineering father, but it also reflects the tenets of the Baptist faith to which Thomson adheres, a faith in which modesty is a virtue.

Ken's son David, the eldest of three children and the heir apparent, has much of his father's personality. Colleagues at Thomson-owned department stores where David has worked describe him as a quiet loner. "He's very nice, extremely shy," says one retailing vice-president. "I've seen him fall asleep at meetings." Another former colleague describes him as pleasant but reticent in social situations. "In a room, David would stand in a corner, talk to people who came up to him, but not approach other people to start a conversation." (Judging from David's recent stints in the executive suites of Zellers and Simpson's, he's learning a lot by quietly observing the way things work.) As David's father will tell him, you can't run a business empire and be the employees' best friend.

No one has ever accused the Thomson empire of being run in a kind, paternalistic style that treats employees like children. As a rule, Thomson steers clear of editorial interference, though he's been known to pick up the phone to express his opinion of a writer to *Globe* publisher Roy Megarry. Thomson is rarely seen in newsrooms. Instead, he remains aloof, leaving his business dealings to a handful of ball-busting, no-nonsense operators with a reputation for making money — and frontline managers and publishers jump — in its far-flung operations. They include, most notably, John Tory, Thomson's longtime lieutenant in Toronto, and Michael Brown, who as chief executive of Thomson Corp. is responsible for the organization's past and future forays into international publishing. Thomson Corp. now ranks as the fourth-largest media conglomerate in the world, and it will primarily be Brown's job to keep it there. Brown won the CEO job at Thomson in 1989, when two wings of the empire, International Thomson Organization Ltd. (ITO) and Thomson Newspapers Ltd., were merged. Brown had impressed Thomson greatly with the way he had turned around ITO since 1985 by selling off dozens of poorly performing companies, getting rid of the company's North Sea oil interests and cranking up profits that remained in the stable.

Thomson Corp. is to the newspaper business what Shoppers Drug Mart is to drug retailing. It has been able to replicate a proven operating style and financial discipline in franchises across North America and Britain. The result has been that critics have accused the chain of turning out hordes of small-town papers that benefit the mind about as much as placebos do the body. The noted exceptions are flagship papers like the *Globe and Mail* and the Winnipeg *Free Press*, whose readers demand much higher quality fare.

Even in the United States, Thomson has a reputation as an organization that makes money out of small papers with tight budgets and fat revenues. An exception was Thomson's 1989 acquisition of the Bridgeport *Post-Telegram* in Connecticut (circulation 80,000) for U.S. $240 million, its biggest daily newspaper acquisition in the United States. Since Thomson didn't immediately slash costs to the bone, a new strategy seemed to be emerging: acquire bigger dailies that will compete through editorial quality. The paradox of newspaper publishing is that while blandness can be a virtue in an owner, it's inexcusable in a newspaper, where blandness is the handmaiden of mediocrity.

Roy Megarry: Being a publisher is not easy. Take too active a part in the newsroom and you end up making your editor look feckless. Target your audience so that the paper can boost circulation, atttract ads and stay profitable, and the newsroom will cry "sellout" and raise serious questions about the quality of coverage. If Roy Megarry didn't know that before his 1989 makeover of the *Globe*'s editorial ranks, when William Thorsell replaced Norman Webster as editor, he knows it now. Whether the *Globe* remains a strong, successful paper depends, in the end, on the judgment and actions of Megarry, the man Ken Thomson relies on to ensure the profitability of his flagship newspaper.

Roy Megarry, above all else, refuses to accept the idea, common in newspapers across the continent, that the papers can afford to stay the same in the way they cover and present the news. The trick has been to convince the newspaper's staff that he's right. In a series of luncheon addresses to staff in the summer of 1989, Megarry preached his gospel of change to his employees. "The pace of change is accelerating," he said at one gathering. "Competition is popping up all around. Therefore, the major threats the *Globe* faces are internal, not external. Are we up to the challenge?"

A tall, well-groomed man who has never been seen at the office in anything other than a suit, Megarry possesses an almost boyish ebullience that can be deceiving. His Irish eyes twinkle in one instant and turn to an intimidating glare the next. He doesn't need a course in assertiveness training (as anyone who has attended his tightly run management meetings can attest). A favourite rumour making the rounds at the *Globe* in the aftermath of the Webster sacking had Megarry bumping into a high-level editor in the halls. The editor said something about "a power struggle" going on at the paper. Megarry's response: "There is no power struggle. I have all the power."

Megarry thinks a lot about the future of newspapers and what readers want. "The role of newspapers in society has changed," he says. "Industry surveys show that readers are cancelling subscriptions because they haven't got time to read. People are busier, it may be playing squash or watching TV. Television is a much more friendly medium. It's an effort to read a newspaper." Another problem for readers, he says, is the complexity of the world. "People are finding that keeping up is just too complicated."

This means a newspaper like the *Globe* can't just present readers with the news. "We have to help readers cope with a complex world. The media has been part of the problem. I would like to see us become more solution-oriented." On top of that, Megarry believes the *Globe* can't afford to be all things to all people. "There are three things we have to be better at than any other paper. National news, international news and business news."

Megarry dismisses talk that the paper has gone soft on business as ridiculous. "Ask any businessmen if they think we're soft," he says. "They don't." And he dismisses any notion that the *Globe* is turning itself into a *Wall Street Journal* North as "foolish" because more than half the *Globe* readers buy it for the news section.

Megarry's confidence in his strategy of targeting the *Globe* to well-off, well-educated readers nationwide rests, in large part, on his strong record at the *Globe* since he took over in 1978. Consider a few of the accomplishments he can take all or partial credit for:

- He quadrupled the paper's profits to more than $20 million during a decade as publisher and increased its circulation to about 330,000, with most of that increase coming in markets outside Ontario.
- He turned the *Globe* into a national paper, in the process spending millions of dollars buying satellite-transmission technology and establishing printing plants in Vancouver,

Calgary, Moncton and Ottawa. ("We would never have survived being a Toronto newspaper," he says.)

• He sanctioned the opening of a handful of national and foreign bureaus, and he oversaw the creation of a clutch of seven magazines. Unfortunately only three, *Report on Business Magazine*, *Destinations* and *Broadcast Week* survived.

Above all, Megarry sees himself an agent of change. This restlessness can be traced to the tough start he had in life. He was born in 1937, the fifth of six children of Protestant parents living in a Belfast ghetto. At 15 he dropped out of Annadale Grammar School and took a job in the cost accounting department of a linen mill to help support his family. Four years later he emigrated to Canada. "Opportunities in Belfast were very limited and the class system was still very much alive in the '50s," he told *CMA Magazine*. Some family members had already made the trip: he had a sister in Boston and a brother in Hamilton. But the major attraction of Canada was a girl named Barbara Bennett, his future wife, whom he met on a bicycling holiday in Killarney.

In Canada, Megarry earned his CMA at night school while working as a comptroller at a succession of small companies. He credits that training, along with a management development course he took at Princeton, as crucial to his rapid climb up the corporate ladder.

By 1969, he had risen to senior consultant at management firm Urwick Currie & Partners (forerunner of Coopers and Lybrand). Then in 1974, when he was only 37, Torstar Corp. recruited him as vice-president of corporate development. He set about figuring out ways to diversify the newspaper business. His most notable success was the acquisition of Harlequin Enterprises.

Today a member of the Establishment, Megarry nevertheless sees himself as an outsider who made it without benefit of the usual credentials. "As open as our society has always been in Canada, unquestionably there was an Establishment here," he has said. "It helped to be part of that Establishment, to be a graduate of a private school or of a prestigious university. I think there's a lot of evidence to suggest that that is not nearly as important a criterion for success today in Canada and North America as it once was."

There is no doubt that Megarry has put in place an editorial team that will assist him in carrying out his vision for the *Globe*. Having such a team is what he calls his first law of management. "A dictatorial manager can achieve, and some of them do achieve, great things. But it seems to me that a lot more would be achieved if that same manager were able to create an environment and a management team that contributes to what he or she wants to achieve," he once said.

Now that his team is in place, Megarry has retreated behind the imaginary wall that separates the publisher's office from the editor's — and none too soon as far as journalists on the newsroom floor are concerned. But his management shakeup at the *Globe* left no doubt in anybody's mind that the publisher has the power to set the course for the paper.

John Fisher: Fisher is a rare breed in the chain-dominated business of Canadian newspapering. He is not only a member of the family that founded the business but he also is the hands-on manager who runs the show. The 63-year-old president and CEO of Southam Inc. is the latest in an unbroken string of family to head to the company since it was founded 114 years ago by his great-grandfather, William Southam. While families like the Thomsons and Atkinsons (Torstar) long ago ceded operating authority to professional managers, Fisher still runs day-to-day operations as chief executive (although he's not known as an interventionist when it comes to editorial content). Critics of Southam's financial performance have long argued that Fisher should cede power to professional managers, despite his efforts to streamline and invigorate the company since he took over in 1985.

Southam ranks as Canada's largest newspaper publisher, with 18 dailies in Canada which account for about 28 per cent of all newspapers sold in the country each day. Southam's other assets include Coles Book Stores Ltd., business magazines and a printing and graphics division.

Fisher is an unlikely media boss. An engineer by training, he took over the top job reluctantly after Gordon, his younger brother and predecessor at Southam, died from cancer. At the time, John was happily settled in Edmundston, N.B., where he ran a pulp and paper mill called Fraser Inc. Fisher took the new job only out of a sense of responsibility to the family, which had no other likely contenders in its ranks. Fisher had no trouble fitting in with Toronto society. After all, he belongs to the favoured Establishment religion, Anglicanism, and is a member of the best private clubs: the Toronto, the Royal Canadian Yacht Club and the Mount Royal.

At first, Fisher was toasted by just about everyone for his get-tough management techniques at the somnambulent company. Methodical and tenacious by nature, he brought management of the newspapers under central control at head office, set profit targets for every division and cut costs rapidly by slashing the workforce.

Six years later, Fisher could be excused if he regretted his decision to take the job. Everyone from family members to investment experts is griping about his management. At the 1991 annual meeting, William Balfour, youngest grandson of the founder, complained that his older brother St. Clair, the family patriarch, former Southam boss and still an honorary director, had not been invited to board meetings. Meanwhile, Stephen Jarislowsky, the outspoken Montreal investment counsellor whose institutional clients hold big chunks of Southam stock, opined to journalist John Partridge that Fisher wasn't taking tough enough rationalization measures and was too nice for the job. Said Jarislowsky, "John Fisher is a very pleasant, nice human being, but I don't think that's how you win. Nice guys finish last. The entire board needs to take a much tougher attitude." The real cause of Southam's woes, however, was a recession during 1990 and 1991 that demolished all the financial progress Fisher had been able to eke out of the conglomerate.

As a result, as much uncertainty hung over Fisher's future as over the future of the company. In the midst of falling profits, Southam's major shareholders — Torstar and the far-flung Southam family, both with about 23 per cent voting control — were growing restless: Torstar was itching to take over and do a better job of managing assets, while some Southam family members were wondering how long they should hold on to their value-eroded shares. Fisher had discovered to his dismay that blood takes a second place to money.

Doug Bassett: Dougie, as his friends call him, is central Canada's blue-blooded broadcaster, a bona fide member of the Establishment. Now chief executive officer of Baton, he is the son of John Bassett, former publisher of the Toronto *Telegram* and owner of the Toronto Argonauts.

Baton is controlled by the Eatons, the Bassetts' blood brothers in business — they sit on each other's boards — through Telegram Corp. Ltd., a company set up by John Bassett and John David Eaton. Later the senior Bassett sold his stake in Telegram Corp. and his three sons, Doug, Johnny F. (who died of cancer in 1986) and David followed suit.

Today, Doug Bassett, 51, has a direct stake in Baton, worth a couple of million dollars, but he runs the company in such a tough, penny-pinching style you'd think he owned the whole thing. "Big John was never interested in detail," Bassett once told journalist Rod McQueen. "I am, because if you can control your costs, you can spend more. If your costs get out of line, it can kill. I'm chintzy because I don't like people at the trough, going to Bucharest, Romania, to some goddam film festival."

Like successful scions everywhere, Bassett knows that if you take care of the pennies in the business, you can afford to spend big dollars in private. He lives in Forest Hill and owns about 90 hectares on Lake Rosseau in Muskoka, playground of Toronto's oldest money, where he keeps his collection of vintage boats, including a sleek Cigarette, the *Silver Bullet.*

Not that Bassett has much time to enjoy his private assets. He's too busy running Baton, the biggest member of the CTV Television Network. It has about $250 million worth of assets tied up in seven CTV affiliates in six cities, including CFTO-TV in Toronto, CJOH-TV in Ottawa and major outlets in Saskatoon, Regina, Yorkton and Prince Albert. Baton also runs a radio station (CFQC-AM) in Saskatoon and has two production companies, Glen-Warren Productions in Toronto and Carleton Productions in Ottawa.

Considering Bassett's flair for running a business profitably — he keeps a list of every employee's salary and date of last raise within reach — it may seem surprising that he spent a good part of his life finding his calling. Education didn't hold much appeal for him. After attending Upper Canada College in Toronto, he went off to the University of New Brunswick (where he roomed with Fred Eaton) but quit after two years and worked for James Lovick Advertising in British Columbia. For a time he was executive assistant to B.C. premier W.A.C. Bennett, then he returned to Toronto to run Inland Publishing Co. Ltd., a string of community newspapers owned by his father. After Inland was sold to the Toronto *Star* in 1978, Bassett began his career at Baton.

Since then he has slowly taken over from his father, who stepped down as Baton chairman in 1985. Judging from the increasingly competitive nature of the television market, Bassett is the right man at the right time to run Baton.

John Cassady: Hustle and muscle. The two words might as well be put on a plaque and hung over the door of CTV's Toronto headquarters, for they're the words that sum up the business philosophy that John Cassady took to the CTV Television Network, Canada's only nationwide network besides the CBC, when he became its chief executive in 1990. A mere 38 going on 50, Cassady, who went from selling soup at Campbell's to selling serials and soaps at CTV, is living proof that television is a thoroughly commercial business where the marketing goes in before the quality (he hopes) goes out.

Cassady was hired by the CTV board, made up of representatives of eight (usually feuding) member broadcasting companies, to reinvigorate the news, current affairs and entertainment fare that CTV central turns out for its members' 24 affiliated stations. For Cassady, the job immediately took on the air of a mission. The way he sees it, television stations are in a fight for survival. "We're all experiencing declining audience shares and we have to be more aggressive in the share game," he told an industry gathering in 1990.

Like all marketing men, Cassady thinks big. His goal is to concentrate on developing cost-effective quality programming to compete with CBC and even CNN, the U.S. cable phenomenon that he considers one of his major competitors. As far as he's concerned, that leaves no room for guesswork. "We have to treat every new program as if the life of the series depended on it," he has said. "There's too much intuition in our business. We need more research."

Marketing research is a tenet of the food and tobacco companies Cassady got his training in. His previous employers include RJR-

Macdonald Inc., General Foods and Campbell Soup Co., where he rose to president of its British subsidiary in 1987. Since he signed on at CTV, Cassady has revamped the network's national news service as well as its popular current affairs programs "Canada AM" and "W5." He brought in veteran print journalist John Macfarlane, former publisher of the *Financial Times* and of *Saturday Night* magazine, to oversee the news and information programming. Cassady also brought in fellow marketing whiz from Campbell, Paul Robertson. But while Cassady led the charge of the bright brigade, his major challenge was to make sure the troops followed him. As ad revenues slumped in 1991, the rank and file among CTV's 380 employees were more worried about layoffs than audience shares.

The Outsiders

The most fascinating group among the media czars is the bootstrap brigade. Mainly of humble origin, they built their media businesses from the ground up. In some cases, they are outsiders who have risen from nowhere to challenge the power of the central Canadian media establishment. For instance, I.H. (Izzy) Asper, owner of CanWest, is the son of a Winnipeg theatre owner who started with a single station in 1976. Frank Griffiths, an accountant who married into money (his wife is daughter of Dr. Ballard of dog-food fame), built WIC, the most powerful western media conglomerate, from a single station in the 1930s. Pierre Peladeau, the son of a lumber merchant, is the king of racy U.S. tabloids and proprietor of *Le Journal de Montréal.*

Other outsiders have parlayed their business success into full membership in the central Canadian media establishment. Allan Slaight, the son of a Moose Jaw newspaper owner, rose to prominence by proving himself a worthy newcomer to the business establishment ranks. An ambitious former reporter, station manager and small-time station owner, Slaight acquired Standard Broadcasting in the mid-1970s, primarily because his obvious drive and talents won him the blessing and backing of Brascan honcho Trevor Eyton, a member of Standard's board. Douglas Creighton, a one-time reporter who oversees Toronto Sun Corp. and its subsidiary, the *Financial Post,* shook up the newspaper industry in 1971 with his creation of the Toronto *Sun*, a daily tabloid. He went on to oversee the creation of *Sun*s in Edmonton, Calgary and Ottawa. His papers were so successful that the media giant Maclean Hunter bought him out. Creighton's boss at Maclean Hunter, Ron Osborne, is a dynamic, British-born accountant who was transformed into one of the most powerful media czars in Canada when he became CEO of the conglomerate in 1986. Another outsider who worked his way from nowhere into the ranks of the media and corporate elite is Beland Honderich, who joined the Toronto *Star* as a reporter in 1943 and rose to serve as its publisher for 22 years. A highly interventionist publisher/owner who ruled the newsroom with an iron glare, Honderich transformed the *Star* into Canada's biggest daily, devoted to three major causes: Liberalism, defending the downtrodden and covering almost every issue from a Toronto perspective. Now chairman of Torstar Corp., Honderich, 73, has passed day-to-day control to publisher David Jolley and president David Galloway. Son John Honderich is the paper's editor, who seems as well liked and respected as his father was feared and respected.

Another working journalist who became a media boss is Patrick Watson, chairman of the CBC, the nation's prime force in public broadcasting, which is a netherworld where the media and political establishments — rather than the media and business — intermingle. Public broadcasting is the only area of media where former bureaucrats are parachuted in as bosses by political fiat. Gérard Veilleux, a career federal civil servant who became CBC president in 1989, is the most notable example. Bernard Ostry, chief executive of TVOntario since 1985, is a peculiar hybrid, with both broadcasting experience and a distinguished bureaucratic career on his résumé.

In the private sector, other outsiders who made good in the central Canadian media elite have proven to be among the most innovative forces in broadcasting. André Chagnon and Moses Znaimer lead the pack.

The following are profiles of some of the most successful of the bootstrap brigade. Their presence in the owners' ranks shows that to a certain extent the media elite has been open to outsiders with talent and ambition.

Frank Griffiths: Chairman and founder of WIC (Western International Communications), Griffiths, western Canada's premier media mogul, keeps track of his $625-million television and radio empire from a seaborne office: his 87-foot mahogany motor launch, *La Feline*. Anchored at April Point, just up the coast from Vancouver, the boat has air-conditioning, a fax machine, a cellular phone and a satellite dish that picks up TV signals from across the continent.

Griffiths is a chartered accountant like his father before him. His Western Broadcasting owns the Vancouver Canucks hockey team and WIC, which operates seven TV stations and nine radio stations in major cities from Vancouver to Toronto. Its major TV outlets include flagship BCTV in Vancouver and CHEK in Victoria, both CTV affiliates, and CBC affiliate CHBC-TV in Kelowna.

The 1990 acquisition of Allarcom Ltd. gave WIC a lock on independent television broadcasting in Alberta. WIC already owned CFAC-TV in Calgary and CFAC-TV 7 in Lethbridge. The Allarcom buy added CITV in Edmonton and CKRD in Red Deer, as well as Superchannel, the western Canadian pay-TV network.

Shy and retiring, Griffiths doesn't fit the mould of the typical Lotusland entrepreneur. He's as low-key as Jimmy Pattison is brash and as conservative in business as Nelson Skalbania is aggressive. Griffiths spends his money quietly. He loves Mercedes-Benzes, a habit he picked up decades ago when he set up Vancouver's first Mercedes dealership with Poldy Bentley. Griffiths recently built a multimillion-dollar home in West Vancouver. Made largely of concrete to fend off the elements, it sits on a point surrounded on three sides by ocean. There's also a condo in Diamond Head in Hawaii, where Griffiths, his wife and two sons, both company employees, spend each Christmas. But from May until September every year, Griffiths spends his time on *La Feline* fishing and taking care of business. "I spend May and June off Alaska," he says. "Then in July and August, I go fishing in the Gulf of Georgia. In mid-September, I tie the boat up." Griffiths says his goal is to have "a strong, audience-responsible TV system in the west." In the process of achieving that goal, Griffiths has changed the balance of power in Canadian broadcasting. With revenues in the $350-million range, WIC is already bigger than other regional giants like Global Communications and Baton Broadcasting.

Doug Holtby: Griffiths's right-hand man, Holtby is president and CEO of WIC, a post he won in 1989 ahead of Griffiths's two sons. Griffiths hired Holtby away from Allarcom Ltd., the Edmonton film and television conglomerate where Holtby learned everything he then knew about the business from his mentor, Dr. Charles Allard, Allarcom's owner. It was that close relationship that smoothed the way for Allard's decision to sell out to WIC a year later.

A beefy, action-oriented man with the imposing presence of a linebacker, Holtby quickly asserted his control over the WIC stable of companies — albeit under the watchful eye of Griffiths, who rigorously goes over the quarterly financial reports. Holtby moved quickly to replace management at two problem radio stations, CJOB in Winnipeg and CFGM in Toronto, which has been transformed into an outrageous rock station that calls itself HOG Radio. WIC's well-known radio call letters include Q-107 in Toronto, CHML/CKDS-FM in Hamilton and CKNW in Vancouver.

Griffiths has given Holtby plenty of leash to set and achieve goals for WIC. One of his priorities is to rearrange the voting power on the board of the CTV network. WIC owns two CTV affiliates, in Vancouver and Victoria, which account for about 16 per cent of the network's annual revenues. At present each affiliate has a single vote no matter how much it contributes to network revenues. Holtby believes that the voting arrangement should be based on regional representation, not revenues, with each major region of the country having a vote. By contrast, Doug Bassett, president of Toronto's Baton Broadcasting, which chips in about 30 per cent of the network's revenues, has long argued that only one station should control the CTV board. Thanks to its recent expansion, WIC is now in a position to walk out of the CTV network if a fight erupts over the matter. But Holtby doesn't see that in the offing. "This company was one of the founders of CTV. It's part of our heritage. If we were asked to leave we wouldn't be happy." Besides, the relationship with Toronto is helpful when it comes to financing movie and TV projects. "It's helpful for us and western producers," says Holtby. "I can phone up [CTV president] John Cassady and say, 'I've got this new project. I'm sending it down for you to have a look at.'"

With or without CTV backing, though, Holtby is determined to be a major benefactor of a flourishing West Coast production industry. That has won him plenty of backers in the film community. "Holtby has a passion for this business, without a doubt," says Wayne Sterloff, chairman of the B.C. Film Fund, the provincial funding agency. "Everybody's optimistic about WIC." Holtby will have to back his passion for new film and made-for-TV projects with attention to the bottom line. Griffiths will make sure of that.

Izzy Asper: Barely more than 15 years ago, I.H. (Izzy) Asper, now chairman of CanWest Capital Group Inc., had just retired as leader of the Liberal Party of Manitoba and was almost broke. His salary as an MLA had been a meagre $14,000. Looking for a new career, the former lawyer and tax expert opted for the communications business. He teamed up with two partners, Paul Morton, like Asper the son of a Winnipeg theatre owner, and Seymor Epstein, a working-class boy from Montreal whose credentials included a stint as head of policy and planning at the CRTC, to set up a local station in Winnipeg. Next the trio formed a partnership with Allan Slaight to raise the money to acquire control of Global Television in Toronto, which at the time was a faltering operation.

Over the years since, Asper's relations with his partners have frayed and snapped, first with Slaight and then with Morton and Epstein. The partnership with Slaight lasted only three years. (Asper, chairman, drove Slaight to distraction by demanding detailed reports on every conceivable subject.) It wasn't until the mid-1980s that Asper's relations with Morton and Epstein began to sour in what was essentially an ego contest over who deserved the most credit for Global's success. After an acrimonious battle for control of Global that ended up in court, Asper emerged the owner.

Today, the chain-smoking, junk-food-loving boss of CanWest oversees a telecommunications empire that includes the Global television network in Toronto, his flagship CKND in Winnipeg, CKVU in Vancouver, CFSK in Saskatoon and CFRE in Regina. Asper has big plans to expand his company's presence to every other major market, either through new stations or by teaming up existing independents. But operating efficiencies are far from being his major motivation. It's all part of his pro-west philosophy. "I believe Manitoba and the west have traditionally been given the short end of the stick by Canadian political and economic forces," he once told *Marketing* magazine. Asper makes no secret of the fact that he's forging a network to compete with the CTV and CBC, one that mixes in a few more western news items and movies with the U.S. serials that pay the bills. Like his counterparts at WIC in Vancouver, Asper views central Canada as the hinterland to be exploited by western-based broadcasters, not vice versa. Asper's motto might as well be Go East, Old Man. As far as he's concerned, that's where the power and profits lie.

André Chagnon: The king of Quebec cable TV has come a long way since he worked as an electrician in Montreal's underground conduit system. Today, he's still running cables, but now they carry TV signals instead of high voltage. As president and chief executive of Montreal's Groupe Vidéotron Ltée, Chagnon runs Quebec's largest cable TV operation (assets: about $800 million), after Rogers Communications of Toronto (assets: about $2 billion). Yet Chagnon is not content to sit back and collect fees from his cable customers like most of his cable peers. He's risking his reputation and a good deal of his firm's money on the concept of interactive TV.

Born and raised in Montreal, Chagnon, whose father was also an electrician, attended l'Ecole Technique de Montréal and later the prestigious l'Ecole des Hautes Etudes Commerciales. At age 29, he cashed in a $7,000 insurance policy and began an electrical contracting firm. He bought his first cable system in Laval in 1964 and expanded outside Quebec in 1986, with his purchase of the Edmonton cable firm QCTV. In 1987, he diversified by buying control of Télé-Métropole, operator of CFTM-TV, a major Montreal outlet.

At 63, with three of his five children working at the company, Chagnon might be expected to slow down a bit, perhaps spend more time on his 15-metre sloop in Guadeloupe, or indulge his talent for gourmet cooking. Instead, Chagnon has launched Vidéotron on expensive gambles. Abroad, he's spending about $1 billion to break into the British cable TV market. At home, he's committed Vidéotron to a project that could transform the nature of TV viewing — if his finances hold out long enough. His Videoway Service is pioneering the concept of interactive TV, in which cable subscribers, armed with a converter and a remote control, can choose from 120 electronic services, including stock prices, grocery store bargains, movies and a dating service. But the unique feature of Videoway is a feature that permits viewers to choose camera angles while they're watching a sports game, or start the news show with, say, sports instead of the lead story. "The advantage we have is the diversity we can offer subscribers," says Chagnon. "It's a win-win situation." Investment analysts don't necessarily see it that way. They worry about the way Chagnon's latest ventures have pushed up the company's debt load. The way Chagnon sees it, though, the company has little choice but to forge into new areas. "The company operates in a mature cable industry," he says, using business jargon that means big companies have divvied up the market and there's little room left to grow. Chagnon adds that without his controversial investments, the company wouldn't have a future. In Chagnon's case, necessity is the mother of innovation.

Moses Znaimer: The headquarters of CITY-TV on Queen Street West in Toronto are located in a squat, massive terra-cotta edifice that used to be called the Wesley Buildings, named in honour of John Wesley, the pious founder of the Methodists. It's hard to imagine Old John being pleased with the menagerie of hip-hopping dancers, swaggering rap artists, cocky DJs and laid-back production crews the building now houses. John meet Moses, your successor as godfather of Toronto's prevailing mores.

This ultra-animated TV station, where anarchy is the rule, is the creation of Moses Znaimer, the man who one leading commentator, Gina Mallet of the Toronto *Star*, has called "the single most influential broadcaster in Canada." There are no studios in Znaimer's headquarters. Cameras can go live to air from virtually any point in the building, thanks to 32 power "hydrants." The youthful battery of on-air announcers, often leaning on their desks, sounds as unscripted and natural as guests at a house party who've suddenly had a microphone thrust at them — sometimes they're just as amateurish, too.

The formula Znaimer has used to redefine broadcasting since he cofounded CITY in 1972 with journalist Phyllis Switzer is to break all the formulas of the TV business. "The channel has a presence, a sensibility and a character that is greater than the sum of its shows" is how he describes his handiwork. "The purpose of my work is to create media character with which people identify." Znaimer has managed to tap in to a kind of fountain of youth, the wellspring of everything new, trendy, gritty and realistic in Toronto. And the way he's done it is to tear away every layer of insulation — the decorum, the production bureaucracy, the elaborate sets — that blunt the effect of mainstream stations. Znaimer has stripped the viewing process down to three simple elements: the scene, the camera and the viewer. On-air hosts are allowed to intervene in this process only if they remain natural and spontaneous conduits for the reality of the cityscape. As long as that is understood, Znaimer gives his hosts free rein; he prides himself in hiring raw talent and letting it loose.

The hardest thing to figure out about Znaimer is whether he's a poseur, with a fine sense of self-promotion, or as much of a genius as he presents himself to be. On air and in person, he comes across as a latter-day prophet decked out in the trendiest of attire. His sentences slide out slowly in earnest tones that suggest they should be written on a stone tablet somewhere. His clothing, usually black variations of the baggy Italian look, helps reinforce his image as a maverick who despises the mainstream. Those who know Znaimer well say the persona is soul-deep, not just an artifice to attract attention. "It's sometimes easy not to get past the style or flash to the substance in Moses," says Ivan Fecan, CBC's programming chief who once worked under Znaimer. "Moses is both a highly structured thinker and a highly lateral thinker," which, translated, means his thinking is rigorous and wide-ranging. His musical tastes run to Hebrew liturgical music from the Middle Ages, his reading runs to serious works like Machiavelli's *The Prince*.

Thinking has always been Znaimer's strong suit. His brightness lifted him out of lower-class life on Montreal's St. Urbain street, an immigrant corridor where his family settled with their young son after immigrating from Tajikistan, in the southern Soviet Union. While his father, Aron, sold shoes and his mother, Helen, worked as a bookkeeper and waitress, Znaimer won scholarships to attend McGill, then Harvard, where he earned an M.A. in government. After a stint as a CBC current affairs producer in his twenties, Znaimer quit and in 1972 set up his own station, where he could put his innovative broadcasting ideas into practice.

CITY-TV made a name fast with blue movies and a whole new approach to covering the news. The premise behind "CityPulse," its news program, was novel. While the traditional way of covering, say, a demonstration, was to set up a camera on a tripod and have a commentator analyse events, "CityPulse" took the cameras right into the crowd and let participants do the talking. In the years since, Znaimer hasn't stopped coming up with new ideas for television programs, most of which have double-barrelled names like MuchMusic, the successful pay-TV music station, its French-language counterpart, Musique Plus, the MusicVideo Awards, and VideoFact. No wonder pundits have taken to calling his endeavours ZnaimerVision.

Znaimer no longer owns CITY-TV. Faced by a climbing debt load, he sold it to Toronto broadcaster CHUM Ltd. in 1981. But he hasn't faded from the Toronto broadcasting — or social — scene in the least. Parties at his home, a stone residence atop a ravine overlooking Grenadier Pond in the High Park area, are a highlight of the social set. Built in 1901, the house is all Znaimer. The living room has a life-size portrait of his longtime companion, actress Marilyn Lightstone, and a giant TV screen on one wall. The house is filled with art nouveau furniture and contains nine TV sets, some from the early 1950s.

The amazing thing is that Znaimer has been doing his idiosyncratic thing at CITY for 19 years now — longer than most of the teenagers who writhe about on his successful dance show, "Electric Circus," have been alive. But that's the beauty of tapping in to the intangible, creative spirit of a city. That creativity is renewed with each new generation of youths who hang out on Yonge Street and slouch down Queen Street West. Revolutions, as chairman Mao observed, can be continual and self-renewing. Moses Znaimer, for one, has proved him right.

Conclusion

As we have seen, it's a dangerous oversimplification to think of Canada's media czars as a homogeneous group of pinstriped businessmen divvying up media markets in private. In two important ways, Canada's media bosses are as diverse as any other business group. They may be capitalists trying to make a profit, but their motives don't stop there. Several see themselves as fighting a power struggle with their counterparts in central Canada. As well, they have differing social origins: more of them rose from lower-class or middle-class origins than inherited their wealth and media domains. But anyone who aspires to join their ranks in the 1990s faces much tougher hurdles. In print, the market is pretty well sewn up by the media conglomerates and regional monopolies. In broadcasting, there are already too many stations and signals fighting for too few viewers and advertising dollars.

Whatever their regional loyalties and social origins, however, the media bosses have much in common. Most are now bona fide members of both the media and business ruling elites. For example, most owners are also directors of major banks and major corporations (John Fisher, Ken Thomson, Conrad Black, Doug Bassett, Martha Blackburn and Pierre Peladeau are examples). The notable exceptions are Moses Znaimer, who wouldn't be caught dead in a pinstripe suit, and Halifax's Graham Dennis, who proudly told me that he has "no entangling alliances."

Most of the group are also members in the most prestigious private business clubs. All but one are men (Martha Blackburn is the exception), and the most powerful are Protestant. (Blackburn, Fisher and Bassett are Anglican, Thomson is Baptist, K.C. Irving is Presbyterian.) The Catholics include Conrad Black, Pierre Peladeau, Philippe de Gaspé Beaubien and Roy Megarry. Several others don't identify with any religion. Only two, Asper and Znaimer, are of Jewish descent; almost all are of British or French descent.

Most of the media owners and their most important lieutenants make a point of staying aloof from the editorial content of the publications they own; their real power rests in choosing the people who run their stations and newsrooms. This is the group to which we now turn.

Chapter 10
Gatekeepers, Newshounds and Pundits

It may seem strange to anyone feeling completely deluged by the flow of information from the print and broadcast media, but there are actually people who exercise judgment about what gets covered as news and what doesn't. They are the gatekeepers of the news media, the men and women who pick which events and issues will be packaged into digestible bits and sent on to the public.

Unlike the columnists, reporters and TV news anchors, the gatekeepers are not household names; they don't turn heads in downtown restaurants, like Peter Mansbridge, for instance, and they don't generally get invited to society galas to add a dash of celebrity, like Allan Fotheringham or Richard Gwyn. In the print media, the most powerful gatekeepers are the editors and their immediate underlings who run the newsrooms. In broadcast media, the top gatekeepers are the information programming vice-presidents and news producers and editors. As a group, they tend to be news junkies hooked on caffeine and news scoops. They lead peculiar lives. The best of them work inhuman hours, surviving on the adrenaline that comes from trying to beat the competition in the timing or quality of coverage. Even in off-hours they can be seen listening intently to news broadcasts or reading newspapers to keep in touch with events. At major dailies like the *Globe and Mail,* senior editors are lucky to get out of the newsroom before 9 p.m. on a normal day, let alone when late news breaks. At *Maclean's* magazine, editors regularly work 50-hour weeks. The editor-in-chief, Kevin Doyle, takes Sundays off — for reading the Sunday New York *Times.* Stress is enormous because news breaks are unpredictable and occur around the world with callous disregard for news deadlines.

The Print Gatekeepers

If the left-wing critics are right, the people who run the nation's news outlets got their jobs because their ethnic backgrounds, as well as social, economic and political perspectives, are compatible with those of the owners. To assess this trickle-down theory of power, I sent a survey questionnaire to a powerful group of media figures: 43 publishers and editors at major dailies across the country. Replies came from 27 publishers and editors representing 21 newspapers. The survey solicited a range of information, including the respondent's sex, birthplace, education, career backround, ethnic background, class origins, religion and club affiliations. It also asked how many women and nonwhites run full departments or are in management positions at each newspaper. The findings indicate who gets ahead in the management of newspapers and who doesn't, and whether the lucky few are a homogeneous group.

More than two decades ago, in *The Vertical Mosaic*, John Porter conducted a similar survey of 35 publishers and editors. He was able to collect information on about half this group. Among his findings: like the ownership group that hired them, they were exclusively male and British in origin; the great majority were university graduates with middle-class backgrounds; and few belonged to private Establishment clubs. In summary, Porter wrote, "The image of Canada, inasmuch as the mass media contribute to that image, is created by the British charter group as represented by the upper-class owning group or the successful middle-class journalists."

While Canada's demography has changed greatly in the decades since Porter did his study, the makeup of the media elite, as represented by the publishers and editors of major dailies, hasn't. The composite picture that emerged from my survey can be summed up in one sentence: Most newspaper powerbrokers are well educated, white Protestant males of British stock, who are upwardly mobile members of the middle class.

The complete survey results can be found in the Appendices, but here are the highlights. Only three women — one publisher and two editors — qualified for the survey (all three responded). Women and nonwhites have very little power in newsrooms. The survey rendered this information for 18 major newspapers. Two newspapers scored the highest in the (confidential) survey, with a combined total of nine women and nonwhites. Fifteen papers reported from one to five women or nonwhites in positions of authority. One paper reported none at all. Most of these responses represented women, since nonwhites are virtually excluded from senior positions and are poorly represented in newsrooms to begin with. A 1985 study of 20 Canadian newspapers revealed that only 30 of 1,731 full-time newsroom employees were nonwhite.

Not only were the top employees at newspapers male, they were also predominantly of British stock (13 of 15 editors and 10 of 12 publishers). The remainder hailed from other European origins. Most were also Protestant (9 of 15 editors and 8 of 12 publishers). There were two Roman Catholic editors and two Roman Catholic publishers. Judaism and other minority religions were not represented. The respondents had high levels of education. Four of the editors and five publishers had attended exclusive private schools, and the vast majority in both groups went on to earn university degrees.

As for social origins, all of the editors (15) had fathers who held middle-class or lower-class jobs. Four publishers had fathers who were also publishers, but six hailed from the middle class and two from the lower class. Once in the media elite, however, a good many editors (4) and publishers (11) joined leading Establishment clubs including the Toronto, the Royal Canadian Yacht Club and the Badminton and Racquet.

The survey findings provide pretty conclusive evidence that the people who run newspapers have a lot in common with the people who hire them. But that only provides a broad-brush impression. Before we despair about the range of news coverage in Canada, we might remember that the quality of news coverage, and the diversity of outlooks and "voices" that it reflects, has a lot to do with the people who report the news and agitate to get events covered and stories written. There are a growing number of women reporters and a good many iconoclasts who take their roles as instruments of social responsibility seriously. (Unfortunately, there are few nonwhites.) The quality and diversity of news coverage has almost everything to do

with the editors' resolve to draw on the creative diversity of the newsroom, to draw a line between the commercial pressures and biases
emanating from above and the news instincts on the newsroom floor.
For a more accurate view of the backgrounds and power of editors,
and their role as gatekeepers to this profusion of ideas and outlooks,
I profile three editors whose decisions help set the nation's public
agenda.

Kevin Doyle, editor, *Maclean's* magazine: Canadians assume that
Maclean's is just there, spat out every week without fail from the
bowels of Maclean Hunter, its corporate parent in Toronto, but the
magazine's appearance 52 times a year is the result of a ferocious
act of will by journalists working in a state of chronic desperation
from one deadline to the next. Getting the magazine out each week
is an act of defiance against an array of obstacles: late-breaking news
that can rearrange the contents of the magazine — including the
cover story; unpredictable writers who don't write on time or on
topic; freelancers who send in unusable files that rehash newspaper
clips. Through it all, *Maclean*ers write till they drop just like marines
march till they drop. The man who has instilled this sense of mission
in successive waves of employees is Kevin Doyle, 48, editor-in-chief
since 1982.

There's more to Kevin Doyle than meets the eye. He looks like
an amiable Donegal storekeeper, with his round face and kind round
eyes with laugh lines at the corners. But the stereotype stops there.
No one would ever say Doyle has kissed the Blarney Stone. Never
glib or insincere, Doyle speaks slowly and thoughtfully, with great
care for accuracy and meaning.

Doyle is one of the most influential opinion makers in Canada.
Every week *Maclean's* massages the minds of Canadians, telling them
what's important in their lives and helping to shape the way they
think about it, whether it be the latest diet craze, the creation of
the new Europe or federal government policies. Every week 600,000
copies of *Maclean's* are read by roughly 2.5 million Canadians —
more than read *Time* or *Newsweek*. A single issue of *Maclean's*
reaches one in three Canadians who are senior managers; one in
four university graduates; and is read by readers with a broad range
of income, living fairly equally spread out in communities of all

sizes. It's not favoured reading among the intelligentsia, who tend to belittle its coverage as too little too late — they've already read all they want in the daily paper. Nevertheless, *Maclean's* shapes the opinions of those who like to sit, read and think about major events rather than watch them flick past as TV images that leave little impression.

Doyle, the man who in a sense runs the largest continuing education course for Canadians, has a personality that exudes a sense of order, calm and unflappability; useful attributes in a person who has to impose order on a constant and chaotic flow of news events. Doyle's favourite expression, usually directed at anxious staff, is "Get a grip!"

He's taken his own advice since he stepped in with a mandate to double the magazine's size and refine its coverage. "The magazine had been launched as a weekly, and very successfully, by Peter Newman," he recalls. "But the process of making it a weekly was so all-consuming that nobody ever had time to stand back from it and ask, 'Exactly what does a weekly newsmagazine do, and is there a consensus about where we should go over the next five years?' That's what I figured I had to do."

The priority was to expand news pages. "We had to basically double the number of pages, quickly — no matter what the cost. We just simply couldn't cover in any adequate way the news of the week." Adds Doyle: "I wanted it to be more, in a sense, predictable in the way it covered events, in the scope of its coverage and in the way it wrote about events." *Maclean's*, he suggests, offers coverage that Canadians can't get anywhere else. It should cover the main stories "from more angles, far more sources, far more locations than a newspaper ordinarily has time to do. In other words, if the prime source of a story is Ottawa, I want us to be able to call in the relevant information from Vancouver, from London, from Moscow, from Halifax." The aim, he continues, is "to be able to identify the repercussions of that event every place they exist, pull that information together and have a writer write it from Toronto in a style that's recognizable as *Maclean's*." That style at its best, he says, is "one-third reporting, one-third analysing and one-third throwing the story ahead."

Doyle has achieved his objectives in the past nine years. He's doubled the size of the magazine, boosted the staff from 50 to 150, opened bureaus in London, Washington and Moscow and pushed the publication into the black. Doyle is backed by managing editor Robert Lewis, a former Ottawa bureau chief for the magazine and an old *Time Canada* hand who has a shrewd mind, a quick wit and a love of the news business that just doesn't seem to quit, no matter how many cover stories he edits.

Then there are the executive editors: Carl Mollins, a kindly, experienced news hand in the truest sense of the phrase, who worked with Doyle at Canadian Press, and Alan Walker, a brilliant eccentric who has a taste for office intrigue and carefully spins an air of dark mystery around himself; for instance, he covers the glass partitions between his office and the hallway with black paper. Aside from being an unbeatable wordsmith with a voluminous memory for names of music and literary greats, Walker is known for his idiosyncrasies, such as the horse whip he used to walk around with to enforce deadlines. He also has a phobia for four-wheeled vehicles, especially cabs, and is rumoured to have not travelled outside the city centre for decades.

Doyle himself has been the target of venom during two legal strikes by *Maclean's* staff, but he is generally well-liked. He directs the news operation with a sure hand, learned in a wide-ranging career in journalism. Born in 1943 near Fitzroy Harbour, a small town in the Ottawa Valley, Doyle grew up on a dairy farm, the second son in a family of six. *Hardscrabble* and *poor* are the words he uses to describe life on the farm. "We'd get up at 5:30 in the morning, do the chores, milk the cows, catch a schoolbus at eight." After school, "you'd repeat the morning chores until 7:30 and then do homework."

A typical farm kid, he went to a one-room schoolhouse with a big stove in the centre. "The last two years I was there I lit the wood stove and swept the floor, and made soup for 15 bucks a year."

Later, at Arnprior District High School, he worked on the school yearbook, but that was the extent of his outside involvements. "I didn't have time to do much because of all the farm work." Like John Kenneth Galbraith, another Ontario farm boy, Doyle wasn't sorry to leave the farming life behind. "I'd certainly never want to be a farmer in the Ottawa Valley," he says with obvious understatement.

For a time, Doyle felt the church was his calling. He went to a Catholic seminary in Kitchener for a couple of years after high school, but didn't stay at it. "We had a tragedy in my family that was fairly profound and led me to a cosmic reassessment," he says. "My dad got killed in a car I was driving."

Doyle doesn't feel he wasted the time he spent studying under the Resurrectionist Fathers. "The lasting value of the seminary was that it did teach me a great love of logic and learning that I probably otherwise wouldn't have had." Doyle finished his B.A. at the University of Ottawa, then enrolled in a graduate course in journalism at the University of Western Ontario. He dropped out after a few months. "I realized that I could be learning whatever I was learning at Western and making a bit of money." A bit of money was right. Doyle landed his first news job at the Cornwall *Standard Freeholder* for $50 a week. He didn't last long. "It was a good little paper, but I couldn't live in rented quarters and eat on 50 bucks a week." He got more money and better work at the Windsor *Star*, where he worked until 1970, then went to earn an M.Sc. at the London School of Economics. The school had a strong intellectual influence on Doyle. "It certainly aroused my interest in Keynes and Keynesian economics. And if that's liberal or left-wing, yes, I guess it influenced me."

In 1971, Doyle signed on full-time with Canadian Press's London office, where he and three or four staffers were expected to cover the world's hot spots. In five years of frequent flying, Doyle covered the fighting in Vietnam, the Middle East war in 1973, Northern Ireland and Rhodesia.

Doyle moved to Washington for CP in 1975 and a year later was hired by Peter Newman to join the team he was building at *Maclean's*. "Newman phoned me and said he was coming to Washington. He was full of idealism, full of ambition for *Maclean's*, which I didn't know much about. He offered me the job of foreign editor." Doyle took it, and by 1978, when *Maclean's* went from a biweekly to a weekly, he had risen to managing editor.

But Doyle still had two more lessons in store about the way the news business works. One was unpleasant. In 1979, he went to Ottawa to set up a news service for what was then the FP chain of newspapers. As editor of the FP News Service, Doyle had hired a team of topnotch reporters when the operation fell victim to the harsh realities of corporate deal-making. The Thomson media conglomerate bought the chain and shut down the news service.

By contrast, Doyle's next experience, as a general editor at *Newsweek* in New York for a year and a half, provided better memories. "It was a formative experience. It was probably the single most professional group of people. They cared so much about the magazine. Maybe they cared too much. They worked unbelievably long, hard hours. They suffered over every page, over every paragraph. They had a style that was recognizable, but they never stopped trying to perfect it." Doyle agrees that he tried to bring those ideals to *Maclean's* when he became editor. "No question. I don't think I tried to copy *Newsweek*, but it certainly gave me some ideals."

The major criticism of Doyle's magazine is that it is *over*-edited. The common view among the Toronto media community, primarily contributing writers, is that *Maclean's* writing is too predictable, too formulaic and contains too many overused phrases. This is enough to frustrate freelance writers who strive to say things in original ways. But it's not at all clear that readers mind the magazine's stylistic predictability. Readership has held its own over the last decade or so. There has been no mass cancellation of subscriptions to protest one too many sentences beginning with "Still" or "At the same time."

Doyle is aware of the cynicism about the *Maclean's* writing style. "It's a legitimate criticism," he says. He also agrees that the editing has been exaggerated. But his eyes are on a higher goal: "The one thing I've been proudest of while I've been here is that the magazine, to my knowledge, has never been biased. And it's to prevent that that it's been so heavily edited."

Like many writers, Doyle has a streak of shyness. He would sooner go to the dentist than give a speech to a local chamber of commerce. Yet he doesn't shrink from wielding the power that goes with the editor's title. In his book, the editor, not the publisher, calls the shot at the magazine. "The tradition at *Maclean's*," he says, "is that the publisher hires an editor and tells him he wants his magazine to be professional, mindful of the profit motive, and he leaves the editor alone to do that. If an editor can't — let's not even talk about it.

"I think the publisher and the editor are on friendly terms and talk about business and journalism all the time. But the publisher would never say 'I want you to do a story' any more than the editor would say 'I think we should be selling more ads to a car company.'"

Reminded of an incident in 1978 when the publisher at the time, Lloyd Hodgkinson, killed a cover of the magazine (a cartoon caricature of then prime minister Pierre Trudeau cowering in a corner like a rat), Doyle says, "The publisher has a right to approve the cover because it's the stamp, the face that the magazine presents to the public. I say that very carefully, that he has the right to approve. Should he disapprove fundamentally, then an editor would have to choose whether he accepted that judgment over his own."

John Fraser, editor, *Saturday Night* magazine: Fraser, 46-year-old journalist and author, appreciates a good tale as much as an oenophile loves a good wine. This one happens to be about the relationship between himself and his controversial boss, businessman Conrad Black. "This is perhaps an inappropriate tale to tell you, but I don't mind. I'll tell it to you anyway," says Fraser with his trademark impish smile. We are in his baronial-style office in downtown Toronto, and he is recalling a conversation with Black about the magazine's May 1989 cover story entitled "Canada's Gay MP," on politician Svend Robinson, who was then rumoured to be an NDP leadership hopeful. Not an obtuse man, Fraser realized that the story and the cover line were not run-of-the-mill *Saturday Night* fare. "I informed Conrad about two weeks before the magazine was going to be in hand — but some time after any changes could be made to it — that we were going to have a piece on Svend Robinson." Black's reaction, he says, was, "What, that faggot?" Replied Fraser, "Yeah, you know, the NDP guy." Both men agreed that they liked the writer of the story, John Lownsbrough, but Black's concern was: "How are you going to bury it?"

Fraser then broke the news. "Well, actually, I'm putting it on the cover." Black, in a choked voice, could muster only a "Wow."

The mood eased when Fraser injected a little humour. "Conrad, you know you're going to sleep easier knowing you did your bit to help Svend Robinson get the leadership of the NDP." Said Black: "I can use that line."

The story illustrates the intimate yet independent relationship between Fraser and Black, the man whom many assumed would turn *Saturday Night* into a right-wing rag after he bought it in June 1987 and hired Fraser as editor. Fraser has held his own as the one who runs the magazine's editorial direction, despite having the most loquacious and opinionated man in Canada for a boss. "Our chemistry is just fine. That's one of the biggest assets I bring to the magazine," says Fraser. "He loves discussing current affairs. He's got, as you know, very strong and decided opinions, and he likes people. He likes debate, so I throw it back at him. I think the worst thing to do is to feel daunted by it."

Fraser's ability to maintain *Saturday Night*'s reputation as an editor's magazine (a tradition of legendary predecessors Hector Charlesworth, B.K. Sandwell, Arnold Edinborough and Robert Fulford) is a result of two things: first, his iron-clad, five-year contract, which lays out a division of powers between the editor and owner; and second, Fraser's idiosyncratic personality, which makes him as difficult to step on, pin down or otherwise control as a darting beetle. "If someone thinks that they've got me nicely under control, then I feel a compulsion to show how out of control I am," he says.

The contract was a condition of Fraser's taking the job. Fraser was in England working as the *Globe and Mail*'s London correspondent when Black phoned him to say he had bought the money-losing publication from Norman Webster. "I said, 'I hope you look after Robert Fulford [editor since 1968],' and added, 'When he's finished, whenever he's finished, don't forget me. I'd love to be editor of *Saturday Night*.'" As it turned out, Black called the next day with the news that Fulford had resigned in dismay (he had decided, after a face-to-face meeting, that he couldn't work with Black). Black offered the job to Fraser. For Fraser, landing the editor's job at *Saturday Night* fulfilled one of the few identifiable ambitions he's had in an otherwise haphazard career. But it took Fraser four weeks to accept, partly because he was working on a book about the dancer Baryshnikov, and partly because of the controversy that had sprung up in Canada over Black's purchase. The contract seemed to be a natural solution in the midst of the anti-Black paranoia. "I think it's a unique contract," says Fraser. "I hope it is a model for the future. It has language of editorial independence in it and I wear it like a robe."

(Fraser's contract stipulates that the editor "is solely responsible for the direction and integrity of the total editorial product, process and staff." The proprietor is allowed to criticize, chastise, admonish, suggest or advise, among other things, but he cannot dictate what goes into the magazine. The 1981 Kent Commission on newspapers recommended that a system of contracts be instituted for editors of newspapers owned by conglomerates. With the exception of Fraser's contract, the idea has been virtually ignored. Most editors' contracts concern share bonus plans, company cars and the like, not independence.)

Fraser is a product of the Establishment, if an unusual one. He's upper-middle-class in origin and did a stint at Upper Canada College, yet he did not proceed directly from the playing field to a bank boardroom or a law partnership as Old Boys are supposed to do. Fraser went directly to a clerk's job at Woolworth's and later followed a highly erratic course through the waystations of journalism before landing at the top of the media elite, where he's matched his Old Boy chums in prestige, if not in wealth.

Fraser was born in Montreal in 1944, and grew up in Toronto, where his father, a chartered accountant, and mother, a writer, moved when he was very young. For a time, he enjoyed a stable, privileged life. The family had a large home on Russell Hill Road just below Forest Hill village. As Fraser tells it, his life was fine until he was 15, when his "family life sort of collapsed." Emotional turmoil at home culminated in his parents' divorce and carried over into John's life, which veered off the route to respectability as laid down by UCC. "I failed at Upper Canada in Grade 11, got a 7 in physics," he says with amusement. "It was the year Conrad Black was kicked out for stealing all the exams."

"I went to Oakwood Collegiate to make up Grade 11, and that big house was sold. My father's business affairs went into decline and I went through a bizarre period where I went to all sorts of schools." It was a lot of upheaval for any adolescent to handle.

The unhappy saga continued for several years. "I convinced my grandmother to send me to Lakefield boarding school for a year," he says, peering from behind dark-rimmed glasses. "Then I came back and went to Jarvis Collegiate, where I failed Grade 13 — I failed twice." It got worse. Fraser went to work as a clerk at Woolworth's head office on Bay Street in Toronto. "I remember my job was taking the mail sacks down to be picked up at 4:30. Once I ran into two Old Boys from UCC and it was the nadir of my sense of social esteem. Then I got angry with myself and I cleared out of Toronto. I went to Newfoundland." (Interestingly, Fraser has not become an opponent of private school education. He describes his view of UCC as being "completely pragmatic." UCC, he says, gave him "the best things private schools have to offer, which is confidence. It gives you contacts and it gives you confidence, and I don't say that state schools can't do that either, but there is such a natural unconscious aura that you're at the top of the heap.")

Fraser's characteristics, including an acerbic, Voltaire-like wit and tendency to talk faster than Woody Allen, finally asserted themselves. He did a B.A. at Memorial University and went on to study at Exeter College at Oxford, where he received a diploma in 1970. The next year he attended the University of East Anglia, where he earned a Master of Arts degree. "I did a Masters degree in literature, focused on drama. I thought I wanted to be an academic and that cured me of it," he says. Fraser returned to Toronto and got a job at the *Telegram*, where he had previously spent a summer working as a copy boy. "I knew Mr. Bassett. I had a foot in the door," he says. "I used to cut classes at UCC, and the only place to hide out was the Badminton and Racquet Club, where I played squash by myself. Bassett thought that was a sign of independence and that seemed to get me my job."

In little more than a year, Fraser rose from the police beat to be music and dance critic at the *Telegram*, just in time for its folding in 1972. "I knew nothing about dance," he recalls, "but fortunately the paper lasted only six months." During that brief interval, Fraser "fell in love with dance," and, after six months out of work, he was hired as a dance critic and feature writer at the *Globe and Mail* by then editor and later senator Dic Doyle. "Doyle is my journalistic father figure," comments Fraser. Over the next two decades, Fraser had a diverse career at the *Globe*. He served, successively, as drama critic, Peking correspondent, national columnist, national editor and London correspondent. In the same period he wrote four books: *Kain and Augustyn*, on the legendary National Ballet lead dancers; *The*

Chinese: Portrait of a People in 1980, which became an international best-seller; *Telling Tales*, a grab bag of portraits of leading Canadians; and *Private View: Inside Baryshnikov's American Ballet Theatre.*

Despite his well-earned reputation in journalism, Fraser arrived at *Saturday Night* as a novice to the magazine business. "I was nervous because of my own inexperience at being a magazine editor, but I was also very cocky," he says. Staff members say his management style reflects the last-minute world of daily journalism rather than the more orderly, long-term approach of magazines. Fraser is the first to admit that his management style is chaotic. "I'm accused of trying to turn this place into a daily newspaper. There are a lot of freaky moments because I leave things until late in the production schedule."

Fraser is equally sure of his strengths. "I knew that one of my assets was enthusiasm and getting the best out of people. I like doing that and I love getting people to work together." Within a year, Fraser had made his mark on the magazine, although he carefully tried to preserve its best qualities. "I came to the magazine very much respecting what it stood for and what Fulford had done." On the other hand, he says, "I had very strong views that it had become boring. I thought it was out of sync with the times." He brought back former staples of the magazine such as poetry, fiction, letters to the editor and a crossword puzzle. He added regular politics and travel coverage. He also gets credit for maintaining the quality of the writing while adding more edge and controversy to the magazine — which very much reflects his own mischievous personality. "We're very much committed to the in-depth investigative journalism that has largely been abandoned in most places. We're on a kind of tightrope, if you like, between being a serious magazine like *Atlantic Monthly* and a much lighter general interest magazine like *Vanity Fair.*"

The dread that the magazine would be turned into a conservative mouthpiece for Black has turned out to be overblown. But Fraser readily admits that his philosophical compatibility with Black was obviously a factor in his being hired. "A publisher or an owner/ publisher or a proprietor has every right — because he owns it under our system — to have his publication reflect his general views. But he does so not through the daily scrutiny of the editorial content, but by the choice of people that he puts in there." (Though they frequently chat on the phone, Fraser doesn't report directly to Black, who spends up to seven months a year in England overseeing his British newspaper interests. Black's point man at *Saturday Night*'s weekly management meetings is John (Jack) Boultbee, president of the magazine and a senior vice-president of Black's Hollinger Inc. And according to Fraser, the magazine's high-profile publisher, former ambassador to Washington Allan Gotlieb, is "a wonderful asset but a part-time publisher.")

"I don't share all of Conrad Black's views. I'm right of centre on economic issues and regarding the general role of government in our lives. On the other hand I'm sort of left of centre on most social issues, and many of my views are really supra-ideological. Nevertheless, I must in some way reflect something of Black because I'll hear from him in those areas that I don't — my views on Quebec, for instance."

Fraser's goal has been to keep the viewpoints expressed in the magazine as wide-ranging as possible. His commitment to opening up the magazine to more "authentic individual voices," as he puts it, whether from the right or the left, and to strong commentary in columns and articles keeps the magazine polemical, controversial and, most important of all — read.

So far, Fraser's *Saturday Night* has one important similarity with the old *Saturday Night*. "It does not make money and it hasn't made money in nearly half a century, really since the war," comments Fraser. "But it's on a solid foundation because it's a small, well-kept welfare case in the Hollinger empire."

The key to profits is attracting more readers, which would allow the magazine to wave more impressive circulation figures at advertisers. With a circulation of only about 115,000, albeit affluent, well-educated readers, *Saturday Night* has had a tough time competing for ads against publications like *Maclean's*.

In pursuit of more readers and profits, Fraser launched the magazine on its most ambitious venture ever in the fall of 1991. Under a deal with Southam Inc., the freshly redesigned magazine was included free with five Southam newspapers across the country. As well, the magazine will be included free in selected markets by the *Globe and Mail*. If advertisers' dollars follow, that should keep the chemistry between Fraser and his proprietor just fine, as befits a couple of Old Boys.

William Thorsell, editor, the *Globe and Mail*: Machiavelli couldn't have envisioned a better scenario of high intrigue. Picture the members of a palace court (the *Globe*) gathering to pay their respects to a departing nobleman (outgoing editor Norman Webster) at a party attended by leading members of the realm (former ambassador Stephen Lewis, lawyer Clayton Ruby, publisher Peter Herrndorf). Only the monarch (*Globe* publisher Roy Megarry) is not there. Held on a cold winter evening in January, the affair proceeds with decorum and civility. The host of the event (*Globe* journalist Patrick Martin) maintains the pleasant atmosphere with a heartfelt speech of appreciation, noting the guest of honour's achievements, presenting him with a cartoon portrait of himself and announcing that his supporters will create a university scholarship in his name.

Then Webster rises. In an emotional speech, he reveals that, contrary to first appearances, he was fired from his job and fears for the wellbeing of others in the room who, he says, are about to suffer the same fate at the hands of the monarch.

Reactions range from tears to acute unease because, watching from a corner of the room, is Webster's successor, William Thorsell, the man chosen by Megarry to carry out these deeds. Thorsell remains the model of composure, even when the gathering is shocked later when Geoffrey Stevens (the *Globe*'s managing editor) reveals that Thorsell has already fired him.

Bloody successions are the stuff of legend in literature and history. Whether the central characters belong to a British royal court, a Chinese dynasty, a Latin American country or a modern newspaper, the elements are the same: cabals, intrigues, back-stabbing, divided loyalties, seething unrest among the masses, decapitations and ultimately a New Order.

This is the context in which the changing of the regime at the *Globe and Mail* in 1989 belongs. It was a tumultuous beginning for the new editor, Thorsell. In the months after his appointment,

there was an outpouring of outrage from some quarters in the journalism community, expressed in numerous articles and columns, over
the way the changes had taken place.

From the start, Thorsell found himself in a difficult situation. The
anxious newsroom lurched between confusion and despondency over
exactly where the newspaper was headed. Very quickly, the overriding
challenge for Thorsell became to prove, primarily to the newsroom,
that he was his own man, not Megarry's puppet.

In person, Thorsell, 45, is impressive. He is a refined man, both
in manner and in intellect. Never the least bit unkempt, he favours
well-tailored suits, sports neatly trimmed blond hair with just a suggestion of curls on top. He speaks in clear, precise sentences with
an engaging, mellifluous cadence that immediately reveals him to
be a man with a potent combination: a powerful intellect and emotional stability. Despite the often horrendous pressure of the daily
news business, Thorsell has never been known to lose his composure
at work.

Reflecting on the tumult that marked the changing of the guard
at the *Globe*, Thorsell is as composed as ever. He doesn't take the
hostility personally; it was a matter of a large number of journalists
becoming alarmed that he would lead the paper to the far right of
the ideological spectrum. "I don't blame anybody for raising the ideological issue at the time," he says. "We were coming out of one
of the most emotional election campaigns since the Second World
War." The debate, he says, was reduced to the single issue of free
trade with the United States, which stood for a whole panoply of
other issues. "I happened to be the person on the editorial board who
wrote all the editorials strongly supporting free trade and therefore
became associated with a certain issue in a very emotional context.

"A few weeks after the free trade issue was settled, I was appointed
editor in the context of Norman Webster's dismissal. Everyone
thought, 'Wow, there's this great ideological lunge.' The wounds were
still fresh from the free trade debate."

For Thorsell, the assumption of many critics that he would turn
the *Globe* into a mouthpiece for the right is intellectually insulting.
"No editor worth his salt is going to impose an ideology, political
or economic, on his columnists and the paper. I think you've seen

some other papers do this as a matter of pride. But readers are too intelligent for that. As an individual, as a journalist, I would take no pride in it."

Critics have expressed the fear that the *Globe* is becoming either a mouthpiece for Big Business or a news wrap-up for budding William F. Buckley types. They fear that the new regime in the editorial offices is a homogeneous group of right-wingers with business journalism backgrounds who will impose their views on news coverage, ultimately making it less worthwhile for readers.

But Thorsell's opinion of what makes a good newsroom doesn't fit either scenario. "To a large degree," he says, "I think a newsroom is a neighbourhood. A good newsroom is very collegial by nature; a bad newsroom is very hierarchical." He elaborates. "A good newsroom thrives for a couple of reasons. One is the initiative of its reporters, who are close to the scene in their areas of expertise. It grants a lot of power to them, it depends on the wisdom and experience of its reporters, so there is an implicit element of decentralization in a good newsroom."

The other reason a newsroom thrives, according to Thorsell, is when the editors are "clear in their own minds about what the readers should be getting from their reporters, from their sections. This requires a lot of communication between editors and writers and perhaps more leadership than there has been."

These principles, of course, leave enormous room for interpretation in practice. The push for more direction from editors could easily translate into the heavy-handed control of news coverage that some staffers at the paper fear. The departure from the *Globe* of well-known writers with left-of-centre views, such as Thomas Walkom, Judy Steed and Linda McQuaig (all of their own volition), as well as the resignation of June Callwood, a noted humanitarian activist, led to worries that the paper was losing a healthy diversity of voices. Soon after the departures, Jock Ferguson, a veteran staff reporter, noted: "One of the great strengths of the *Globe and Mail*, historically, was that there was a lot of room for different opinions and voices at the newspaper. That is shrinking rapidly." Since then, however, the outflow of reporters and writers with reputations for shaking up the powers that be has ceased.

The acknowledged voice of a newspaper is the editorial page. Under Thorsell, editorials have usually supported the policies of the federal Conservative government, but the editorial stance has not become relentlessly right-wing, as many journalists feared. The editorial denouncing the American invasion of Panama in December 1989, an invasion supported by the Conservative government in Ottawa, was a notable example. Nor has the editorial board suddenly stopped speaking out on behalf of the needy, as was made clear by its editorials on the plight of children in poverty.

Early in Thorsell's tenure, the most fascinating question was whether he had the wherewithal and the will to reassert the power of the editor's post not just in the eyes of the newsroom but in the eyes of Megarry.

Thorsell's own career refutes the idea that he is a yes man of modest abilities and limited ego. His life story isn't quite a generic log-cabin-to-White-House tale, it's more accurately the tale of one man's rise from unheated garage to editor's office. He was born in Camrose, Alberta, in 1945, the son of a Swedish father and a Norwegian mother. Thorsell spent the first year of his life living with his family in a garage with no running water. His father, who had spent the war years repairing planes on a base south of Calgary, was trying to start a new life. By 1947, he had landed a job in a lumber store in Edmonton and was busy building his own house on land granted to him under a veterans' program. Thorsell grew up on the outskirts of Edmonton, just about two blocks from the countryside.

His ability to express himself eloquently showed up early. He became president of the student council at his junior high school and then at his secondary school, Strathcona High. Clearly a BMOC (Big Man on Campus) in the making, Thorsell earned a B.A. in history by 1966 at the University of Alberta, where he also found time to co-edit the yearbook.

During the summers, Thorsell further developed his elocution skills by working as a travelling tourism promoter for the Government of Alberta. For two summers, his job was to travel with a team on the North American fair circuit espousing the attributes of Alberta. That was only a warm-up for something better. In late 1966, at age 21, he applied for and got the job of manager for the Western Canada Pavilion at Expo 67 in Montreal. "The job at Expo was really exciting," he recalls. "There was no commissioner on site from western Canada. I became the sort of ambassador for western Canada." Thorsell spent much of his time attending formal events for heads of delegations of the countries at the fair. "Here I was, this 21-year-old kid attending these functions. It was really kind of symbolic of the west."

After Expo, Thorsell returned west to do an M.A. in twentieth-century intellectual history at the University of Alberta. His thesis was on the development of pacifism during the First World War.

Thorsell's fascination with intellectual history partly explains why, in 1968, he set off with a friend for a two-month car trip through the Soviet Union. "This was the '60s, the counterculture movement was coming into full force, and we were all pretty sceptical about our own system," he recalls. "The people were wonderful, the landscapes were incredible. Every day was fascinating. But you could see how terribly stultifying the system was in almost every way." The trip left a lasting impression. "It turned me into a capitalist," he says.

For a time, it appeared that Thorsell was destined to become an academic. He lectured in history at the University of Alberta from 1968 to 1969, then went to the Woodrow Wilson School of Public and International Affairs at Princeton (after taking another summer off to serve as head of protocol for the Canadian delegation at Expo 70 in Osaka, Japan). Thorsell specialized in U.S. domestic affairs. "I had a lot of catching up to do in economics, statistics and analysis of public policy," he says. He graduated in 1972 with an MPA. For the next two years, Thorsell worked as the executive officer of the University of Alberta's senate, then joined the staff of the Woodrow Wilson School to assist the dean in reorganizing the curriculum.

The switch to journalism came in 1975, when Thorsell reassessed his career plans and took a job as an editorial writer at the Edmonton *Journal* at the invitation of publisher Ross Munro. Within a year, though, he was back in Toronto, applying for a job at the *Globe and Mail*. "I came down to Toronto in the summer of '76, and Dic Doyle hired me on the spot."

Thorsell was not entirely happy in his new job. "I was used to much more freedom in Edmonton. Here you went into the boardroom and you were basically assigned your topic and almost your point of view." He returned to the Edmonton *Journal* the next year to become associate editor in charge of the editorial and op-ed pages. He stayed for seven years before landing at the *Globe* again, in 1984, as an editorial writer. "I wanted to get back to a more demanding environment," he explains. "I returned to the *Globe* at a substantial cost to myself — a 15 per cent drop in salary — but I thought that was a very good investment in being in the right place as a journalist." It was — considering Thorsell was appointed editor-in-chief less than five years later.

On his appointment, Thorsell immediately became a major focus of interest among the Toronto cultural elite. His coming-out party, so to speak, was held in February 1989 at the home of Barbara Frum, host of CBC's "The Journal" and the reigning doyenne of power networkers in Toronto. The guests who turned up to give Thorsell the once-over were drawn from a cross-section of central Canada's ruling power groups. There were businessmen (Conrad Black, Robert Campeau and Hal Jackman), current and former politicians and diplomats (Marcel Masse, Allan Gotlieb, Gerry Caplan and David Crombie), book publishers and authors (Anna Porter, Sondra Gotlieb, Peter Herrndorf, Margaret Atwood, Graeme Gibson and Robert Fulford) and TV personalities (Wendy Mesley and her husband, Peter Mansbridge). For Thorsell the evening was a success. Making a good impression on the newsroom was proving a much more difficult task.

By any measure, Thorsell's first attempt at winning the loyalty of the newsroom was an impressive display of serene confidence in the face of enormous pressure. On January 30, 1989, he called a general meeting of staff of the newsroom floor. The newsroom by that point had almost reached the point of anxiety paralysis as rumours, and rumours of rumours, about changes to come had multiplied rapidly.

Thorsell spoke in an intimate and engaging manner, surrounded by a mass of about 100 reporters and editors whose moods ranged from acute worry to outright hostility. His words were well chosen to soothe frayed nerves and play upon the grievances that had built up under the old regime.

Media coverage to that point had painted the putsch in black and white: before the deluge, everyone in the newsroom was happy; after it, everyone was up in arms. In fact the newsroom had been seething with discontent under the leadership of Webster and Stevens. The cafeteria grumblers were continuously criticizing Stevens for being aloof and playing favourites, and Webster, a pleasant man with a thoughtful though distant manner, for being too removed from the newsroom. The saving grace of both men, for even the most vitriolic critics, was that they were fine journalists, who could be counted on to preserve the editorial integrity of the newspaper no matter what pressures might come from the enemy (read the advertising side of the paper).

In his newsroom talk, Thorsell first tried to allay the fear that he was Megarry's yes-man. He reviewed the paper's major strengths but said one of its weaknesses was "the emotional gap between the senior editorial staff and the newsroom." This point hit a responsive chord among those who felt the previous managers had lost touch with the staff.

As for the rumours, he said no, he didn't have a list of people to fire; and no, Megarry didn't give him a to-do list. The publisher gave him only one goal, he said: to carry out a two-year attrition process in the newsroom so that staff numbers would shrink.

Thorsell's personal goals, he said, were to improve relations between the editors and management; to have fair and open competition for bureaus on the basis of talent, not personal favouritism; to redesign the paper; and to improve working conditions in the newsroom.

Probably the most important thing Thorsell had to say concerned the balance of power between the publisher and the editorial managers. He compared the newsroom to Canada's North. "You have to populate it to claim sovereignty," he said. "Similarly, in the newsroom you have to provide strong editorial policy to prevent the need for intervention by the publisher."

In an interview several months later, Thorsell elaborated on his relationship with Megarry. What he said revealed that, if the *Globe* universe was so far unfolding according to the publisher's vision, it was primarily because Thorsell agreed with Megarry on the priorities for the paper. Megarry and Thorsell meet at least once a week for long chats over tea, usually in Thorsell's office. "We have a very engaging relationship," says Thorsell. "We talk on and on, especially about the future of newspapers, about this newspaper, where the information-gathering and dissemination is going." In any organization, he said, "there has to be an element of chemistry within management to make it work." He added: "Chemistry is a short-hand word for some kind of sharing of assumptions, values and outlooks. That chemistry has to be there and, so far, we certainly have that chemistry. I think it's good for the newsroom, it's good for reporters, and it's good for the readers in the long run."

Thorsell has a high regard for the initiatives Megarry has taken in the last 10 years as publisher. "Roy Megarry has been a friend of the newsroom," he says. "Look at the initiatives and innovations he has taken for the *Globe and Mail*."

If the *Globe* had not gone national in 1982, says Thorsell, "I doubt very much that it would look the same today. It would probably be more like a business newspaper." The reason, he explains, is that circulation in the Toronto area would not have been large enough to pay for the whole newspaper and it would have had to concentrate on the more lucrative business coverage, which has always generated most of the paper's advertising revenues. "So the *Globe*'s extension as a nationally distributed newspaper is much more than a pretension on the part of the paper — it's a lifeline for the paper. It supports the broad reach of the editorial in terms of foreign coverage, our sports and all the rest."

Thorsell also believes that the paper must concentrate on reaching a well-defined readership to prosper. "I use three words to describe the personality of readers," he says. "Independent, intelligent and informed." *Globe* readers, he says, are people across Canada with "high needs for information at a fairly complex level. Not all of them need to be wealthy, not all of them need to be professional/managerial. There are many of our readers who are middle class, for example teachers, who are, however, very demanding readers."

Specifically, a 1988 survey of *Globe* readers carried out by the paper revealed that 53 per cent are university graduates, 85 per cent are employed, 24 per cent are either senior managers or professionals, and 23 per cent earn more than $50,000 a year. "The demographics of our readership are fairly well known to us and to our advertisers," says Thorsell. In his view, the papers that are having the most difficulty are the large, middle-class newspapers like the Toronto *Star*, "because their readership is quite heterogeneous and therefore they have difficulty defining their own identity, defining their target readership and projecting an identity to the readership."

The big success story of readership growth in Toronto, he says, is the Toronto *Sun*. "It targets its audience, which is relatively homogeneous and tends to be blue-collar and fairly young. We are, ironically enough, in the same situation as the *Sun*. We have a fairly clear idea of who our readers are."

This does not mean, in Thorsell's view, that the paper should become, as critics allege it has, the mouthpiece of the powerful. It also "has a role to describe the Establishment's failures."

Thorsell's words show that he understands the fine line an editor must walk between striking up a partnership with the publisher on one hand and appealing to the news instincts of the newsroom on the other. He's succeeded with the first part, and he's working hard on the second part.

Doyle, Fraser and Thorsell are among the most powerful editors of Canada's mainstream print media, particularly because their mass-circulation publications serve a national audience. But they are by no means the only extremely influential print gatekeepers. Most of the others run highly respected city dailies that serve regional audiences.

Norman Webster, editor, Montreal *Gazette*: Erudite, well-heeled and low-key, Webster has run the *Gazette* since he lost his job at the *Globe and Mail* in 1989 after a career there that began in 1965. Born in Summerside, PEI, he's a grandson of the late senator Lorne Webster, the Scots founder of one of Canada's largest business fortunes. Norman Webster is independently wealthy but made journalism his career after an education at Bishop's University (B.A.) and Oxford (M.A.), where he was a Rhodes scholar. Unlike so many news bosses, Webster doesn't bully or browbeat to get his way. He rules on cool-headed logic. Known for his fierce belief in editorial independence, he is a role model for a generation of younger journalists.

John Honderich, editor, Toronto *Star:* Honderich is the heir to one of the most successful newspaper franchises in Canada and the largest-circulation daily. The son of Beland Honderich, long-time publisher of the *Star* and now chairman of the paper's parent, Torstar Corp., Honderich began his career determined to "stay as far away from journalism as possible." But after a law degree at the University of Toronto, he gave in to a hankering for journalism and in 1973 started as night copy boy at the Ottawa *Citizen* for $83 a week. He joined the *Star* in 1976 as a reporter and rose to his current post after serving as business editor and editorial page editor. Under John, the Star is still a miasma of rivalries. But unlike his father, John doesn't rule with an iron hand, and is striving to soothe the war-like, paranoid mood that pervaded the *Star* newsroom for years. He's pushing for more investigative stories from his staff, as long as they relate to the paper's longtime motto, What Does It Mean for Metro?

Lise Bissonnette, "hands-on" publisher, *Le Devoir:* Situated in an ancient stone building on Saint-Sacrement street in Old Montreal, *Le Devoir* has been one of the most respected and influential papers in Quebec since it was founded by Henri Bourassa in 1911. Bissonnette became publisher in June 1990, when her predecessor, Benoit Lauzière, left after a newsroom mutiny. The strongly nationalist news staff were irked with Lauzière because he was a Trudeau-style Liberal whose passionate beliefs in the rights of the individual led him, for instance, to write an editorial in December 1988 opposing Quebec's French-only sign laws. Under Bissonnette, the paper has resumed its tradition as a fervent nationalist, although not sovereigntist, voice. Bissonnette was raised in Rouyn-Noranda, Quebec, the daughter of a secondhand goods store owner. With an M.A. from the Université de Montréal and a Ph.D. from a French university, Bissonnette worked as a planner at the Université de Québec before beginning a distinguished career as a journalist in the mid-1970s. She now runs what is considered the most independent paper in Canada. To keep it free of commercial pressures from advertisers and owners, it is run by an independent, self-perpetuating board of directors. That leaves Bissonnette plenty of editorial freedom; her major constraint is the paper's roughly $1.5 million debt, which she's trying to reduce through fund-raising campaigns.

Other Noteworthy Print Gatekeepers (in approximate order of influence):

Diane Francis, editor, *Financial Post*; Roger Landry, editor, *La Presse* (Montreal); Murray Burt, editor, Winnipeg *Free Press*; Gillian Stewart, editor, Calgary *Herald*; Linda Hughes, editor, Edmonton *Journal*; Ian Haysom, editor, Vancouver *Sun*; Tim Pritchard, managing editor, *Globe and Mail*; Margaret Wente, editor, Report on Business, *Globe and Mail*; Robert Lewis, managing editor, *Maclean's*; Bill Peterson, editor, Saskatoon *Star Phoenix*; Neil Reynolds, editor, Kingston *Whig-Standard*; Ken Foran, editor, Halifax *Chronicle-Herald*; William Callahan, editor, St. John's *Evening Telegram*; David Bailey, editor, Edmonton *Sun*; Bob Poole, editor, Calgary *Sun*; Yvon Lamare, editor, *Le Journal de Montréal*; Steve Lawrence, editor, *The Financial Times of Canada*; Philip McLeod, editor, London *Free Press*; Link Byfield, editor/publisher, *The Alberta Report*; Katherine Ashenberg, arts editor, *Globe and Mail*.

The Television Gatekeepers

All the regional TV stations in the country have their gatekeepers, but the most influential among them produce and edit the news and current affairs programs of the two major networks, "The CTV National News" and the CBC's "The National." CTV news regularly pulls in 1.2 million viewers in its 11 p.m. time slot; the CBC news regularly pulls around 1.5 million viewers in its 10 p.m. slot. Both shows are hosted by outstanding journalists: the CTV has the venerable Lloyd Robertson, probably the news anchor with the most credibility since Walter Cronkite, and the CBC has Peter Mansbridge, who has the intelligence and pleasant looks to match CBS megahost Dan Rather but fortunately lacks Rather's frenetic edge. Both Robertson and Mansbridge are far more than talking heads and contribute to the news selection process. But they are really the figureheads for massive news-gathering machines presided over by the gatekeepers.

The names of the gatekeepers are well known only to fellow journalists and public decison makers who have an interest in knowing where the real power lies in the media. At CTV, for instance, the behind-the-scenes decisions are made by men like John Macfarlane, managing director of news, features and information programming, and his boss Tim Kotcheff, vice-president of news, features and information programming. In Quebec, the most powerful TV news gatekeeper is Pierre O'Neil of Radio-Canada, the French-language arm of the public broadcaster. On the English-language CBC, everyone in Ottawa, from politicians to bureaucrats, knows that Elly Alboim, the national political editor, is the guy who has first say in determining whether they will get national exposure on the nightly newscast and how they will be portrayed. Alboim has first-line input into the CBC's Ottawa coverage. But before it goes on air, he has to compete for air time on "The National" with other news from around the country and the world. The men with the final authority over coverage are his bossess, and fellow gatekeepers, Tony Burman, chief news editor for CBC-TV, and David Bazay, executive producer of "The National." Another of the CBC's most influential gatekeepers is Mark Starowicz, the executive producer and creator of "The Journal," and the man who made CBC Radio's "As It Happens" a nationwide success.

For the most insightful, provocative and iconoclastic views of the gatekeeper's role, it's difficult to surpass Elly Alboim, chief of CBC-TV's parliamentary bureau since 1977.

Elly Alboim: Alboim is devouring a club sandwich and Coke in his Toronto hotel room. But he's not the kind of guy who can simply set aside some time for eating. There's too much wasted time between bites. So, between taking in ravenous gulps, he pours out a torrent of words. All day, he's been going over the results of a CBC-*Globe and Mail* opinion poll with *Globe* editors. Right now, he's talking about his job and offering a critique of TV news for an interviewer. When it's done, he'll work past midnight writing up the results of the day's meetings. Just another day in the life of the man who has become a bit of a legend in CBC circles and beyond.

As parliamentary bureau chief, Alboim runs a bureau of about 60 people and decides which stories are covered, how they're covered, what resources are used to cover them and ultimately what they say. He has been responsible for CBC-TV's coverage of four federal elections, four federal leadership conventions and two provincial leadership campaigns, all economic, constitutional and aboriginal first ministers' conferences, the Quebec referendum of 1980 and all provincial election-night broadcasts since 1983.

You'd think that after all that, Alboim, age 44, would have taken on a "Mr. CBC" persona, that he'd be imbued with the mission and mandate of the public broadcaster, convinced that the so-called Mothercorp (as CBC types call their employer) could no more do wrong than his own mother. Nothing could be further from the truth. A tall man with shaggy hair and a greying beard, Alboim would be no more comfortable adopting a bureaucratic mindset than he would be wearing a pinstripe suit. The word *homeostasis* doesn't seem to be in his vocabulary. When he talks, it's as if a hard disk in his mind is switched on, the output of thoughts is so rapid, but it's not preprogrammed with officially endorsed software. The way he sees it, television news, and the media in general, is engaged in a massive breach of trust with its audience. "It's no secret in the industry that I'm really terribly dissatisfied with the news television does," he says. "If it communicates as badly as the studies seem to indicate, in terms of comprehension, attention, then I think it has the responsibility to clean up its house. We have a responsibility to understand what its impact is and influence is and then to develop ways of communicating both more effectively and more neutrally."

Network news is the main source of information for its audience, and helps define public policy issues, he says, but the public has little or no idea of the assumptions underlying the coverage they watch. "People really do approach 'The National' on a given night and assume that by the end of 22 minutes they will have been told everything they need to know and they will have been told in appropriate sequence, with appropriate relative weight and that there is no editorial overlay, no prism different than the one they normally use to view the world. That's clearly and demonstratively not true any more."

The root of the problem is that television news (and Alboim's arguments sweep in other media as well) has become too dollar-driven. "TV's driving assumptions have become increasingly commercial," he laments. "We are consumer-driven in a marketplace, and it's no different for a Crown corporation. In order to convince our shareholders that we are relevant, we've got to demonstrate audience and ratings. It's as much survival strategy for CBC as it is for the CTV and the *Globe and Mail*."

In Alboim's view, this commercialism has distorted news coverage. Instead of news being selected for its intrinsic importance, it is selected for its audience appeal and the ease with which it can be pummelled into a tight little story with beginning, middle and conclusion. "We don't use the word *important* anymore, we use the words *relevant* or *interesting*." Time was, he says, when editors decided on a news line-up based on what people *should* know at the end of a day. Instead, "We've all repositioned ourselves to answer what the audience *wants* to know."

The dangers of this approach become more apparent as Alboim describes the effects of the drive for ratings on what gets covered and how. The model used for news selection, he explains, requires personalization, some sort of drama or conflict, and narrative structure. As a result, worthwhile issues, whether in politics, business or other fields, never make it on to "The National" or other news shows. "Because of the narrative structure, because of the model, legislation tends to be covered at the point of initiation and at the point of conclusion. But the policy debate, the legislative process — unless it's a contest of wills — it doesn't get covered."

Business and economic issues are sometimes harder to cover than politics using this model. "Take the market crash of 1987. Had you been a consumer of 'The National' you would not have heard about an overheated market, overextended corporations, leveraged buyouts, intrinsic instability in the market. If you were a pensioner on a fixed income and most of your assets were in stocks and bonds, you wouldn't have been aware of the threat."

Some critics are less worried about the effects of commercial pressures on CBC-TV and more concerned about what they perceive as its unacceptable bias in the public broadcaster's coverage of the major issues of the day. Critics such as the Fraser Institute's Michael Walker have said that the CBC's coverage of the free trade issue, which rose to the fore during the 1988 federal election, was biased in opposition to the imminent agreement with the United States. Asked if he was motivated to discredit free trade, Alboim asserts, "No, no. In fact, the company bends over backwards [to avoid bias]. There's a lot more discussion about fairness, content and balance within the CBC than there is in most places."

Controversy also erupted over the CBC's coverage of the Meech Lake accord. David Taras, a University of Calgary professor, analysed the CBC's coverage of the issue from the signing of the accord in 1987 until just after the Langevin meeting. Taras was highly critical of the CBC's coverage and argued that television's focus on the drama of how the agreement was reached rather than on its long-term ramifications distorted the national debate.

"The point that Taras makes is very true," says Alboim. "Until there was a real conflict there was no coverage." Alboim points out that the CBC did step up its coverage in the months before the accord's June 1990 deadline for passage and after Taras completed his study. "We tried to clean up our act. We did a five-part series on Meech Lake in the fall of 1989, where we studied each component. On 'Sunday Report' we did extended discussions and background pieces."

Tougher criticism of the CBC's coverage came from Rick Salutin, a Toronto author and journalist who contributes to the left-wing *This Magazine*. In a November 1990 *Saturday Night* article entitled "Brian and the Boys," Salutin castigated the CBC for the alarmist coverage in the month leading up to the accord's deadline. In fact, the CBC's coverage was clearly pro-Meech, and Salutin did a thorough job of pointing out just how pro-Meech it was. For example, Salutin cited a CBC-TV special ("three hours of anxiety on the subject") in which Barbara Frum opined, "It's as if the fuse has been lit on a time bomb." Standing beside Frum, Peter Mansbridge intoned, "There's a widespread feeling that this is a decisive time, that the days ahead could be the most important we've ever lived through as a nation. Canada has endured for 120 years, but all of that is now on the line. . . . Can Canada work, or is Canada drifting apart?" Salutin's point is that the CBC was unquestioningly parroting the Mulroney government's line. He complains that CBC-TV failed to adequately explore the idea that Meech was not just "the Quebec Round" (a deal to address Quebec's concerns and bring it into the 1982 Constitution), that the accord "gave every province what Quebec requested, thereby undermining national institutions."

Yet Salutin's thinking seems to be just as distorted by emotions — in his case, against the accord — as was the CBC's. There is a smug I-told-you-so undertone to Salutin's comments, as if he's riding on the current wave of popular antagonism to the accord and the Mulroney government. His real point is, "See, I told you so. The country didn't fall apart when Meech failed."

It's ironic, given these objections to the CBC's pro-Meech coverage, that a controversy erupted during 1991 over comments Alboim made about the accord before an academic audience in 1987. One of the academics present, John Meisel, a Queen's University professor, later wrote a book in which he castigated Alboim for his comments. According to Meisel, Alboim criticized the Meech Lake process as "a highly political and highly cynical exercise that had very, very little to do with reconstitutionalizing Canada. Brian Mulroney needed, for his own purposes, to establish that he could do in Quebec what Pierre Trudeau could not." Alboim even described how he had scoured the country for dissenters. Meisel wrote that he was "aghast and shocked by what struck me as the appallingly arrogant and facile stance of one of the most senior CBC journalists." Alboim's outspokenness had landed him in trouble again. But the fact that the CBC's coverage ended up being pro-Meech, especially in the run-up to the accord deadline, showed that in the crunch, the views of his superiors — like current affairs boss Trina McQueen — held the day.

Despite his willingness to castigate the government, Alboim is worried that media-government relations have deteriorated to the point that news coverage is suffering. As an example, he cites media coverage of Mulroney's controversial 1990 appointment of eight senators, which gave him the majority he needed to pass the Goods and Services Tax. "They were not all Tory hacks, flacks and bagmen," says Alboim. "When we can with impunity collectively write that they are all Tory hacks coming in to save the GST, there's something wrong with our characterization."

There is a vicious cycle of distrust, he says. "For every action, there's a reaction. Government has become a lot more manipulative, a lot more secretive, it governs by risk avoidance, it governs by stealth, and it does that because it cannot be convinced that there can be an honest debate [in the media]. So media gets upset and gouges harder and government retreats more. I don't know what's the chicken and what's the egg."

Alboim dismisses the notion that CBC-TV's news coverage falls prey to ideological bias, either left or right. However, he thinks it has an anti-institutional bias. This is because the media is consumer-driven and begins to resonate with the dominant feelings in the community. "There isn't a shared value system," he argues. "It comes as a shock to bureaucrats when the media says that if the government falls down tomorrow it's a news story as opposed to a Canadian tragedy."

Alboim himself could never be accused of being in the government's pocket, or anybody else's, if his lower-class background and days as a student radical are any indication. He was born in Montreal in 1947, the son of a butcher whose own parents had immigrated from Poland after the second war. Alboim grew up in Snowdon, just on the fringe of the immigration corridor in Montreal, and went to high school at a tough downtown school. "The school was very good for me. It was my first exposure to visible minorities. It was a very poor school, and I was one of the richest kids. My friends went shoplifting at Eaton's at lunch and police cars were always around." Alboim was a straight-A student and went on to McGill University in the mid-1960s, where he became a student radical, demonstrating against the Vietnam War in front of the U.S. consulate and joining peace marches. As a member of the McGill newspaper's managing board, he was one of those fired and put on trial for seditious libel after the paper printed William Manchester's "obscene satire" on former presidents Lyndon Johnson and John Kennedy. "The Quebec attorney general threatened us with criminal libel and there was an internal witch-hunt at McGill. . . . We got fired from the paper and went through a tribunal. We were eventually exonerated and got the paper back." After graduating in anthropology and sociology, Alboim attended the Columbia School of Journalism, where he won a Pulitzer fellowship at graduation.

In 1970, Alboim returned to Montreal and landed a job as a reporter for the local CBC-TV supper show. He soon was given the job of line-up editor for the show, an experience he calls the lowest point in his career. He says he managed to drive down the show's audience from about 150,000 when he took over to 25,000 when he left. "Every night we had one monstrous technical difficulty after another. At one point we put the mayor of Montreal on a talk show for 72 minutes and could not get the phones to work — didn't get a single phone call." CBC brass sent some show doctors in and Alboim was informed that his coverage was all wrong. "They brought me a list of what audiences want to see. Weather was number one, then health and medicine were number two, and politics, economics and labour — anything you'd regard as the news of significance — were in the bottom quintile."

In 1976, Alboim fled to Toronto and did a stint as assignment editor for the national news service. A year later, he became Ottawa bureau chief. In the years since, Alboim has been pivotal to CBC's coverage of just about every major political event in the country, orchestrating a team of reporters in a country-wide network. Not only that, he's survived the turf wars at CBC, such as a late-1980s purge of the ranks of his bureau, with his dignity reasonably intact.

Increasingly, Alboim has emerged as one of the most articulate critics of the way CBC and other television outlets cover the news. The real question is: How does the CBC put up with his outspokenness? He has the answer. "The CBC, God bless it, accepts, tolerates dissonance better than any other organization I know of. It accepts people at war with each other, it accepts the clash of ideas. There is a social purpose in the company even though it goes wrong in a whole variety of ways."

Trina McQueen: Early in her career as a television news reporter, Trina McQueen, now vice-president of news and current affairs at CBC-TV, confronted attitudes that would make the current generation of TV newshounds gasp with disbelief. In the late 1960s, McQueen was the first female on-air reporter in the media capital of Toronto, and she didn't confine her coverage to fashion shows or show-biz chatter either. Crime was one of her favourite beats. At one point she was assigned to cover the trial of a judge who was accused of impropriety. "What he did, in fact, was invite hookers into his chambers and ask them to take their clothes off while he masturbated in front of them," she recalls. "I went on air and I did use that word on air. There was a lot of protest from people who didn't feel that a woman should be covering that kind of thing. However, the CBC supported me."

More than 20 years later, McQueen, the highest-ranking woman in Canadian television, finds the episode vaguely amusing. Today, it's difficult to imagine anyone not taking McQueen seriously. At 48, she is extremely comfortable with her post. She is poised and articulate. It's easy to see why she has a reputation in CBC ranks as a bright manager who doesn't shy away from tough decisions. Blonde and petite, McQueen has the good looks of an Angie Dickinson. But it is her intellectual intensity that commands attention.

McQueen's opinions count enormously in what makes it onto the public policy agenda of the country. She presides over the news and current affairs programming at the dominant news source for most Canadians. The staff who produce shows as diverse as "Marketplace," "Newsworld," "The Journal" and "The National" are under her purview. She holds the purse strings and editorial control over these shows and all other CBC current affairs programming. More important, McQueen is responsible for the future of programming in these areas, developing strategy about what kinds of shows and what kinds of issues will be on our TV screens in the future.

McQueen was appointed to her post in April 1989 but didn't really begin until January 1990. Until then she was cleaning up loose ends on her previous job, director of network television, and filling in for her boss, Denis Harvey, the recently retired vice-president of English television, while he was recovering from heart surgery. Interviewed late in 1990, she had already begun to influence the CBC's current affairs programming. McQueen has a strong sense of what types of programming she'd like to see. One of her goals is more "point-of-view" television. A good example is a series of documentaries called "Witness," which explored such controversial issues as the shortcomings of Western press coverage of Nicaraguan politics and the lack of freedom in Castro's modern-day Cuba. These are ideologically loaded issues sure to offend the right or left depending on what point of view is taken. It was a risky area for a public broadcaster to wade into, and McQueen knew it. Yet she was surprised when these and other films in the series, on Albania, Angola and Philippine rebels, failed to generate controversy. "I was disappointed because there wasn't more flack," she says. "Maybe that's because I underestimated the sophistication of the television audience."

McQueen also has ambitions to, as she puts it, expand the range of journalism on CBC-TV; promote "journalism that explores various aspects of society that are not considered journalistically." The approach is refreshingly new. Early in her tenure, she oversaw the development of a show called "Life, the Program." "It really deals with personal choices," she says. It covers such topics as mother-daughter relationships, the life of a man raising young children, the difficulties faced by a man with a wife suffering from Alzheimers. "They're really stories about progressions through life. They don't involve political choices, economic choices or business choices — all of which are clearly outlined in journalism. They are personal choices, the kind of choices that everybody has to make and can understand."

McQueen is also a proponent of more CBC coverage of workplace issues. "Working is an activity that most of us spend most of our waking hours doing, but there is little coverage of it in journalism," she says. Another subject McQueen thinks deserves more coverage in the media is the whole area of decision-making by powerful people.

McQueen sees this type of show as filling an important mandate for television. "I want to play a part in expanding the freedom of the individual to be the best she can be, to have the most possible choices in life. I really believe that Canadians need much more of a sense of their own options. They need to understand very much more of who they are and why they are; what the forces are that shaped them and continue to shape them. That's really why I got into television."

Yet her ambition is not to produce shows that proselytize. Dealing with choices about life ethics and values in TV programs is obviously a tricky area for a public broadcaster. McQueen says that such programs develop a point of view, but only after copious amounts of research. How does she expect her producers to avoid unfair biases or half-truths? "I find the basic rules of journalism are pretty good," she explains. "You do your research. You check it out, you talk to a lot of people, and you make sure you can back up what you say."

On a broader scale, McQueen rejects the notion that CBC television should cast itself as a watchdog over the Establishment, supporting or opposing its views. "That's very much a print question," she says, alluding to newspapers that are openly Liberal or Conservative in slant. "It's not a public broadcasting question. I don't think that public broadcasting should either consistently support or consistently oppose. Our role is to shine a light on what is happening so that people can decide for themselves."

Of course, even with such noble intentions, it is impossible for the public broadcaster to avoid controversy and accusations of unfair bias, such as during the Meech Lake crisis. Says McQueen: "I will plead guilty to thinking that this organization did regard the Meech Lake negotiations as a real touchstone in this country's history, that Meech Lake really became a focus for all the grievances in the country." As a result, "we felt that it was really important to give it the most comprehensive coverage. We probably gave more background, more analysis and more explanation of the issues involved in Meech Lake than we've done on most complicated stories . . . . I don't know how we would have made it into more of a crisis than it was." The Meech Lake issue did prompt McQueen to reconsider some of her traditional notions of what the public wants from news coverage. "I find what people want from journalism now is something beyond balance, and I don't think we have figured out yet what it is." McQueen does, however, have a good idea. "People want to have their views reflected very, very clearly. In old-fashioned journalism, if you interviewed all three party leaders you could pretty well be sure that you could cover the full range of public opinion. I don't think that is true any longer." This gives the CBC great difficulties, she adds. "One of the crucial tasks that we have to come to grips with is a political system that does not necessarily reflect the views of large segments of the population and to find ways in which we can regularly hear the views of the nonpoliticized segments of society."

McQueen certainly has the intellect needed to carry out her job well. But as most women who've made it to the top in any career will attest, brains alone aren't enough to break down the barriers against women in the male-dominated workplace. McQueen was born Trina Janitsch in 1943 in Belleville, a modest-sized city in southeastern Ontario. Her father, a professional engineer, was Yugoslavian in ancestry, her mother was Czech. McQueen was the eldest of five children born into the comfortable middle-class family, and in her youth she showed every trait of leadership usually associated with first-borns in large families. At high school she was, at various times, a cheerleader, a member of the students' council, president of the drama club and a member of the Glee Club. On the side she wrote a weekly high-school activities column for the city newspaper. (Her co-writer was Stevie Dahl, now Stevie Cameron, a noted journalist.) Yet McQueen considers herself a late bloomer. Asked if she enjoyed her high-school years, she responds rhetorically, "Have you ever met anyone who will say, 'Yes, I was popular in high school?' No? Me neither. My theory is that the ones who were popular kind of disappeared along the way."

After completing a political science degree at the University of British Columbia and a journalism degree at Carleton University, McQueen started in a graduate Canadian studies program but dropped out. "I got tired of poverty," she explains. "In my last year I had four part-time jobs." After working for about a year at the now-defunct Ottawa *Journal*, McQueen, then in her early twenties, signed on at CTV to co-host "W5," its newly created current affairs program. The job didn't last long. "I was hired for 'W5' by Peter Wiley, who was a legend in television at the time. But about four months later he was fired in one of those enormous blowouts, and I left with him and went to CFTO news full-time." At CFTO, the

Toronto CTV affiliate, McQueen became the station's first woman news reporter. She soon had her first unpleasant experience with male chauvinism. "The boss told me I didn't have the authority to be there," she recalls. "My boss's boss really didn't want to have a woman around the place." Certain that she was about to be fired, she went to complain about her treatment to the station's owner, at the time, John Bassett. "He saved my job. But I knew the writing was on the wall." Shortly afterward, in 1967, McQueen left for the CBC and is still there.

At the time, McQueen was still the only female reporter in the region. One of the first jobs she had at the CBC was covering the 1967 Conservative leadership convention. McQueen's assignment was to cover the activities of women, which included commenting on the colour of Olive Diefenbaker's dress. There was clearly only one direction for her career to go — up. Over the next two decades she recorded a series of firsts for women in TV. In 1976, she became executive producer for "The National"; in 1978 she added production duties for "Newsmagazine" and news specials to her turf; she directed coverage of the 1979 and 1980 federal elections and the 1980 referendum in Quebec. McQueen stepped up into the nether regions of the CBC bureaucracy in 1980 when she became program director for the network, responsible for day-to-day operations of the entertainment program departments and for the program schedule. Between 1984 and 1989, McQueen was director of network television, in charge of the business and planning activities of English television.

In her new job, McQueen is the most powerful woman in Canadian television. For all her responsibility, she leads a low-profile life. She lives with her husband, Don McQueen, a CTV producer, whom she met in the 1970s when they worked together at CBC, and one daughter, Jennifer. She says reading, especially Victorian novels, is her favourite pastime. She also enjoys her family's annual summer sojourn in France, where they rent a house in Provence. Like a great many leaders of the media elite, McQueen has religious beliefs. She attends Lawrence Park Community Church, a United Church near her Toronto home. She owns four television sets.

McQueen is the closest thing to a role model that aspiring female TV journalists have. Yet she rejects the idea that there are easy prescriptions for women to get ahead in the business. "I guess my advice is, 'Don't take a lot of advice.' There are four factors that I think predict success. One is your talent, another is timing, a third is luck and the fourth is hard work, and that is the only one you can control." Otherwise, she says, she stays away from trendy ideas for women. "I don't network. I don't do power lunches, I don't dress for success. I'm basically an introvert, I just stay home with a good book." McQueen's career has been helped enormously by the confidence that Denis Harvey, retired vice-president of English television, had in her abilities. She credits Harvey with teaching her a good deal about journalism early in her career when she was a reporter and he was an editor. But she is careful to discredit the conclusion that she has advanced at the CBC because of any one person's favours. "Even though I have had some very good bosses, I don't look on any one of them as a particular mentor."

The career of Trina McQueen may not fit the model prescribed for ambitious women in innumerable self-help books and articles. Ultimately, she's been propelled upward by her own hard work and a profound sense of mission. This sense of mission, which she doesn't admit to easily, is rooted in a sense of nationalism she developed early in life. "When I went to university and started looking at Canadian history and Canadian literature, I realized the enormous richness that we are denied. Every other country has its birthright. You understand who the heroes and villains are, you understand the triumphs, you understand the national failures except here. If I have a mission, it is an understanding of the place where we are and the time in which we live. To me that's a contribution to individual freedom." She adds with an embarrassed laugh, "That may sound sort of highfalutin."

The Eight Most Influential
Television News Gatekeepers

Trina McQueen, director, TV News and Current Affairs, CBC; David Bazay, executive producer, "The National"; Mark Starowicz, executive producer, "The Journal"; Tim Kotcheff, vice-president, Features and Information Programming, CTV; John MacFarlane, managing editor, News and Information Features, CTV; Elly Alboim, Ottawa bureau chief, CBC; Doug Small, Ottawa bureau chief, Global TV; Pierre O'Neil, news chief, Radio-Canada, Montreal.

Newshounds and Pundits

Newsrooms are the libido of the media; at their best, they are imbued with irrepressible instincts for a good story. In a good newsroom, the reporters are a polyglot group with critical minds and a diversity of outlooks that make a paper dynamic and ultimately readable. The unspoken rule among most reporters is that they are doing a good job if they can regularly horrify the advertising department with critical articles. It's a tradition of dissent that has been in newsrooms since the beginning.

Yet the common thread of good newsrooms is curiosity, not simply anti-Establishment attitudes. Newsrooms have their doyens, who are highly respected for their insights and experience both inside and outside the organization; they also have their iconoclasts of both left and right persuasion who share a penchant for challenging mainstream political, economic and social views.

There follow profiles of some of the doyens of the media establishment and several leading iconoclasts. How do you become a doyen of the media establishment? You start out as a young rabble-rouser and stay in the business until you're older or more experienced than everyone else. Peter Newman, Michael Enright and Barbara Frum, three of the more fascinating journalists in Canada, are typical examples of this phenomenon.

Peter Newman: Imagine Canada without Peter Newman. That simple exercise is perhaps the fairest way to assess the influence of the man who has held some of the top jobs in journalism in his career and has made a name for himself chronicling the private lives and public power of the corporate and political establishments in a string of record-selling books. Without Newman, Canadians might guess our knowledge of the manners and mores of the capitalist class would surely be severely limited without *The Canadian Establishment.* Our impressions of legendary politicians like John Diefenbaker (*Renegade* *in Power*) and Lester Pearson (*The Distemper of Our Times*) would be a little dimmer and probably more derived from dry textbooks. Newman has, quite simply, created human icons in Canadian society that are an integral part of our view of the country and how it works.

Newman has always had detractors. Diefenbaker struck back at him by calling him "The Bouncing Czech." Most of his detractors, however, are journalists, and their main complaint is that the books, like the two volumes on the Canadian Establishment, are soft on his subjects. Instead of portraits of the rich and famous, they would have preferred a more critical approach. This is an unfair criticism, so far as Newman is concerned: "*The Canadian Establishment* could be read at two levels. You could read it as a kind of great whaling story, a *Moby-Dick*, or just a great interesting gossipy read. Or you could read it as an indictment of the capitalist class of this country, which is what I meant it to be."

Newman, formerly an editor of the Toronto *Star* and *Maclean's* and author of more than a dozen books, is without doubt the most talked-about and written-about author and journalist of his generation. His personal habits are regurgitated in countless profiles. Samples: he awakes at 4 a.m. to write his best-selling books; he writes with Stan Kenton music blasting through his earphones; he loves sailing on his 35-foot yacht *Indra*, when he's not shuffling around in his spectacular 15-level home overlooking Indian Arm Inlet near Vancouver. Yet he remains an enigma to those who know him or have worked with him.

This is understandable. Consider his complexity. Newman has a dark, foreboding presence, enhanced by the way he walks along stooped over, peering out from beneath bristling black eyebrows. He cultivates the image of intrigue by wearing long dark overcoats that somehow drape him in an aura of mystery. In personality, he is normally shyer than the average librarian — an impression accentuated by his curious habit of barely opening his jaws when he speaks so that his words emerge like tiny, flat projectiles. But in a flash, Newman can become as wrathful as an ayatollah, as anyone who has felt his anger can attest.

I knew none of this when I first met Peter Newman, in the summer of 1978. I had applied for the position of researcher at *Maclean's* magazine, which was hiring additional staff in preparation for its transformation from a biweekly to a weekly that fall. Having passed muster with the chief of research, Arlene Arnason, I still needed the approval of Newman, the editor. I appeared at his door at the appointed hour and peered inside. Across a vast expanse of floor, he sat behind his trademark crescent desk puffing on a pipe. He motioned me to enter.

Newman speaks little but has a stunning intellect. The interview went well. But it was only afterwards that I realized that I — an outgoing 26-year-old — had done almost all the talking.

Life at *Maclean's* under Newman was a thrilling, high-speed ride down an endless bobsled run. Week after week, month after month, the whole place pursued the news, working horrendous hours for low pay. Newman presided over the mad rush from a lofty vantage point. He was the unrivalled overseer of the operation, although he had numerous detractors in his employ. Each Monday, the whole staff would wait nervously for his memo, praising or castigating them by name for their contributions or slips in the latest issue. At story meetings of editors, who included some of the brightest stars in journalism, Newman ruled by intellectual intimidation. Sitting at the head of the board table, he said little and listened a lot before giving a story idea the go-ahead or killing it with a curt word. At these meetings, there was always a competition between editors for page space in the next issue. Any editor lacking the self-confidence to pitch his or her stories well ended up with little space.

Newman's accomplishments at *Maclean's* during his editorship from 1971 to 1982 were considerable. He expanded it from an 11-person operation with gross revenues of $2 million into a weekly newsmagazine with a staff of 70 and annual revenues of nearly $30 million.

His tenure ended in controversy, though, after poor morale and paranoia about recent firings led to a successful organizing drive by the Southern Ontario Newspaper Guild. Shortly afterwards, Newman retired to write books in British Columbia, although he has remained a columnist and senior contributing editor of the magazine. After the upheaval, he expressed no regret at leaving, saying he had fulfilled his mandate at the magazine. But in his parting editorial he did make one, now immortal, comment about the staff: "Sometimes the staff functioned with the cool precision of a crew on an attacking submarine. At other times I wondered how I came to preside over Canadian journalism's most elaborate day care centre."

Newman is now where he feels he has always belonged: on the outside looking in. He's felt like an outsider since 1938, when the Germans overran his wealthy family's home in the Sudetenland — they turned it into a casino — and forced the family to flee. Peter, his mother and his father emigrated to Canada because, he explains, "nobody else wanted us. We were Jewish and we didn't have much money." Newman says that Canada's acceptance of him and his family was the root of his fierce Canadian nationalism. Since he knew nothing of his new country, he set about studying up on it. He's been studying it from an outsider's vantage point ever since. "I've always been the outsider, at first by definition and then by choice," he has said. "I've always been the fellow with his nose pressed against the window looking in."

Michael Enright: Michael Enright folds himself onto the couch like a man on stilts. The long lean limbs of his six-foot-two frame protrude over the boundaries of the furniture. But it's not Enright's height that fixes your attention. It's the eyes. Set in a smallish face fringed by a brown beard, they never seem to dart or evade contact. When Enright is listening to someone, the eyes are fixed in a quizzical, attentive stare, brows arching. This has the pleasant effect of making anyone he's conversing with feel worthwhile.

Yet it's Enright's voice that has made him the dinner guest of up to 1 million radio listeners every night. It's a deep baritone, sometimes slightly nasal, sometimes slightly theatrical, but always engaging. His vowels are round and well shaped like those of a Shakespearean actor. As co-host of "As It Happens," CBC Radio's nightly current affairs show, Enright conducts phone interviews with all manner of people caught up in the vortex of news around the world. Whether he's linked to the president of Israel or a fisherman in Newfoundland, his interview subjects usually find themselves drawn into his web of intimacy. "I look at radio as a very intimate thing," he says. "You're talking into someone's ear. I don't think about the mass audience. If I thought I was talking to 700,000 people a night, I'd freeze. Nobody can talk to 700,000, you'd go out of your mind. So you're usually talking to one or two people. There's a closeness. I guess that's why telephone sex is popular."

Enright ranks as one of Canada's few radio megahosts who reach a national and international audience each day. (The others are Peter Gzowski and Vicki Gabereau.) Beyond Canada's borders, the show is broadcast by dozens of public radio outlets in the United States and around the world on Radio-Canada International.

Every evening, Enright goes on air with co-host and announcer Alan Maitland for a 90-minute romp of interviews with the people behind the headlines. The show is packaged in the sense that its aim is not just to cover the news but to make sense of it in a distinctive way. "I keep saying we're not here to cover things," says Enright. "That's the job of the news department. We're here to put our particular spin on it."

There's been a consistency to that spin ever since the show was created in 1969, as a once-a-week program hosted by Phillip Forsythe. At the time, simply phoning up people at the centre of events anywhere in the world and chatting with them was a novel idea that immediately caught the imagination of radio listeners. Beginning in 1971, when Barbara Frum took over as host, the show reached a level of national prominence that it has largely maintained ever since.

In the jargon of the trade, the tone of "As It Happens" is savvy, upbeat and, at its best, very witty. Enright, who joined the show in 1987, brings those qualities and more to the job. As a result, he has a personal influence over the way his listeners relate to or care about news events. He interprets events and makes them relevant to his listeners on a human scale, which is no small service in an information-glutted world. But neither he nor the producers of the show have any overt political agenda in mind, beyond the liberal assumptions that underly the workings of most of the media in Canada. Political guests, whether federal MPs or foreign prime ministers, are grilled with questions that could, or should, be asked by any informed, reasonable citizen.

Enright loves the thought of making people sit up and listen to new tidbits of information. "It's instantaneous. To get somebody to say 'I didn't know that.' I don't care if they get mad or happy; just to have an impact." There's also the hobnobbing with fascinating people. "It's great. I talk to the most interesting people in the world that day."

Although Enright works in an information-filled medium, he suggests that radio is not the best medium for passing information. "What it excels at," he says, "is conveying emotion and drama." This suits Enright's interviewing style. He's at his best when his subject is at the centre of an emotionally charged event. He recalls covering the story of Jessica McClure, the child who fell down a well in Texas and was trapped there for days. "At one point, I interviewed a paramedic who was going down the hole to try to get Jessica out. He was the man, in fact, who did finally get her out. In the interview, he was very straightforward, you know, like cops are: 'Yes sir, we're going down 58 feet and then we'll go in the transverse thing.' He was very calm, so I thought, 'I've got to get through to this guy because he can't be as robotic as he sounds.'" Enright, who has three children of his own, changed direction and asked, "Do you have any kids?" There was a long pause, and the paramedic's voice cracked when he said, "Yes sir, I've got four." Enright continued, "I guess you think about them every time you go down that hole." The paramedic replied, his voice cracking again, "Yes sir, I do." At that point, recalls Enright, "I frankly almost cracked, too. It was a very difficult moment for both of us, and the instant it went on air it was a stopper. It was a great story because two days later he went down and got Jessica out of the hole."

Despite the stress and pace of 10-hour days, Enright loves his job. "I love live radio because you're working without a net. You never know what's going to happen." Enright has high praise for his co-host. Maitland introduces Enright's interviews and engages in continual banter with him. "Alan is wonderful. He's 70 per cent of the show," says Enright. The two men only compete when it comes to crossword puzzles, which they race to complete between interviews.

Enright arrived at the microphone of a nationwide current affairs show after hopscotching through a succession of journalism jobs. He represents the old school of journalists, in that he got ahead with limited formal education but an exceptional ability to work with words on paper or in thin air. He's had the sort of erratic career that would make a high-school guidance counsellor blanch and a fellow journalist envious.

He was born in Toronto in 1943, and attended St. Michael's, a Catholic boys' school, but dropped out and took a job at 19 as a reporter with the Brampton *Times and Conservator.* "I was a cub reporter, but in a weekly newspaper in a small town you did everything," he says. "I was a photographer, a city hall reporter. I wrote a sports column, editorials, the drama critic . . . ."

From Brampton he bounced to the Kitchener-Waterloo *Record,* where he worked as religion editor for a while. "I always had this burden of being considered the bright young thing, the boy wonder, because I could move words around on the page. I was amazed that people would pay me to write."

In 1966, after a year spent soul-searching — and starving — in England, Enright landed a job at the *Globe and Mail.* He was turned down at first. "I talked to [managing editor] Clark Davey and he said, 'We're not going to hire anybody without a university degree.'" But Davey, who went on to become a publisher in the Southam chain, did give Enright a two-week freelance job on the city desk. "At the end of two weeks they hired me because I did some stuff and they liked it." Enright still regrets never having gone to university, although he did win a prestigious Southam Fellowship award in 1978. But his lack of formal education didn't endanger his career once he was signed on at the *Globe.* Thereafter, he held some of the best jobs in Canadian journalism and worked with some of its most talented practitioners.

At the *Globe,* Enright served as Washington correspondent during the upheavals of 1968. "I got beat up in Chicago during the riots. I got kicked around by the cops and tear-gassed. I covered the invasion of Czechoslovakia in August that year." He was also in Washington to cover the shooting of Bobby Kennedy and the resignation of Lyndon Johnson. "It was a great time."

In the following years, Enright worked as a writer with the *Globe Magazine* (with Ken Bagnell and Martin O'Malley) and as an editorial writer for the paper. He worked for *Time Canada* in Montreal for a year, then landed his first radio job, as host of a CBC Radio show in Montreal called "Daybreak." Recalls Enright: "I did that for a year. I got up at four in the morning and trudged down to work in the snow and crap. The show ran from six to nine. I was tired the entire year. After the show we'd go over to Toe Blake's tavern and I'd drink draft beer, have bacon and eggs and then go home and fall into bed. It was awful."

In 1973, Enright jumped to the Toronto *Star*, where he worked on an insight section run by Shirley Sharzer, along with well-known journalists Tom Harpur, Sid Katz, Trent Frayne and Hartley Stewart. Enright was soon asked to join the paper's editorial board by George Bain, head of the editorial page at the time. Enright didn't like the job. "Writing editorials at the *Star* was not like writing them at the *Globe*," he recalls. "At the *Globe and Mail* you were required to think. At the *Star*, you were required to take dictation for [publisher Beland] Honderich."

In 1974, Enright jumped back into radio when he was hired to succeed Peter Gzowski as host of the CBC morning show, then called "This Country in the Morning." (Gzowski quit to briefly dabble in his own TV interview show, "90 Minutes Live.") "It was very interesting. We had great ratings and a great audience, but Margaret Lyons, who ran Current Affairs then, didn't like me for some reason. Margaret and I are great friends now, but she didn't think I was warm."

Enright's contract wasn't renewed next season, which put him on the job market just when Peter Newman and a band of talented writers and editors were beginning the task of turning *Maclean's* magazine, then a monthly feature publication, into a newsmagazine.

Enright stayed with the magazine through its transition to a biweekly in 1975 and to a weekly in 1978. By that time, Enright was assistant managing editor. He says he didn't get along with Newman. "Peter and I had terrible fights about the direction of the magazine and so on. Then I won a Southam Fellowship in 1978 — the prize was an all-expenses-paid year of study at the University of Toronto — and at the end of it I really didn't want to go back."

Enright had one more fling with the magazine business from 1980 to 1984, when he served as editor of *Quest*. His tenure was a tremendous editorial success. When he took over *Quest* it was basically a self-help magazine with articles, he says, on subjects such as how to have a healthier lawn, how to fire your secretary, how to have an affair. "We made it into a writer's magazine, a general-interest feature magazine." Under Enright, the magazine won plenty of journalism awards but not enough advertising. In 1984, it was folded by its owners, Bell Canada Enterprises, parent of the phone company, which had recently acquired the magazine from Comac Communications. Enright learned the bad news in the morning newspaper.

Once more Enright landed on his feet. From 1984 to 1987, he served as managing editor of CBC Radio's national news operation, with an annual budget of about $7 million and a staff of about 300, including foreign correspondents. "The bureaucracy wasn't terribly charming," says Enright, a man whose flamboyant personality makes him the antithesis of the bureaucratic man. But overseeing coverage of world news was a nonstop rush for a news junkie. "They phoned me at 2:30 in the morning in my first week and they said, 'Chernenko has died and we want to extend the "World Report" by five minutes.' I said go ahead and went back to bed. Then I thought, wait a minute, this is a big story. So I got up and drove down to the office in the middle of the night and I walked in with coffee and doughnuts, and they were thunderstruck — they had never seen a manager do that."

It didn't surprise anyone in the business when Enright left the manager's job to go back on air in 1985 as co-host of "As It Happens." "I grew up in the pre-television age listening to radio," he says. "In fact, when I went to my first hockey game at Maple Leaf Gardens I was so disappointed at how small the arena was, because in your brain, it's the whole universe and Foster Hewitt is God." With television, you just sit there, he says. "With radio you have to be a participant. You've got to engage yourself in order to listen to radio and particularly the CBC because we don't do background radio. We don't do wallpaper radio." In that case, "As It Happens" is in good hands, because Michael Enright never has been nor ever will be a wallflower.

Barbara Frum: Barbara Frum had never experienced anything like it. The famous guest in her TV studio was making no sense at all.

Sitting in front of the camera, Hunter S. Thompson, known as America's gonzo journalist for his bizarre articles and personal habits, was virtually unintelligible. All Frum's probing, thoughtful questions could elicit from him were grunts. "The interview began with monosyllabic answers and went that way for 10 or 15 minutes," recalls Frum. "Then he gradually started to rev his motors and went from an absolute crawl to speed demon. So the interview was totally schizoid." Only later did Frum learn the explanation. Thompson had arrived in Toronto from Denver in the depths of depression; he was scooped off the plane by a producer, who was desperate to revive his famous interview subject. "Thompson said that he was not going to be revived unless the producer could serve him up fast some cocaine and bourbon," says Frum. "He rounded up some cocaine — I have no idea how and I don't want to know — and some bourbon, so by the time Thompson walked into the studio at 10 p.m. for makeup, he was nearly awake." Unfortunately for Frum, Thompson revived the rest of the way as the show was being taped. It was a disaster that even heavy editing couldn't salvage before it went on air. "I think I've never been more terrified. I was totally helpless," she recalls.

Frum, host of "The Journal," CBC-TV's flagship current affairs show, is recalling the worst interview of her 33-year career as a radio and television host. The Thompson one-on-one took place in 1974, while she was a fledgling TV host working on a current affairs show called "Barbara Frum," in Toronto. Nothing she experienced in radio, as host of "As It Happens," the nationwide current affairs show, or in her current job has been nearly so bad.

The most revealing thing about Frum's worst-interview anecdote is that she's had to reach back 16 years to find it. There were other close calls in her early days on TV, and there have been reams of tough interviews — the irascible Margaret Thatcher smugly questioned Frum's facts, and Paul McCartney deftly deflected her queries with his whimsicality. But Frum has never really lost control of an interview since Thompson's drug-induced performance. "I must confess that I don't embarrass easily," she says. "I think it's one of the best things I've got going for me."

It's also a quality that has helped make Frum one of the most influential broadcast journalists in Canada. Every weekday night almost 2 million Canadians coast-to-coast tune in to watch Frum interview the people who make the news, like politicians or business executives, or the innocent people who get caught up in it, like freed hostages or disaster victims. Yet Frum dismisses the notion that she has any real power. "I have never accepted the idea that I have influence," she says. "I have always seen myself as a surrogate for others. I'm there to get the viewers the answers they want. I don't enjoy telling people what to think." The biggest danger for people in her position, she adds, is that they often let their ego get the better of them. "You have no right, night after night, to sit there and use public air time as a vehicle for your own ego, and frankly, ego display is one of the great traps that almost everybody who's there a long time starts to fall into."

However much Frum hates to admit it, she helps shape public opinion, probably as much as any of her colleagues on air or in print. Air time on "The Journal" alone guarantees that an issue becomes of national importance. The questions Frum asks, and the *way* she asks them — sceptically, accusingly or even meekly — help determine what Canadians think about her interviewees and their views. Hosts of current affairs programs must convey the worries, concerns and questions of their audience to earn its trust. Dispassionate types don't last two shows. And Frum could never be accused of leaving her personal opinions in the makeup room. Interviewing Prime Minister Mulroney in 1988, on the eve of a federal election, Frum dropped her interviewer's mantle and urged him to drop the free trade initiative. A couple of years later, when the topic was the Meech Lake accord, Frum, her critics said, was very soft on the prime minister.

Predictably, such incidents open Frum up to accusations of partisanship. She counters that it is absurd to accuse her of partisanship. "Do you see how lunatic that is?" she says. "If you're a hard-working journalist who cares deeply, as a citizen and as a journalist, about the future of the country, why can't you work through ideas, test ideas and present them to the viewer, shape the story so that the viewers get it? Remember everybody kept saying that Meech was so tough nobody could understand it? Well, that was just a great big cop-out."

But developing a point of view on an issue does not make you a political partisan. "The longer I stay in journalism, the more resistant I am to partisanship, the more it upsets me. I've never been a political partisan. I don't understand partisanship, to tell you the truth. In my inner soul I don't understand how one can put party advantage any more than personal advantage over mastering a problem and working for the best solution."

For Frum, getting to the essence of an issue should have nothing to do with ideology. "I think looking at every issue fresh without ideological baggage is the essential of my trade. I'll confess to being a bleeding heart, I can't bear human suffering. But I'm also open-minded about how to relieve human suffering, the best way to do it."

Frum, 54, is one of those rare people we've all met who seem to have their adult characters fully formed from their childhood, as if they had an old soul in a new body. In Frum's case, her essential personality traits were in place from the time she was a little girl, in Niagara Falls, where her father was a well-to-do store owner.

"I never was anything other than a miniature version of what I am now," says Frum. This was driven home to her when she read a long-lost cache of letters she had written as a child. "They were letters I wrote throughout my childhood starting at the age of seven, right through until I went to university." In them, Frum saw a continuity of character. "I was just confounded by how similar I am now to what I was then. It was quite unnerving to read this responsible seven-year-old writing home from camp about how she's looking out for her brother and sister."

Probably more important for Frum's career as a celebrated radio host on "As It Happens" for 10 years and "The Journal" from 1981 was her refusal to keep her mouth shut. "I had a very strong sense of equal rights from the earliest time I can remember. I did not know why a five-year-old shouldn't have as much say as a 35-year-old or why my judgment wasn't as good as anybody else's. When people treated me like a child I refused to accept it. I would argue with them and debate with them and say, 'Tell me why I'm wrong.'"

Ever since her youth, Frum has enjoyed affluence in her life, but she's never accepted comfort as her lot. As a girl, she couldn't. For the first year of her life she had to wear a brace for a shoulder that was damaged at birth and is still semiparalyzed. "There are worse handicaps," her mother, Florence, has said, "but a little bit of that kind of punishment goes a long way."

Now in the prime of her life, Frum is still throwing her energy into her career, even though she could relax if she wished. There are three anchors in her life: her mother, with whom she keeps in daily touch by phone; her family, made up of three grown children and husband Murray, a real estate developer she married 34 years ago while both were attending the University of Toronto; and her house. Rather than move into a mansion in Rosedale or Forest Hill, the Frums still live in the York Mills house they bought when they married. Many additions later, their home is the site of some of the best parties in Toronto. As columnist Allan Fotheringham has put it, "If you want to know where power is in Toronto, go to a Barbara Frum party." Fotheringham calls Frum "the den mother, the traffic-cop, among loving (and sometimes warring) personalities in broadcasting, journalism, the book industry and the arts world in general. She mediates feuds, has all the hot new gossip, watches who's on the way up and who's on the way down and generally knows everything that's going on."

When they're not hosting soirees for the powerful, the Frums like to dine with circles of close friends like Julian and Anna Porter (lawyer and publisher respectively), Robert Fulford (a noted journalist and ex-editor of *Saturday Night*) and Gerry Caplan, the NDPer who has been a buddy of Murray's from university days.

For Barbara the home is more of a personal retreat than a venue for socializing. Asked if she has any favourite vacation spots, she replies: "No. That's why I love my house, because we've turned the house into a kind of year-round vacation home. Every place we could, we've punched in a big window. And I've worked on the garden every year now for 10 or 12 years, so it's just beautiful outside those windows every day of the year."

The house is suddenly a lot roomier than it used to be since Frum's three children have moved out on their own. David is making his name in New York at the *Wall Street Journal* as a neoconservative journalist; Linda is the author of a recent book on Canadian universities, which upset academics and students alike; and adopted son Matthew, a native Indian, is making his own way on the West Coast. Rather than let the rooms sit unused, Frum has turned each one of them into an office. "One of them has become a kind of family picture museum. All the pictures I've found of my ancestors are hanging on one wall." (Frum's Jewish forebears emigrated from Kielce, Poland, on her father's side and Odessa, Russia, on her mother's side.) Frum has turned another room into a children's library: "I love children's books and I've never thrown out books that I had from the time I was a child." The third room, Frum describes as "a sort of guest room and an extra cupboard for me."

Yet most of Frum's energy still goes into her 13-hour workdays at "The Journal." Asked to name the highest point in her career, she responds: "I don't think I've reached the highest point yet. Every time I do something well I think, gosh, that's better than I could have ever done it before."

Some would say Frum sounds like a driven individual. She counters: "I don't consider myself driven. I think I'm demanding of myself. I have nothing to prove, and driven suggests something to prove. I'm satisfied with myself. I'm a person I'm proud to be." It's more accurate to explain her energy as a refusal to approach life with complacency. As in her television interviews, Frum gets the last word. "I just really enjoy the topics, and I really care about the truth, and I really care how things turn out."

Other Media Doyens

Peter Gzowski: Gzowski may be the most fantasized-about journalist in Canada. He's the live-in companion, the elusive sensitive male in the lives of millions of women who tune in every weekday morning to "Morningside," his nationwide CBC radio talk show. Toronto-born Gzowski has been a leading light of journalism ever since he became editor of *Maclean's* magazine at the astonishingly young age of 28. He also worked as entertainment editor of the Toronto *Star* and as editor of the now-defunct *Star Weekly*. The print experience never rubbed off — to this day he describes himself as "a magazine person."

His broadcasting experience included stints as host of "This Country in the Morning" and a two-year job as host of a TV talk show, "90 Minutes Live," which flopped. Host of "Morningside" since 1982, Gzowski is known to his staff as a tough, demanding perfectionist. "He's able to walk into the studio at 5:30 a.m., read through his background notes and write his opening commentary; all before he goes on air," says a former producer. On air he's all honey. His warmth brings out the best in his guests; his presence is magically soothing. That combined with his ever-present curiosity makes for good conversation, as his loyal listeners can attest.

Robert Fulford: Fulford is the resident intellectual of Canadian journalism, a noted interlocutor with philosophers, poets and authors on the TV show "Realities," which is remarkable for a Grade 12 dropout. In private, he's also one of the biggest gossips in journalism. At present, he's a professor at Ryerson Polytechnical Institute and a weekly columnist for the *Financial Times of Canada* in Toronto, a position he took after leaving a 20-year tenure as the editor of *Saturday Night* magazine. Like other journalists of his generation, Fulford worked from the ground up without benefit of the advanced education that is required to even get a job interview in journalism today. He grew up in the Beach area of Toronto, son of a reporter and editor of the Canadian Press whom he describes as a "functioning alcoholic." As a teenager, he talked the programming director at CHUM radio into letting him host a program for teens. His first job in newspapers came when he signed on as a copy boy at the *Globe*. That was the beginning of a peripatetic career that took him through most of the major news organizations in Toronto. Among the publications he wrote for: the Toronto *Star* (twice); *Mayfair*, a now-defunct Maclean Hunter magazine; *Canadian Homes and Gardens*; and *Design Engineering*. Along the way, he was a voracious reader, which explains why he now has one of the most fertile minds in journalism.

June Callwood and Trent Frayne: This noted couple have, in their own ways, brought heart and humor to Canadian journalism for decades. Callwood has been a prolific writer on social justice issues in magazines, newspapers and books since the 1950s. She's also a ubiquitous humanitarian and founded Toronto's Jessie's Centre for Teenagers and Casey House Hospice. Frayne, her husband since 1944, is the doyen of sports journalist in Canada noted for his humour and lyrical writing. He is the author of several books.

George Bain: Bain is the id of Canadian journalism, the voice of sober second thought on journalism's strengths and flaws. From his seaside home on Nova Scotia's scenic Mahone Bay, Bain now writes a media watch column for *Maclean's* magazine. Over the past decades, he's served as an editor for major publications including the *Toronto Star* and the *Globe and Mail*.

Richard Gwyn, London correspondent, Toronto *Star*: Before his posting in London, Gwyn spent 12 years as the *Star*'s Ottawa columnist. Tremendous contacts and solid research made him the capital's pundit-in-chief.

Peter Cook, economics editor, *Globe and Mail*: Cook is a cerebral, Cambridge-educated writer who's viewed as being the brightest individual in the *Globe* newsroom. His fresh, generally right-of-centre insights into economic issues have made him the most widely read economic columnist in Canada.

David Crane, business editor, Toronto *Star*: Crane is one of the country's most eloquent spokesmen for the liberal perspective on the economic issues of the day, from free trade to industrial strategy. He and Cook are social friends despite their differing perspectives.

Jeffrey Simpson, Ottawa columnist, *Globe and Mail*: Professorial in mien, rigorous in intellect, Simpson specializes in sober analysis of weighty issues. He tends to lay out the pros and cons of government policies and actions with a fairness that sometimes borders on equivocation. Simpson is the strongest contender for Gwyn's mantle as Ottawa pundit-in-chief.

Carol Goar, Ottawa columnist, Toronto *Star*: Goar's reasoned and balanced analysis of national issues makes her a must read for Liberals and Conservatives alike. An intense, dedicated reporter, who rarely cracks a smile, her single-mindedness pays off in the quality of what she writes. Typical was an assessment of free trade with the United States, written in 1990. The feature was so balanced that the anti-trade deal editors at the *Star* must have been nonplussed.

Marjorie Nichols, syndicated Ottawa columnist, Ottawa *Citizen* and 17 other Southam-owned papers: Nichols has been described by Allan Fotheringham as "the most uncompromising journalist in Canada." She carves up issues (more frequently than people) with barbed words, incisive put-downs and generally unrestrained descriptives.

Don McGillivray: Another Southam columnist, McGillivray is known for his dislike of leaving his file-filled office for the sort of schmoozing that other scribes thrive on — and for his lucid dissections of Tory flaws.

Doug Fisher, Ottawa columnist, Toronto *Sun*: A one-time MP, Fisher has been a columnist for more than 25 years, and his far-right views haven't altered much during that time. A some-time guest of the Mulroneys, he lashes out at everyone from leftist journalists to feminists and gays. He's criticized the "large-scale nastiness of the media assessment of the Mulroney government" and the "pervasive anti-conservatism of the press."

Charles Lynch: A columnist for about 30 years, Lynch has seen eight prime ministers come and go and never asked one of them for an interview. Throughout a career that took him to London during the Blitz, the Normandy invasion and South America, he has outlived any number of dilettantes.

Michel Vastel, Ottawa columnist, *Le Soleil* (Quebec City): The author of two controversial books on Pierre Trudeau and Robert Bourassa, Vastel sways opinion in a *Le Soleil* column and on his personal talk show, "Sans Detour." He's one of several leading Québécois political commentators with loyal audiences. The others are Pierre Nadeau, a former Radio-Canada reporter who now hosts a political talk show on Télé-Métropole; Francine Pelletier, a *La Presse* columnist who makes regular nationwide appearances on CTV's "Sunday Edition"; and Alain Dubuc, the most popular columnist at *La Presse* and a regular commentator on French TV.

William Johnson, Ottawa political columnist, Montreal *Gazette*: A Jesuit-trained mind and a dedication to intellectual rigour make Johnson must reading for bureaucrats and politicians in Ottawa. Johnson developed his skills in stints as the *Globe*'s correspondent in Washington and Quebec. He's known as a die-hard Trudeau-style liberal.

Stewart MacLeod, Ottawa columnist, Thomson News Service: MacLeod doesn't generally make big waves with his criticisms of government, but what he does say sends ripples a long way. His words reach 1 million readers in 49 small papers across Canada. He's the primary source of political comment for voters in 80 federal ridings. MacLeod's journalism hasn't gone entirely unnoticed by the media elite. In 1990, a guest column in *Maclean's* magazine won him the Gold National Magazine Award for humour writing.

David Halton, political correspondent, CBC-TV: Halton was part of the CBC Parliament Hill team from 1976 and was recently posted to Washington to cover U.S. government policy. Along with former CBC colleague Mike Duffy, now a CTV commentator, Halton ranked as the journalist with the best contacts on the Hill. They aren't nearly so good in his new beat — just give him time. Halton's place has been taken by Joe Schlesinger, who brings to Ottawa his ability to make even the most mundane news event sound mysterious.

The Leading Iconoclasts

Whether they're called investigative reporters, left-wingers or raving right-wingers, the iconoclasts are the writers and commentators who buck the mainstream and unsettle the minds of the politically comfortable.

Walter Stewart: Now running his own magazine, *Policy Options*, Stewart is the premier gadfly of Canadian journalism. Quick-tongued and sharp-witted, Stewart has managed to upset just about everyone in power he's ever written about during his 38-year career. He's done it through best-selling books like *Shrug: Trudeau in Power*, *Towers of Gold, Feet of Clay* (on banks) and *Uneasy Lies the Head* (on Crown corporations). And he's done it at a variety of publications ranging from the Toronto *Telegram* to the *Star Weekly* and *Maclean's*, where he was managing editor. Stewart is the nagging voice of conscience sitting on the shoulder of Canadian journalism.

Allan Fotheringham, columnist, *Maclean's* and the Toronto *Sun*: Fotheringham is Canada's master of artful invective, the country's lighthearted answer to H.L. Mencken. The man who coined such phrases as "the chin that walks like a man" (to describe Mulroney), the "regressive Conservatives" and a thousand other crafty turns of phrase, Fotheringham is a specialist in tweaking the noses of anyone who has political power. He describes himself as a "card-carrying limousine liberal," but his friendship with Mulroney grew so close during a tenure in Ottawa that he banished himself to Washington for a spell to regain his objectivity.

Sometimes Fotheringham's attacks backfire, especially when they're against fellow journalists.

Jack Webster: The Vancouver-based T.V. talk-show host is the leading iconoclast in British Columbia. Raised in Glasgow and trained on Fleet Street, Webster emigrated to Canada in 1947 and landed a job as a junior reporter at the Vancouver *Sun*. He moved to radio in 1963 and quickly built a reputation as a talk-show host. His dense Scottish brogue and aggressive style earned him the sobriquet: the Haggis McBagpipe. When he moved his performance to television, viewers were delighted to be able to watch him in action as well as hear him as he pricks the bubbles of the powerful.

Barbara Amiel, columnist, *Maclean's*: Angel of the right, defender of individual rights against fuzzy-minded social-fixers, Amiel enrages even middle-of-the road thinkers with her columns. Her favourite targets are the thought police of the left and human rights activists who seek to remedy society's ills with government intervention. Now contemplating life from an English garden (which she shares with

her British businessman husband), Amiel also writes a column for *The Times* of London.

Terence Corcoran, business columnist, *Globe and Mail*: Corcoran's far-right economic views have enraged liberal-minded thinkers ever since he left an early career in banking to become a journalist. His opinions emerge in a pure strain of conservative thinking that caused one critic, Allan Fotheringham, to muse, "He seems to feel that capitalism would be better served if the children went back into the mines."

Conclusion

There is little doubt that the gatekeepers in print and television have earned their positions by merit and ambition. Yet this is only part of the story. In print, those with the "right" backgrounds (that is, male, white and Protestant) hold most of the positions of authority in the editing offices. There is more diversity among the television gatekeepers, illustrated by the presence of women like Trina McQueen and iconoclasts like Elly Alboim in the inner circles of power. But study after study has shown that women and nonwhites are making only plodding progress up the ranks of power in television news.

Thus, there is only a limited openness to newcomers among the gatekeepers of the media elite. However, the views expressed by the gatekeepers regarding editorial independence and the need for the media to objectively assess news events are reassuring for those concerned about the independence of the media.

So it's an oversimplification to characterize the news media as the servant of society's ruling elites. To be sure, these are strong forces working against editorial independence. At the top of the power structure, corporate concentration works hand in hand with the commercial concerns of owners as a constrictive force on editorial diversity. The homogeneity of the gatekeepers, especially in the print media, and the lack of women and nonwhites, in both print and television, is another factor that works against the media conveying a diversity of "voices." Countering this is the widespread determination of the gatekeepers to respect the line between commercial concerns and editorial content, especially at larger organizations with the financial means to risk constantly offending advertisers or other powerful interests. But the strongest force for editorial independence comes from the journalists themselves. They have many common traits: generally, journalists are small "l" liberal in persuasion, they come from the middle class, and their ranks are still dominated by white males. This isn't cause for equanimity, but it's at least partially reassuring that the circle of power represented by the media elite isn't in anyone's back pocket.

The more unsettling question is whether the people who make up the news media in particular are qualified as a group to serve as our new priestly class. Journalists have no catechism, no ten commandments to guide their conduct; they have only a broadly defined sense of social responsibility, which varies in intensity depending on the individual. Yet, the news media can hardly be blamed for its growing influence over society. In large part, that influence has been magnified by the diminishing respect of the citizenry for Canada's religious and political institutions. Power always expands to fill a vacuum.

Chapter 11

The Film Industry

It's one of those glorious summer days that make Haligonians feel that Mother Nature has chosen their city for her private little arboretum on the Atlantic. Everything is just right: a hot sun, plenty of ancient shade trees, and a cool breeze off the ocean. The splendid day doesn't do a thing, however, for the mood of Paul Donovan, 35, successful film director and Halifax resident. He's come to a trendy little bistro for lunch and a conversation about the state of the Canadian film industry — and he's at his bilious best. "Films in this country are made for tax reasons, for lobbying reasons," he says. "But what about the merits of the script?"

Filmmakers pride themselves on their role as observers and critics of human affairs, but few of them in Canada are willing to risk financial purgatory by criticizing the system that nourishes them. Donovan is. The outspoken filmmaker is one of three partners (the others are his brother, Michael, and Maura O'Connell) who run Salter Street Films, the Atlantic region's largest and most successful producer of films for theatres and TV.

While brother Michael is best known as the producer of the CBC comedy series "Codco," Paul has carved out a niche writing and directing films, from early B-movie moneymakers like *Siege* and *Def Con 4*, to artistic successes such as the award-winning TV drama *Squamish Five* and the children's movie *George's Island*.

"The Canadian film industry is in an artificial stage," says Donovan. "It exists on subsidies. Telefilm has $130 to $150 million to spend each year. That's incredible power." Donovan thinks it's a mistake to have career bureaucrats running the system. "There's a complete lack of filmmaking talent in the bureaucracy. It needs a real turnover at the top. We need to put filmmakers at the top."

But the real *bête noire* of the business, as Donovan sees it, is the insidious, all-pervasive power of Hollywood over the Canadian film industry. "Ninety per cent of all money that changes hands in the film industry changes hands in Los Angeles. The key agents, key actors and studio heads are the centre of power. They're all in the same party circuit, the parties at Brentwood, Pacific Palisades and Beverly Hills. I have contempt for these people. And their influence in Canada is enormous. They can make a bad movie and play it for three weeks at my local movie house. They have the power to ram films down the public's throat."

Donovan has a point. It is an act of faith to even talk about the Canadian film industry as an elite group. A sceptic might ask just how much influence over our culture our filmmakers can have when almost all the movies available in our theatres, on TV and in our video stores are products of the Big Six Hollywood studios (Columbia, MGM/United Artists, Paramount, 20th Century-Fox, Universal and Warner Brothers). In 1989 alone American companies raked in $360 million at Canadian box offices and made almost $300 million selling us TV programs and another $1 billion or so in video sales and rentals. The average Canadian probably couldn't even name a few good home-grown movies or top filmmakers. The country has a strong tradition in documentaries, dating from the days of John Grierson, who founded the National Film Board in 1939. But that has left us in the strange situation, as one pundit put it, of recording our realities on film and importing our fantasies.

This has hardly been necessary, since the basic ingredients of most people's fantasy lives — sin, sex, romance, scandal, betrayal, violence, greed, hatred and crime — can just as easily be set in Saint John, Montreal or Saskatoon as in Miami or Manhattan. Canadian cities are a fertile ground for any film-writer's imagination. It's hard to beat Toronto for avarice and power-lust, Montreal for sensuousness, Vancouver for the celebration of health and the outdoors or Winnipeg for human endurance. Nor do American filmmakers have any corner on the ability to spin tales that uplift the spirit or speak to universal human experience.

There are forces at work that should cheer up filmgoers who are tired of endless car-crash scenes and flying bullets at their local cinema. Canada's film industry is enjoying a tremendous surge of creative energy, and it's not entirely tied to tax write-offs like the 1970s tax-shelter boom.

Today, more talented filmmakers are working in Canada than ever before. The auteur-directors, like Atom Egoyan, Patricia Rozema and Denys Arcand, are making films that put their distinctive creative visions ahead of commercial tastes. And, to the surprise of everyone, they're making money at it.

Changes are also under way in the style and content of Canadian film. Piers Handling, a Toronto critic and film historian, believes that Canadian film has been typical of colonized countries, often dwelling on "marginal people who are perceived as victims." Our films have been marked by a strong sense of social and often political conscience, he says. "Absent is the sense of optimism in the individual and the ability to effect change, which is so prevalent in American literature and cinema."

The new generation of filmmakers is breaking out of the old aesthetic straitjacket. Their production styles are more diverse. They shock (David Cronenberg's *Dead Ringers*), they are tinged with surrealism (Atom Egoyan's *Family Viewing*) or they tell conventional tales with a distinctive reflective and atmospheric rhythm (William MacGillivray's *Life Classes*).

"There is a growing maturity and authority at work," notes Handling. "A distinguishing mark of our cinema has been its adolescent nature expressed in the number of films that have dealt with the rite of passage into adulthood. There are signs that this is changing. Recently, the terrain has shifted to the more complex problems of middle age, indeed to the middle class that wields power." The works of Edmonton's Anne Wheeler (*Bye Bye Blues*) and Montreal's Denys Arcand (*Decline of the American Empire, Jesus of Montreal*) are good examples.

So will this talent have room to flourish? Certainly, Canada is still Hollywood's back yard, but at last the federal government is taking steps to ensure Canadian companies have a patch of grass to play on. The major problem has been that U.S. distributors lump Canada together with the U.S. market and typically buy North American rights for independent films — virtually shutting out Canadian distributors — and rely on moneymakers from Hollywood to fill screen time. New federal laws have been designed to make sure the Canadian market is treated separately, thereby giving Canadian distributors a shot at winning distribution rights. If ever they are passed into law, they would prove a financial bonanza for Canadian distributors — the money can be poured back into local production — and would result in more screen time for home-grown films.

The Canadian film industry is an elite in the making, one that should and could have an enormous influence on the values of Canadians. "Film is an incredibly powerful medium," says Wayne Clarkson, executive director of the Canadian Centre for Advanced Film Studies. "The average Ontarian goes to about four or five films a year, and that's true generally about North America. But look at the impact of, say, *Batman* on world culture, let alone the North American culture." TV has a long-term insidious influence, he adds, "but movie-making is the single most important medium, dramatically speaking."

No one is expecting Canadian filmmakers to turn out megamillion-dollar productions like *Batman*. A typical big-budget Canadian movie runs in the $4- to $5-million range. But just about everyone (except Jack Valenti, the head flack of the American movie makers) understands the importance of winning more screen time for movies that reflect Canadian realities and fantasies, or simply make some comment on the human condition in the late twentieth century without resorting to Hollywood formulas.

So who has the power in Canada's emerging film elite that intends to define our cultural values? How do they wield that power, and who's shut out?

Donovan is right to locate the centre of power at the desks of bureaucrats who hand out taxpayers' money, which remains the lifeblood of the industry. Professional mandarins at federal government funding agencies like Telefilm Canada and the National Film Board, as well as various provincial bodies that have sprung up across the country to fund local productions, control the destinies of the majority of filmmakers, who rely on public money to finance the lion's share of their production costs. These mandarins team up with broadcast executives to fund made-for-TV movies, dramatic series, variety specials, children's programs and documentaries. The most influential of these broadcast executives is Ivan Fecan, programming chief for English-language CBC-TV. Between them these bank-rolling bureaucrats and broadcast executives are the arbiters of taste in the Canadian film and TV industry. They have broad powers to define the type of work that gets made, from low-budget schlock to high-brow fare, and to define what is appropriate cultural content.

The second tier in the power rankings is made up of the bankable producers and directors — mostly men — who have shown that they can make money for their investors in the public and private sectors.

Because the most powerful of the movie moguls (mandarins, broadcast executives and producers) work in Toronto and Montreal, directors and producers in the rest of Canada feel alienated from the action. They've grown tired of the $500-cup-of-coffee syndrome — the cost of a plane fare just to win a 15-minute chat with a central Canadian powerbroker.

In contrast with the other elite groups studied in this book, the film industry is peopled by a polyglot collection from diverse backgrounds. Explains Wayne Clarkson: "It has always been a fly-by-the-seat-of-your-pants industry, and it can't afford to be restrictive in its attitudes toward racial backgrounds. By and large, if you're prepared to work for nothing, stick your neck out and work 24 hours a day, get in here. If you're lucky, six months from now you might be a filmmaker or run the company."

Clarkson sees the efforts of people from minority cultures as crucial to the vitality of the industry. "One of my long-standing fears is that perhaps there is something in our character that's a hindrance to making good films." Canadians, he says, are "contemplative, considerate and informed. Our tradition has been documentary filmmaking." But movie-making, he says, is "Big Screen. It's big, it's brash, it's loud." Clarkson hopes that as Canada's Calvinist tradition breaks down, as the racial makeup of the country changes, there will emerge "some incredible stories that must be told." But even if race matters little in the movie business, gender still does. "Producers are still predominantly men," says Clarkson. "They run the power end, they have access to the pools of money, the access to banks." Clarkson's comments are backed up by a 1990 study published by Toronto Women in Film and Video. The study showed that women made up 35 per cent of the 40,708 people working or available for work in Canadian film and independent television production. But they did not have a proportionate share of the public funds or senior jobs. Women received only 9 per cent of the $72.5 million handed out to Canadian producers in 1987-88 by Telefilm Canada. In the private sector, women represented only 29 per cent of producers, 16 per cent of directors and 38 per cent of writers. They dominated clerical positions and wardrobe, makeup and hairstyle jobs. While the film industry has traditionally been very open to a hodge-podge of ethnic groups, and still is, women have only recently entered the production end of the business, where the money, and hence the power, lies.

Bureaucrat Power

"The Canadian film industry," says one Canadian film director, "is run by career bureaucrats. The successful film, the one that gets made, is the one for which the most lobbying has been done."

The Mogul in Mandarin's Clothing

Pierre DesRoches: Sitting in the reception area of Telefilm Canada is not a reassuring experience for any director who has made it to the fourteenth-floor office of the federal funding agency in downtown Montreal. A menacing, abstract mural, used in the movie *Un Zoo, la nuit* (*Night Zoo*), hangs on one wall. A sinister eye, with a drop of blood trailing down, peers out at waiting supplicants, making sure they have a good case of the jitters before they enter the inner sanctum of Pierre DesRoches, executive director.

DesRoches is a very powerful man. He's Canada's version of a Hollywood movie mogul. His outfit, Telefilm, functions as the country's major studio, deciding the fate of films and their directors by picking who will get cash and who won't. Telefilm typically turns down three out of four proposals for feature films, TV dramas and videos. That makes for a lot of unhappy would-be directors. The lucky 25 per cent share roughly $150 million, mostly provided by taxpayers.

In person, DesRoches, 60, doesn't look the part at all. With his bushy eyebrows and bright, owlish eyes he resembles the Wizard of Oz more than David O. Selznick. He's a portly man with a double chin, but one senses he got it from his wife's cooking, not from consuming too many martinis while talking to breathless starlets.

DesRoches is a phlegmatic career bureaucrat who survived a couple of decades at the CBC intact, which makes him something of a rarity. He joined the CBC's record library in his twenties and progressed through the ranks, eventually becoming a vice-president with eight vice-presidents reporting to him and a budget of about $700 million.

When DesRoches took the Telefilm job in June 1988, at the request of Flora MacDonald, then communications minister, he walked into a nasty situation of infighting and political turmoil. Telefilm's finances were in a mess, its reputation had been tainted by political interference from above and it had almost completely lost the confidence of the film industry.

The scandal burst into the open in the fall of 1987, when executive director Peter Pearson was forced to resign under pressure from Telefilm's board. Pearson's political masters had decided that his management abilities left something to be desired. This was made clear by Pearson's boss, Telefilm chairman Jean Sirois (a lawyer whose independence was doubted in some quarters because he was a buddy of Prime Minister Brian Mulroney and a Tory fund raiser). Just after Pearson left, Sirois startled the film community by announcing with dismay that the agency had overcommitted itself financially for the fiscal year. The implication: Pearson had botched up the agency's finances.

Privately, Pearson got off a volley of his own. In his resignation letter to Flora MacDonald, he charged Sirois with politically interfering in Telefilm's operations.

As it turned out, Pearson had a point. Writing about the spat, Toronto *Star* columnist Sid Adilman reported at least two occasions when Telefilm decisions were overturned by calls from MacDonald's office. In one case, Telefilm had decided not to give any more funds to the TV series "Diamonds" because it didn't like the financial terms offered by the series' private investor. The investor, Barry Young, of Toronto's Sklyd Group, went over the bureaucrats' heads, and in no time one of MacDonald's senior aides called the agency to demand that the decision be overturned. Another time, MacDonald and her aides pushed Telefilm's staff to go ahead with an investment in *Bethune: The Making of a Hero*, despite Telefilm's reluctance, because she had to sign an official film agreement with China and *Bethune* was the lynchpin. (Eventually Telefilm sunk $8 million into the problem-plagued, repeatedly delayed production of the movie, which was finally released to mixed reviews in 1990.)

These are all memories DesRoches is trying to put behind him at Telefilm. He is willing to explain what went wrong under Pearson in order to lay the controversy to rest. The financial problems arose, he says, because in the five years until 1987, Telefilm ended up each year with money left unspent. (Ending a year with a surplus can mean the next year's budget is cut back. Spend It or Lose It is the motto of good bureaucrats everywhere.) The unspent cash for the 1987 fiscal year totalled $17 million. Indeed, the government did refuse to let the agency have the $17 million for the following year.

As a result, DesRoches explains, the Telefilm executives said, "Listen, it's not going to happen any more" and asked filmmakers to send in more projects. The line-up of supplicants at Telefilm's door turned into a crowd in June when Finance Minister Michael Wilson scaled down tax write-offs for investments in Canadian movies, scaring off private investors and sending producers running to Telefilm for more funds. But when a rush of projects was submitted and approved, it suddenly looked as though Telefilm had accepted too many projects. (It was hard to tell for sure because of the agency's sloppy administration methods. Between April and September, for instance, about $33 million had been promised to producers on the strength of "verbal assurances" instead of proper documentation.) Alarmed, the agency shut the spigot abruptly, causing panic in the subsidy-reliant industry. As it turned out, that was an overreaction. "By year end, they found they had too much money left, so they started to zoom the machine again," says DesRoches.

When DesRoches arrived at Telefilm in June 1988, he moved to smooth out the financial roller coaster at the agency. He stopped the policy of funding projects on a first-come, first-served basis. Now Telefilm spreads its investments more evenly through the year. He's also revamped the departments at head office and given more autonomy to the four regional offices.

Everyone agrees that DesRoches has accomplished his goal of stabilizing Telefilm and has helped it regain some credibility with the film industry. He has earned a reputation as a man who can make order out of mayhem, and that's one reason he was widely touted as a strong candidate for president of the CBC in 1989, a job that eventually went to broadcaster Patrick Watson.

The greatest challenge that DesRoches faces is to prove to the industry that Telefilm isn't a thoroughly politicized beast that fulfils the whims of its political masters. In the past it earned a reputation for doling out funds to the producers who had the tightest connections with cabinet ministers. DesRoches asserts that he does not have any potentially compromising political connections.

Has Telefilm cast off its reputation as a political animal? "Well, I can tell you, I have been here for 16 months. I haven't had one call from any minister's office, including my own minister," DesRoches said in a 1989 interview. No doubt true. But all that means is that DesRoches himself didn't take the call from the Prime Minister's Office to find some funds for a movie being produced by Halifax filmmaker Paul Donovan in 1988. Perhaps DesRoches's underlings did. When Donovan applied to Telefilm for funds for a children's adventure called *George's Island* in midyear, he was turned down because the agency had already spent its budget for the year. But Donovan's major investor, Halifax stockbroker J.W. Ritchie, the wealthy owner of Scotia Bond, wouldn't take no for an answer. A well-connected Tory, Ritchie had two avenues of influence. He was good friends both with Mulroney crony Fred Doucet (whom Ritchie talked to about the problem) and with Edmund Bovey, chairman of Telefilm at the time. No one, including Donovan, will talk about the episode or reveal who called the PMO, but a little arm-twisting did the trick. *George's Island* got its funding.

DesRoches may have some way to go in ridding Telefilm of its political stigma, but his management skills are uncontested; he's a master bureaucrat who has come a long way from his origins as a draftsman's son from central Montreal. One of five children, Des-

Roches took the favoured route for upwardly mobile Quebeckers. He attended Collège Sainte-Marie, a private classical college run by the Sisters of Providence. After earning a B.A. in humanities, he went to work for the CBC's record library with hopes of producing a music program. He worked for a while as a film director in the children's department before he found his calling as an administrator. At 29 he became head of the CBC's youth department for French Canada, overseeing 35 programs a week. From there, his career path went straight upwards till he arrived in the CBC stratosphere, serving as executive vice-president of planning and then vice-president and general manager of French services.

Running Telefilm is not just another stop in DesRoches's progress up the bureaucratic ladder. He deeply believes in the importance of film to Canadian culture. Leaning forward in his chair, DesRoches speaks with a passion and eloquence that could convert Sylvester Stallone to the cause of Canadian cultural nationalism. "We spend billions and billions of dollars educating our children, and yet we don't have the guts to spend enough money for our children to see things, at movie theatres or on television, that carry our values," he says. "The fantasies and fiction in feature films and television dramas carry our values as a society. They have more influence on our values than anything else that is done culturally, including hockey or baseball games. So when we do a feature film, when we do television, it is the basis of building a society."

It is a little known fact that DesRoches's passion for film extends to his private life. When he's not deciding on the fate of projects by well-known producers, he is a filmmaker himself, using an 8-mm Sony. DesRoches refers to his films as "small documentaries" to distinguish them from the sort of family movies fathers are shooting everywhere. But don't expect to see a DesRoches movie appear at a theatre near you. Reluctant to talk about his amateur efforts, DesRoches says he shows his films only to a few close friends.

Anyone who has any doubt about the significance of Telefilm to the film business need only consider some of the movies and TV dramas that cash from the agency has made possible. In 1987 and 1988 Telefilm poured $22.6 million and $36.8 million respectively into such well-known titles as *My American Cousin, American Boy-*

friends, Bye Bye Blues, Cold Front, Malarek: A Street Kid Who Made It, Speaking Parts, Jesus of Montreal, A Winter Tan, The Outside Chance of Maximilian Glick, Palais Royale, Tommy Tricker and the Stamp Traveller, La grenouille et la baleine, and *Trois pommes à côté du sommeil.* Then there are lesser-known productions, such as *Dykes on Bikes.*

On the TV drama front, Telefilm has provided crucial funds for just about every worthwhile production in Canada. In 1988 it invested $60.1 million in 142 series and programs. They included such dramas as "Degrassi Junior High," "Danger Bay" and "Glory Enough for All," kids shows such as "Raccoons," "My Pet Monster," "The Care Bears," "Babar" and "Sharon, Lois and Bram's Elephant Show" and important documentaries such as "The Struggle for Democracy," "The World Is Watching" and "A Rustling of Leaves: Inside the Philippine Revolution." The irony, of course, is that most Canadians aren't aware that many of the best movies and TV shows they and their children watch are Canadian rather than American productions.

Telefilm sits like a Mother Sow over the industry, suckling filmmakers like so many offspring that haven't been weaned. It is the single largest investor in Canadian productions, providing vital sustenance for artists who couldn't survive on the cash trickling in from other public and private investors. For example, in 1988, Telefilm supplied more than $22 million for feature films. Other public agencies, the National Film Board and various provincial film development agencies invested only $14.7 million combined. Private distributors chipped in about $13 million. Broadcasters, including the major networks CBC and CTV, should be ashamed of their stinginess; they invested only $5.1 million in Canadian feature films, and $4.4 million of that was provided by pay-TV companies. Private investors anted up an inadequate $19.1 million.

With figures like that, it is inevitable that the film industry will remain firmly in the public sector's debt (in both senses of the word), rather than in the private sector's. The rules of the game will be laid down by bureaucrats rather than businessmen. And what are the rules of the game laid down by Pierre DesRoches?

He favours funding established filmmakers over aspiring ones; he favours films with a high degree of Canadian cultural content; he intends to continue Telefilm's policy of pouring about two-thirds of its money into English-language productions and one-third into French-language productions; and he will continue to fund films on the merits of their quality, not according to politically inspired considerations of spreading money equally among the country's regions.

This last principle is, predictably, the most controversial with anyone outside Toronto and Montreal, the nation's two largest film production centres. But DesRoches is adamant. "I'm against setting aside any regional envelopes [of cash]," he says. "We're going on quality of product. If the B.C. people don't feel they can come up with a good idea for a film, then that's just too bad for them."

Ivan Fecan: Taste-maker for the Nation. It's a boring Saturday night in 1978, and Ivan Fecan, a rookie news producer for a Toronto TV station, is at home listening to police reports on his radio-wave scanner when he hears of a disaster in the making. A CP freight train has derailed and exploded in Mississauga, just west of Toronto. Police and emergency crews are rushing to the scene. Fecan calls for a camera crew, then rushes to the scene and arrives even before police roadblocks are set up. His camera crew arrives moments later. Fecan beckons his sidekick, Fred Mahon, a cameraman, to follow him, and the two make their way closer to the inferno for a good tight shot. They are not aware that the overturned freight cars are leaking poisonous chlorine gas that will later prompt the evacuation of 250,000 people.

Edging closer to the flames, the pair reach a wire fence. As Fecan jumps the fence, carrying a hand-held camera, another explosion erupts, and he lands hard, snapping his ankle. He lies in the searing heat, just metres from the flames, as Mahon gets good footage for the news.

Even though it sounds like a plot for a TV show, the episode was a real-life adventure of Ivan Fecan in the days before he became a TV mogul. The 1978 mishap occurred while he was the producer of "Citypulse" news in Toronto. Today, at 38, Fecan is director of programming at CBC-TV, where he presides over the life and death of CBC's cultural fare, from "Street Legal" to "Degrassi Junior High" and "Road to Avonlea." His power stretches from Halifax to Vancouver, since he alone has the final say over whether in-house or independently produced series, variety programs and made-for-TV movies will receive funding and be shown on the CBC network. This highly centralized system is his creation and makes him the most powerful director of programming in the history of the CBC.

Fecan's made-for-TV bravado at the Mississauga train disaster partly explains why he has shot to the top of the industry. Recalling the incident, he explains: "Every time I've ever worked at something, I throw myself into it entirely, because I don't think you can do anything well if you only do it for a few hours a day. It has to be all-consuming." Yet there's obviously a lot more to his success than zeal, which is a fairly common trait among hungry young media types. In a career that has taken Fecan from CBC Radio to CITY-TV and CBLT in Toronto, to NBC in Los Angeles and then back to the Mother Corp. (CBC) in Toronto, he has been propelled upward by his instincts for what makes a good show that will attract large audiences. As the cultural czar of the CBC, Fecan's instincts, and the values that he thinks television should nurture, have become crucial to Canadian culture in the country's most powerful medium.

Canadians' evolving cultural identity rests to a great extent in Fecan's hands, whether they like it or not — and some Canadians decidedly don't. One of his most vocal critics is John Haslett Cuff of the *Globe and Mail*, who has written: "In its continuing, dollar-driven quest for the mass audience, the CBC English network has become increasingly vapid, imitative, and distressingly commercial. Most of the new Canadian shows it has developed derive from the American TV series formula and seem designed to be as slick and generic as possible reflecting almost nothing of the reality Canadians face today."

Four years into his mandate at CBC, the question still hanging over the head of Ivan Fecan is black and white: Is he the *wunderkind* who is rescuing CBC or the *enfant terrible* who is wrecking it?

The CBC's cultural taste-maker developed his values in an immigrant enclave in Toronto. Fecan was born in 1953 to a Ukrainian father and a Russian mother, who immigrated separately to Canada in the late 1940s and met shortly afterward. They split up while their only son was still a toddler. Fecan grew up near College and

Bathurst in Toronto, a low-income area, populated by a myriad of ethnic groups. "The neighbourhood was completely polyglot," he says. "A big mystery in my life was 'What was a WASP?' because there were none there. There were people from Jamaica, from Italy, Greece, Eastern European Jewish, and lots of Romanians, Poles, Russians. It wasn't a rich neighbourhood, but it wasn't a violent neighbourhood." (Fecan still has a multicultural outlook. He encourages his producers and heads of development to regularly ride the Carlton streetcar in Toronto to avoid white, yuppie myopia, and he was a strong backer of "Inside Stories," a series of dramas developed to reflect the lives and concerns of visible minorities in Canada.)

Fecan was raised by his mother, who worked as an operating-room aide, and his grandmother. It was a religious home (Eastern Orthodox) and a natural spawning ground for a high achiever. Fecan says that, together, his mother and grandmother had by far the largest influence on his life. "They were the toughest two women I have known in my life. Whatever I did, I was told I could do better. I would give any rock or wrestling promoter 10 seconds in the room with them and they could take care of him."

Fecan was educated at local schools, then enrolled in York University's Fine Arts program. He never graduated, though he aced the program's third- and fourth-year courses. The problem was he was too impatient to take some first-year courses that were prerequisites for a degree.

After leaving York, he landed a job with CBC Radio in Toronto in 1974 and worked successively as a producer on three hit shows, "Identities," "Quirks and Quarks" and "Sunday Morning." The radio experience taught him the tricks of story-telling that he's used ever since in judging scripts. "I learned the narrative form. Most people miss that when they try to pigeon-hole me as a television person."

Fecan jumped over to television in 1976, when Moses Znaimer hired him to help produce a fledgling news show, "CityPulse." "There was a basic philosophy at 'CityPulse' that there is more truth on the street talking to real people," says Fecan.

From 1980 to 1982 he served as program director for CBC's largest local TV station, CBLT in Toronto. Next, he moved over to the network operation to become director of program development, then head of variety programming. In those jobs, he set out to re-establish the star system in Canadian television: he wooed celebrities like Anne Murray, Toller Cranston and Murray McLauchlan back to the network to do variety specials. Aside from those mass-audience hits, he backed such shows as "Second City's 25th Anniversary," and more artistic endeavours like "King of Friday Night," "I Am a Hotel" and "Indigo."

By the mid-1980s, Fecan's reputation had spread to NBC, where in 1985 NBC's head of entertainment, Brandon Tartikoff, hired Fecan as his vice-president of creative affairs. At the age of 32, Fecan found himself working at the epicentre of American network television. His job was a combination of developing show concepts and firefighting in problem areas. Despite the title and responsibilities, Fecan saw his two-year stint at NBC as an apprenticeship. "When I went to NBC, in many ways I had to start over. I had to entirely relearn the business, and a lot of things I thought I knew I didn't. So a fair amount of humility was called for."

Fecan values part of what he learned at NBC. "I learned how to bring something in on budget and to increase market share. If you are to survive you have to learn to do this very well." But he didn't become an unquestioning disciple of American-style programming and was eager to return to Toronto when Denis Harvey invited him back in 1987. "I had to leave because I didn't believe in everything they believed in and I wanted to try a different way," he says. "There are a lot of shows that I do here or have some influence on which run against everything that American television teaches you." The style of Canadian shows, he says, "is much more blunt, it's rougher in texture, it doesn't have blonde, blue-eyed leads, it wears its heart and its soul on its sleeve a lot more and is a lot more emotionally confrontational than American television." Fecan says CBC's productions are also "a lot less violent" than U.S. shows and don't offer giggle-and-jiggle fare.

The move back to Toronto hurt Fecan financially — the cut in salary was enormous — yet was rewarding emotionally and intellectually. For one thing, it ended the constant commuting between him and his wife, Sandra Faire, a CBC producer in Toronto. It also gave him a chance to pursue his vision for Canadian TV.

It's easy to understand why Fecan has been tagged the boy wonder for the past decade or so. In person, he fits the image perfectly. He is strikingly handsome in an old-world European way. Two generations back, his maternal ancestors were members of the Russian intelligentsia, which probably helps explain why he looks and carries himself like a member of the czar's court. The face is fine-boned, with an aquiline nose that curves down gracefully to a mouth of perfect proportions. (The lips are narrow, but not so thin as to suggest dourness.) Light-brown hair sweeps back from his high forehead in undisciplined locks that he brushes back with sweeps of his hand. The dashes of premature grey hair at his temples complete the refined image. Fecan's dress and office decor provide hints of a perfectionist, stand-offish personality. The aquamarine walls of his office, the blue-green coffee table, and white leather couches set a perfectly cool mood for a practitioner of the cool medium, as media types call television. A large TV screen in one corner and a smaller set on his desk flicker soundlessly.

Sitting behind his modern glass-topped desk, Fecan talks about his goals for CBC programming, what kinds of show he wants to run and how he decides whether to fund the proposals for shows that flood into his office. "When I came here in 1987, everybody said that no Canadian drama can compete with the American. Our audience will never watch them. The other assumption was that the only chance we had was to make 'Europlays,' programs that would be seen around the world if they were a little American, a little British, a little French and set somewhere over the mid-Atlantic. My personal beliefs were and still are that our audiences will watch our shows if they have quality and they are culturally specific and if we don't make compromises for foreign sales. The world will watch them as well if we do our job right."

Those convictions have made Fecan the torch-bearer for the CBC's Canadianization targets. Shortly before he was hired in 1986, the upper management of CBC English television had decided that it was time for the public network to make a drastic break with its past. For 30 years the CBC had been making on-and-off progress toward increasing its Canadian programming but had never been able to afford it. (Buying ready-made U.S. shows is immensely cheaper than producing shows at home.) But in 1986, the brass decided to cut back on U.S. fare and push for 95 per cent Canadian programming within three years.

In August 1987, Denis Harvey, the irascible vice-president of English television, hired Fecan away from his job as vice-president of creative affairs for NBC in Los Angeles. Continued budget-slashing at CBC has prevented Fecan from meeting his three-year deadline, and the goal is now 1992 or beyond, yet there's no disputing that he has moved relentlessly toward fulfilling his mandate.

As vice-president of programming, Fecan spends a lot of time deciding on time slots for the entire CBC weekly schedule. His most crucial influence has been over new program development. Early on, he made some of his most important moves behind the scenes. It was apparent to him that funding program development, which traditionally had been the first to suffer from spending cutbacks, was the *sine qua non* for reaching his goal. Fecan didn't simply want to boost the budgets of his underlings, who would then decide whether to spend the cash on in-house productions or on those of independent producers; he wanted to make all the final calls himself. By late 1989, he had completely reorganized the departments under his control. On paper, his scheme looked simple. He split up the multi-armed drama department and ended up with six key positions: head of drama series, head of movies and mini-series, head of children's television, head of variety, head of comedy and sitcoms and head of arts, music and science. He was turning the lethargic, wasteful culture of those operations on its head. Previously, department heads were given budgets and spent them as they saw fit. Unfortunately, says Fecan, "that meant that there was a great deal of waste because everybody wanted to use their money and their air time for territorial reasons."

Under the new system, department heads are expected to champion ideas for new projects, but the final decision for which ones are funded rests with Fecan. "I've tried to create a system of advocacy where there is a pool of money that any number of people can go for," he says. "What I've said is that nobody has fixed money or fixed air time. The best idea gets it." Fecan agrees that the system concentrates power in his hands "because I'm the one that says yes or no," but argues that power is diffused at the same time because there are more department heads who can champion a project.

While Fecan was stirring up the highly politicized power structures of the CBC, he was also making programming decisions that showed up on Canadian's TV screens. "I figured my first order of business was to get programs on the air that people wanted to watch and that measured somewhere in the cultural mandate. I certainly haven't made the most commercial decisions possible," he says, explaining that he's tried to strike a balance between backing shows for commercial reasons and backing shows he feels the CBC "oughta be doing for cultural reasons." (Fecan's habit of dropping letters from his words betrays both his addiction to TV and his upbringing in the Kensington market area of Toronto.) This is not to say that Fecan thinks mass appeal and quality are mutually exclusive. Mass audience hits like "Anne of Green Gables," "Degrassi Junior High," "Road to Avonlea" and *Love and Hate* (a movie based on the Colin Thatcher murder case) all prove the point. 'Street Legal,' the CBC's answer to "L.A. Law," is more contentious. Some critics say it has gone too low-brow and lusty. Fecan views it as one of his bigger successes. "'Street Legal' is a show that was dead on arrival when I arrived here. It was a show that was going down for the count." Fecan brought in a spin doctor, Carla Singer, former vice-president of drama development for CBS, to put glitz and pace in the show, changed its time slot and has watched its ratings rise ever since. His answer to critics who decry what they see as American-style programming: "I make no apologies for shows that are slick or entertaining. I think that is a style rather than a substance question. I think if people are used to seeing a thing in a particular style, you are wasting your time trying to change the style."

The critics have Fecan figured all wrong if they think his pupils dilate only at the sight of huge audience ratings. He's particularly fond of shows like "Adrienne Clarkson's Summer Festival," an outstanding arts program that began as a summer special and went year-round in 1990. "A show like Adrienne's is not meant to get huge audiences," he says. Nor, he adds, are shows he backs such as "Codco" or "Kids in the Hall," both featuring quirky, far-edge comedy troupes. He also points to theatrical Canadian movies the

CBC has aired, such as Patricia Rozema's *I've Heard the Mermaids Singing*. "Look, we know when we schedule them that they are not going to get big audiences, but it is important that we have these shows available because there is no other real distribution system for them in the country."

Asked to respond to the criticism of some media experts who say that TV is in the business of conveying images that convey affluence and promoting the blind pursuit of material possessions, Fecan talks about the line between fantasies and values. "There's a fine line when you're in the business of entertainment," he says. "You can't be too far from where your audience is because you begin to proselytize at that point. At the same time you have to put in values that may be more useful to people in their daily lives than materialistic things that may be impossible for people to reach. Even in our flashiest show, 'Street Legal,' Leon lives on the Island [Toronto Island, which appeals to bicycle-riding, middle-class types]. Nobody is running around in Mercedes like they are on 'L.A. Law.'" Fecan cites other examples from CBC's roster of successful shows. "Look at 'Degrassi Junior High' where everyone in the show is solidly rooted in working-class values. Look at 'Mom P.I.' and 'Max Glick,' where the protagonists are solidly honest working-class people who have dreams." Pressed further to reveal his normally unspoken attitudes to the unavoidable issue of what values underlie even the most glitzy, well-produced series and dramas, he sums up his viewpoint. "I think that the heart of every show still has to have a value system that strikes a chord and that — and this sounds difficult — will help people in their lives, because by suggesting false values you may be doing damage."

Fecan rejects the notion that the CBC should become PBS North, catering exclusively to a select audience. "It strikes me that that particular view would probably not only be financial ruin but would lead to mainstream cultural ruin, because at that point the public won't see themselves reflected in any way. They will just see some intelligentsia reflected, and I think that's a very scary prospect." He adds: "I have no interest in making shows that are watched by 10 people. I think this is the wrong craft to be in if you don't want an audience."

Fecan sees himself as a participant in the Canadian myth-making industry. "When you are living right next door to the huge American myth-making machine, the huge danger is that the only myths you end up learning are American. Shows like 'Road to Avonlea' exist, in part, to get our myths out there. Your kids aren't watching some story about Davy Crockett that was actually shot in the B.C. Interior. If that's all there is, then our generation of young people is growing up with only the myths of another country, and that's a scary proposition."

This isn't an argument to get bad Canadian dramas and variety shows on the air, he says. "You have to put quality in the writing and have some slickness so people are not watching out of obligation to the flag. They are watching because it speaks to them in some way, because it is as good as anything else, but there is a special value added because of its Canadian qualities."

Fecan's record has shown that he has the talent to realize his goals. He's had only two shows bomb so far — "Mosquito Lake" and "Not My Department" — and he has the power. Now if he can keep his domain clear of the axes that are swinging at CBC operation costs . . .

Wayne Sterloff: West Coast Promotion Man. "If we're going to have a culturally elite group of men, by and large, in central Canada defining our cultural existence, they sure as hell better be sophisticated, intelligent and have a hell of a lot of integrity. And they better be on the road a lot learning about our country." Wayne Sterloff, 42, speaks from the perspective of a Vancouver native who has spent the past two decades in the film business, including a stint running Telefilm's western regional office. Since late 1987 he's served as chairman of the B.C. Film Fund, a private, nonprofit operation set up by the Social Credit government that year to invest in the province's film business. B.C. Film is one of several funding organizations set up by provincial governments across the country. All of them are supposed to promote local culture and make some degree of profit. B.C. Film ranks as the most profit-motivated of the bunch.

(The other provincial agencies are in Alberta, where Lorne Mac-Pherson runs the Alberta Motion Picture Development Corporation;

Manitoba, where Jimmy Silden runs the Canada Manitoba Cultural Industries Development Office; Quebec, where Charles Denis runs the Société générale des industries culturelles; and Ontario, where the Ontario Film Development Corporation was looking for a boss as of mid-1991. Saskatchewan and Nova Scotia are setting up similar agencies. New Brunswick, Newfoundland and PEI fund films through cultural ministries.)

B.C. Film was largely the creation of Barry Kelsey, assistant deputy minister of culture. "He pushed and pushed and pushed to get the Social Credit government to fund such a cultural body," says Sterloff. The free-market-minded Socreds agreed to put up the seed money, but after that is spent the fund is on its own. "Unlike Alberta, Quebec or Ontario," says Sterloff, "where the film funds have become permanent parts of a government bureaucracy, we are private sector and we battle for funding on a year-to-year basis."

And private investors, unlike governments, expect returns on their investments. "We'd be happy if we got a third of our money back each year," says Sterloff. "The province made a three-year commitment, and if we get a third of each year's funding back in profit, that would give us a revolving fund to help new filmmakers."

Sterloff's agency has already added some adrenaline to the West Coast industry, which has long been dominated by U.S. producers. "In 1987, before the fund was in business, there was less than $1 million worth of indigenous production, and only about $150,000 of that was private money," he says. "In 1988 there was about $33 million worth of indigenous production, with about $6 million worth of private money."

More than any other provincial film agency, B.C. Film was born out of discontent with Telefilm's policy of pouring the lion's share of funds into central Canada. It's always been a vexing issue in B.C. that Telefilm, which is funded by a tax on cable TV services across the country, collects about 16 per cent of its revenues from the province but spends only about 5 per cent of its budget there in a good year.

As Sterloff sees it, B.C. Film is an antidote to Telefilm's neglect. He formed his opinions while working as Telefilm's point man for the four western provinces from 1984 to 1987. "It was as close to insanity as you could ever get," he recalls. "Western Canada was a hotbed of talent just dying to take part in this huge federal cultural fund. There were strong producer-directors in places like Edmonton and Calgary. Vancouver was just crazy with talent. Every meeting with regional filmmakers was just screaming and yelling," he says. "I felt like a guerrilla bureaucrat, doing what I could just to get a couple of bucks out of central Canada and into those western cities."

On a larger scale, Sterloff sees B.C. Film as a way to help fight off the cultural imperialism of central Canadian powerbrokers whose knowledge of Canadian culture extends about as far west as Mississauga. "I don't think there's a mandarin alive who should be given the power to kill a project or advance it based on cultural content." The problem, he says, is that eastern bureaucrats have notions of culture based on life in Toronto or Montreal. He uses a B.C.-produced movie, *The Trap*, as an example. "It's a story about the Indian culture and the exploitation of Indians on the West Coast. The images are more culturally rich than any script evaluator from the east could understand. We've got to be so careful about this. Otherwise you get this elitism where bureaucrats start killing off scripts because they don't fit their cultural definitions."

French Power

Roger Frappier: The Maestro of Max Films. Every once in a while, when film producer Roger Frappier needs to get away from it all, he leans back in his office chair and stares at an oil painting on the far wall. It's a portrait of his brother-in-law, lolling back in a rowboat with a dreamy grin and a bottle of beer in his hand. "I look at it whenever I'm working too hard," says Frappier. "I think to myself, Now *that's* life."

For the past few years, Frappier, 45, has had plenty of need for this visual escape. He's been frantically busy building Canada's closest thing to a movie hit-making machine. *Jésus de Montréal, Le déclin de l'empire américain, Un Zoo, la nuit, Pouvoir intime* — Frappier has been the maestro behind a series of back-to back hits that are the envy of filmmakers across Canada. He and his partner, Pierre Gendron, are the country's hottest producers.

The resurgence of Quebec cinema in recent years owes much to the organizational machinations of Frappier, who has managed to inspire some of the province's most promising directors to work together in a unique experiment in collegiality. Most of the press for the creations that followed has gone to the directors, Denys Arcand, Léa Pool, Yves Simoneau, Jean-Claude Lauzon. A lot of the credit for their success goes to Frappier.

It all began in 1984, when the National Film Board asked him to sign on with Studio C with the title of executive producer and head of programs. After a decade or so in the film business, directing and producing everything from documentaries to commercial videos, Frappier had come to the conclusion that Quebec filmmakers were better than the films they were making. Frappier says he took the job "on the grounds that I would have the freedom to work with the directors as I saw fit."

For Frappier, that meant trying something that hadn't been tried before: he formed Le groupe de travail cinématographique, a collection of talented directors who would help each other out in every step of the filmmaking process. But for the group to be successful, he needed a financial commitment from the NFB to produce the films developed by the directors. He got it.

"I contacted each director separately to discuss the project," he says. "We held the first meeting in June 1984 around a large boardroom table at the National Film Board. It was fantastic because, all around the table, they had decided that they wanted to be part of the experience." That seminal group consisted of three NFB staffers, Jacques Leduc, Bernard Gosselin and Tahani Rached, and three of Montreal's most promising directors, Léa Pool, Denys Arcand and Pierre Falardeau. Their interests ranged from making documentaries to more commercial fare.

"We began to meet one day a week. We just started by discussing ideas," remembers Frappier. There was no effort to follow the Hollywood model. "I wanted to make low-budget, contemporary movies dealing with our problems, with our lives. A lot of things were happening to us that we never saw on the screen," he says. After a few weeks, they had some solid ideas. "I went to the head of the NFB and said, 'We have our first few films on the go. Denys Arcand is writing a movie on sex and Pierre Falardeau is writing a movie on the death of Pierre Laporte. I'm telling you now because the scripts will be coming in in three months and we will be shooting in six or seven months and I don't want any surprises along the way.'"

The little group turned out to be a hothouse for idiosyncratic, high-quality cinema. Among its successes: *Anne Trister* by Léa Pool, *Trois pommes à côté du sommeil*, by Jacques Leduc, and Denys Arcand's *Déclin*, produced at a cost of only $1.7 million but which turned into a worldwide hit that grossed $22 million.

Not that *Déclin*'s success came easily. Arcand's script, for instance, went through several rewrites. Each time Arcand submitted a draft, the group would spend a day critiquing it. Even when the movie was finished no one was sure anybody would pay money to see it. "It was not obvious that having intellectuals talking in a kitchen about sex would become such a success," comments Frappier.

Nor did the movie get a good reception at first. When Frappier and co-producer Réné Malo submitted it for acceptance at the 1986 Cannes Film Festival, the jury rejected it and sent it back with eight pages of suggested changes.

Fortunately, Frappier, Malo and Arcand stuck with their instincts and ignored the experts. Arcand, suffering a bad case of creator's anxiety, agreed. Says Arcand, "Frappier has an extraordinary enthusiasm, which surmounts anguish and doubt."

Déclin didn't make the main competition at Cannes, but it was selected for the Directors' Fortnight, where it won the International Critic's prize. It was also nominated for an Oscar. Frappier didn't become rich on the film's earnings; he was a salaried employee of the NFB. But he has some vivid memories of his trip to Hollywood. "Just to be there and see all the people I'd seen on screen, to talk to Jack Nicholson, to have a discussion with Oliver Stone. I thought to myself, 'You're a producer, too. You're part of the industry even if you're located so far away.' That night meant more to me than winning the Oscar itself."

With the success of *Déclin* behind him, Frappier left the NFB and teamed up with Pierre Gendron. Their first production, *Un Zoo, la nuit*, directed by Jean-Claude Lauzon, met with just as much scepticism as *Déclin*. Things got off to a bad start when it was panned by journalists at an advance screening for the Directors' Fortnight.

Then, three days before the Directors' Fortnight, the main organizer told them he regretted slotting the movie in for the first night. "We went to the screening that night with our stomachs like this," Frappier says, twisting his fists. "But it received such an ovation. It was received so warmly that it became history." The movie, produced for $1.9 million, went on to gross $3 million.

Jésus de Montréal was the third smash hit in a row for Frappier. It was a box-office hit in both French and English Canada, where after six weeks it had topped $2 million and $500,000 in profits respectively. But, shockingly for anyone who enjoyed the movie's deft swipes at everything from organized religion to the excesses of the media, the major American distributors were reluctant to sign a deal. (Apparently, they were put off by its use of subtitles and worried that the movie might provoke a backlash from religious leaders similar to the controversy caused by *The Last Temptation of Christ*.) Without access to U.S. theatres, the earning power of *Jésus* was seriously crippled, considering it had to gross over $4 million just to recoup production costs.

Success hasn't padded Frappier's pocketbook, or gone to his head. Apart from the painting of his brother-in-law, Frappier's office looks more like an unused industrial storeroom than the headquarters of Canada's hottest producer. The decor consists of a few filing cabinets and a large round plywood table, painted black. The building itself sits among run-down factories in Montreal's garment district. "I'd rather spend extra money on making better films," says Frappier.

Frappier views success with an almost Calvinist suspicion. Rather than bask in the media attention that inevitably followed *Déclin* and *Jésus de Montréal*, he and his colleagues shut it out of their minds. "When we win prizes," he says, "the very next day we pay attention to the next project." He compares the experience to a hockey team winning the Stanley Cup. "Right after the victory, the players know they have to begin training for the next season."

Frappier spent too many years fighting to get where he is now to relax just yet. He's loved movies since he was a child growing up in Sorel, Quebec, where he was born in 1945, the son of a hard-working welder. "From when I was five or six onwards," he says, "every Saturday was movie time." Either his aunt took him to a movie at the local cinema, where she was an usher, or he went to the free movies at a nearby orphanage. He did so well in primary school that the priests picked him out as a good prospect for the church and offered to pay for his education at Saint-Hyacinthe, a classical college.

Once there, though, he fell in love with literature instead of liturgy, thanks mainly to the influence of a teacher who took him under his wing after his father died of lung cancer. At 18, he went off to university in Montreal intent on becoming a novelist. Instead, he became enraptured with movies. "I was seeing at least two movies a day," he recalls. "Every day of the week I would skip the first class and go to a movie. Then I'd go to another one at night. I knew I would become a filmmaker." After learning the business at the London Film School, he arrived back in Montreal to pursue the profession that remains his obsession. "I cannot imagine myself doing anything else," he says. "It's my only passion. Even now, at 9:30 at night I go and see a movie, and if it's good, I come out afterward and I'm all upside down."

Frappier is a rarity among producers: directors enjoy working with him. His great quality is that he doesn't needlessly impose his creative ideas on the film. "He's truly creative and he doesn't need to prove it," comments Arcand. "Frappier is not a man who gives orders," adds another director, Marie-Hélène Roy. "To get what he wants, he is capable of incredible charm. It's his feminine side." Frappier explains his approach this way: "If I work with Denys Arcand, if I work with Jacques Leduc, it's because I like their universe. I like their story. And my task is to make that story, that universe, on the screen."

Norman Jewison: The Guru. When Norman Jewison was working as a CBC-TV producer in the early 1950s, broadcaster Gordon Sinclair described him as "the pixie of Jarvis Street," for his size (five-foot-eight) and twinkling eyes. Years later, Burt Reynolds speculated that Jewison was possibly Hollywood's nicest director, adding, "But he must be able to kick the shit out of people at meetings." Reynolds was right. During a career that has spanned almost four decades in Toronto, New York, Los Angeles, London and then Toronto again,

Jewison has worked the system with a potent blend of moxie, talent, integrity and above all, passion.

Today, Jewison is known by virtually everyone as the country's unchallenged film guru. "If there is a figurehead of the film business in Canada, it would have to be Norman Jewison," says Wayne Clarkson.

In his early years it looked as though Jewison was destined to be under the klieg lights, not behind them. He was born in East Toronto in 1926, the son of a general store merchant. By age seven, he had recited (imperfectly) the entire "Shooting of Dan McGrew" onstage. At Malvern Collegiate in East Toronto, he wrote and acted in minstrel shows. But when he directed and co-wrote his first major stage production, while studying at the University of Toronto, he discovered he had a special knack for directing performers.

The major stops in Jewison's career after that are well documented: his first job in TV production at the BBC; his jump to the CBC when it started up in 1952; the move to CBS in 1958, where he became the highest-paid director in North America, directing specials for the likes of Judy Garland, Andy Williams, Harry Belafonte and Jimmy Durante (he left because "Madison Avenue regarded television as an extension of the advertising industry. They were only interested in how much money it would generate"); his sign-on with Universal Studios in Hollywood in 1961, where he directed *Forty Pounds of Trouble, The Thrill of It All* and *Send Me No Flowers*; and from 1964 his towering success as an independent director/producer.

The most remarkable aspect of Jewison's career is that he has achieved international success while staying true to principles that he thinks make his films worthwhile. "I use honesty as a standard for everything," he has explained. "Dishonest films sometimes make money, but making money is not the criterion for success." Of course, recent hits like *Moonstruck* are successes on both the commercial and artistic fronts. He's in the rare position of having had the "final cut" on his films for decades. That means he has creative control, the right to have the final say over how the film looks.

Jewison's movies usually combine a compelling narrative with an underlying "important idea" or social comment, such as underdogs and outcasts fighting the system (*The Cincinnati Kid, And Justice*

for All); racial tension (*In the Heat of the Night*); anonymous corporate control over society (*Rollerball*); musicals with social messages
(*Fiddler on the Roof, Jesus Christ Superstar*); and the social legacy
of the Vietnam War (*In Country*).

Jewison explains his philosophy this way: "When I was a young
man I wanted to change the world. I now know that there's very
little possibility of me being able to deflect it one millimetre from
its course. But if I ever stop trying, or if I ever stop believing that
it's worth trying, then I will cease to make films that have any value."

Jewison cemented his guru status in 1988, when he opened the
Canadian Centre for Advanced Film Studies, at Windfields, the former estate of E.P. Taylor in North York. Explaining why he created
the centre, Jewison said, "Most countries have had 30 or 40 years
of making movies. We've got to play catch-up. We have made amazing
progress with the infrastructure, and we have developed great technical crews. Our real need is in the area of writers, producers, directors and cameramen — people on the artistic side who control
the quality of a film."

At the centre students learn just as much about how to play the
movie-making system as about how to light a set. In Jewison's opinion, knowing how to pitch a movie to investors is a key to success.
"If you aren't a good salesman you can't possible convince people
to give you millions of dollars to make your dream."

David Cronenberg: The Horror King. The University of Toronto
prides itself on being the breeding ground for such Canadian note-
worthies as Northrop Frye, Marshall McLuhan and Glenn Gould. Compared to them, however, filmmaker and fellow U of T alumnus David
Cronenberg stands out like the mutant progeny of an aberrant gene.

Since Cronenberg's student days in the 1960s at U of T, where
he studied literature, he has turned out a stream of science-fiction
horror flicks that have been called everything from sleaze to mas-
terpieces. No matter, at 48, the Toronto-born writer/producer/di-
rector ranks as the most bankable filmmaker ever to build a career
without leaving Canada.

Cronenberg's penchant for breaking taboos and destroying complacency showed up in his early experiments with science-fiction, like

Stereo and *Crimes of the Future*. In *Scanners*, a bunch of nasty fetuses turn into violent monsters after their mothers take a drug that gives the little darlings telepathic powers. And so on. Cronenberg claims that making scary films isn't easy. "A lot of people think it's a breeze," the self-taught director has explained. "It's pointless to just have a lot of gore and bodies being chopped up."

For the longest time, critics couldn't agree on whether Cronenberg was brilliant or depraved (as Robert Fulford once alleged in a *Saturday Night* column). But Cronenberg's most recent critical and financial hits, *The Fly* and *Dead Ringers*, have proved that he's probably both.

Money Power

Robert Lantos: Lantos, a 42-year-old Hungarian émigré who runs Alliance Communications Corp., Canada's biggest independent film and television production company, has achieved staying power in the Canadian film industry using a simple four-letter formula: FFFF — *flesh, flesh, fun* and *flash*. Lantos has trampled on prudish Canadian sensibilities with relish ever since he got into the movie business distributing a soft-core porn flick in 1973. Since then, he has parlayed his instincts about what audiences want to see into a string of hits on the large and small screens.

With a series of business partners that has included Stephen Roth, John Kemeny and Denis Héroux, Lantos has managed to make a lot more money than he's lost, which alone makes him an exception in the business. From his first movie, *L'Ange et la femme*, known for a steamy scene in which Quebec enchantress Carole Laure copulates with Lewis Furey, to his more recent hits like the prime-time TV series "Mount Royal," Lantos has operated on the principle that sensuality, sin and slickness sell. "If you want to kick the Americans off the air," he has said, "you have to give audiences the scope and the slickness they expect."

Sample hits: *In Praise of Older Women* (grossed $10 million); *The Gate* (grossed $60 million). Then there are small-screen winners like "Mount Royal," "The Sword of Gideon," "Night Heat" and "E.N.G."

Sample bombs: *Joshua Then and Now*, adapted from the book by Mordecai Richler, was a financial and critical failure; *Your Ticket Is No Longer Valid*, a feature starring Richard Harris and Jennifer Dale, then Lantos's wife, was ruined by fighting on the set.

Lantos easily attracts money from private networks, Telefilm and the Ontario Film Development Corporation. That gives him plenty of power in the business, and many directors end up working with him whether they like it or not. He's not Mr. Sensitive on the set, and directors who pride themselves on their role as creators don't like his commercial approach. Producers like Lantos, grumbles one director, "don't have taste, but they insist on imposing their choice of actors, changes in the script and the way of shooting."

Lately, Lantos is trying to tame the party-boy, wheeler-dealer image he once enjoyed. After all, he runs a vertically integrated business with a distribution business and in-house investment banking operation as well as a production arm. "He's trying to downplay that perception of him now," says an industry insider. "He's constantly emphasizing his role as a responsible corporate officer. He's matured."

Harold Greenberg: The hyperbole flowed as copiously as the wine when about 380 people gathered at the Ritz Carlton in Montreal in late 1989 to pay tribute to Greenberg, president and CEO of Astral Bellevue-Pathé entertainment conglomerate. The Montreal World Film Festival organized the event to present Greenberg with an International Achievement Award for his contribution to the film industry in Canada, and the guest list gave an indication of how far Greenberg's clout extends beyond his Montreal base. A sampling: Keith Spicer and André Bureau, former chairmen of the CRTC; Marcel Masse, then federal communications minister; former prime minister Pierre Trudeau; and Quebec cultural affairs minister Lise Bacon, who praised Greenberg for playing "a major role in the cultural industries" and called him "a great Canadian, an authentic Quebecker, and a man with a profound social conscience."

The last comment must have been especially satisfying for Greenberg, who first made a name for himself bringing the world the culturally retarded hit *Porky's* (though it grossed $150 million) and its sequels. But then Greenberg has made his contribution to the industry as a businessman, not as a proponent of high-brow culture. To use the businessworld's informal measure of power, Greenberg "makes things happen" in the film business, and he's been doing it for almost 30 years.

Greenberg commands an entertainment network with annual revenues of about $265 million and a staff of 1,500. The company is in pay-TV: it has controlling interest in First Choice and Super Ecran channels and a 50 per cent interest in Family Channel. It's in TV distribution: subsidiary Astral Television handles U.S. imports such as "L.A. Law" and is the largest supplier of English and French programming in Canada. It's in movie distribution to theatres: Astral Films handles mostly U.S. titles but distributes such Canadian movies as *Dead Ringers* as well. Then there's the empire's video distribution, post-production services and a chain of 125 photo-developing shops.

Greenberg started out in 1962 with a string of camera shops, which he ran with his brothers, Harvey, Sidney and Ian. They added a photo-processing business in 1963, with the help of Edper Investments, the holding company of Edward and Peter Bronfman, which chipped in $100,000 for a one-third interest. In 1974, Greenberg and the Bronfmans collaborated further when they folded Astral Films, a theatre and TV distribution company, into one huge company with Greenberg at the helm and his brothers running various branches. Today, the major shareholders are the Greenberg family (Harold's two sons, Stephen and Joel, are also in the business) and the Bronfmans.

During the 1970s, Greenberg became involved in producing movies, mainly, he says, because he had to repeatedly step into bail out productions using his film labs. Starting with a few made-for-drive-in losers, he went on to produce or coproduce some mostly forgettable movies, such as *Ritual*, *City on Fire* and *Terror Train*. Efforts like *In Praise of Older Women* and a TV mini-series, "A Man Called Intrepid," were more memorable, but Greenberg never claimed to put his directors' interests above those of his investors.

Greenberg got out of production after the CRTC made it a condition of his winning pay-TV licences. As a distributor, though, he's still heavily involved in swinging financial deals for made-in-Canada movies. And he still doesn't like the suggestion that he's done little to contribute to Canadian culture. As he put it recently: "We've supported individual producers right across Canada, but that doesn't get played up in the papers. I don't know of any company in the last 15 years which has more supported the cultural undertakings of filming than my company."

Perhaps. But it was Greenberg's deal-making smarts and his gruff, irascible manner that opened doors for him at the Hollywood majors. Treating studio executives like office boys came naturally to Greenberg. ("You know he likes you if he insults you," says a friend.)

These days, Greenberg has legendary clout in political circles in Quebec City and Ottawa. "Harold has a direct line to the politicians," says a film-industry veteran. "You know that if the government is planning any film policy or program, Harold is going to have a voice in that decision."

Michael MacMillan, Seaton McLean: Since founding Toronto-based Atlantis Films in 1978 with $300, these former film students from Queen's University have accomplished the remarkable: they've given films with middle-class, English-Canadian values a good name in artistic circles. With MacMillan as the financial impresario and McLean concentrating on the creative side, along with Janice Platt, a third co-founder who has since left the company, they built Atlantis into Canada's second-largest independent film and TV production house, with annual revenues of about $40 million. They made their name making successful films with a leisurely pace and lyrical mood based on books by Canadian authors. They include *The Olden Days Coat* (Margaret Laurence), *Boys and Girls* (Alice Munro), *All the Years* (Morley Callaghan) and *Cat's Eye* (Margaret Atwood). *Boys and Girls* won an Oscar in 1984.

From that base, though, they're concentrating on developing international coproduction efforts. Their TV productions include "Airwaves," a serial that flopped, "Airwolf," produced for the U.S. market in association with MCA, and 30 episodes of "The Twilight Zone." In 1989, the company picked up six major U.S. television awards, including the prize for best dramatic series for the "Ray Bradbury Theater."

Remarkably, they've achieved success without the usual formula of sex and sin. They pride themselves on making films that families can watch without fear of being offended by sex and violence.

Other Bankable Filmmakers

The foregoing are only the best-known of Canada's film deal makers. Here are the country's other most bankable producers and producer/directors.

Phillip Borsos (Mercury Pictures Inc., Toronto); Gilles Carle (Les Films Gilles Carle Inc., Montreal); Zale Dalen and Laara Dalen (Highlight Productions Ltd., Gibsons, B.C.); Jack Darcus (Exile Film Productions, Vancouver); Rock Demers (Les Productions La Fête Inc., Montreal); Atom Egoyan (Ego Film Arts, Toronto); Niv Fichman and Barbara Willis-Sweete (Rhombus Media Inc.); Graeme Ferguson (Imax Systems Corp., Toronto); Beryl Fox (Beryl Fox Productions, Toronto); John Frizzell (John B. Frizzell Inc., Toronto); Claude Héroux (Les Productions Lance et Compte Inc., Montreal); Michael Hirsh (Nelvana Ltd., Toronto); Thomas Howe (Thomas Howe Productions, Vancouver); Lulu Keating and Christopher Zimmer (Red Snapper Films Ltd., Halifax); Peter Kroonenberg (Filmline International Inc., Montreal); William MacGillivray (Picture Plant, Halifax); Réné Malo (Malofilm Production Inc., Montreal); William Marshall (Marshall Arts, Toronto); John McGreevy (John McGreevy Productions Ltd., Toronto); Peter O'Brian (Independent Pictures Inc., Toronto); Roger Racine (Cinéfilms Inc., Montreal); Peter Raymont (Investigative Productions, Toronto); Stephen J. Ross (Cinexus Capital Corp., Toronto); Patricia Rozema and Alexandra Raffé (VOS Productions Inc., Toronto); Paul Saltzman and Deepa Saltzman (Sunrise Films Ltd., Toronto); Peter Simpson (Norstar Entertainment Inc., Toronto); Kevin Sullivan (Sullivan Films Inc., Toronto); Sandy Wilson (Fineline Productions Ltd., Vancouver).

Woman Power

Gail Singer: Gail Singer recalls, in a did-you-expect-anything-better tone, the time she was asked to trade sex for a job. She's a successful director who, after two decades in the film business, is surprised by very little. At 47, she can no longer be shocked, only disgusted, with the proposition that was put to her in 1971 when she applied for a job making films for the Institute of Urban Studies at the University of Winnipeg.

"The night before the interview," she recalls, "I got a phone call at about 12:15 a.m. from a guy who was on the interview board. The man, an employee of the National Film Board, said: 'I understand you're interested in the job.'"

Singer: "Yes."

The man: "Well, why don't you drop by [to my hotel room] and we'll talk about it."

Singer: "I'm in bed. I'm supposed to meet you at 8:15 tomorrow morning."

The man: "So you're not really interested in the job."

Singer: "I'll see you in the morning."

The next morning, Singer went to the interview, which went very well, despite the presence of Mr. X. in the room. At the end, Singer, not known to be cowed by anyone, said: "You know, I would have been much more alert and much more articulate if Mr. X here hadn't called me late last night."

Singer got the job. Mr. X kept his.

Singer is one of a growing group of women who are emerging as major creative forces in the Canadian film industry. They are carrying on the legacy of important female filmmakers from earlier eras, such as Nell Shipman, who made *Back to God's Country* in 1919, Donna King Conway, one of the few women filmmakers in the 1920s, and Evelyn Spice Cherry, Jane Marsh and Judith Crawley in the 1940s. Then there were the documentary filmmakers nurtured by the NFB in the 1940s: Bonny Klein, Patricia Watkins, Margaret Perry and Anne-Claire Poirier. By the 1970s, directors such as Beryl Fox (who made the landmark *Mills of the Gods*, on the Vietnam War) and Joyce Wieland, probably the country's best avant-garde filmmaker, had taken their place as godmothers of the industry. Singer is part of the latest wave of important women filmmakers, many of whom have now branched into feature films. They include Mireille Dansereau, Paule Baillargeon, Micheline Lanctôt, Léa Pool, Patricia Rozema, Anne Wheeler and Sandy Wilson.

Does this mean women are at last taking their rightful positions in the power structure of the film industry? Not at all, according to Singer and any other woman in the business. They've moved from the role of starlet to director, but the producers, who have sweeping say over every aspect of filmmaking, are virtually all men. There are only rare exceptions, such as Alexandra Raffé, producer of Patricia Rozema's movies.

No one denies that it is vital to our culture that women continue to increase their contribution in the film industry. Precisely *why* this is vital is not easily put into words without wandering into the verbal minefield of sexual stereotyping. The issue is best clarified by posing questions: Could a male director have created *My American Cousin*, Sandy Wilson's award-winning film dealing with a girl's coming-of-age? Could a man have created the wonderful character of Polly, the secretary in Patricia Rozema's internationally acclaimed *I've Heard the Mermaids Singing*, or sensitively portrayed the dilemmas faced by the heroine of Anne Wheeler's *Bye Bye Blues*? Could a female director ever be bothered with creating a piece of cultural trash like *Porky's*, about young males with sex on the brain? These are extreme examples, of course, but they make the point. Canadian culture, in film as in other spheres, is a glass only half-full without the contributions of women.

Singer has made a successful career in the film business despite the odds. It's taken an ability to cope with the men who call the shots on the set, the persistence to deal with paper-loving bureaucrats who decide the fate of proposals, the ability to deal with the financial insecurity endemic to the business and the self-confidence to be happy with an essentially rootless existence.

A large woman ("I'm not the sexpot I used to be") with an irrepressible mirth, Singer laughs when she recalls what her father, a Winnipeg podiatrist, and mother, a traditional wife, wanted her to do with her life. "I grew up in a conventional household," she says. "My parents wanted me to marry a nice Jewish doctor and raise children . . . . But I imagined a life in Winnipeg, I looked around me and saw some kind of a vacancy that was unbearable. I saw getting married and settling down in Winnipeg as death. It was a terrifying prospect."

Singer opted instead for some world travel, working a year in England during the mid-1960s, and later travelling, like thousands of other youths of that era, to Morocco and Israel. She was back in

Winnipeg by 1969, the proud proprietor of a kitchenware shop. In 1971, she took a gamble and landed the job at the University of Winnipeg's Urban Studies Institute, as an executive producer. Singer had picked up some film experience on an underwater shoot in Israel but, essentially, she was a complete ingénue. "I knew absolutely zero about what I was supposed to do," she says of the Winnipeg job. "I took the job in a state of terror." Singer pulled it off, with the help of some very experienced co-workers. Then she moved on to a job as a researcher, and subsequently a director, for the CBC in Winnipeg.

Singer made a name for herself making films, mainly on environmental and native issues, and in 1978 she attracted the attention of the local National Film Board office. A special unit, Studio D, had been formed in 1974 to focus on women's issues, and it signed up Singer to make a film on wife-battering. It was the first of three critically acclaimed documentaries by Singer, who went on to make *Portrait of the Artist as an Old Lady*, a poignant, mesmerizing film on the life of Canadian artist Paraskeva Clark, and *Abortion: Stories from North and South*, a film with an international perspective.

The making of *Abortion* illustrates the difficulties Singer and others have had getting a controversial, if timely, topic past hand-wringing bureaucrats and onto the screen. The idea for the film was a result of Singer's travels in the Third World, where she had gained a new perspective on the significance of abortion in ordinary people's lives. "If you have seven children and another mouth to feed would mean the end of the mother — either she'd die or she'd kill herself — abortion is just a practical decision," says Singer. "I took my idea to the National Film Board in Toronto, and I sensed their resistance to anything beyond the most narrow, banal production. They just wanted to follow the old idea of getting a bunch of people together on screen and having them talk about how good it is or bad it is to do."

Singer received a better reception when she took the idea to Studio D. To get the movie approved by head office at the NFB, they resorted to a little subterfuge. "On the books it was called *The History of Medicine*, in order not to arouse ire before the film was made."

Singer considers herself a feminist ("It's only in this century that women have been recognized as persons"), but she doesn't want to be marginalized because of her sex. She's foremost a filmmaker and views it as creatively stifling to make films solely to argue a feminist viewpoint. For a time, she says, "the feminist movement interfered with my creative juices, my creative imagination. Now I feel free to explore topics according to my instincts." Her latest pursuits allow her to do that. They include a film on women comics called *Wisecracks*, and a feature film, *True Confessions*, on growing up in Winnipeg. "I want to illuminate, shed new light," says Singer. "I want to say something in my films that nobody thought of before but that makes you go, ahah!" So far, she's succeeded.

Hottest Directing Talent (by region)

Quebec:

Denys Arcand (*Le Déclin de l'empire américain*; *Jésus de Montréal*); Rock Demers (*The Dog Who Stopped the War*; *The Tadpole and the Whale*); Jean-Claude Lauzon (*Un Zoo, la nuit*); Jacques Leduc (*Trois pommes à côté du sommeil*); Léa Pool (*Anne Trister*; *Straight to the Heart*); Tahani Rached (*Haiti-Québec*); Yves Simoneau (*Pouvoir intime*); Micheline Lanctôt (*Sonatine*); John Smith (*Welcome to Canada*).

The West:

Sandy Wilson (*My American Cousin*; *American Boyfriends*); Zale Dalen ("Beachcombers"; *Terminal City Ricochet*); Richard Martin (*Matinee*); Charles Wilkinson (*Quarantine*); Allan King (*Who Has Seen the Wind*; *Termini Station*); Anne Wheeler (*A War Story*; *Loyalties*; *Cowboys Don't Cry*; *Bye Bye Blues*).

Ontario:

Atom Egoyan (*Next of Kin*; *Family Viewing*; *Speaking Parts*); Patricia Rozema (*I've Heard the Mermaids Singing*; *White Room*);

Janice Cole and Holly Dale (*P4W: Prison for Women*; *Hookers on Davie*; *The Making of "Agnes of God"*); Gail Singer (*Portrait of the Artist as an Old Lady*; *Abortion: Stories from North and South*; *Wisecracks*); Peter Mettler (*The Top of His Head*); Kay Armitage (*Striptease*; *Storytelling*; *Artist on Fire*); Joyce Wieland (*Reason Over Passion*; *Rat Life and Diet in North American*; *The Far Shore*; *Birds at Sunrise*); Vic Sarin (*So Many Miracles*; *Cold Comfort*); Bruce Pittman (*Where the Spirit Lives*); Barry Greenwald (*Who Gets In*).

The Atlantic Provinces:

William MacGillivray (*Stations*; *Life Classes*); Paul Donovan (*Siege*; *Def Con 4*; *The Squamish Five*; *George's Island*); Lulu Keating (*Midday Sun*); Kevin Sullivan (*Anne of Green Gables*; *Road to Avonlea*).

The Impresarios

Wayne Clarkson and Helga Stephenson: Wayne Clarkson is in fine networking form. It's the opening-night gala of Toronto's 1989 Festival of Festivals, and money, fame and talent have converged on the Eglinton Theatre for the world premiere of Norman Jewison's latest movie, *In Country*, a Vietnam War retrospective starring Bruce Willis. Outside, stretch limos roll up to the door to disgorge international stars onto a red carpet bordered by security guards, paparazzi and swivelling search lights. Inside the theatre, Clarkson darts from celebrity to celebrity as though he has jet-packs in the cowboy boots he never seems to take off, even for black-tie affairs like tonight's. One moment he's crouching beside Shelley Peterson, actress and wife of David, then Ontario premier. The next instant, he's off to get in a few quick words with other luminaries, from real estate deal maker Eddie Cogan to CITY-TV boss Moses Znaimer. Clarkson is only halfway through a long night of chatting up the film stars, politicians, media celebrities and socialites who have turned up for the opening night of the film festival he helped put on the film world map.

The other impresario responsible for the festival's success, Helga Stephenson, is also hard at work this night. Stephenson's busy evening of networking started before the show at a pre-gala bash at the Bellair Café in the fashionable Yorkville district and ended with a crowded bash at Harbourfront, where the luminaries of Canadian film and entertainment mingled with a couple of hundred Warner Brothers heavies flown in especially for the night from Los Angeles. Swaggering producers with insolent lips mingled with young directors outfitted in black clothes and pony tails. Starlets and socialites bounced about in some of the most outrageous fashions this side of L.A.

Clarkson and Stephenson don't attract the cameras, star-watchers and social columnists the way the actors and directors do at the annual festival, but more than anyone else they stand at the epicentre of the creative commotion that rattles Toronto out of the closet each year, transforming the city from an ageing dowager into a drag queen for a night. In their roles as behind-the-scenes impresarios, Clarkson and Stephenson are almost single-handedly responsible for the vitality of the Toronto festival and, for that matter, for the English-language Canadian film industry. Film writer Martin Knelman notes that the Toronto Festival of Festivals now ranks among the top 10 of the world's 300 or so film festivals.

Clarkson served as festival director between 1978 and 1985, during which time he built it into an internationally recognized event. Then he went on to serve as chairman of the Ontario Film Development Corporation, the provincial funding body, from 1985 until 1991. In that job he provided money and encouragement to directors like Atom Egoyan and Patricia Rozema who would later win acclaim on the festival's screens and at festivals abroad. Currently he is executive director of Norman Jewison's Canadian Centre for Advanced Film Studies, which trains aspiring directors.

Stephenson, as executive director of the festival since 1987, has taken what Clarkson started and made it bigger, better and more international in flavour. The Toronto festival has rivals in other major Canadian cities, including Montreal, Vancouver, Halifax and Banff. But everyone except perhaps the organizers of those festivals would concede that Toronto has them outclassed in drawing power — of movies, producers, deal makers and stars — in the international scene. Some industry insiders view Toronto as an unbeatable place to get a fix on what's happening in world film, even taking Cannes and Venice into account.

The feature Clarkson and Stephenson have in common is their *style* of operating: they are both polished cultural diplomats, capable of moving effortlessly among politicians, Hollywood moneymen, cultural bohemians, auteur-directors, in Toronto, New York, Cannes or anywhere else the film industry swarms to. Clarkson is the Peter Pan of the film industry, quixotic, quick-witted and never letting his shadow catch up with him; Stephenson is the Wendy, well-loved but unmistakably in control of her words.

Clarkson shows up for an interview wearing a brown leather jacket, blue jeans and cowboy boots and carrying his version of a power lunch: a bag of chips and a Pepsi. It's a week after the 1989 film festival, and Clarkson, head of the OFDC at the time, feels like stale popcorn. "Everybody wants something at the festival," he moans. "Directors or producers who've had their application for funds turned down use it as an occasion to protest and try to reopen their case. 'By the way . . . ' When I hear that I think, 'Oh no.'" Since he left the OFDC in 1991 to run Jewison's film centre, Clarkson won't have to put up with money-seeking producers, but he will continue to have an influence over the industry as a guru to an annual crop of some of the country's most promising directors and producers.

The common thread in Clarkson's career has been his love of film, though it was not always obvious that it would become more than a hobby. His family background wasn't conducive to a life in the fringe world of film. Clarkson's father was a deputy minister of economics in the Ontario government. But there was not much doubt that Clarkson's passion lay in the creative arts, not the dismal science. He was born in 1946 in Amherst, Nova Scotia (his father was attending Mount Allison), and he was raised in Toronto. Although Clarkson majored in English at Ottawa's Carleton University in the late 1960s, he spent a lot of his time making movies with the campus film society. Not that he had his career all figured out. "I went to university because that's what every good middle-class kid did." He graduated in 1970, after taking a year off to chase his future wife, Marg, around Europe and North Africa.

Next, Clarkson got a job as an information officer at the Canadian Film Institute in Ottawa, which at the time had one of the finest film archives in North America. The real appeal of the place for

Clarkson was its tremendous collection of films, and books and magazines about films. "In the basement there was this incredible library of films. So I'd stay after work and look at all the movies. I saw all the great Chaplins. I read all the magazines, and for the first time in my life I realized that I really wanted to learn." After two years at the CFI, Clarkson went off to the Slade School of Fine Art in London to do an M.A. "I was interested in film history, film theory, film aesthetics, less the production side of it."

When he returned to Canada in 1975, he rejoined CFI and ran their film programs. While there, he ran the Ottawa International Film Festival for three years and made a reputation and connections that landed him a job as boss of the Toronto film festival.

Clarkson ran the Toronto festival, which William Marshall had launched in 1976, from 1978 to 1985, building it into an internationally renowned success. The numbers tell part of the story. In 1978, the festival had a budget of $198,000, and showed about 75 films to roughly 35,000 people. In 1985, the festival's budget topped $2 million and it showed more than 200 movies to about 200,000 film lovers.

Then came the call from the premier's office. Premier David Peterson's government was setting up the OFDC, and he thought Clarkson was the man for the job. For six years, Clarkson ran a relatively smooth show at the OFDC, handing out about $12 million a year to directors and projects he judged talented. His only critics tend to be a few independent producers who feel shut out of the social milieu he operates in, or are jealous of the attention Clarkson pays to certain stars, like Atom Egoyan and Patricia Rozema.

But Clarkson's personality, which blends oodles of social tact with an almost boyish wonder at the *amazing* experiences life holds, have helped him stay well liked in an industry riddled with jealousies. His energy and sense of adventure have seen him through Outward Bound trips and a three-month solo journey down the length of South America in 1988, armed only with a smattering of Spanish and a book of handy travel tips.

Clarkson has applied the same restless energy for the past 15 years to making Ontario the centre of the Canadian film industry. It's also helped that Telefilm has poured about 80 per cent of its annual funds for English-language film into the province. This is as it should be, as far as Clarkson is concerned. "The centre for English-language production in this country is Ontario," he asserts. "No question about it. We are the third-largest production centre in North America, after Los Angeles and New York."

Credit for that (or blame, depending on your regional loyalties) also goes to Helga Stephenson, successor to Clarkson as head of the Festival of Festivals. Her main contribution has been to make the film festival a showplace for international as much as Canadian talent. Stephenson was at first passed over as a replacement for Clarkson when he vacated the job in 1985. A seasoned publicity agent, she had worked for Clarkson since 1982 as director of communications. She was also well connected. That same year she married William Marshall, a former aide to Toronto mayor David Crombie and the man who founded the festival in 1976. Yet the board of directors of the festival felt Stephenson lacked the requisite experience. Instead they chose Leonard Schein of the Vancouver Film Festival. Schein, an abrasive ex-Californian draft dodger, managed to alienate just about everybody associated with the festival over the next nine months before he was dumped at a stormy board meeting. Schein's most powerful backer was movie mogul Garth Drabinsky, then owner of the Cineplex Odeon chain, whose theatres were key venues for festival showings. Even a temper tantrum by Drabinsky couldn't save Schein's job.

When Schein left, the board asked Stephenson, who had stayed on as communications director, to replace him. But even then there were doubters. "We had some unspoken reluctance because she was a woman," one former director admits candidly, aware of how unfounded that bias proved to be. Stephenson proved herself shrewd very quickly. She divided the director's job in two, making herself executive director and appointing Piers Handling, the festival's resident film expert and programmer, as artistic director. It's a partnership that's worked wonders ever since.

Stephenson's main attribute has been her organizational and networking skills. She's a social chameleon, able to move from black-tie social events to black-shirted film gatherings with ease. This has something to do with her social origins. She grew up in Montreal's affluent Mount Royal district, the daughter of Harald Stephenson, an Icelandic Lutheran from Winnipeg whose sister Signy married John David Eaton. Helga's mother, Mary, was a strong Irish Catholic who sent her daughter to French convent schools. For a time, after her father's retirement, Helga's family lived in Switzerland. There, Helga took to going to movies as an escape from the rigours of her education at the hands of Dominican brothers. Film became her passion, even though as a girl she had aspired to being a nun. Back in Canada in the mid-1960s, she studied communications at McGill University. After a stint as director of programming for the National Arts Centre, she moved to Toronto and launched her career as a publicist.

A gregarious woman with a smile that's all mouth, Stephenson exudes a sincerity in her dealings with people that has made her remarkably well liked in the community. She is in her best form working the Cannes Film Festival, where she goes each year to massage her film-world contacts and keep on top of the best offerings different countries have to offer. At Cannes, Stephenson has said she feels like a kind of "bag lady," wandering around having conversations with contacts about which films she might select for the Toronto festival. Informal understandings are reached at elegant receptions, over lunch or at the bar of the Majestic Hotel, and are usually formalized months later. Between her Cannes contacts and her unchallenged role as queen of the screenings in Toronto, Stephenson has the power to make or break a movie in Canada.

Conclusion

Canada's film industry is a riotous blend of opposites, of bureaucratic power and artistic energy, of commercial schlock and creative genius, of centralist bias and regional resentments, of white middle-class angst and immigrant iconoclasm. Despite — and perhaps because of — this state of dynamic tension, the industry has a surfeit of productive energy. Pity that so few Canadians have the opportunity or motivation to sample the films and made-for-TV movies and serials it produces. Since our industry is so overwhelmed with American fare, Canadian producers and directors have more potential than actual influence over the cultural consciousness of Canadians. Canadian-content television regulations are the best route to redressing the situation, although the high cost of producing shows here rather than just buying them off the shelf from the United States makes the Canadianization process slow and arduous. Yet the Canadian film industry has a record of artistic and commercial successes that justifies continued support with taxpayers' dollars.

One of the most powerful arguments for encouraging the industry to a position of greater influence is the diversity of ethnic and social backgrounds of its leading lights. As the profiles illustrate, the film industry is a cultural elite (in the making) that has a higher degree of social mobility than any other elite studied in this book. The majority of its major players come from humble backgrounds, and a good many are first-generation Canadians with exotic backgrounds. Atom Egoyan was born in Cairo to Armenian parents; Vic Sarin (*Cold Comfort*) hails from Kashmir, India; Phillip Borsos (*The Grey Fox, Bethune*) is from Tasmania; Robert Lantos is a Hungarian refugee who immigrated to Montreal via Uruguay; Ivan Reitman, who brought the world *Animal House*, is Czech-born; John Kemeny (*The Apprenticeship of Duddy Kravitz, Quest for Fire*) fled Budapest in 1956. Even filmmakers with more traditional French or British ancestry tend to come from lower-middle-class backgrounds. Bill Marshall hails from the slums of Glasgow; Ted Kotcheff (*Joshua Then and Now*) grew up in Toronto's Cabbagetown, the son of a Bulgarian immigrant grocer; Denys Arcand hails from Deschambault, a small Quebec town.

The Canadian film industry is arguably the most powerful force for multiculturalism now at work in the country. It's something politicians should remember when they're deciding whether to pour money into yet another ethnic dance competition or the film business.

Chapter 12

The Publishing Industry

Fortunately, Canadian publishers have a talent for self-deprecation that helps to keep them sane. Take, for example, the annual "No Returns Cabaret and Revue," a satirical romp through the industry's star system put on each year by the Book Publishers Professional Association. At the December 1990 show, emcee Peter Waldock (president of Cannon Book Distribution) announced, "You'll know you've made it in publishing when you're horribly abused at the 'No Returns Cabaret and Revue.'" His intent, no doubt, was to lessen the blow to the show's victims. Anna Porter, president and publisher of Key Porter Books, was portrayed by Sarah MacLachlan, a marketing executive with a rival company, who imitated Porter's aloof air, tossed back her hair à la Anna, and brought the house down with a song adapted from *Evita*: "Don't Cry for Me, Little People." Malcolm Lester and Louise Dennys, publishers of Lester & Orpen Dennys, were portrayed making a pitch for their struggling company like public television fund raisers. In a swipe at the publisher's parent company, the actors promised viewers a prize for the largest donation — "a Hees executive bound and gagged and hung with Christmas lights." Within a month, Lester & Orpen Dennys was closed.

The satire was easy to take for members of an industry where survival requires a capacity for self-flagellation, or at least an indifference to adversity. Canadian publishing is a chronically endangered business, made up of a collection of men and women who make mostly modest livings by cajoling authors into completing manuscripts, then selling the books to a mostly uninterested and unappreciative public. As nourishment for the educated imagination, to use a favourite phrase of the late Northrop Frye, publishers serve up a wholesome buffet that, year after year, gets passed over by most people for intellectual fast food: TV sitcoms, Hollywood blockbusters and the like.

The main problem is not lack of talent in the publishing houses, it's the modest size of the Canadian market. "The market base is incredibly small, around 15 million," says Linda McKnight, a literary agent and former publishing executive. "Many of the audience don't have English as a first language. Most don't read books, compared to Europe where, typically, 85 per cent of the public buys books." The entire Canadian market is smaller than that of California.

Commenting on the economic state of the industry, literary critic William French summed up the situation concisely: "Too many books for too few readers, at too high a price." Added to that, the offerings of Canadian publishers are swamped by foreign titles. Every year, about $1.4 billion worth of books are sold in Canada. Of those, 70 per cent come from the United States, 20 per cent from Canada and most of the rest from Great Britain.

With the market for Canadian books so small, the publishers with the greatest financial stability are those that have been around long enough to have huge backlists of steady sellers, a lucrative mass market division to move paperbacks or, best of all, the distribution rights to market foreign titles in Canada.

Little wonder that the economics of book publishing have more in common with a crap shoot than corporate finance. Bankers are the publishers' best friend (after grant-giving governments). Lines of credit are the lifeblood of an industry that has to borrow to produce books with no assurance that sales will be sufficient for them to break even. To add to the uncertainty, book sellers take books only on consignment; that is, they have the right to return books to the publisher if they don't sell within a few months. And so, every year, publishers are swamped with returns accompanied by demands from the retailers for repayment. Under these conditions, publishing accountants find it absurdly impossible to make trustworthy revenue projections, let alone profit projections.

Measuring the influence of the Canadian publishing industry on our culture is akin to measuring the effects of spring sunlight on a Winnipeger's winter-hardened soul. There is no tangible way to measure the process, but the beneficial effects are undeniable. Publishers in a sense are star makers in the same way that film producers are: they decide which authors merit publication, how they will be promoted and how much they will earn in advances and royalties. Behind every great Canadian author there is a publisher with the gall and determination to make that author great. They have the power to introduce new talent to the Canadian publishing scene. As well, it is next to impossible for an aspiring or established author to score a best-seller without the efforts of a publisher that has the leverage to get the book on store shelves.

Publishers aren't the only ones with the power. At the beginning of the process, publishers have to contend with some of the most sophisticated literary agents in the world. At the other end of the process, they are at the mercy of the two largest bookstore chains, W.H. Smith and Coles, which together account for up to 45 per cent of the market.

For all its fragility, the publishing industry makes an enormous contribution to Canadian culture. It publishes the books that give Canadians a sense of place, both geographic and spiritual. The characters and locations of Canadian fiction and nonfiction are as diverse as the country and its people. Even a passing familiarity with the best books the country's writers have produced gives a reader an intimate look at Canada that no amount of city-hopping could ever provide. Readers can experience W.O. Mitchell's prairies, Mordecai Richler's Montreal, Michael Ondaatje's Toronto; journey through popular history with Peter C. Newman and Pierre Berton; reflect on the human condition through the characters of Gabrielle Roy, Margaret Laurence and Margaret Atwood.

In *The Bush Garden: Essays on the Canadian Imagination*, Northrop Frye writes: "It is obvious that Canadian literature, whatever its inherent merits, is an indispensable aid to the knowledge of Canada. It records what the nation's imagination has reacted to, and it tells us things about this environment that nothing else will tell us." The nation's imagination, as Frye termed it, should not be confused with nationalism, which Frye called "the parody of the reality of cultural identity."

This influence is ideological only in its broadest sense, in that literature helps shape readers' values in a whole variety of ways. Authors also exert influence in the context of political or economic ideology, through nonfiction books or by speaking out on public issues. Authors Margaret Atwood, Timothy Findley, Rick Salutin, Farley Mowat and Alice Munro are among those who have spoken out passionately on such issues as free trade, the government's handling of the Oka crisis, the Goods and Services Tax and more.

Yet this advocacy role is an addendum to the deeper, more important role of publishing: to cultivate cultural identity. As journalist Stephen Godfrey has noted, members of Canada's cultural community, from authors to filmmakers, "spoke with a new and unapologetic sense of place" during the 1980s. He observed that a younger generation of writers, such as Guy Vanderhaeghe in Saskatchewan, David Adams Richards in New Brunswick and Sandra Birdsell in Manitoba, "stuck close to home and wrote about what they saw there."

English-language publishing in Canada took firm root at the turn of this century. Numerous publishing houses were founded, including the University of Toronto Press (1901), Oxford University Press (1904), Macmillan of Canada (1905) and McClelland and Goodchild (1906), the precursor of McClelland and Stewart. For French-language publishing in Quebec, the Second World War marked a turning point. Many French writers fled to Montreal, and quite a number of publishing houses sprang up.

Despite the growth in publishing houses, Canada was far from a literary-minded nation. North America was a book-poor continent compared with Western Europe. No more than 500,000 books were sold in Canada in any year before the Second World War, according to one estimate. Throughout the first half of the century, Canada was a publishing backwater exploited by publishers in Britain and the United States. After the war, the country was flooded with cheap foreign paperbacks. By that time, the United States had built a prosperous industry by simply pirating books from other countries and marketing them at home without bothering to pay the authors. (Charles Dickens exhausted himself campaigning against U.S. infringement of his copyright.)

Much of the credit for the development of CanLit, as it became known, goes to Jack McClelland, who in 1946 began his career at the company his father had founded at the turn of the century. With his flair for promotion and loving care of authors, McClelland became the godfather of publishing in Canada, despite the perpetually precarious financial state of his company, McClelland and Stewart. "The Canadian Publisher," as M&S began calling itself in the 1950s, launched one writer after another onto the national scene. Among them: Pierre Berton, Farley Mowat, Irving Layton, Margaret Laurence, Leonard Cohen, Peter Newman, Mordecai Richler, Margaret Atwood and Sylvia Fraser.

McClelland's contribution didn't stop there. Before he sold M&S to financier Avie Bennett in 1986, he hired and trained talents that later emerged as respected figures in publishing, most notably Anna Porter, publisher of Key Porter Books, and Linda McKnight, who was publisher at both M&S and Macmillan of Canada before her latest incarnation as literary agent. A third of McClelland's protégées, Janet Turnbull, now the wife of novelist John Irving, faded from the scene after moving to New York as a literary agent.

During the 1960s and '70s, there was not only a growth in the number of authors, but the number of leading publishing houses outside Toronto grew as well. In Montreal, the other major centre of publishing in Canada, Sogides became a strong force in an already well populated French-language industry. Fiddlehead emerged in Fredericton, Hurtig Publishers set up shop in Edmonton, and on the West Coast, Vancouver's Douglas & McIntyre emerged as a major publisher of B.C. authors. The biggest players in the industry, however, remained based in Toronto, home of more large Canadian- and foreign-owned publishers than any other city in the country.

For all its eccentricities and foibles, the publishing industry is an elite group. Its leading figures and rising stars are virtually all well educated, mainly foreign-born and most often with graduate degrees or at least B.A.s in English or the humanities from major universities. Unfortunately, high salaries have never gone hand in hand with the high qualifications. Starting copy editors with M.A.s rarely earn more than $25,000 a year and can work their way up to $35,000 in eight years. Editors-in-chief have been known to make $50,000 or less a year, despite handling responsibilities as taxing as any chief operating officer's in another business. Publishers rarely make six-figure incomes. One female publisher who left for better-paid pastures says that the low pay probably explains the predominance of women in the business.

Publishing has traditionally been a sanctuary for well-bred, well-educated people who disdain the hurly-burly of business. In Great Britain, it evolved as a supremely civil, gentlemanly pursuit conducted with less intensity than an after-dinner chat at a private club. Predictably, the Americans added their characteristic hustle and braggadocio to the business (rather like stripping down a British-made Bentley and turning it into a stock car). But the English-language Canadian publishing business is somewhere in between, a hybrid of both, probably because most of its influential executives were born and educated either in Great Britain or the United States or worked for companies based there. Aside from that, the New York aggressiveness is seeping northward as ambitious Canadian publishers make regular junkets there to acquire distribution rights for Canada or peddle their books to the huge American market. The French-language publishing business, like most of Quebec culture, is also a hybrid, but of American hustle and French sophistication.

Without a doubt, Canadian publishing is in transition from its days as a mainly literary pursuit to a commercial business. This is not to say that publishing will ever be a business like any other, but with the book-buying public shrinking steadily, production costs soaring and tax breaks vanishing, the publishers who are likely to succeed are those who have both business acumen and authors who write good prose. This trend is already apparent in the people who have emerged as publishing's most influential leaders.

Publishing's Powerbrokers

The Colberts: Literary agents turned publishers, the Colberts have been shaking up the somnambulent Canadian publishing industry since the late 1970s. Critics and rivals sometimes attack them as being too aggressive, too oriented to deal-making in a business where talk of money should be hushed and polite. Born and bred in New York, they make no apologies for pursuing profits, but they are much more complicated than the generalizations suggest.

Nancy, founder of the agency business, can be as graceful and charming as any woman who frequents the Rosedale Golf Club, favourite watering hole of old money Toronto. The razor blades beneath her charm show only when she's talking deals. Husband Stan is much more L.A. in style. For all his killer instincts, developed during his days as a CBC executive, he tends to listen more than he talks, all the better to assess when and how to make his move. Son David is far more aggressive and made a name for himself as an agent by cowing publishers into giving the authors he represented record high advances (including this author, it should be noted for the sake of declaring my biases). No wonder they grumbled about his pushiness.

Nancy pioneered the literary agency business in Canada. She set up her Toronto agency in 1977, roughly the same time as another well-known and successful agent, Lucinda Vardey, was hanging out her shingle. Together, they paved the way for other major agents such as Peter Livingston, Beverley Slopen and Carol Bonnett, a protégée of the Colberts now working with Linda McKnight. But while other agents operated with laid-back, intellectual styles, Colbert's style was all New York. Her business was already a thriving success when Stan left his CBC job to join her as partner. Together with David, they finished what Nancy began: they changed the balance of power in Canadian publishing. Before the Colbert revolution, aspiring and even recognized authors were financially at the mercy of publishers. For all their egos, writers are notoriously inept at promoting themselves or bidding high for their work.

The Colberts changed all that and were largely responsible for a flow of bargaining power to the authors and agents. In the process they built their agency into the largest and most successful in Canada, with more than 250 clients and close to $5 million in gross annual revenues at its peak. The rest of the industry didn't know whether to admire them or deride them, so it settled for the latter, in a virulent case of publishing envy. "With their New York style, they really put the cat among the pigeons," comments an industry veteran.

It was all the more surprising, therefore, when in February 1989 the Colberts changed hats to become publishers. They bought a controlling stake in the Canadian arm of Scottish publisher William Collins PLC, after the parent company was bought out by Australian media magnate Rupert Murdoch. Rich, but not media moguls in their own right, the Colberts bought Collins in partnership with a big New York publisher, Harper & Row, which came on as a minority partner. They then christened their new publishing company Harper & Collins (since abbreviated to HarperCollins) Publishers Ltd. At the same time, acutely aware that the easiest money in the business comes from distributing books for foreign publishers, the Colberts set up a distribution arm, called Harper & Collins Books of Canada Ltd. Nancy Colbert was publisher of the first company, Stanley was chief executive of the distribution arm. David became editor under Nancy, but before long went down to New York to learn the ropes as a senior lieutenant to Harper's chief, George Craig.

By all accounts, the Colberts have done extremely well as publishers. "It's poacher turned gamekeeper," says Nancy. "It's wonderful." HarperCollins has already topped the best-seller lists with books by Timothy Findley and Wayne Gretzky. To top it off, they're making a profit. The company lost $1.7 million the year before the Colberts took over, but they've turned it around. "Both sides of the company are profitable," says Nancy.

In 1991, to bolster their reputation as publishers, they hired Ed Carson as executive vice-president. Carson had made a name for himself at Random House Canada, where as vice-president of publishing he built a Canadian list in three years flat. At HarperCollins, Carson is working directly with Stanley on the business side. There is already talk of him succeeding the Colberts if they step aside to pursue other interests in New York or Canada. "If he stays two or three years, he'll have all the training he needs to become head of the house," comments an observer, who gives him high marks for likability. "He knows his own mind and is easy to get along with."

The mudslinging by industry insiders who think that self-promotion is for car salesmen continues. A *Globe and Mail* writer poked fun at the Colberts for repeating the word *profitable* 15 times in a news release announcing Carson's appointment. Yet that's nothing like the jabs the Colberts took when they first became publishers. Success tends to silence critics. "They all said we were going to fall on our faces," comments Nancy. "Once they realize you're here to stay they stop griping."

Anna Porter: "In her way, she is as complex a character as Jack McClelland," says literary agent Linda McKnight. "If anyone has inherited Jack McClelland's mantle, she has," says Doubleday Canada editor-in-chief John Pearce. "She has the best information network on writers and writing in the country, the way McClelland used to." They are talking about Anna Porter, a perpetually restless soul who has climbed from landed-immigrant status to Establishment in just a few decades. Poet Irving Layton has called Porter a butterfly with steel wings, but the metaphor is a little too suggestive of awkwardness to capture the Porter persona. A falcon with steel talons is a more accurate comparison. The falcon, after all, combines an aloofness with majestic beauty, a sense of fragility with killer instincts.

Falcons are also hard to hold for long, as Porter's foreign partners in Doubleday Canada discovered in early 1991. The industry was shocked when Porter walked away from the owner's seat at Doubleday to focus her energies on Key Porter Books. Porter said she was "signing back" the shares she acquired in Doubleday Canada in 1986 from Bertelsmann A.G., a German media conglomerate that had just bought Doubleday's New York parent. (The 1986 sale of 51 per cent interest in Doubleday Canada to Porter was in keeping with the federal government's 1985 Baie Comeau policy, which requires foreign interests who buy Canadian book publishers or retailers to transfer majority ownership and control to Canadians within two years. Porter had clearly owned the shares, but her foreign partners had financed the sale.)

Porter's decision to scale back her publishing ambitions showed that she is governed more by pragmatism than by pride. After she acquired her majority stake in Doubleday in 1986, Porter was toasted as a mini-*conglomerature*, the Canadian industry's albeit modest answer to Australia's Rupert Murdoch or Britain's Robert Maxwell.

Since 1982, she had built up a publishing empire without parallel in Canada. She was publisher and 50 per cent co-owner of Key Porter Books, a successful publishing house that has steadily expanded since its creation. As chairman and 51 per cent owner of Doubleday Canada, she added to her domain a big house with seven major book clubs as well as a paperback subsidiary, Dell. Porter also owned (and still owns) 75 per cent of Seal Books, a mass market paperback company with close ties to Bantam Books of New York.

Buying into Doubleday was probably the most ambitious thing Porter has ever done, but getting out may prove to be the smartest thing from her perspective. Insiders at Doubleday report that Porter was an absentee owner anyway, rarely seen around the office, and was clearly spreading her talents too thinly. Publishing is a relationship-intensive business, and Porter was hard-pressed to maintain contact with even the most important of the authors she signed up. Financially, she couldn't have picked a worse time to juggle so many responsibilities. With book publishers going through the industry's equivalent of a Third World famine, Porter was constantly being hounded by the accountants working out of Doubleday U.S.'s New York headquarters. Fed up, she left to concentrate on expanding Key Porter into the United States. Porter left just weeks after Doubleday Canada's president, David Kent, had accepted a lucrative offer to become president of Random House Canada. Fortunately, however, Doubleday could count on editor-in-chief John Pearce to run the place and get the company's fall list out without hiccups. Pearce, a thoughtful, Cambridge-educated publisher, was left to work hand in hand with financial and administrative types parachuted in from New York to oversee a "reorganization" of the company that was still underway at time of writing.

Porter's abdication may have diminished her empire, but not her reputation as a smart publisher with sharp business instincts. In all areas of business, conglomerates have proven too big and cumbersome to maximize profits. Unlike some empire builders, Porter was smart enough to realize that publishing is no different. Peers in her field give her high marks for hard work and ability. "She built up her own company with a lot of blood, sweat and tears," says McKnight. One rival publisher has called her "ruthlessly and aggressively commercial." But Pearce has a more balanced view. "What is so impressive about Anna is that she combines editorial instinct with creative marketing."

Porter's ability to coax reluctant authors to write books for her is legendary. The consummate pitch, usually made over lunch, is reserved for the already famous in other walks of life. Porter employs a combination of intellectual stimulation and intoxication (which doesn't come from the alcohol) to strike a deal. The clincher comes, as one editor describes it, "when Anna leans over the table and says in her throaty Hungarian accent" — he imitates it — "'You *must* write me this book.'"

Most authors who succumb never regret it. Allan Fotheringham, the wit from the west with a huge, devoted audience for his newspaper and magazine columns, overcame a phobia of writing books and turned out several best-sellers for Key Porter. Jean Chrétien scored a remarkable success with his memoirs, *Straight from the Heart*, which sold more than 120,000 hardcover copies in a country where most books sell from 2,000 to 10,000 copies. Feisty journalist Claire Hoy topped the best-seller lists with his provocative look at the Mulroney government, *Friends in High Places*, which endeared neither Hoy nor Porter to Mulroney. Fortunately, however, Porter is simply too important a force in publishing for the bureaucrats in Ottawa to ignore. "Anna has influence in Ottawa," says Pearce. "She is appreciated and listened to. She helps shape the government's view of publishing."

In the pursuit of profits and the sort of prestige that most immigrants can only hope their children achieve, Porter works hours that verge on the inhuman. She divides her time between offices and countries. She's a respected figure in London, in Frankfurt, home of the world's largest book fair, and in New York.

In between office- and country-hopping, Porter has found time to write two well-received novels, *Hidden Agenda* and *Mortal Sins*. These she wrote evenings at the substantial home she shares with noted libel lawyer Julian Porter and their two children in Toronto's Moore Park. The area is fashionable, but the home's decor would make it into *Architectural Digest* only with the help of a few coats of paint and a team of Molly Maids. The Porter house is kept in the perpetually dishevelled state common among people of Julian's old money origins (his father was Ontario chief justice Dana Porter). Old money leaves the lint-free, wall-to-wall carpeting, slick leather furniture and bathroom skylights to the nouveau riche in Don Mills.

Porter's energy and ambition can be traced to her origins. "She's got that central European fatalism," former CBC producer and fiction writer Geraldine Sherman has remarked, "that disbelief in the continuity of good fortune. It makes her work hard and enjoy life enormously. If she woke up tomorrow and everything had disappeared, as long as she had her family and her health, she'd start again."

Porter was born Anna Szigethy 48 years ago in Budapest. She has no childhood memories of her father, who was taken away by the Russians when she was a toddler, leaving her and her mother, Maria, to survive as best they could in a one-room apartment. (Decades later, she learned that her father had made his way to Winnipeg. He reluctantly agreed to a brief meeting at her insistence, but it was, as she put it, "awkward.") After the 1956 Hungarian uprising, Maria and her 12-year-old daughter emigrated to New Zealand. Porter attended a convent boarding school, then completed an M.A. in English at the University of Canterbury in Christchurch. There, she first read the Canadian authors she would later edit: Margaret Laurence, Mordecai Richler, Leonard Cohen.

The workaholic nature was apparent early on. To put herself through school, Porter held down a variety of part-time jobs, ranging from modelling to washing the toilets in a mental institution. In the late 1960s, she continued her transcontinental travels by leaving for London, where she found a job with Collier Macmillan publishers. In 1968, Collier transferred Porter to Canada and, just one year later, she was hired away to M&S by Jack McClelland.

Porter signed on as an executive editor responsible for the production (logistics, printing, etc.) of books. By the time she left in 1979, she had risen to vice-president and editor-in-chief, and her public reputation as a golden girl was well established. By 1978, *Chatelaine* magazine had already named her one of the 10 most powerful women in Canada.

After a stint working for McClelland as president and publisher of McClelland-Bantam (Seal Books), a company she would later buy from McClelland, Porter set out on her own. In 1982, she became publisher and president of Key Porter Books, a company she launched with *Key* magazine publisher Michael de Pencier. As head of Key Porter, Porter soon did a remarkable thing: she showed that publishing companies can make money year after year. At first, Key Porter's bread-and-butter publications were assorted how-to books, coffee-table books and the like, but she soon built up a list of more prestigious titles by respected Canadian writers.

Porter has evolved from McClelland's pampered protégée to become his successor as the godparent of Canadian publishing.

Jack Stoddart: Soft-spoken yet innovative, Stoddart runs what is perhaps the most surprising success story in Canadian publishing, Stoddart Publishing Co., which he formed in 1984. The new venture was quite a gamble for a guy who could have chosen instead to lead a more docile life running General Publishing, the company founded by his father, Jack, Sr., in 1957. But Jack, Jr., wanted more challenge than he thought he could find running General, one of Canada's biggest distributors of books and now a perpetual profit maker for Stoddart. Launching his own line was a chance for Stoddart to put his stamp on the family business and get out of his father's shadow. Seven years after the launch, the verdict is in: Stoddart Publishing is a success. But not for the reasons you'd expect.

Stoddart has been successful by bucking conventional wisdom in the industry. The firm doesn't have a publisher. It has an editorial board of six with equal power to bring in authors and approve publishing decisions. Stoddart doesn't go in for flamboyant promotions, it doesn't make a big Christmas sales push, and it tends not to offer its authors multi-city promotional tours. Jack Stoddart's low-key, tight-fisted style has even won him admiration from rivals in the business. As Edmonton publisher Mel Hurtig has commented, "He's an important player because he's one of the few publishers in Canada who has good business sense."

Good luck has helped too. Revenues at Stoddart ($8 million annually at last count) have benefited from the sales of books like Claire Hoy and Victor Ostrovsky's *By Way of Deception*, an exposé of the Israeli secret service that made No. 1 on the New York *Times* best-seller list and sold more than 400,000 copies. Launching a line of children's books by geneticist David Suzuki was another profitable move.

Stoddart is the sphinx of Canadian publishing. In one sense, he's as conservative as his father. Balding, low-key and usually dressed in a business suit, he looks every inch the businessman, just like his father was. He belongs to his father's club, the Donalda, and even lives in his father's house. In another sense, Stoddart is a maverick, both for his unconventional attitudes about publishing and for his nonconformist past.

After he was kicked out of Upper Canada College for feigning a faint on the battalion field in the presence of Field Marshal Montgomery, he set out to make it big in the music world, playing bars with Robbie Lane and the Disciples. By 1964, though, he had given up on a music career and went to work for his dad. He became president of General in 1977, bought the company from his father in 1983, then launched the Stoddart line the next year.

In recent years, Stoddart has emerged as something of an icon in Canadian publishing. He's become a vocal spokesman for the industry causes and shown he's on the look-out for growth opportunities. In 1990 he bought Anansi Press, which first published authors like Michael Ondaatje and Anne Hébert. And he also bought a 49 per cent interest in Macfarlane Walter & Ross, a dynamic new publishing venture launched by three high-profile writers and editors, John Macfarlane, Jan Walter and Gary Ross.

For all his business acumen, Stoddart sees publishing just as much as a cultural enterprise. "If I decided to put a warehouse operation in Buffalo, it would probably save us a quarter of a million dollars a year," he once told the *Financial Post Magazine*. "But I don't think that's being Canadian . . . . You're not going to have the Hugh MacLennans and the Morley Callaghans of this generation coming forward unless you've got Canadian publishers publishing them."

The Colberts, Porter and Stoddart are the best-known publishers in the business who combine literary appreciation with bottom-line instincts. There are others.

In Quebec, Pierre L'Espérance heads a multi-armed publishing company, Sogides, that he founded in 1977. He has since subsumed eight lines of books into his corporate fold (including les Quinze Editeur, Les Editions de l'Homme and Editions la presse). He publishes a full range of books, from biography to fiction, strictly for the French market at home and abroad. Known for his deadpan face — "He never smiles," says a colleague — and Gallic charm, he's a respected fixture at the annual book fair in Frankfurt. L'Espérance has emerged at the forefront of Quebec's substantial publishing industry, which also includes Libre-Expression and Quebec's other premier publisher, Jacques Fortin, whose company, Québec-Amérique, has published numerous French-language best-sellers, including *Les Filles de Caleb*, *Le Matou*, and René Lévesque's memoirs.

In British Columbia, Jim Douglas and Scott McIntyre's company, Douglas & McIntyre, has emerged as the province's premier publisher since its founding in 1971. Douglas & McIntyre has been primarily responsible for getting B.C. writers into print. They also scored a major coup when they signed up Andrew Cohen, whose book on Meech Lake became a national best-seller.

Some smaller fry in the business are also known as smart financial operators, including Cyril Hayes, who runs Durkin Hayes, a small, profitable house in Toronto (Hayes peddles the sort of books known as "cheap and dreadfuls" to the Canadian and U.S. markets and recently acquired Listen for Pleasure); Michael Burch, of Whitecap Books in Vancouver; and Lionel Koffler, of Firefly Books in Toronto.

It shouldn't come as a surprise that so few book publishers can be relied on to make profits with any degree of regularity. Literature and commerce are antitheses that rarely find synthesis in one mind. Imagine William Shakespeare having a conversation with the hustler Donald Trump, Dr. Johnson chatting with defrocked real estate king Robert Campeau, and you get the picture in the extreme. That is why most publishing houses in Canada operate in a perpetual state of manic depression, their denizens lurching between bouts of acute anxiety, brought on by nightmares of insolvency, and ecstasy, brought on by dreams (occasionally realized) of literary glory. Which brings us to the rest of our leading lights in publishing.

Mel Hurtig, of Hurtig Publishers in Edmonton, knows all about financial nightmares. Hurtig is a national gem, a seemingly unstoppable force for Canadian publishing, culture and national pride who keeps bumping into an immovable object: financial reality. Born in Edmonton in 1932, Hurtig began his career in the book-selling business in 1956 in his native city. Since 1972, he has devoted his career to publishing Canadian books at Hurtig. He's become equally well known for his nationalistic crusades and is the author of *The Betrayal of Canada*. He was a founding member of the Committee for an Independent Canada and later the founding chairman of The Council of Canadians, an anti-free trade group formed in 1985. Two of Hurtig's publications in particular have made an invaluable and lasting contribution to Canada: *The Canadian Encyclopedia* and *The Junior Encyclopedia of Canada*. For the first time, they gave Canadians source books for Canadiana, past and present. Unfortunately, in 1991, Hurtig was forced to sell his company to McClelland & Stewart because of insurmountable financial difficulties. A botched marketing campaign for the *Junior Encyclopedia* had combined with a recession and the Goods and Services Tax to slash sales of the excellent and overdue publication — proving once again that in publishing, the road to oblivion is paved with good intentions.

Financial reality is just as unpleasant a spectre at the Toronto offices of Penguin Canada. In a state of panic, its New York parent opted in 1991 to put a financial expert in charge of operations. Steve Parr, youthful accountant, was appointed publisher to replace Sandra Hargreaves as the once-profitable company fell further into the red. The losses were a legacy of an expansionary phase at Penguin during the 1980s, led by its former boss Morton Mint. Comments a veteran: "You don't have two bosses within 15 months without damage." On the editorial side, Parr's main asset is Cynthia Good, whom one industry insider describes as "an extremely lively and creative marketing editor and a great fighter. If she believes in a collection of short stories, she'll fight for it." For the next few years, though, Parr will be doing most of the fighting, digging out from annual losses that are rumoured to have grown to almost $4 million.

There are also plenty of good intentions but no profits these days at the doyen of Canadian publishers, McClelland and Stewart. Since being bailed out by real estate developer Avie Bennett in 1986, the firm has continued to lose money, at an estimated rate of $1 million to $2 million a year. This has caused at least one pundit to remark, "In one sense Jack McClelland was a better businessman. There was no way that Jack lost $8 million in five years."

But then, Bennett has never claimed that profits were his only concern. About 18 months after taking control of M&S, Bennett talked to journalist David Olive about his goals for the company. "If we failed to publish first novels and poetry, if we didn't do essays about the future of this country, M&S would be nothing special." He continued: "My two pressing concerns are to stop the financial hemorrhaging, but also to retain the position the company bears in Canadian publishing. I know it sounds shmaltzy, but if profit were the underlying motive I wouldn't have bought the company, because there are a lot easier ways of making money. It's not worth my saving M&S unless I try to save what Jack started."

The industry dreaded what Bennett might do to Jack's tradition when he took over; after all, his expertise was in strip malls, not prose. Bennett, though, has first-hand experience at the sort of personal tragedy that makes for great literature. He is the scion of one of Canada's first large real estate empires, which was forced into bankruptcy by its bankers in the early 1960s. Bennett, who had dropped out of the University of Toronto to learn the ropes of the business from his uncle, had the family heirloom snatched out from under him. To his credit, he never dwelled on the injustice of it all. Instead, he bought some of the pieces of the fallen empire himself, and by the time he acquired M&S in 1986, he had assembled himself a modest little domain of apartment buildings and plazas. Nothing grand, mind you, but enough to make him a wealthy man.

For a businessman like Bennett, propping up M&S is an extreme form of philanthropy. Instead of a one-time hit to the pocketbook like a donation to the theatre or the symphony, it's a constant drain on resources, and there isn't a lot of room to manoeuvre, either. The costs of reneging on the support can be fatal to one's reputation, as the Hees group found out when it cut loose Lester & Orpen Dennys. Yet the intangible rewards of playing cultural sugar daddy seem to far outweigh the tangible costs. Only a businessperson who has spent a lifetime devoted to the soulless nuts-and-bolts game of making money — after a while the deals all seem the same — can fully appreciate the psychic payback of cultural philanthropy. What's one more apartment building when you can pass the great books you've published on to posterity?

Bennett's greatest asset at M&S is Doug Gibson, publisher since 1988. Born in Scotland in 1943, Gibson is well bred and well educated (he went to a public school, then earned two M.A.s, first at the University of St. Andrews, then at Yale). Gibson came to Canada in 1967 to work as an administrative assistant to the registrar at McMaster University in Hamilton. Just a year later, he began his publishing career as an editorial trainee at Doubleday Canada. Since then, he's served as managing editor of Doubleday and publisher of Macmillan of Canada. He was hired away by Avie Bennett in 1986 and for two years was publisher of his own line of books, Doug Gibson Books. In 1988, when Adrienne Clarkson ended her brief tenure at M&S, Gibson became publisher. "Doug Gibson's list is small, but he is a first-class publisher/editor, although he's a dreadful businessman and numbers person," says one colleague. A witty Scot, Gibson is left to handle authors, not profit ratios and sales projections. They're Bennett's responsibility — and everyone's headache.

Louise Dennys and Malcolm Lester can also attest to the danger of financial headaches becoming terminal. For slightly more than a decade until its closure in 1991, their company, Lester & Orpen Dennys, was a celebrated publisher of international authors and built up a respectable list of Canadian writers as well. They are both in this book because they have by no means vanished from publishing. In fact, Lester has already re-emerged with a new, small company, and Dennys became publisher of a new imprint, Alfred A. Knopf Canada, in September, 1991.

An industry veteran says of Louise Dennys: "She's the only other person besides Anna Porter who is a credible figurehead for the industry. She floats around internationally. All the men who run large houses would like the same kind of profile." Like Anna Porter, Dennys is noted for her clout in the international publishing marketplace. But there is a difference. Porter is best known for her commercial acumen; Dennys is known primarily for her dedication to literature with a capital "L." "Lester & Orpen Dennys was frequently in financial trouble," says John Pearce, editor-in-chief of Doubleday Canada, "but Louise did something, she spearheaded something innovative: the treatment of this country as a separate marketplace for international books. Their Canadian list wasn't bad, but what made them a stellar company was their publishing of international authors, among them Graham Greene, Josef Skvorecky and P.D. James. There are too many books in this world. There has to be a filter. New York publishers do this for the American public. Here Lester & Orpen Dennys said, 'Hey Canada, this is what you should be reading.'"

Like so many other leading figures in the industry, Dennys developed her taste for literature elsewhere and put it in practice after immigrating to Canada. Born in Egypt, where her father was head of British Intelligence in the Middle East, she spent her earliest years in Turkey and France. The family returned to England when she was in her teens. Educated at public school and Oxford University, where she received a B.A. in 1968, Dennys fell in love with publishing while selling books, before and after graduation, at Blackwell & Sons, the famous Oxford bookstore. After a brief fling working as a blackjack croupier in a London casino owned by Penthouse, Dennys landed a job as manager at the Oxford University Press in Charing Cross Road.

In London, Dennys met Canadian Eric Young, a student at the London Film School. When Young returned to Canada in the early 1970s, Dennys came with him and began her career in Canadian publishing. She worked in Toronto first as an editor at Clarke, Irwin & Co., then at antiquarian book seller Anson-Cartwright. While there, she published two novellas by Czech émigré Skvorecky, who was brought to her attention by her uncle, the novelist Graham Greene. By the end of the '70s she had come to the attention of publisher Malcolm Lester and his partner, Eve Orpen. In 1979, the firm of Lester and Orpen became Lester & Orpen Dennys (LOD).

As vice-president, Dennys formed an excellent publishing team with president Malcolm Lester, who brought to the bargain editorial skills that he had picked up in a career in Canadian publishing. Born in Toronto in 1938, Lester was educated at the University of Toronto and at Hebrew Union College, where he earned a Bachelor of Hebrew Literature. His career had spanned both publishing (he was managing editor of Holt, Rinehart and Winston of Canada from 1964 to 1970) and sales (as general manager of Coles, 1970–71). While Dennys graced the international stage, Lester proved himself adept at signing new authors at home. Over the next decade, LOD made an international name for itself publishing Canadian authors such as Josef Skvorecky and Joy Kogawa as well as international talent.

Unfortunately, the two principals' forte did not lie in corporate finance. As Lester himself once put it, "We're in the business not just to make money. We're in the business to publish books. The publishing of books is what's important." In the end, publishing good books wasn't enough. LOD ended its life in 1991 with $2 million in bank debt and other liabilities.

The company's death was slow and protracted. The beginning of the end came in August 1988, when international financier Christopher Ondaatje, through his company Pagurian Corp., bought LOD from Lester and Dennys. For a brief four months Lester and Dennys thought they had it made: Ondaatje agreed to back the company's debts and told the pair to think big. Then suddenly, that December, Ondaatje sold half of Pagurian — and with it LOD — to a merchant banking company, Hees International Bancorp, controlled by Peter and Edward Bronfman and their senior managers. After that, LOD was left rudderless.

To the Hees managers, LOD was a little bit of a nuisance. They were more preoccupied with restructuring the Hees empire, in which Pagurian was used as a vehicle to buy out Edward Bronfman's 50 per cent holding in key companies in the Bronfman orbit. LOD was lost in the shuffle. Ondaatje was soon out of the picture completely, eventually selling the rest of Pagurian to Hees and resigning as chairman of LOD.

LOD's demise came about in a tangled web of accusations and counter-accusations between the Hees managers and Lester and Dennys. The two publishers wanted to buy out the company but were rebuffed. Hees tried to sell off the company to any other publisher but had no takers. And a government bailout was out of the question for a company owned by the mighty Bronfman dynasty.

LOD's death is a testament to the futility of trying to match a purely literary enterprise with the mindset of shrewd accountants.

The Government Giveth and the Government Taketh Away

The publishing industry is one of the least influential elite groups studied in this book, if the traditional measures of power are financial clout or political leverage. That probably explains why entry into its upper echelons is comparatively open. There is plenty of room at the top for first-generation immigrants of various ethnic groups, although the industry's powerbrokers are virtually all white. Women are not precluded from power, as they are in almost every other elite. Indeed, women predominate in the industry, from top to bottom.

The influence of the industry lies in its contribution to the evolution of Canada's polygot personality. But because publishing is a cultural industry, it is not like a business that makes products for consumers. Book publishers shouldn't be treated like, say, cereal makers. Books impart a cultural heritage that can be passed from generation to generation; cereal, at best, imparts fibre.

Writer and publishing policy consultant Roy MacSkimming has concisely summed up the tenuous relationship between books and economics. "For two decades now," he wrote in 1991, "managing Canadian publishing has been predicated on the belief that culturally valuable books are what economists call 'merit goods' — products that have intrinsic value to society but aren't sustainable from market revenues alone, and so merit public support." This has been the assumption behind government support for the industry, especially since the mid-1970s, when an Ontario Royal Commission concluded that the Canadian industry required public action to survive in a small market saturated with imported titles and populated by undercapitalized publishers.

The federal government, through the Department of Communications and the Canada Council, spends about $15 million a year on the publishing industry. In Ontario, home of most of the major publishers, the province spends about $1.5 million a year helping publishers pay interest on their debts, guaranteeing bank loans and parcelling out little grants averaging $14,000 each to 55 publishers. (A paltry sum compared to the $15 million the Ontario Film Development Corporation receives each year.) Given these insufficient handouts, it is patently absurd that the federal government imposed the 7 per cent Goods and Service Tax on books. The tax placed the government in the silly situation of giving out money with one hand and taking it back with the other.

In the summer of 1991, the publishing industry was still hoping for relief from the GST and awaiting a package of tax incentives from the federal government that would help improve publishing's financial outlook. The outcome promised to have major implications for the health of the industry, but it also promised to say a lot about the government's appreciation, or lack of it, of the lasting merits of a good book.

Conclusion

Toward a Just Society

The day Edward Plunket Taylor left this world went almost unnoticed. Only a hundred or so friends and family showed up for the service at St. John's Anglican Church in York Mills on Tuesday, June 14, 1989. There were no reports in the social columns, there were no moving descriptions of the ceremony in the news media. It was a discreet affair: black limousines, Jaguars, Porsches and Mercedes glided past the side door of the historic stone chapel to disgorge guests who had come to pay respects to the man who had symbolized the Canadian Establishment for decades. By the time E.P. Taylor died at 88 in his Bahamas retreat, the other business greats of his generation were long gone. Roy Thomson, Garfield Weston and Bud McDougald all had died by the late 1970s. The social and business notables who attended the service were sons of Taylor's business associates. Fred and James McCutcheon were there, sons of Senator Wally McCutcheon, who served as Taylor's axeman at Argus Corporation. Montegu Black, elder brother of Conrad, came to pay respects to his father's Argus business partner. Austin Taylor, chairman of Scotia McLeod, was there, and Michael Burns, son of investment dealer Charles Burns, attended with his mother, Janet.

Power in Canada's upper class passes quietly from one generation to the next. It's like a many-coloured coat that fits only those with the right upbringing and attitudes.

If he were alive, E.P. Taylor would still be very much at home in the corridors of money and social power in Canada. The atmosphere at the private clubs is the same; there are so few women on corporate boards that they can be ignored; and there may be people of many colours and races on the city streets, but they certainly aren't making inroads into the Establishment.

The business and social establishments of Canada have been the slowest to change of any of Canada's ruling elites, but across the spectrum, social mobility is a goal rather than a reality.

In *The Vertical Mosaic*, John Porter concludes that "ethnic and religious affiliation in Canadian society have always had an effect on the life chances of the individual." He goes on to predict that "Canada will always appear as an adaptation of its British and French charter groups, rather than as one of a new breed in a new nation."

The main conclusion to be drawn from my study of Canada's elites is that Porter's assessment still rings true, with the added observation that gender, as much as ethnicity, plays a role in sorting out who gains admission to the circles of power. Canada's ruling class — especially the political, bureaucratic and business elites — is still very much the domain of the two so-called charter groups, English and French, no matter how much the makeup of the population has been diversified by immigration, and despite all the rhetoric and taxpayers' dollars that have gone toward promoting multiculturalism.

It is possible to take the conclusion a step further. Canadians with British ancestry and at least nominal affiliation with the Protestant Church still hold sway in the business and political affairs of the nation as well as in the print media. The only significant inroads have been made by other white Europeans who tend to blend in well at the boardroom tables. The popular assumption that Canada has become a smorgasbord of competing cultures transplanted from foreign lands may be true of our inner cities but not of the inner sanctums of power.

Certain of the elites have been more open to newcomers than others, most notably television, film and publishing. Yet even in those fields, women at the top are more the exception than the rule.

As a result, there is a vast pool of Canadians who have been largely shut out from power in Canadian society. They are the women who find themselves bumping into a so-called glass ceiling that limits their progress up the ranks of the organization. They are non-whites or members of Jewish and other minorities whose ethnic background, religion or even accents keep them from assimilating smoothly into the ruling groups. They are the truly disinherited who feel that their social mobility is limited by hermetically sealed elites that govern them.

Yet they are not the only ones who feel disinherited. In the 1930s, Gaetano Mosca wrote: "In all societies . . . two classes of people appear — a class that rules and a class that is ruled." In Canada, those who are ruled, regardless of their sex or ethnic background, share a widespread sense of alienation from the ruling elites. There is a sense that structures of power need a massive renovation in order to restore the faith of ordinary Canadians — from all regions, ethnic backgrounds and genders — in their legitimacy.

Our faith in political, bureaucratic and religious elites has never been lower. These elites are in decline, insofar as their capacity to lead the country by suasion — rather than simply by (generally unpopular) policies, rules and regulations — is vastly diminished. The business elite, whose power rests ultimately on its control over the movement of capital and goods and not popular support, has held its own in general and, if anything, increased its influence over the political agenda of the country. Likewise, the media has increased its influence over societal values in recent decades as the churches' role has declined.

On the whole, the social contract that has bound the rulers and the ruled in Canada for generations is in disrepair. But how can we fix it? Just what are the legal principles, practical policies and underlying ethical values needed to make Canada a more just society?

Political philosophers, not to mention theologians, have been mulling over how to create a just, or model, society since the beginning of recorded history. Some of their best works contain the philosophical underpinnings of our modern democratic traditions. Most of these thinkers were motivated to write by their disgust with the ways things worked in the societies they knew. Plato, who was upset with the Athenian democracy that had been responsible for the execution of his friend and teacher Socrates, penned *The Republic* to show how an ideal state should work. His model state was class-based and ruled by a talented minority and an all-wise philosopher-king. The importance Plato placed on justice, education and ethics in the state has inspired democratic thinkers ever since.

Many centuries later, Sir Thomas More updated Plato's thesis with his own best-seller, *Utopia*. More's fictional state comprises a homogeneous society made up of 54 towns, all alike in language laws, customs and institutions, and all located the same distance from the capital, Aircastle. Economic production is organized so well in this model state that there is more than enough of everything to go around. No unproductive occupations are allowed, except for elected politicians. In this perfect world, no one is greedy and one consumes only what one needs — without paying, since there is always a surplus. The inhabitants all enjoy religious freedom, and most believe in a supreme being. Their definition of the pursuit of happiness is to follow the will of this god.

Jean Jacques Rousseau was so upset with the way societies worked in the mid-1700s that he was moved to write his famous treatise *The Social Contract*. Rousseau had two main reasons for condemning existing societies: they made men dependent on other individuals (or what we would call power groups), and they were competitive, not cooperative. In his view, it was impossible for men to co-exist in a competitive society without "deceiving each other, betraying each other, destroying each other." The way Rousseau saw it, the best way to rein in the selfish and aggressive instincts of human beings was to submit people to the authority of the general will of the state. By entering this social contract, the individual loses his natural liberty and the unlimited right to everything he tries to get and succeeds in getting. But he gains moral liberty, civil liberty and the right to hold property and possession by law rather than by beating off others who would take them from him.

At first glance, the thoughts of these philosophers and others may seem to have little relevance today, but the ideas they explored, primarily the principle that human beings have natural rights by virtue of being human beings, are hugely important in modern democracies, including Canada's. Yet even the legal enshrinement of fundamental human rights is not enough to ensure a truly just society.

The Limitations of Law

Canadian politicians have had high hopes that by enshrining citizens' rights and freedoms in law, a just society could be achieved.

In 1960, John Diefenbaker, the Prairie populist, gave Canada its Bill of Rights. His motivations were twofold: he feared the potential of expanding federal and provincial bureaucracies to limit individual freedoms and procedural safeguards, and he abhorred racial discrimination. Diefenbaker saw the bill as a way of promoting his dream of "one Canada"; he envisioned his beloved Bill of Rights as a symbol that would transcend regional identities and apply to "all, including the poor, the dispossessed, the ignored and the shut-out." The Bill of Rights laid out several basic rights and freedoms that are "to exist without discrimination by reason of race, national origin, colour, religion or sex."

For Pierre Trudeau, entrenching a charter of rights in the Constitution was a key ingredient of his government's nation-building strategy between 1967 and 1982. Trudeau got his Charter, but national unity eluded him.

The 1982 Charter of Rights and Freedoms entrenches some wonderful-sounding principles in the newly patriated constitution. They include fundamental freedoms: freedom of conscience and religion; freedom of thought, belief, opinion and expression, including freedom of the communications media; freedom of peaceful assembly and freedom of association. Other sections lay out "democratic rights" such as the right of citizens to vote in federal and provincial elections; "mobility rights," ensuring every citizen the right to move from province to province to find work; "legal rights," such as a prohibition on unreasonable search and seizure; and "equality rights," including the principle that every individual "is equal before and under the law and has the right to equal protection and equal benefit of the law without discrimination."

For decades, then, Canadians have had the benefit of fundamental freedoms laid down in specific laws and, since 1982, in the Constitution. Numerous provincial bills of rights have also been enacted.

So there is little doubt that all Canadians enjoy equality before the law (with the noted exception of English-speaking Quebeckers). But the Charter could hardly be expected to create a just society on its own, one in which gender, race or national origin are not handicaps to advancement. The Charter, after all, applies only to relations between a person and the government (federal, provincial and municipal), not to private relations between persons. Private relations are covered by eleven provincial human rights codes and the common law. There is also the federal Canadian Human Rights Act, enacted by Parliament in 1977, to control private discrimination within federally regulated workplaces. Laudably, the Charter specifically makes affirmative action programs legal, and there is a smattering of them in government and educational institutions across the country.

Yet, judging from the makeup of the country's ruling elites, there remains much progress to be made in ensuring equality of *opportunity* in Canada, and hence realizing the dream of social mobility. Creating a society where the ethos is everyone for themselves (provided they stay within the limits of the law) is a step up from the jungle but hardly an admirable state of affairs. Two additional principles make for a better society. First, the rights-bearers must accept the responsibility of tolerating the rights of others. Second, the rights-bearers also have a responsibility to take action to ensure that others have the *opportunity* to exercise their rights; that is, to pursue self-realization. Another way of putting this is that we should be our brother's or sister's keeper. This is a difficult concept to codify in law, since it has a lot more to do with personal ethics than legally defined civil liberties.

Practical Policies

There are no quick fixes or even bold policy initiatives, either in the private or the public sector, that can suddenly change the structure and makeup of Canada's ruling elites. But there are some more modest steps that can be taken.

Legislation, of course, has limited uses. Since we do not live in a dictatorship, it is neither realistic nor wise to suggest that laws could be passed forcing, say, banks to make sure their boards represent the makeup of the population, with half of the directors women, or one-third of them of other than British or French descent. Less ambitious policies, however, like affirmative action programs, can help. (Sometimes these are involuntary, as is the case of government employees, or voluntary, in private sector organizations.)

Affirmative action programs are, of course, one of the more controversial ways to redress the way women and minorities are underrepresented in the leadership ranks of most fields. Ultimately, they relate directly to the notion of equality of opportunity for everyone. In its most simple terms, the debate raises the question: should groups that have suffered from a lack of equality be helped along by measures that infringe on the equality of others, such as males or whites? Should a well-qualified woman be given an advantage in career promotions above an equally well-qualified male, or even a better qualified one?

All three of the philosophers discussed above accepted the notion of the natural rights for human beings — rights they are born with rather than granted by legislatures — although all three wrote at times when male dominance in society was unquestioned. But one is tempted to think that, if he were alive today, Plato's concern for justice and the lot of the underprivileged would have led him to say yes to some form of affirmative action programs. Thomas More's vision of a model society didn't take account of real-world blemishes like prejudice and is just as utopian now as it was when he wrote it. But perhaps Rousseau's belief in the need for an all-powerful state might lead him to recommend state intervention to deal with discrimination. This is all speculation, of course, since the notion of human rights has been greatly advanced in modern-day democratic theory.

The findings of this book illuminate the degree to which those advances in theory, however, have not been fulfilled in practice in Canada. My view is that to redress the effects of decades of discrimination, affirmative action programs in private and public organizations are very necessary. These programs, however, should be voluntary, and not involve arbitrary quotas, since the latter can lead to horribly unjust situations where better qualified candidates are

systematically passed over for poorly qualified contenders. This solution is, at best, a workable compromise between groups demanding
equality of opportunity. It infringes on the notion of equality of opportunity, but it doesn't trample on it.

As we have seen, though, some institutional power structures are
so exclusionary that they must be changed before other voices will
ever be heard in their deliberations. For example, whether women
in the Roman Catholic Church will ever be treated as equals is up
to the Pope to decide. As for the United Church, the problem lies
with a faulty power structure that has permitted an ad hoc power
grab by well-organized bureaucrats.

The elitist nature of the federal government, however, is everybody's problem. At present, Canada's leaders are preoccupied with
the question of national unity and the constitutional division of powers between the provinces and Ottawa. Yet in their deliberations, the
politicians, bureaucrats and scholars concerned would be wise to consider parliamentary reform that would help reduce regional grievances
and restore the faith of the population in how well the government
represents voter interests. The three-way triad that rules Ottawa —
the cabinet, the mandarinate and the most powerful lobby groups
— should be opened up to allow the voices of the regions and general
population to wield some influence.

Such steps would not change the fundamental nature of federal
politics, the government's need to broker between the demands of
different interest groups and regions and its love of handing out patronage plums to party faithful. They would simply open up the game
to more players.

The Ethical Imperative

Thomas Hurka, a University of Calgary philosopher, writes in his
Globe and Mail column: "We've built Canada on tolerance, a respect
for diversity and a willingness to share with those who are less for-
tunate. We created a medicare system that makes health care a right
of all citizens and we are justifiably proud of it. We took special
steps to preserve the way of life in Newfoundland outports and among
the Dene in the Mackenzie Valley. We instituted equalization pay-

ments to share the wealth of rich provinces with those who are worse off."

Hurka's comments crystallize a central myth that has bound Canadians together for generations. Until recently, that is. The central ingredients of this myth are tolerance and compassion, and as everyone from Tuktoyaktuk to St. Catharines knows, those qualities seem forgotten these days. Yet without them, any efforts to create a more just society in Canada, or for that matter reconstruct the federation, are imperilled. Granted, people with different skin colours, religions or styles of dress are *tolerated*, but not gladly, to judge from the rise of racial tensions in our major cities. In Vancouver, anti-Asian sentiment is running high. In Toronto, tension between blacks and whites is at a new high. In Halifax it erupted in riots. In Montreal, French-language laws have made Greeks, Italians and Anglos feel like second-class citizens. Compassion seems even more scarce than tolerance, which, after all, takes no effort except to leave people alone. Many sociologists agree that compassion is on the decline in Canada. They say we are born with the need to help others, but it's subverted by the competitive drive to be the best. Some experts blame the situation on our high-tech culture. As Tony Richards, a Dalhousie University professor, has warned, "The further we get into industrialization, into high technology, the less we as individuals connect, the less there is to be compassionate about." Evidence of this declining compassion is not hard to find. In major cities, it is becoming difficult to board a bus without using your elbows. Pause for a moment in your car when the light turns green and blaring horns will alert you to your misdemeanour. It's no coincidence that Canadians are making more money than ever but giving less to charity.

But more than anything, the decline in compassion can be traced to the waning of religious values in Canadian society. By this I do not mean straitlaced Protestant virtues that crimp the soul and confine the mind. I mean the most redeeming feature of all Canada's major religions, love of fellow human beings. This love should not be confused with sentimentality. It is very clearly expressed in the Christian notion of love, called agape, which is divinely inspired, unselfish love. It is different from other kinds of love, such as friendship and erotic passion. Agape is the product of an intellectual decision, not emotion. It is more an aspiration for human beings than an easily recognizable quality. Yet the pursuit of it lays the ground for reconciliation where possible, and at least tolerance where reconciliation seems impossible.

Religious values have other important contributions to make. A belief in a divine being gave rise to the notion, incorporated in liberal democratic traditions, that the human being has intrinsic worth and hence fundamental rights in society. To strip away the notion of the divinely inspired worth of individuals is to undermine the philosophical underpinnings of the importance of the individual in democratic societies. Legal definitions of rights become just that, mere legal definitions that can be changed by judges or legislators.

As the religious convictions of Canadians have withered away, so has their capacity to get along with one another. Of course, religious beliefs have never guaranteed harmony or just treatment of fellow human beings. Look at the Spanish Inquisition, or the way established religions have condoned slavery or apartheid. But such misuses of religion do not negate the potential of religions to inspire compassion and tolerance.

Whatever their source — Christianity, Judaism, Hinduism, Islam, secular humanism or plain old pragmatism — the qualities of tolerance and compassion are needed more than ever in Canada. They are the qualities that will motivate Canada's ruling elites to welcome newcomers into the inner sanctums of power and help make the myth of social mobility a reality. Tolerance and compassion are also the qualities that will have to underlie the deliberations over Canada's federation, if they are to be successful.

There are no guarantees on either score. Tolerance and compassion are not much good if they're not reciprocated. But they do offer hope.

Appendix 1

Political Elite Survey Results

Survey of the 39 members of the federal cabinet.
Date completed: December, 1989
Sources: 13 responded to biographical questionnaire; information on the remaining 26 individuals was derived from phone calls and biographical texts including, *Ottawa's Senior Executive Guide*, published by Info Globe and the *Canadian Who's Who*.

Gender

known: 39 (100%)
Men: 33 (84.6%)
Women: 6 (15.4%)

Age

known: 39 (100%)
Between 60–69 years: 2 (5.1%)
Between 50–59 years: 22 (56.4%)
Between 40–49 years: 12 (30.8%)
Between 30–39 years: 3 (7.7%)

Birthplace

known: 39 (100%)
Foreign-born: 2 (5.1%) (West Germany and Czechoslovakia)
Canadian-born: 37 (94.9%)
  The West: 9 (23.1%)
  (British Columbia: 2; Alberta: 4; Saskatchewan: 2;
  Manitoba: 1)
  Central Canada: 23 (59.0%)
  (Ontario: 11; Quebec: 12)

  The East: 5 (12.8%)
  (New Brunswick: 2; Nova Scotia: 2;
  Newfoundland: 1)

  The Yukon and Northwest Territories: 0

Education

Secondary
known: 32 (82.1%)
Attended public school: 19 (59.4%)
Attended private school: 13 (40.6%)
Private schools attended:
  Upper Canada College: 2 (6.2%)
  Academie Ste. Emilie: 1
  Trinity College: 1
  Appleby College: 1
  Ste.-Anne de la Pocatière College: 1
  Ecole Superieur St. Stanislas: 1
  Valleyfield College: 1
  Albert College: 1
  Academie St. Joseph de St. Quentin: 1
  Seminaire de Sherbrooke: 1
  St. Andrew's College: 1
  Jesuit School: 1

Post-Secondary
known: 37 (94.9%)
No post-secondary education: 4 (10.8%)
Some post-secondary education: 33 (89.2%)
Completed post-graduate degrees (masters level and above):
  11 (29.7%)
Professional degrees or designations: 22 (59.4%)
  (law: 12; accounting: 1; engineering: 3; other professional qual-
  ifications: 6)
Universities attended most frequently (many ministers attended more
than one:)
  University of Toronto: 6 (16.2%)
  Laval University: 5 (13.5%)
  University of Montreal: 4 (10.8%)
  Queen's University: 3 (8.1%)
  University of Western Ontario: 3 (8.1%)
  McGill University: 3 (8.1%)
  University of Alberta: 3 (8.1%)

University of New Brunswick: 3 (8.1%)
Dalhousie University: 2 (5.4%)
St. Francis Xavier: 2 (5.4%)

Career Backgrounds (Some ministers combined more than one career)

known: 39 (100%)
Law: 12 (30.8%)
Business: 11 (28.2%)
Academics (including two secondary school teachers): 9 (23.1%)
Journalism: 3 (7.7%)
Engineering: 3 (7.7%)
Farming: 2 (5.1%)
Politics only: 2 (5.1%)
Pharmacy: 1 (2.6%)
Physiotherapy: 1 (2.6%)

Ethnic Background (individual may fit into one or more categories)

known: 23 (59.0%)
At least one parent of British descent: 8 (34.8%)
At least one parent of French descent: 11 (47.8%)
Other European: 4 (17.4%)

Religion

Of the 39 ministers for whom information was available, 25 (64.1%) listed a religious affiliation; of those claiming adherence to a particular faith, the distribution was as follows:
Protestant: 18 (72.0%)
   (Anglican: 7; United Church: 7; other Protestant: 4)
Roman Catholic: 6 (24.0%)
Jewish: 1 (4.0%)

Social Origins (based on occupation of father)

known: 20 (51.3%)
Blue collar or working class: 7 (35.0%)

White collar, managerial or clergy: 10 (50.0%)
Other major elite group: 3 (15.0%) (corporate: 2; judge: 1)

Private Clubs

known: 39 (100%)
Ministers who list membership in one or more: 11 (28.2%)
Ministers who list membership in five or more: 1 (2.6%)
Most popular clubs:
   The Albany (Toronto): 6 (15.4%)
   The Rideau (Ottawa): 3 (7.7%)
Other clubs listed: The Toronto, Mount Royal, Ranchmen's,
   Garrison, University

Appendix 2

Bureaucratic Elite Survey Results

Survey of the 27 federal deputy ministers who run full government departments.
Date completed: December, 1989

Sources: 17 responded to biographical questionnaires; information on the remaining 10 individuals was derived from phone calls and biographical texts, including *Ottawa's Senior Executive Guide*, published by Info Globe, and the *Canadian Who's Who*.

Gender

known: 27 (100%)
Men: 20 (74.1%)
Women: 7 (25.9%)

Age

known: 27 (100%)
Between 50–59 years: 10 (37.0%)

Between 40–49 years: 16 (59.3%)
Between 30–39 years: 1 (3.7%)

Birthplace

known: 27
Foreign-born: 4 (14.8%) (England, Ireland, Czechoslovakia and The Netherlands)
Canadian-born: 23 (85.2%)
   The West: 6 (22.2%)
   (British Columbia: 1; Alberta: 3; Saskatchewan: 2)

   Central Canada: 17 (63.0%)
   (Ontario: 8; Quebec: 9)

   The East: 0
   The Yukon and Northwest Territories: 0

Education

Secondary
known: 16 (59.3%)
Attended public school: 11 (68.8%)
Attended private school: 5 (31.2%)
Private schools attended:
   Rupert Landing Girls School
   College Classique de Rouyn
   St. Joseph's College
   College Stanislas
   Lower Canada College

Post Secondary
known: 27 (100%)
No post-secondary education: 0
Some post-secondary education: 27 (100%)
Completed post-graduate degrees (masters level and above): 16
   (59.3%)

Professional degrees or designations: 8 (29.6%)
  (law: 5; engineering: 2; medicine: 1)
Universities attended most frequently (many deputy ministers attended more than one:
  Queen's University: 5 (18.5%)
  University of Ottawa: 5 (18.5%)
  University of Alberta: 4 (14.8%)
  University of Toronto: 3 (11.1%)
  University of British Columbia: 3 (11.1%)
  Oxford University: 3 (11.1%)
  Harvard University: 2 (7.4%)
  University of Montreal: 2 (7.4%)
  Laval University: 2 (7.4%)

Career Backgrounds

known: 27 (100%)
Spent *entire* career in civil service: 14 (51.9%)
Spend *most* of career in civil service: 22 (81.5%)
Spend some time in other fields: 13 (48.1%)
  (other fields: academics: 4; law: 3; business: 2; engineering: 1; geology: 1; public health: 1; airforce: 1)

Ethnic Background (individual may fit into one or more categories)

known: 22 (81.5%)
At least one parent of British descent: 9 (40.9%)
At least one parent of French descent: 9 (40.9%)
Other European: 5 (18.5%)

Religion

Of the 27 deputy ministers for whom information was available, 13 (48.1%) listed a religious affiliation; of those claiming adherence to a particular faith, the distribution was as follows:
Protestant: 6 (46.2%)
  (United Church: 3; Anglican: 2; other Protestant: 1)

Roman Catholic: 5 (38.5%)
Jewish: 2 (15.4%)

Social Origins (based on occupation of father)

known: 17 (63.0%)
Blue collar or working class: 3 (17.6%)
White collar, managerial or clergy: 12 (70.6%)
Other major elite group: 2 (11.8%) (corporate director and professor)

Private Clubs

known: 27 (100%)
Deputy ministers who list membership in one or more: 9 (33.3%)
Deputy ministers who list membership in five or more: 0
Most popular clubs:
  Five Lakes Club: 3 (11.1%)
  Rideau Club: 2 (7.4%)
Other clubs listed: Le Cercle Universitaire, Royal Montreal Golf,
  Britannia Yacht, Alpine

Appendix 3

Corporate Elite Survey Results

Survey of the 251 directors of the 20 largest (by assets) Canadian corporations. The total number of positions represented is 278 but 22 individuals sit on boards of two of the top 20 and four sit on boards of three of the top 20 corporations:
Date completed: October, 1989
Sources: 94 responded to biographical questionnaires; information on an additional 71 individuals was derived from personal biographies, the *Directory of Directors*, published by *The Financial Post* and the *Canadian Who's Who*.

Bank Group

Survey of the 181 directors of the five largest (by assets) Canadian banks. Forty-four of these individuals were also part of the corporate group as they held directorships on the top 20 corporations as well. Date completed: October, 1989.

Sources: 57 responded to biographical questionnaires; information on an additional 74 individuals was derived from personal biographies, the *Directory of Directors*, published by *The Financial Post* and the *Canadian Who's Who*.

Gender

Corporate Group
known: 251 (100%)
Men: 229 (91.2%)
Women: 22 (8.8%)

Bank Group
known: 181 (100%)
Men: 172 (95.0%)
Women: 9 (5.0%)

Age

Corporate Group
known: 170 (67.7%)
Between 70–79 years: 11 (6.5%)
Between 60–69 years: 79 (46.5%)
Between 50–59 years: 53 (31.2%)
Between 40–49 years: 26 (15.3%)
Between 30–39 years: 1 (0.6%)

Bank Group
known: 136 (75.1%)
Between 70–79 years: 8 (5.9%)
Between 60–69 years: 84 (61.8%)
Between 50–59 years: 35 (25.7%)

Between 40–49 years: 8 (5.9%)
Between 30–39 years: 1 (0.7%)

Birthplace

Corporate Group
known: 162 (64.5%)
Foreign-born: 16 (9.9%)
(USA: 8; UK: 3; Australia: 2; Jamaica: 1; Switzerland: 1;
Austria: 1)
Canadian-born: 146 (90.1%)

The West: 29 (17.9%)
(British Columbia: 5; Alberta: 7; Saskatchewan: 9;
Manitoba: 8)

Central Canada: 104 (64.2%)
(Ontario: 52; Quebec: 52)

The East: 13 (8.0%)
(Nova Scotia: 9; New Brunswick: 4)

The Yukon and Northwest Territories: 0

Bank Group
known: 128 (70.7%)
Foreign-born: 14 (10.9%)
(USA: 6; UK: 5; France: 1; South America: 1; Austria: 1)
Canadian-born: 114 (89.1%)
The West: 42 (32.8%)
(Saskatchewan: 13; Manitoba: 13; British Columbia: 10; Alberta:
6)

Central Canada: 58 (45.3%)
(Ontario: 34; Quebec: 24)

The East: 14 (10.9%)
(Nova Scotia: 8; New Brunswick: 5; Newfoundland: 1)

The Yukon and Northwest Territories: 0

Education
Corporate Group
known: 131 (52.2%)
Attended public school: 82 (62.6%)
Attended private school: 49 (37.4%)
Private schools attended most frequently:
    Collège Jean de Brébeuf: 9 (6.9%)
    Upper Canada College: 6 (4.6%)
    University of Toronto Schools: 3 (2.3%)
    Ridley: 2 (1.5%)
    Lakefield: 2 (1.5%)
    Seminaire de Québec: 2 (1.5%)
    Selwyn House: 2 (1.5%)
    Trinity College: 2 (1.5%)

Bank Group
known: 106 (58.6%)
Attended public school: 63 (59.4%)
Attended private school: 43 (40.6%)
Private schools attended most frequently:
    Upper Canada College: 6 (5.7%)
    Ridley: 6 (5.7%)
    Ravenscourt: 3 (2.8%)
    University of Toronto Schools: 2 (1.9%)
    Collège Jean de Brébeuf: 2 (1.9%)
    Notre Dame: 2 (1.9%)
    St. George's: 2 (1.9%)

Post-Secondary
Corporate Group
known: 159 (63.3%)
No post-secondary education: 13 (8.2%)

Some post-secondary education: 146 (91.8%)
Completed post-graduate degrees (masters level and above): 47 (29.6%)
Professional degrees or designations: 79 (49.7%)
(law: 33; accounting: 21; engineering: 21; medicine: 2; pharmacy: 2)
Universities attended most frequently (individuals often attended more than one):
   University of Toronto: 27 (17.0%)
   McGill University: 25 (15.7%)
   Harvard University: 19 (11.9%)
   Laval University: 13 (8.2%)
   University of Montreal: 10 (6.3%)
   University of Western Ontario: 10 (6.3%)
   Osgoode Law School: 8 (5.0%)
   Queen's University: 8 (5.0%)
   Dalhousie University: 7 (4.4%)
   University of Manitoba: 7 (4.4%)

Bank Group
known: 125 (69.1%)
No post-secondary education: 9 (7.2%)
Some post-secondary education: 116 (92.8%)
Completed post-graduate degrees (masters level and above): 29 (23.2%)
Professional degrees or designations: 59 (47.2%)
(law: 27; engineering: 21; accounting: 8; medicine: 3)
Universities attended most frequently (individuals often attended more than one):
   University of Toronto: 20 (16.0%)
   Harvard University: 16 (12.8%)
   McGill University: 15 (12.0%)
   Queen's University: 11 (8.8%)
   University of British Columbia: 10 (8.0%)
   University of Manitoba: 9 (7.2%)
   University of Alberta: 8 (6.4%)
   University of Western Ontario: 6 (4.8%)

University of Saskatchewan: 6 (4.8%)
Dalhousie University: 5 (4.0%)
Cambridge University: 5 (4.0%)
Laval University: 5 (4.0%)

Career Background (former careers of individuals who came to
the corporate elite from another major elite)

Corporate Group
Politicians: 11
Academics: 6
Bureaucrats: 5

Bank Group
Politicians: 7
Bureaucrats: 2
Academics: 1
Senators: 1

Ethnic Background (individual may fit into one or more
categories)
Corporate Group
known: 110 (43.8%)
At least one parent of British descent: 67 (60.9%)
At least one parent of French descent: 35 (31.8%)
Other European: 16 (14.5%)

Bank Group
known: 67 (37.0%)
At least one parent of British descent: 50 (74.6%)
At least one parent of French descent: 12 (17.9%)
Other European: 12 (17.9%)

Religion
Corporate Group
Of the 165 corporate directors for whom information was available,

117 (70.9%) listed a religious affiliation; of those claiming adherence to a particular faith, the distribution was as follows:
Protestant: 75 (64.1%)
  (Anglican: 34; United Church: 28; other Protestant: 13)
Roman Catholic: 35 (29.9%)
Jewish: 7 (6.0%)

Bank Group
Of the 131 bank directors for whom information was available, 90 (68.7%) listed a religious affiliation; of those claiming adherence to a particular faith, the distribution was as follows:
Protestant: 70 (77.8%)
  (Anglican: 27; United Church: 26; other Protestant: 17)
Roman Catholic: 14 (15.6%)
Jewish: 3 (3.3%)
Other: 3 (3.3%) (Unitarian: 2; Christian Science: 1)

Social Origins (based on occupation of father)

Corporate Group
known: 94 (37.4%)
Blue collar or working class: 22 (23.4%)
White collar, managerial or clergy: 46 (48.9%)
Other major elite group: 26 (27.7%)
  (corporate directors: 20; politicians: 2; publishers: 2; diplomat: 1; professor: 1)

Bank Group
known: 55 (30.4%)
Blue collar or working class 8 (14.5%)
White collar, managerial or clergy: 32 (58.2%)
Other major elite group: 15 (27.3%)
  (corporate directors: 14; deputy minister: 1)

Private Clubs

Corporate Group
known: 165 (65.7%)

Directors who list membership in one or more clubs: 118 (71.5%)
Directors who list membership in five or more clubs: 37 (22.4%)
Directors who list membership in ten or more clubs: 2 (1.2%)
Most popular clubs:
  The Toronto: 36 (21.8%)
  Mount Royal: 33 (20.0%)
  York: 25 (15.2%)
  The Granite: 20 (12.1%)
  Toronto Golf: 13 (7.9%)
  St.-Denis: 11 (6.7%)
  Mount Bruno: 10 (6.1%)
  Rosedale Golf: 10 (6.1%)
  Forest and Stream (Dorval): 8 (4.8%)
  Canadian: 8 (4.8%)
  Halifax: 8 (4.8%)
  Toronto Badminton and Racquet: 8 (4.8%)

Bank Group
known: 131 (72.4%)
Directors who list membership in one or more clubs: 101 (77.7%)
Directors who list membership in five or more clubs: 39 (29.8%)
Directors who list membership in ten or more clubs: 4 (3.1%)
Most popular clubs:
  The Toronto: 46 (35.1%)
  Mount Royal: 34 (25.9%)
  York: 32 (24.4%)
  Toronto Golf: 17 (13.0%)
  Granite: 15 (11.5%)
  Toronto Badminton and Racquet: 8 (6.1%)
  Vancouver: 8 (6.1%)
  Ranchmen's: 8 (6.1%)
  Rosedale Golf: 7 (5.3%)
  National: 7 (5.3%)

Appendix 4

Religious Elite Survey Results

Roman Catholic Church
Survey of the 123 Bishops, Archbishops and Cardinals of the Roman Catholic Church in Canada.
Date completed: September, 1990
Sources: 41 responded to biographical questionnaires; information on an additional 18 individuals was derived from personal biographies and the *Canadian Who's Who*.

Anglican Church
Survey of the 43 Bishops, Archbishops and the Primate of the Anglican Church of Canada.
Date completed: September, 1990
Sources: 21 responded to biographical questionnaires; information on an additional five individuals was derived from the *Canadian Who's Who*.

Gender

Roman Catholic Church
known: 123 (100%)
Men: 123 (100%)

Anglican Church
known: 43 (100%)
Men: 43 (100%)

Age

Roman Catholic Church
known: 56 (45.5%)
Between 80–89 years: 6 (10.7%)
Between 70–79 years: 15 (26.8%)
Between 60–69 years: 21 (37.5%)

Between 50–59 years: 11 (19.6%)
Between 40–49 years: 3 (5.4%)

Anglican Church
known: 24 (55.8%)
Between 60–69 years: 12 (50.0%)
Between 50–59 years: 10 (41.7%)
Between 40–49 years: 2 (8.3%)

Birthplace

Roman Catholic Church
known: 56 (45.5%)
Foreign-born: 4 (7.1%)
   (USA: 2; Yugoslavia: 1; Ukraine: 1)
Canadian-born: 52 (92.9%)
   The West: 9 (16.1%)
   (Alberta: 4; Saskatchewan: 2; Manitoba: 2;
   British Columbia: 1)

   Central Canada: 33 (58.9%)
   (Quebec: 23; Ontario: 10)

   The East: 10 (17.9%)
   (Nova Scotia: 4; New Brunswick: 4; Newfoundland: 2; Prince Edward Island: 0)

   The Yukon and Northwest Territories: 0

Anglican Church
known: 26 (60.5%)
Foreign-born: 6 (23.1%)
   (England: 4; Germany: 1; Northern Ireland: 1)
Canadian-born: 20 (76.9%)
   The West: 6 (23.1%)
   (Manitoba: 3; British Columbia: 2; Saskatchewan: 1; Alberta: 0)

Central Canada: 10 (38.5%)
(Ontario: 8; Quebec: 2)

The East: 4 (15.4%)
(Newfoundland: 2; Nova Scotia: 1; New Brunswick: 1; Prince Edward Island: 0)

The Yukon and Northwest Territories: 0

Education

Secondary
Roman Catholic Church
known: 47 (38.2%)
Attended public school: 11 (23.4%)
Attended private school (includes Catholic separate schools)
  36 (76.6%)

Anglican Church
known: 19 (44.2%)
Attended public school: 18 (94.7%)
Attended private school: 1 (5.3%)

Post-Secondary
Roman Catholic Church
known: 59 (48.0%)
Some post-secondary education: 59 (100%)
Completed post-graduate degrees (masters level and above): 29
  (49.2%)
Professional degrees or designations (other than religious): 1 (1.7%)
  (law)
Institutions attended most frequently (many attended more than one):
  Laval University: 12 (20.3%)
  Angelicum University (Rome): 12 (20.3%)
  Gregorian University (Rome): 10 (16.9%)
  Holy Heart Seminary (Halifax): 7 (11.9%)

Ottawa University: 7 (11.9%)
Catholic Institute of Paris: 6 (10.2%)
St. Augustines Seminary (Toronto): 5 (8.5%)
University of Montreal: 4 (6.8%)
University of St. Paul: 4 (6.8%)
Grand Seminary of Montreal: 4 (6.8%)
St. Francis Xavier: 4 (6.8%)

Anglican Church
known: 26 (60.5%)
Some post-secondary education: 26 (100%)
Completed post-graduate degrees (masters level and above): 10 (38.5%)
Professional degrees or designations (other than religious): 0
Institutions attended most frequently (many attended more than one):
    Trinity College (U of T): 7 (26.9%)
    Huron College (Western): 5 (19.2%)
    University of Toronto: 4 (15.4%)
    University of Saskatchewan: 3 (11.5%)
    University of Emmanual College: 3 (11.5%)
    King's College: 3 (11.5%)
    McGill University: 3 (11.5%)
    University of Manitoba: 2 (7.7%)
    University of British Columbia: 2 (7.7%)
    Montreal Diocesan Theological College: 2 (7.7%)
    Queen's College: 2 (7.7%)
    Bishop's College: 2 (7.7%)

Ethnic Background (individual may fit into one or more categories)

Roman Catholic Church
known: 50 (40.7%)
At least one parent of French descent: 33 (66.0%)
At least one parent of British descent: 14 (28.0%) (of these, 12 were
    Irish, although they did not specify Northern or Southern Ireland)
Other European: 6 (12.0%)

Anglican Church
known: 22 (51.2%)
At least one parent of British descent: 21 (95.5%)
Other European: 2 (9.1%)

Social Origins (based on occupation of father)

Roman Catholic Church
known: 40 (32.5%)
Blue collar or working class: 26 (65.0%)
White collar, managerial or clergy: 12 (30.0%)
Other major elite group: 2 (5.0%) (deputy minister and judge)

Anglican Church
known: 21 (48.8%)
Blue collar or working class: 9 (42.9%)
White collar, managerial or clergy: 12 (57.1%)
Other major elite group: 0

Responses to questionnaires on the influence of the Church

Influence of the Church on Moral Values (in last 20 years)

Roman Catholic Church
responses: 41 (33.3%)
influence fallen: 24 (58.5%)
influence risen: 5 (12.2%)
influence stayed the same: 6 (14.6%)
influence on Quebec fallen/in the rest of Canada risen: 2 (4.9%)
influence on moral values in private life fallen/on moral social values
    risen: 2 (4.9%)
influence has changed in nature: 1 (2.4%)
no influence: 1 (2.4%)

Anglican Church
responses: 21 (48.8%)
influence fallen: 17 (81.0%)
influence risen: 0

influence stayed the same: 3 (14.3%)
influence fallen in some areas/risen in others: 1 (4.8%)

Influence of the Church on Government Policy

Roman Catholic Church
responses: 41 (33.3%)
influence is indirect: 18 (43.9%)
influence is direct: 4 (9.8%)
influence is both direct and indirect: 17 (41.5%)
little or no influence: 2 (4.9%)

Influence over government policy over the last 20 years:
responses: 38 (30.9%)
Influence has:
risen: 13 (34.2%)
fallen: 14 (36.8%)
stayed the same: 5 (13.2%)
fallen in Quebec/risen in Ontario: 2 (5.3%)
don't know: 2 (5.3%)
yes: 2 (5.3%)

Anglican Church
responses: 21 (48.8%)
influence is indirect: 8 (38.1%)
influence is direct: 1 (4.8%)
influence is both direct and indirect: 9 (42.9%)
little or no influence: 3 (14.3%)

Influence over government policy over the last 20 years:
responses: 21 (48.8%)
Influence has:
risen: 5 (23.8%)
fallen: 12 (57.1%)
stayed the same: 2 (9.5%)
don't know: 2 (9.5%)

Appendix 5

Media Elite Survey Results

Publishers

Survey of the 20 publishers of major daily newspapers across Canada.
Date completed: December, 1989
Sources: 12 responded to biographical questionnaires; information on an additional two individuals was derived from the *Canadian Who's Who*.

Editors

Survey of the 23 editors of major daily newspapers across Canada.
Date completed: December, 1989
Sources: 15 responded to biographical questionnaires; some information was derived from the *Canadian Who's Who*.

Gender

Publishers
known: 20 (100%)
Men: 19 (95.0%)
Women: 1 (5.0%)

Editors
known: 23 (100%)
Men: 21 (91.3%)
Women: 2 (8.7%)

Age

Publishers
known: 12 (60.0%)
Between 60–69 years: 4 (33.3%)
Between 50–59 years: 5 (41.7%)
Between 40–49 years: 3 (25.0%)

Editors
known: 9 (39.1%)

Between 40–49 years: 8 (88.9%)
Between 30–39 years: 1 (11.1%)

Birthplace

Publishers
known: 14 (70.0%)
Foreign-born: 4 (28.6%)
 (England: 2; Northern Ireland: 1; Australia: 1)
Canadian-born: 10 (71.4%)
 Central Canada: 8 (57.1%)
 (Ontario: 7; Quebec: 1)

 The East: 2 (14.3%)
 (Nova Scotia: 1; Newfoundland: 1)

 The West: 0

 The Yukon and Northwest Territories: 0

Editors
known: 15 (65.2%)
Foreign-born: 6 (40.0%)
 (England: 4; Scotland: 1; New Zealand: 1)
Canadian-born: 9 (60.0%)
 The West: 4 (26.7%)
 (British Columbia: 1; Alberta: 1; Saskatchewan: 1; Manitoba: 1)

 Central Canada: 4 (26.7%)
 (Ontario: 3; Quebec: 1)

 The East: 1 (6.7%)
 (Prince Edward Island: 1)

 The Yukon and Northwest Territories: 0

Education

Secondary
Publishers
known: 13 (65.0%)
Attended public school: 8 (61.5%)
Attended private school: 5 (38.5%)
Private schools attended:
  Scotch College (Australia)
  Beauharnois and Bourget Colleges
  Mount Allison Academy
  Havergal College
  Trinity College School

Editors
known: 15 (65.2%)
Attended public school: 11 (73.3%)
Attended private school: 4 (26.7%)
Private schools attended:
  Séminaire de Saint-Hyacinthe
  Upper Canada College
  Neuchâtel Junior College
  Bishop's College School

Post-Secondary
Publishers
known: 14 (70.0%)
No post-secondary education: 2 (14.3%)
Some post-secondary education: 12 (85.7%)
Completed post-graduate degrees (masters level or above): 2 (14.3%)
Professional degrees or designations: 3 (21.4%)
  (accounting: 1; engineering: 1)
Universities attended most frequently (some attended more than one):
  Western: 3 (21.4%)
  University of Toronto: 3 (21.4%)
  Queen's University: 2 (14.3%)

Editors
known: 15 (65.2%)
No post-secondary education: 2 (13.3%)
Some post-secondary education: 13 (86.7%)
Completed post-graduate degrees (masters level or above): 4 (26.7%)
Professional degrees or designations: 1 (6.7%) (law)
Universities attended most frequently (some attended more than one):
   University of Toronto: 5 (33.3%)
   Oxford University: 2 (13.3%)

Career Background

Publishers
known: 12 (60.0%)
Rose through editorial side: 6 (50.0%)
Rose through business side: 4 (33.3%)
Rose through editorial and business side: 2 (16.7%)
Taught at university level: 2 (16.7%)

Editors
known: 15 (65.2%)
Newspaper background: 13 (86.7%)
Academics: 2 (13.3%)
Taught at university level: 7 (46.7%)

Ethnic Background (individual may fit into one or more categories)

Publishers
known: 12 (60.0%)
At least one parent of British descent: 10 (83.3%)
At least one parent of French descent: 2 (16.7%)
Other European: 1 (8.3%)

Editors
known: 15 (65.2%)
At least one parent of British descent: 13 (86.7%)
At least one parent of French descent: 1 (6.7%)
Other European: 3 (20.0%)

Religion

Publishers

Of the 14 publishers for whom information was available, 11 (78.6%) listed a religious affiliation; of those claiming adherence to a particular faith, the distribution was as follows:

Protestant: 8 (72.7%)

(Anglican: 4; United Church: 2; other Protestant: 2)

Roman Catholic: 2 (18.2%)

Other religion: 1 (9.1%)

Editors

Of the 15 editors for whom information was available, 11 (73.3%) listed a religious affiliation; of those claiming adherence to a particular faith, the distribution was as follows:

Protestant: 9 (81.8%)

(Anglican: 3; United Church: 3; other Protestant: 3)

Roman Catholic: 2 (18.2%)

Social Origins (based on occupation of father)

Publishers

known: 12 (60.0%)

Blue collar or working class: 2 (16.7%)

White collar, managerial or clergy: 6 (50.0%)

Other major elite group: 4 (33.3%) (all 4 were publishers)

Editors

known: 15 (65.2%)

Blue collar or working class: 3 (20.0%)

White collar, managerial or clergy: 12 (80.0%)

Other major elite group: 0

Private Clubs

Publishers

known: 14 (70.0%)

Publishers who list membership in one or more clubs: 11 (78.6%)

Publishers who list membership in five or more clubs: 0
Most popular clubs:
 The Toronto: 2 (14.3%)
Other clubs listed:
 Calgary Petroleum, Canadian, Centre, Edmonton, Galt Country,
 Granite, Kingston Yacht, London Hunt and Country, Manitoba,
 Ranchmen's, Rideau, Royal Dart Yacht and Ocean Cruising,
 Royal Montreal Golf and Country, St. Charles Country, St. John's
 Curling, Toronto Cricket, Union, University (Toronto), University
 (Montreal), Victoria Golf, Wig & Pen (UK)

Editors
known: 15 (65.2%)
Editors who list membership in one or more clubs: 4 (26.7%)
Editors who list membership in five or more clubs: 0
Most popular clubs: no preference shown
Clubs listed:
 Assiniboia, Badminton and Racquet, Osler Bluff Ski, Regina Golf,
 Royal Canadian Yacht, Royal Glenora, The Toronto, Toronto Golf

Women and Non-whites Who Run Departments

Number of newspapers: 18
With none: 1
With 1-5: 13
With 6 or more: 1

Notes

Introduction

1. C. Wright Mills, *The Power Elite* (New York, 1956), p.4. Mills's early twentieth-century precursors in the study of societal elites were Vilfredo Pareto *(The Mind and Society)*, Gaetano Mosca *(The Ruling Class)* and Roberto Michels *(Political Parties)*.

2. B.R.Blishen and H. McRoberts, "A Revised Socioeconomic Index for Occupations in Canada", *CRSA* 13 (February 1976): 73–79; Dennis Forcese, *The Canadian Class Structure* (Toronto: McGraw-Hill Ryerson, 1986), p. 18.

3. The discussion on social mobility in Canada in this section is drawn from three major texts by Canadian sociologists. They are: *Ascription and Achievement: Studies in Mobility and Status Attainment in Canada*, by Monica Boyd, John Goyder, Frank E. Jones, Hugh A. McRoberts, Peter C. Pineo and John Porter (Ottawa: Carleton University Press, 1985); *The Canadian Class Structure* by Dennis Forcese (Toronto: McGraw-Hill Ryerson, 1986); and *Ethnic Inequality in a Class Society*, by Peter S. Li (Toronto: Wall & Thompson, 1988).

Chapter 1

1. For a lucid discussion of Canadian parliamentary traditions, see C.E.S. Franks, *The Parliament of Canada* (Toronto: University of Toronto Press, 1987).

2. Franks, *The Parliament of Canada*, p. 17.

3. In the past two decades, more women than ever before have emerged as top contenders in the political field. Here are some federal landmarks:
• 1975: Rosemary Brown, a Jamaican-born social worker, almost upset Ed Broadbent in the federal NDP leadership contest. She came within 300 votes of winning.
• 1976: Flora MacDonald became the first woman to contest the leadership of the federal PC Party. She lost to Joe Clark after much of her so-called committed support vanished in the voting booths, giving rise to the phrase "the Flora factor."

• November 1988: Ethel Blondin (Liberal, Western Arctic) became the first native woman elected to federal Parliament.

• December 1989: Audrey McLaughlin, a 53-year-old rookie MP from the Yukon, beat NDP stalwart Dave Barrett and became the first woman in Canada to lead a national party.

• January 1990: Sheila Copps, a 37-year-old MP from Hamilton East, became the first female contender for the national Liberal leadership. A former MPP in the Ontario Legislature, Copps ran for the provincial leadership in 1982 and placed second. She has been a federal MP since 1984 and is now Deputy Leader of the party. She is also the first MP to have a baby while in office.

• February 1990: Kim Campbell became the first female minister of justice.

• April 1991: In B.C., Rita Johnson became Canada's first female premier when she stepped in as interim Social Credit leader after the resignation in disgrace of William Vander Zalm. She was confirmed as leader in July 1991.

Women's progress hasn't been limited to the federal arena. Provincial powerhouses have also emerged. Alex McDonough, a former social worker, became NDP leader in Nova Scotia in 1980; Sharon Carstairs, the Liberal leader in Manitoba, was the first Canadian woman to become leader of an official opposition; Lynda Haverstock heads the Liberals in Saskatchewan; Barbara Baird Filliter leads the Conservatives in New Brunswick.

There are signs that the male hegemony is breaking down in the party organizations. Iona Campagnolo has served as president of the federal Liberals. Johanna den Hertog became NDP national party president in 1987. A West Coast union activist, Hertog ran in the 1988 federal election in Vancouver Centre but lost to Kim Campbell. Katheryn Robinson became president of the Ontario Liberal Party in 1988. Previously a lawyer with Goodman & Goodman in Toronto, she is viewed as a strong contender for provincial or federal election.

4. Peter A. Hall and R. Peter Washburn, "Elites and Representation: A Study of the Attitudes and Perceptions of MPs," in Jean-Pierre Gaboury and James Ross Hurley, eds., *The Canadian House of Commons Observed: Parliamentary Internship Papers* (Ottawa: University of Ottawa Press, 1979), p. 294.

5. Charlotte Gray, "Secret Servant," *Saturday Night*, April 1991.

Chapter 2

1. As of early 1991, there have been 119 reports and studies related to affirmative action, employment equity and women in the public service. The major ones were:
• The 1967 Royal Commission on the Status of Women, chaired by Florence Bird. Published in 1970, the report made 167 recommendations. Among them were the introduction of pay equity and the expansion of part-time work.
• A 1970 study, "Sex and the Public Service," done by Kathleen Archibald for the Public Service Commission, recommended a host of measures, including the establishment of an equal opportunity program for recruitment, selection and placement improvements, and expansion of part-time work.
• In 1984, the Royal Commission on Equality in Employment, chaired by Rosalie Abella, issued a report that recommended that federally regulated industries be required by legislation to implement employment equity.

2. For an excellent survey of the building of the civil service, see J.L. Granatstein, Irving M. Abella, David J. Bercuson, R. Craig Brown and H. Blair Neatby, *Twentieth Century Canada* (Toronto: McGraw-Hill Ryerson, 1983), chapter 9.

Chapter 3

1. For a good discussion of regional political cultures in Canada, see Rand Dyck, *Provincial Politics in Canada* (Toronto: Prentice-Hall Canada, 1986).

Chapter 4

1. For a detailed analysis of Cockwell's rise in Canadian business, see Patricia Best and Ann Shortell, *The Brass Ring: Power, Influence and the Brascan Empire*, (Toronto: Random House, 1988).

2. By far the most lucid and thorough analysis of the Edper Group's modus operandi was done by *Globe and Mail* reporter Kimberley Noble in a series published in late 1990 and early 1991. Her well-documented conclusions:
In recent years, through careful legal planning, Edper companies have:

• Acquired a number of large public companies without triggering public disclosure requirements or takeover provisions;

• Transferred partial control of the entire Edper empire to its managers without triggering public disclosure requirements or takeover provisions;
• Mixed and matched memberships in the boards of directors of companies with large minority shareholdings to achieve specific goals;
• Established a large network of private or officially arm's-length public companies that are closely linked to and financed by the Bronfman empire, and used those companies to help make acquisitions that do not trigger public disclosure requirements or takeover provisions.

3. The pairings are as follows: the Royal Bank of Canada with RBC Dominion Securities; the CIBC with Wood Gundy; the Bank of Montreal with Nesbitt Thomson Deacon Inc.; the Bank of Nova Scotia with Scotia McLeod Inc.; and the National Bank of Canada with Lévesque Beaubien Geoffrion Inc.

4. For the most insightful piece of writing on Dick Thomson's career, see Jacquie McNish, "Dick Thomson's Born Again Bankers," *Report on Business Magazine*, October 1989.

Chapter 5

1. In 1989, the Canadian Centre for Policy Alternatives released a study of women in Canada's five major chartered banks. It showed that women made up 73 percent of the banks' full-time workforce in 1987, but their average pay was only $22,368, compared with $39,984 for men. The study found that 69.4 percent of women's jobs were clerical, compared with only 15.8 percent of men's jobs. There were no women in the top echelons of the five institutions. Since then, one or two women have risen to vice-president.

Chapter 6

1. Beutel and Goodman teamed up to form a widely respected investment counselling company under their names, and Goodman later assembled a diverse fortune in financial services and mining conglomerates at Dynamic Capital. Baker became a cofounder and principal of Gordon Capital.

Chapter 7

1. To be fair, generosity of spirit is becoming rarer in all classes of Canadian society, not just among the wealthy. Consider these facts. Canadians are giving 30 per cent less to charity than they did 20 years ago. On average, individual Canadians give one-third as much of their pre-tax income as Americans do. Canadian corporations give only 0.45 per cent of their pre-tax profits to charity. American corporations give four times that figure.

Chapter 8

1. The study notes that the biggest losers in the trend were the mainstream Protestant churches. In 1981, 35 per cent of all Canadians were affiliated with either the Anglican, Baptist, Lutheran, Presbyterian or United Church denominations, down from 40 per cent in 1971 and 49 per cent in 1941. Between 1971 and 1981, the number of people calling themselves Presbyterian fell by 7 per cent, Anglican by 4 per cent, United Church by 1 per cent. Only the Baptists were up, by 4 per cent.

2. In all 41 clerics completed the detailed questionnaires and one sent a biography. Information on another 17 was compiled from the *Canadian Who's Who*.

Bibliography:

Auden, W.H., ed. *The Portable Greek Reader*. (Markham, Ontario: Penguin Books Canada Ltd., 1977.)

Bejermi, John. *Canadian Parliamentary Handbook*. (Ottawa: Borealis Press, 1990).

Best, Patricia and Ann Shortell. *The Brass Ring: Power, Influence and the Brascan Empire*. (Toronto: Random House, 1988).

Bibby, Reginald W. *Fragmented Gods: The Poverty and Potential of Religion in Canada*. (Toronto: Irwin, 1987).

Bibby, Reginald W. *Mosaic Madness: The Poverty and Potential of Life in Canada*. (Toronto: Stoddart Publishing Co. Ltd., 1990).

Bliss, Michael, *Northern Enterprise: Five Centuries of Canadian Business*. (Toronto: McClelland and Stewart, 1987).

Boyd, Monica, John Goyder, Frank D. Jones, Hugh A. McRoberts, Peter C. Pineo and John Porter. *Ascription and Achievement: Studies in Mobility and Status Attainment in Canada*. (Ottawa: Carleton University Press, 1985).

Brodie, Janine. *Women and Politics in Canada*. (Toronto: McGraw-Hill Ryerson Ltd., 1985).

Burnet, Jean R. and Howard Palmer, eds. *"Coming Canadians": An Introduction to a History of Canada's Peoples*. (Copublished in Toronto: McClelland and Stewart and Ottawa: The Multicultural Directorate, 1988).

Cameron, Stevie. *Ottawa Inside Out: Power, Prestige and Scandal in the Nation's Capital*. (Toronto: Key Porter Books Ltd., 1989).

Canada. *Beneath the Veneer: The Report of the Task Force on Barriers to Women in the Public Service, Volume 1.* (Ottawa: Ministry of Supply and Services, 1990).

Carty, R. Kenneth and W. Peter Ward, ed. *National Politics and Community in Canada.* (Vancouver: University of British Columbia Press, 1986).

Chomsky, Noam. *Necessary Illusions: Thought Control in Democratic Societies.* (CBC Massey Lectures, 1988).

Christian, William and Colin Campbell. *Political Parties and Ideologies in Canada.* 3rd ed. (Toronto: McGraw-Hill Ryerson Limited, 1990).

Clandfield, David. *Canadian Film: Perspectives on Canadian Culture.* (Toronto: Oxford University Press, 1987).

Clement, Wallace. *The Canadian Corporate Elite.* (Toronto: McClelland and Stewart, 1975).

Clift, Dominique. *The Secret Kingdom: Interpretations of the Canadian Character.* (Toronto: McClelland & Stewart Inc., 1989).

Cohen, Andrew. *A Deal Undone: The Making and Breaking of the Meech Lake Accord.* (Vancouver: Douglas & McIntyre, 1990).

Couture, Pierre, ed. *Ottawa's Senior Executives Guide.* (Toronto: Info Globe Inc., 1990).

Crocker, Lester G. *Rousseau's Social Contract: An Interpretive Essay.* (Cleveland: The Press of Case Western Reserve University, 1968).

Curtis, Michael, ed. *The Great Political Theories, Volume 1: From Plato and Aristotle to Locke and Montesquieu.* (New York: Avon Books, 1981).

Curtis, Michael, ed. *The Great Political Theories, Volume 2: From Burke, Rousseau and Kant to Modern Times.* (New York: Avon Books, 1981).

Donno, Daniel, ed. and translator. *The Prince and Selected Discourses: Machiavelli.* (New York: Bantam Books, Inc., 1971).

Dumas, Jean. *Current Demographic Analysis: Report on the Demographic Situation in Canada 1986.* (Ottawa: Ministry of Supply and Services Canada, 1987).

Dyck, Rand. *Provincial Politics in Canada.* (Scarborough: Prentice-Hall Canada, Inc., 1986).

Eaman, Ross A. *The Media Society: Basic Issues and Controversies.* (Toronto: Butterworths, 1987).

Ehrenreich, Barbara. *Fear of Falling: The Inner Life of the Middle Class.* (New York: Harper Perennial, 1990).

Fetherling, Douglas, ed. *Documents in Canadian Film.* (Peterborough, Canada: Broadview Press Ltd., 1988).

Forcese, Dennis. *The Canadian Class Structure.* (Toronto: McGraw-Hill Ryerson Ltd., 1986).

Fotheringham, Allan. *Birds of a Feather: The Press and the Politicians.* (Toronto: Key Porter Books Ltd., 1989).

Francis, Diane. *Controlling Interest: Who Owns Canada?* (Toronto: Macmillan of Canada, 1986).

Franks, C.E.S. *The Parliament of Canada.* (Toronto: University of Toronto Press, 1987).

Fraser, John. *Telling Tales.* (Don Mills, Ontario: Collins Publishers, 1986).

Frye, Northrop. *In the Bush Garden: Essays on the Canadian Imagination.* (Toronto: House of Anansi, 1971).

Fulford, Robert. *Best Seat in the House: Memoirs of a Lucky Man.* (Don Mills, Ontario: Collins Publishers, 1988).

Gabourg, Jean-Pierre and James Ross Hurley, eds. *The Canadian House of Commons Observed: Parliamentary Internship Papers.* (Ottawa: University of Ottawa Press, 1979).

Graham, Jean, ed. *Directory of Directors.* (Toronto: The Financial Post Company Ltd., 1988).

Graham, Ron. *One-Eyed Kings: Promise and Illusion in Canadian Politics.* (Toronto: Collins Publishers, 1986).

Granatstein, J.L. *The Ottawa Men: The Civil Service Mandarins 1937–1957.* (Toronto: Oxford, 1982).

Granatstein, J.L., Irving M. Abella, David J. Bercuson, R. Craig Brown and H. Blair Neatby. *Twentieth Century Canada.* (Toronto: McGraw-Hill Ryerson Ltd., 1983).

Greene, Ian. *The Charter of Rights.* (Toronto: James Lorimer & Company, 1989).

Gregg, Allan and Michael Posner. *The Big Picture: What Canadians Think About Almost Everything.* (Toronto: Macfarlane Walter & Ross, 1990).

Guindon, Hubert. *Quebec Society: Tradition, Modernity, and Nationhood.* (Toronto: University of Toronto Press, 1988).

Halli, Shiva S., Frank Trovato and Leo Driedger, ed. *Ethnic Demography: Canadian Immigrant, Racial and Cultural Variations.* (Ottawa: Carleton University Press, 1990).

Handling, Piers. "Canadian Film From Yesterday to Tomorrow." In *O Canada: L'Amour du Cinema From North to South.* (New York: Museum of Modern Art, 1989).

Henrie, Maurice. *The Mandarin Syndrome: The Secret Life of Senior Bureaucrats.* (Ottawa: University of Ottawa Press, 1990).

Herman, Edward S. and Noam Chomsky. *Manufacturing Consent: The Political Economy of the Mass Media.* (New York: Pantheon Books, 1988).

Hiller, Harry H. *Canadian Society: A Sociological Analysis.* (Scarborough, Ontario: Prentice-Hall of Canada, Ltd., 1976).

Hoy, Claire. *Friends in High Places: Politics and Patronage in the Mulroney Government.* (Toronto: Key Porter Books Ltd., 1987).

Hunter, Alfred A. *Class Tells: Social Inequality in Canada.* (Toronto: Butterworths, 1986).

Innis, Harold A. *Essays in Canadian Economic History.* (Toronto: University of Toronto Press, 1956).

Jackson, Robert J. and Michale M. Atkinson. *The Canadian Legislative System.* (Toronto: Gage Publishing Ltd., 1980).

Jaher, Frederic Cople, ed. *The Rich, the Wellborn, and the Powerful: Elites and Upper Classes in History.* (Secaucus, New Jersey: The Citadel Press, 1975).

Kilgour, David. *Inside Outer Canada.* (Edmonton: Lone Pine Publishing, 1990).

Kilgour, David. *Uneasy Patriots: Western Canadians in Confederation.* (Edmonton: Lone Pine Publishing, 1988).

Knelman, Martin. *Home Movies: Tales from the Canadian Film World.* (Toronto: Key Porter Books Ltd., 1987).

Kornberg, Allan et. al. *Representative Democracy in the Canadian Provinces.* (Scarborough, Ontario: Prentice-Hall Canada Inc., 1982).

Lapham, Lewis H. *Money and Class in America: Notes and Observations on the Civil Religion.* (New York: Ballantine Books, 1989).

Lee, Desmond, transl. *Plato: The Republic.* (Markham, Ontario: Penguin Books Canada Ltd., 1974).

Leslie, Peter M. and Ronald L. Watts, eds. *Canada: The State of the Federation 1987–88.* (Kingston, Ontario: The Institute of Governmental Relations, 1988).

Li, Peter S. *Ethnic Inequality in a Class Society.* (Toronto: Wall & Thompson, Inc., 1988).

Lorimer, Rowland and Jean McNulty. *Mass Communication in Canada* (Toronto: McClelland and Stewart, 1987).

Lynch, Charles. *The Lynch Mob: Stringing Up Our Prime Ministers.* (Toronto: Key Porter Books, 1988).

March, James H., ed. *The Junior Encyclopedia of Canada.* (Edmonton: Hurtig Publishers Ltd., 1990).

McIntosh, Dave. *Ottawa Unbuttoned: Or Who's Running This Country Anyway?* (Toronto: Stoddart Publishing Co. Ltd., 1987).

McLuhan, Marshall. *Understanding Media: The Extensions of Man.* (Scarborough, Ontario: The New American Library of Canada Ltd., 1964).

More, Thomas. *Utopia.* Translated by Paul Turner. (Markham, Ontario: Penguin Books, 1965).

Morgan, Nicole. *The Equality Game: Women in the Federal Public Service (1908–1987).* (Ottawa: Canadian Advisory Council on the Status of Women, 1988).

Morrison, Ann M., Randall P. White, Ellen Van Velsor and the Centre for Creative Leadership. *Breaking the Glass Ceiling: Can Women Reach the Top of America's Largest Corporations?* (Reading, Massachussetts: Addison-Wesley Publishing Co., 1987).

Morton, W.L. *The Kingdom of Canada: A General History from Earliest Times.* (Toronto: McClelland and Stewart Ltd., 1982).

Muggeridge, Anne Roche. *The Desolate City: Revolution in the Catholic Church.* (San Francisco: Harper & Row, 1990).

Newman, Peter C. *The Canadian Establishment.* (Toronto: McClelland and Stewart, 1979).

Newman, Peter C. *The Canadian Establishment, Volume Two: The Acquisitors.* (Toronto: McClelland and Stewart Ltd., 1981).

Olsen, Dennis. *The State Elite.* (Toronto: McClelland and Stewart, 1980).

Osbaldeston, Gordon. *Keeping Deputy Ministers Accountable.* (Scarborough, Ontario: McGraw-Hill Ryerson, 1989).

Pareto, Vilfredo, ed. by Arthur Livingston. *The Mind and Society.* (New York: Dover, 1963).

Porter, John. *The Vertical Mosaic: An Analysis of Social Class and Power in Canada.* (Toronto: University of Toronto Press, 1985).

Rutherford, Paul. *The Making of the Canadian Media.* (Toronto: McGraw-Hill Ryerson Ltd., 1978).

Sawatsky, John. *The Insiders: Government, Business, and the Lobbyists.* (Toronto: McClelland and Stewart, 1987).

Simpson, Kieran, ed. *Canadian Who's Who.* (Toronto: University of Toronto Press, 1990).

Valaskakis, Kimon. *Canada in the Nineties: Meltdown or Renaissance?* (Ottawa: World Media Institute Inc., 1990).

Verney, Douglas V. *Three Civilizations, Two Cultures, One State: Canada's Political Traditions.* (Durham, North Carolina: Duke University Press, 1986).

Watts, Ronald L. and Douglas M. Brown, eds. *Options for a New Canada.* (Toronto: University of Toronto Press, 1991).

Index